KARATE
AS THE ART OF
KILLING

A Study of Its Deadly Origins, Ideology of Peace,
and the Techniques of Shitō-Ryū

Masayuki Shimabukuro and Leonard J. Pellman

BLUE SNAKE BOOKS
HUICHIN, UNCEDED OHLONE LAND
AKA BERKELEY, CALIFORNIA

Published by Blue Snake Books, an imprint of North Atlantic Books
Berkeley, California
Cover art © Elina Li/Shutterstock.com
Cover design by Jasmine Hromjak
Book design by Happenstance Type-O-Rama

Printed in the United States of America

Karate As the Art of Killing: A Study of Its Deadly Origins, Ideology of Peace, and the Techniques of Shitō-Ryū is sponsored and published by North Atlantic Books, an educational nonprofit based in Berkeley, California, that collaborates with partners to develop cross-cultural perspectives, nurture holistic views of art, science, the humanities, and healing, and seed personal and global transformation by publishing work on the relationship of body, spirit, and nature.

North Atlantic Books' publications are distributed to the US trade and internationally by Penguin Random House Publishers Services. For further information, visit our website at www.northatlanticbooks.com.

PLEASE NOTE: The creators and publishers of this book disclaim any liabilities for loss in connection with following any of the practices, exercises, and advice contained herein. To reduce the chance of injury or any other harm, the reader should consult a professional before undertaking this or any other martial arts, movement, meditative arts, health, or exercise program. The instructions and advice printed in this book are not in any way intended as a substitute for medical, mental, or emotional counseling with a licensed physician or healthcare provider.

Library of Congress Cataloging-in-Publication Data

Names: Shimabukuro, Masayuki, 1948– author. | Pellman, Leonard J., author.
Title: Karate as the art of killing / Masayuki Shimabukuro and Leonard J. Pellman.
Description: Berkeley, California : Blue Snake Books, 2022. | Includes index. | Summary: "A comprehensive exploration of the deadly origins of karate-dō--and its accompanying philosophy of peace, self-sacrifice, compassion, and service"—Provided by publisher.
Identifiers: LCCN 2021036244 (print) | LCCN 2021036245 (ebook) | ISBN 9781623176617 (paperback) | ISBN 9781623176624 (epub)
Subjects: LCSH: Karate—History. | Karate—Philosophy.
Classification: LCC GV1114.3 .S465 2022 (print) | LCC GV1114.3 (ebook) | DDC 796.815/309—dc23
LC record available at https://lccn.loc.gov/2021036244
LC ebook record available at https://lccn.loc.gov/2021036245

1 2 3 4 5 6 7 8 9 KPC 27 26 25 24 23 22

This book includes recycled material and material from well-managed forests. North Atlantic Books is committed to the protection of our environment. We print on recycled paper whenever possible and partner with printers who strive to use environmentally responsible practices.

To future budoka

未来の武道家の為に

We struggled for months over whom to dedicate this book to. We had already dedicated *Katsujinken* to Shimabukuro Hanshi's Shitō-Ryū *sensei*, Mabuni Kenzō and Hayashi Teruō, so it would have been redundant to dedicate *Karate As the Art of Killing* to them as well. Another logical choice would have been Mabuni Kenwa, the founder of Shitō-Ryū, whose desire to unify karate-dō, rather than splinter it into the many styles and factions it has become, was a major inspiration to the authors.

Following his untimely death, another excellent choice would have been Shimabukuro Hanshi, but as the coauthor of the book, it might have seemed self-aggrandizing to do so.

Eventually, the answer to a simple question provided the solution to our dilemma: who did we actually write this book for, and why? We wrote it for the future generations of *karateka,* hoping that it would inspire them to return to the roots of the art in their training.

So, it is to those future generations—the karateka who are just now beginning their training, as well as those yet unborn—to whom we dedicate this book. We do so in the earnest hope that the maturing karateka who are reading it now will devote themselves to nurturing those future karateka as their *sempai* and sensei to become generations who practice karate-dō as the art and lifestyle it was intended to be.

謝辞
Shaji

ACKNOWLEDGMENTS

This book would not have been possible without the support, encouragement, and assistance of countless people whose contributions were no less important than those we have named in these acknowledgments—karateka on whom the techniques in this book were tested, beta readers who provided valuable feedback on its contents, and those who worked behind the scenes to create it. We are grateful to and for them all.

SPECIAL APPRECIATION

A special word of thanks is due to Shimabukuro Kanako sensei, widow of the late coauthor, Shimabukuro Masayuki Hanshi, for authorizing its publication and providing support and advocating its completion, without which it would not have been possible.

PHOTOGRAPHY

The photographs used in all the instructional portions of this book were taken by Bill Villarreal. He contributed far more than merely pressing the shutter button. His professionalism, his eye for lighting, layout, and presentation, and his appreciation for the concepts we were trying to convey were essential to the clarity of the information presented.

MODEL

Mr. Samuel Mills, a student of coauthor Pellman *shihan* for over fifteen years, was the model assisting Pellman shihan in the instructional photographs. He endured hours in the heat and glare of studio lights to help make this book possible, and the authors are deeply grateful for his assistance.

COVER DESIGN

The cover initially envisioned by the authors was austere—merely the title and authors' names without any images in order to strike readers with its simplicity and uniqueness. However, the design created and proposed by Ms. Jasmine Hromjak so vividly captured the essence of the book and so greatly impressed the people asked to critique it that it was immediately recognized as visually superior. We are immensely grateful to Ms. Hromjak for her stellar contribution to this work.

目次
Mokuji
CONTENTS

前書
Maegaki
PREFACE

When Shimabukuro Masayuki Hanshi and I wrote *Katsujinken: Living Karate and the Way to Self-Mastery* in 2006, we were not attempting to write a treatise specifically about Shitō-Ryū karate-dō. Instead, as we emphasized in its Authors' Note, *Katsujinken* was intended from the outset to serve as a generic overview of the principles, philosophy, and fundamentals of karate-dō that would apply and appeal to practitioners of every style of karate and every form of fisticuffs. In that Authors' Note we stated, "You will find that the principles taught in this book will readily apply to any Japanese or Okinawan style of karate, as well as to tae kwon do, tang soo do, hapkido, soo bahk do, kenpō, kung fu, American free-style, kajukenbo, boxing, and savate." Our goal in writing *Katsujinken* was essentially twofold: to provide a reference resource that would benefit practitioners of any form of hand-to-hand combative art, and to encourage them to adopt a peacemaking and life-preserving attitude and philosophy in their practice of those arts.

Even while we were writing and editing *Katsujinken*, we began discussing the need for a book specific to the Shitō-Ryū style. Almost immediately after the first printing of *Katsujinken* was released in 2006, Hanshi and I began work on the second edition of *Flashing Steel: Mastering Eishin-Ryu Swordsmanship*, which was published in 2008. Soon after that, Hanshi suggested that we begin work on the follow-up to *Katsujinken* with a specific focus on Shitō-Ryū. By that time it was clear that *Katsujinken* had appealed primarily to practitioners of Shitō-Ryū, but not to those practicing other styles to the extent we had hoped and expected. Since *Katsujinken* wasn't serving its primary purpose of reaching an audience outside the Shitō-Ryū community, Hanshi decided that we should produce a book that would describe Shitō-Ryū as he had come to understand it from his extensive conversations and training with Mabuni Kenzō.

In February 2009, we began outlining a second book on karate-dō, which we tentatively titled *Advanced Shitō-Ryū Karate*. The original concept for *Advanced Shitō-Ryū Karate* was that it would be both a successor to *Katsujinken* and a presentation of the more advanced concepts of the Shitō-Ryū style specifically. Month by month, chapter by chapter, we began assembling our new book in the manner we had done our first two books together—except that we were now working by phone and email instead of face-to-face. However, the further we got in writing *Advanced Shitō-Ryū Karate*, the more dissatisfied Hanshi became with that concept due to the evolution of his own thinking and research of the art. By the middle of 2011 we had scrapped and rewritten most of what we had written during our first ten or twelve months of work on the book.

To understand his reasoning, it might help to review Hanshi's growth and development as a karateka. Shimabukuro Hanshi began his study of karate in 1963 as a student of Sō Dōshin, the founder of Shōrinji Kempō. Shōrinji Kempō incorporates a considerable amount of grappling, throwing, and joint-locking techniques in its curriculum. In 1965 he became a direct student of Hayashi Teruō, who later founded the Hayashi-Ha branch of Shitō-Ryū karate-dō. Hayashi sensei was a strong proponent of karate tournament competition, so Shimabukuro Hanshi's emphasis for decades in his personal training and later in his teaching was the sports aspect of karate-dō, and many of his students in the 1980s, 1990s, and even into the early 2000s were local, regional, and national tournament champions. In the mid-1990s, however, Shimabukuro Hanshi aligned himself with Mabuni Kenzō, son of the founder of Shitō-Ryū karate-dō, Mabuni Kenwa, and his training, research, and teaching emphasis began to shift away from the sporting applications of karate-dō to its historic and pragmatic aspects. The process of expressing his knowledge and ideas in print caused him to completely reevaluate his approach to teaching and explaining karate-dō. This fundamental reassessment was reflected in the revisions to the text of *Advanced Shitō-Ryū Karate*.

It also caused him to reconsider the title of the book. We realized we were no longer writing a sequel to *Katsujinken*. We were now writing a book that presents an entirely different perspective on karate-dō than the one we had presented in *Katsujinken*, and Hanshi wanted the title of the book to reflect that significant change in perspective. By the time we had rewritten the first five or six chapters, it was clear that such a bland title as *Advanced Shitō-Ryū Karate* wasn't suitable for the content we were creating, nor would it attract the audience for which we were writing it. Over the process of revising and refining each chapter several times, the book had taken on a character quite different from our original concept. It had morphed into an entirely different perspective on the art of karate-dō. Where *Katsujinken* is essentially the *omote* view of karate-dō—the "face" of the art that everyone sees—this book is the *ura*: the opposite side of that coin that had rarely, if ever, been presented in print. His inspiration ultimately came from a conversation in which Mabuni sensei was urging Hanshi to discontinue training his students for participation in karate tournaments and said bluntly, "Karate is not a sport. Karate is for killing." A lengthy explanation of that remark followed, but the result was the eventual change in the title of this book to *Karate As the Art of Killing.*

We first toyed with at least a dozen other titles, like *Okuden Karate-dō* ("Deep-Level Karate") and *Karate-dō no Himitsu* ("Secrets of Karate"). Hanshi ran several such names by the students at his *hombu* (main) *dōjō*, but none of them elicited much enthusiasm. Instead, the feedback was that nearly every martial arts book now claimed to contain "secrets" or heretofore unknown techniques. Hanshi wanted to be sure that this book would stand out from all the others. He had always liked the title of *Flashing Steel,* because it expressed the essence of both the book and the art of iaijutsu: that in a battle with samurai swords a sudden and brief flash of steel was the culmination of a lifetime of training and the end of a human life. He wanted the title for this book to be similarly evocative of the nature of the art of karate-dō itself, and in his customary fashion Hanshi contemplated that idea for months as we continued writing.

We discussed a few titles trying to capture the notion of a blur of fists and feet, but most of them—like *Lightning Feet* and *Fists of Thunder*—just left us laughing out loud. Then in late 2011, Hanshi called me with an idea: "I've been thinking, Len *san*—why are we writing this book? We're trying to explain that real karate is simple. Brutal. Deadly. No fancy stuff. No mystery. Right, Len san? So title of book should be same way. Mabuni sensei always says karate is not sport; karate is for killing, so maybe we should just call book *Karate for Killing*. What you think?"

I initially balked at the idea. I was concerned that the title might imply that the book, and we as its authors, were either advocating the use of karate-dō to kill people or that the book would be a detailed instruction manual on killing techniques. On the other hand, it perfectly reflected my own beginnings in Japanese *budō*. Although I had been bullied quite a bit in elementary school, I had never sustained any serious injuries—only occasional bruises and bloodied nose and lips. But in the early weeks of junior high school I befriended several of the first Black children to move into a previously all-White school district. One became my best friend. After school one day early in the semester, we were attacked by several boys who objected to our friendship. We were both severely beaten, and my parents finally agreed that something needed to be done about it. For about two years since seeing the henchman Oddjob easily defeat James Bond in the 1963 movie *Goldfinger*, I had been asking my parents to enroll me in a karate program. Now they were seriously considering it. My father worked for a company that subcontracted work from an Okinawan named Higa Yetsuō who had immigrated to Hawaii in the 1930s. With me listening on his office speaker phone, he called Mr. Higa and asked what he thought of enrolling me in karate. I will never forget Mr. Higa's reply: "Karate is for killing, Jack. I would recommend jūdō instead. With jūdō, Lenny can defend himself without leaving corpses on the playground."

Although I was still uncomfortable with the name, and even said that we might as well call it *Satsujinken* ("Murdering Fist") in contrast to *Katsujinken* ("Life-Giving Fist"), after a few more weeks of discussion and reflection we settled on *The Art of Killing*. At our publisher's suggestion, this was later expanded to *Karate As the Art of Killing* to include "karate" in the title for clarity.

After that, work on *Karate As the Art of Killing* progressed sporadically. In 2010 and 2011 I had gone through two job changes and the death of my mother. Serving as executor of her estate and moving twice had distracted me considerably from my work on the book. Although I continued working on the book and occasionally sent Hanshi updated drafts, we only completed two or three chapters during that time. And unknown to me, Hanshi was beginning to suffer the effects of the cancer that would eventually take his life, so our phone conversations and emails were hit-and-miss for much of those two years.

Then in mid-2011 Hanshi inundated me with a flurry of activity. I was unaware at the time that it was a period in which his cancer was in remission. For two or three months, he called at least twice a week with new material to add to the book—so much that I couldn't keep up with him in producing new and revised drafts from our discussions. "Don't worry about that," he told me. "Just write down what I say for now and send chapters later." At the time I thought he was just trying to give some leeway in which to catch up on my writing. In hindsight, however, it seems clear that he suspected he might have little time left in which to complete the book, and he wanted to get his ideas into my hands. I visited him in November 2011, but he was only able to see me briefly. He did not tell me at the time that his cancer had recurred. His calls suddenly stopped around Christmas, and not understanding why, I was grateful for the opportunity to focus on the work of assembling some of Hanshi's thoughts into manuscript form.

I first learned of Hanshi's cancer during a phone call around his birthday in March 2012 after sending him a couple of recently completed chapters. He was characteristically upbeat and expressed confidence that surgery to remove his gallbladder and bile ducts, followed by a regimen of chemotherapy, would fully restore his health. It was months later that I learned the illness was far more extensive than he was telling me at the time. In late April I sent him some updated material to review while he was recuperating from the surgery. We spoke again in mid-May and I could hear the weakness in his voice, but he assured me that he was recovering well and would soon be back to full health.

Our last conversation was in early July 2012, just a few days after I was laid off by my employer of eleven years. I explained that my severance package would give me ninety paid days in which to complete the book. Hanshi was greatly enthused by that, so we planned to go into high gear as soon as he returned from the *gasshuku* (training camp) scheduled for July 27. But it was not to be. He contracted pneumonia at or immediately following the gasshuku and was hospitalized for treatment. He never fully recovered from the pneumonia and its complications, and passed away on September 7, 2012.

Hanshi's death left the manuscript with nine chapters completed in first-draft format, my hand-scribbled notes for an additional five chapters, and our outline of the contents for the remaining eight or ten chapters. It also left me grieving, unemployed, and filled with a sense of aimlessness. I lost all enthusiasm for completing the book. It seemed pointless without Hanshi to share it with. On top of that, I had my own problems to deal with, not the least of which was finding a new job. After applying for more than 200 faculty and administrative positions over a six-month period in Indiana, I ended up moving to Texas and teaching online. By the end of 2013, finishing *Karate As the Art of Killing* was relegated to the "maybe someday" category, together with visiting Machu Picchu and the Great Wall of China.

There it remained until 2019, when I realized that the twenty-fifth anniversary of the publication of *Flashing Steel* was just a year away. It had been eleven years since the second edition of *Flashing Steel* was released, so it was due for an updated— perhaps final—edition, which seemed like an opportunity to make the 25th Anniversary Edition a tribute to the memory of Shimabukuro Hanshi. As work on that edition was coming to a close in early 2020, it occurred to me to do essentially the same thing with *Karate As the Art of Killing*. I remembered Hanshi once mentioning the concept of *isho* sometime in 2011. An isho (遺書) is a work, often the culmination of a lifetime of study serving as the author's masterwork or final word on a subject, and it seemed fitting that *Karate As the Art of Killing* be published as Hanshi's isho on the topic of karate-dō. The more I thought about it, the more it became an imperative rather than just befitting. You now hold the result in your hands.

Those who have read *Flashing Steel* or *Katsujinken* will notice that we have included a few topics from each of those books in *Karate As the Art of Killing*. This was both unavoidable and deliberate, not only for the sake of readers who are not yet familiar with our previous works, but also because those topics are essential for a full understanding of karate-dō. While there is some overlap or duplication from our previous books, we attempted to add further depth and breadth to our explanation of those topics, and did not simply transfer them verbatim into this book.

As with our previous collaborations, *Karate As the Art of Killing* contains the teachings of Shimabukuro Masayuki Hanshi as understood and expressed in English by me with the occasional use of familiar Western cultural icons and examples. Accordingly, it presents Hanshi's culminating thoughts on karate-dō following a significant transformation in his understanding of, and approach to, the art after coming under the tutelage of Mabuni Kenzō for roughly ten years. The ideas expressed in *Karate As the Art of Killing* are not mine, except to the extent that I have assimilated them from Shimabukuro Hanshi, having been a student of his for some twenty-three years. They are essentially his thoughts—a product of his study, training, and contemplation for nearly fifty years—to the best of my ability to comprehend and explain them. Any of my own thoughts I have contributed to this work are merely a by-product or extension of Hanshi's teaching. He was the sage. I am but the scribe.

It is a task I have undertaken with enormous trepidation, since it represents his final and ultimate words—his isho on the art and the style to which he devoted most of his life.

Leonard J. Pellman
December 15, 2020

内容紹介
Naiyō Shōkai
INTRODUCTION

For the benefit of any readers who are as yet unfamiliar with the Japanese language, here are a few of the key terms in the early chapters of this book. We strongly encourage karateka to become familiar, if not fluent, in the Japanese terminology for karate techniques and training methods. Since karate is a Japanese art, Japanese is its lingua franca. Knowing the Japanese terms not only facilitates training in Japan or Okinawa periodically, but allows karateka from anywhere in the world to train together and exchange knowledge of the art.

KARATE AND KARATE-DŌ

Karate is a term that should be familiar to most readers of a book on the art. Since the end of World War II, the word *karate* has practically become part of the English language. Nevertheless, since it is the subject of this book, it warrants a clear definition and an explanation of the distinction between our use of the terms *karate* and *karate-dō*.

Karate is written 空手 in Japanese, and it is a difficult term to precisely define. *Kara* (空) has several meanings and pronunciations that are usually derived from the context in which the symbol appears. It can mean "air," "sky," "space," "weather," "emptiness," "vacant," "blank," "void," "open," "vast," or "limitless." *Te* (手) means "hand" or "hands." Given the Japanese penchant for symbolism and multiple layers of meaning, *karate* is probably intended to convey both the concepts of empty hands and limitless hands for a combat art that employs no other weapons than the human body and is limited in that use only by the knowledge and ingenuity of the individual karateka.

Dō (道) means "way of life." It is the same symbol that is pronounced "tao" or "dao" in Chinese. In this context, *dō* is used to identify a comprehensive lifestyle, as opposed to an art, method, skill, or technique. So, karate-dō is more than merely a fighting system; it is a way of life based on the concept of facing life's challenges with only one's skill and ingenuity.

Thus, we typically use the word *karate* when referring primarily to the physical skills of the art, and *karate-dō* when speaking of the lifestyle and philosophy of a kara-teka in a more comprehensive way.

BUDŌ AND BUJUTSU

Throughout this book you will find frequent references to *budō* or *bujutsu*. Both of these terms are typically translated into English as "martial arts," but this is an inaccurate translation that fails to convey the true meaning of *budō* or *bujutsu*. We therefore believe it is worthwhile to understand the significant difference in meaning between *budō* or *bujutsu* and "martial arts."

The word *martial* means "military," so in the truest sense, the term *martial arts* means any form of warfare training—armed or unarmed combat, and irrespective of its use for offensive or defensive military campaigns. The *bu* (武) in *bujutsu* (武術) and *budō* (武道), however, means "peacemaking." *Jutsu* (術) means "art" or "skill" and *dō* (道) means "way of life." Thus, bujutsu is the art or skill of peacemaking and budō is the way of life of peacemaking. Since their purpose and intent is peacemaking, budō and bujutsu seek first to avoid or prevent conflict or war, and only engage in physical combat if forced to do so. If combat is unavoidable, then bujutsu and budō strive to end the conflict and restore peace as quickly and with as little harm to others as possible. Thus, true budō and bujutsu are entirely defensive and protective in nature, whereas martial arts, in the strictest sense, can be either aggressive or defensive, for peace or war, for deterrence or conquest.

Throughout this book, we use the terms *budō* and *bujutsu* to identify Japanese arts of peacemaking and only use *martial arts* when referring to military combat or combative arts that have both offensive and defensive applications.

BUSHI AND BUSHIDŌ

We devote an entire chapter each to the origins of the *bushi* and *bushidō*. Bushi (武士) is typically mistranslated into English as "warrior." Again, the *bu* (武) in *bushi* means "peacemaker." *Shi* (士) has several nuances, including "gentleman," "scholar," "sage," and "samurai" (see below). A bushi, therefore, is not merely a fighter, as the term *warrior* suggests, but a well-educated and refined person of accomplishment who is dedicated to peacemaking and serving others. *Bushidō* (武士道) is the way of life (dō) of the bushi: the ideals, guiding principles, personal character, and habits of a bushi.

SAMURAI

Another widely misunderstood term is samurai. Probably due to the influence of *chanbara* (sword-fight) and *jidaigeki* (historical drama) movies depicting fierce battles between them, the word *samurai* has also come to be synonymous with *warrior* outside Japan in much the same way *cowboy* more often evokes the image of a gunfighter than a cattle rancher or drover. The *kanji* (Chinese symbol) for *samurai* (侍) is a mash-up of 人 ("human being") and 寺 ("temple"). The verb form of *samurai* is *haberu* (侍る), which means "to serve." Just as the priests in a temple devote their lives to serving both the god or gods of that temple and the people who worship there, the samurai devoted their lives to serving both the emperor (once considered a god) and the people of Japan. Although for centuries samurai were trained in combative arts as part of their preparation for service, the majority of them actually served as clerks and administrators, as explained in greater detail in chapter 4.

RYŪ, HA, AND RYŪHA

The Japanese word *ryū* (流) literally means "flow" or "current," as in the flow of a river or stream. It denotes the passage of something—water, electricity, knowledge, culture—from a source to one or more recipients. When appended to another word, as in Shitō-Ryū or Gōjū-Ryū, it is generally taken to mean "style," "school," "type," or "system."

Ha (派) is a word closely related to *ryū* that originally referred to a "tributary" or "branch" of a stream, but has evolved to mean "faction" or "sect." So in the context of budō, a ryū is a style or school, such as Shitō-Ryū, and a ha is a branch, sect, or derivative of a ryū, such as Hayashi-Ha Shitō-Ryū.

Combining the words *ryū* and *ha* forms the word *ryūha* (流派), which is used as a general and collective term for schools and their branches, as in "all the ryūha (schools and their branches) of karate-dō."

KORYŪ AND GENDAI-RYŪ

Koryū means "ancient ryū" and *gendai-ryū* means "modern ryū." To our knowledge there is no authoritative definition of "ancient" and "modern" with respect to the ryū of budō, but in general parlance, koryū are those ryū that were established prior to the Meiji Era (1868–1912) and gendai-ryū are those ryū that were established during or after the Meiji Era. This is the context in which those terms are used in this book.

BUDŌKA AND *KARATEKA*

Budōka and *karateka* are common terms used to identify the practitioners *(ka)* of budō or bujutsu and karate-dō, respectively. *Ka* (家) means "household," so a karateka is a member of the household—or family—of karate-dō, and a budōka is a member of the household of budō. For reasons explained earlier in this chapter, we prefer and use the term *budōka* rather than the English term *martial artist*, to distinguish karateka and practitioners of other forms of classical Japanese budō from those who train in martial (military) disciplines or warfare.

KIHON, *KATA*, *KATACHI*, AND *KUMITE*

It is said that there are three *k*'s in karate: *kihon*, *kata*, and *kumite*. These terms are so widely used in karate and in this book that the reader should understand them from the outset. *Kihon* means "basics" or "fundamentals." The term usually refers to individual strikes, blocks, kicks, throws, and the principles that make them effective. A kata is an example, template, or model, typically a set of twenty or more techniques performed in a specific sequence for individual performance and training. The authors occasionally use the term *katachi* ("pattern") for a series of solo movements performed as a training drill, to differentiate those drills from kata, which are examples or templates for practical self-defense. A katachi may or may not have practical self-defense application, but its primary purpose is usually to develop speed, timing, balance, stamina, agility, and similar athletic traits. *Kumite* means to "cross hands" or "intertwine hands" and refers to a training activity in which two or more people practice simulated attack and defense against each other.

Three closely related terms frequently used in karate are *waza* ("techniques"), *kata* ("methods"), and *hō* ("ways"). Examples are: *atemi waza* ("striking techniques"), *keri kata* ("kicking methods"), and *jūhō* ("soft ways").

GŌHŌ AND *JŪHŌ*

Gōhō means "hard methods." *Jūhō* means "soft methods." In typical usage, gōhō are striking techniques, and jūhō are nonstriking techniques, such as foot sweeps, throws, joint locks, grappling, and pins.

SENSEI AND SHIHAN

Sensei (先生) literally means "previously born," but in common usage refers to a teacher or mentor. The term undoubtedly derives from the fact that older people generally have greater knowledge and life experience than younger people. *Shihan* (師範) means "exemplary teacher," implying one who leads by example or epitomizes the qualities being taught. It is usually applied to older or high-ranking instructors to show a greater degree of respect than *sensei*. It is also frequently used in reference to an instructor who has several sensei among their students.

SŌKE AND SŌSHIHAN

These are terms for the leaders of a ryū. A literal reading of *sōke* is "family origin," but in normal usage a sōke is the leader of a religious or philosophical sect. Technically, it should be—as "family origin" suggests—a hereditary position passed down within a family, but in practice there are many ryū that use the term *sōke* for an appointed or elected leader. *Sōshihan* means "supreme teacher" and is the equivalent of the English words *headmaster* (leader of a school) or *grandmaster* (leader of an order of knighthood). In English, "grandmaster" sounds pretentious, so the authors prefer to use "headmaster" as the English translation of *sōshihan*.

AITE AND TEKI

Aite (相手) literally means "other hands" and designates another person. In the dōjō, *aite* is the appropriate term for a training partner—a person who performs the role of an enemy or opponent, but is in fact an ally.

Teki (敵) means "enemy." A teki is the person we are training to defeat when we practice with aite. We treat aite with care, always being mindful of their safety during training. But in combat, we utterly destroy teki.

SHIKATA AND UCHIKATA

Shikata (使方) means "using person" and is the term we prefer for the person who utilizes the technique being practiced when performing *yakusoku kumite* and other partner exercises.

Uchikata (打ち方), sometimes written 受方, means "striking person" or "receiving person." Uchikata is the person who receives, or is struck by, shikata's technique during practice. The term *uchikata* also implies that uchikata is the one who initiates the attack—the first to (attempt to) strike—during partner exercises.

As a courtesy during training, the first to perform the role of uchikata is usually the *kōhai* (lower-ranking) partner, and the sempai (higher rank) is first to be shikata. When teaching, however, the sensei takes the role of uchikata.

OTHER USEFUL TERMS

A few other basic Japanese words that will help the reader understand our extensive use of Japanese terminology in this book are:

dōjō: the building in which budō training is conducted

sempai: a senior student

kōhai: a junior student

seito: a student

deshi: a disciple, often implying a strongly committed student

kanji: Chinese ideograms (漢字) used in writing the Japanese language

PRONUNCIATION GUIDE

For the benefit of those readers with a limited knowledge of the Japanese language, here is a brief guide to the pronunciation of Japanese words and how they are written in *rōmaji* (the Latin alphabet) in *Karate As the Art of Killing*:

The vowels in Japanese are always pronounced the same way, as follows:

a: "ah" as in "father"

i: "ee" as in "bee"

u: "oo" as in "tool"

e: "eh" as in "red"

o: "oh" as in "go"

Doubled vowels (*aa, ii, uu, ee, oo*) or vowels written with a bar above them (most commonly *ū* and *ō*) are simply voiced twice as long as single vowels, like a half-note instead of a quarter note in music.

Diphthongs (*ai, ao, au, ae, ao, ia, iu, ie, io, ua, ui, ue, uo, oa, oi, ou, oe*) are pronounced by pronouncing both vowels in normal fashion, so that *ai* sounds like "eye," *au* sounds like "ow," and so forth. Although they are technically different sounds, *ō* and *ou* are so similar that they usually sound alike.

Most Japanese consonants, as written in rōmaji, are also pronounced like their English equivalents:

k: "k" as in "kick"

s: "s" as in "see"

sh: "sh" as in "she"

t: "t" as in "toe"

ch: "ch" as in "chair"

ts: "ts" as in "nuts"

n: "n" as in "no"

h: "h" as in "hot"

m: "m" as in "me"

y: "y" as in "you"

w: "w" as in "way"

g: "g" as in "go"

z: "z" as in "zoo"

d: "d" as in "day"

j: "j" as in "jar"

The two Japanese consonants that give English speakers the most difficulty are *f* and *r*. The *f* in Japanese is pronounced as a cross between an English *h* and *f*, like the sound made when blowing out a candle. The *r* in Japanese is like a cross between the English *r* and *l* and is made by pressing the tip of the tongue against the roof of the mouth—not the back of the incisors, like an English *l*—and trying to say an *r*, so *ra* should sound halfway between "raw" and "law."

Also troublesome for English speakers are the Japanese digraphs *ky, ny, my, hy, ry, gy, by,* and *py*. These should be pronounced with its accompanying vowel as one syllable, so *kya* is pronounced "kyah" rather than "key-ah." Thus, the capital of Japan is Tōkyō (two syllables, "toh-kyoh"); not "toh-key-oh." *Kyōto* is likewise only two syllables, "kyoh-toh," not "key-oh-toh."

Japanese syllables always end with a vowel or *n*. So *Toyota* is pronounced "Toh-yoh-tah" and not "Toy-oh-tah."

Karateka should never call the art they practice "kuh-ROT-ee." That is like fingernails on a chalkboard to a traditional sensei. It is pronounced "kaw-raw-teh," with equal emphasis on each syllable.

Kanji
CHINESE IDEOGRAMS

We devote a considerable portion of this book to explaining the deeper and nuanced meanings of many of the Japanese terms for karate principles and techniques, including the meaning of the word *karate* itself. We have done so because the Japanese language is fundamentally different from the English language, and the Japanese words often convey more complex meaning than the English words into which they are most often translated.

English is a phonetic language. The letters of our alphabet convey no meaning of their own. They merely represent sounds, and we translate those sounds into meaning. This is why it requires such an enormous vocabulary to be fluent in the English language. The unabridged Webster's dictionary contains more than four hundred thousand English words and their definitions. Each word must sound different from nearly all others to avoid confusion. For instance, in English there is only one word that is pronounced "show," and it is either a verb meaning "to display or present" or a noun meaning "presentation." In Japanese there are roughly 150 words pronounced "shō," most of which have greatly differing meanings.

This is because Japanese is a pictorial language. It is written in symbols (kanji) that often represent complex and heavily nuanced meanings—meanings that are often metaphors rather than direct descriptions. The Japanese word for the solar plexus, for example, is *suigetsu*, which is literally "water moon." As we explain in more detail in chapter 2, even the word *karate* is chiefly metaphorical. It doesn't mean "fist-fighting" or "boxing" or "pugilism"; it simply means "empty hands" or "empty-handed." If you did not already know that karate is a method of hand-to-hand combat, you would never be able to guess it solely from the symbols 空手, pronounced "karate."

For this reason, we believe it is important for karateka to have a working knowledge of the Japanese words that are most commonly used in karate-dō. The terminology used in karate is, in many cases, more than merely convenient labels by which to identify concepts and technique. The words themselves are often the key to understanding the deeper levels and even practical applications of the art.

Now that you are fluent in Japanese, you are ready to delve deep into the history, philosophy, culture, traditions, techniques, and mysteries of Shitō-Ryū karate-dō.

Chapter One

一撃必殺

Ichi Geki Hissatsu

Killing with a Single Strike

One of the most famous maxims of karate is *ichi geki hissatsu* (一撃必殺), which can be translated as "one attack, inevitably kill." In many respects, it is the essence of karate to develop the ability to kill an enemy with a single blow. Yet, anyone who has been training in karate for a few years is familiar with cases in which a karateka has been soundly beaten by a street punk with almost no formal training. How can this happen if karate is truly so effective that ichi geki hissatsu is a reality? That is the question that prompted us to write this book.

No unarmed attacker should ever be able to defeat a properly trained karateka because the purpose of karate, in a nutshell, is to make the karateka all but unbeatable in hand-to-hand combat. Nevertheless, even some "world champion" karateka have been handily defeated in real fights in recent years. We are convinced that the reason for this is because the purpose and nature of karate training changed dramatically in the decades following the Meiji Restoration. Prior to the Meiji Era, karate was strictly a form of bujutsu, and its techniques had only one purpose: to disable or kill another human being with one's bare hands. It was a brutal and devastating art whose practitioners could—and did, on some occasions—kill with a single blow.

The complete history of karate will never be known. It is a combative art whose origins have become shrouded in the mists of history and clouded by myth, legend, and even some fantasy. If the full, true story of its origins was ever known or recorded, it has long been lost to the ravages of time, conquest, and warfare. What we are left with are relatively recent accounts drawn chiefly from oral tradition and considerable speculation about the origins and early history of karate.

What little we do know with some certainty is that a form of empty-handed combat originated in the Ryūkyū Islands at least a thousand years ago. Originally called *ti* ("hands") in the Okinawan dialect or *te* in Japanese, it assuredly developed progressively over a period of centuries, and was influenced by many sources and cultures. Anthropologists believe that the early people of the Ryūkyū Islands were an eclectic group—a collection of Polynesian, Japanese, and continental Asians who explored or wandered into the four-hundred-mile-long chain of islands and settled there over a period of thousands of years. Archaeologists have found evidence of habitation of the Ryūkyū Islands that may be as much as thirty thousand years old. Chinese documents from the Sui Dynasty (AD 581–618) mention the people of the Ryūkyū Islands. Artifacts found at various sites in the Ryūkyūs suggest that they were engaged in extensive trade with most of Southeast Asia well before AD 1000. Archaeological evidence also indicates that each inhabited island probably began as an independent clan or tribe. Over the centuries, these isolated tribes banded together for mutual defense and cooperation with those of nearby islands to form small kingdoms, gradually coalescing through merger and conquest into larger island groups under common rule by a single king or chieftain.

Genetically, the Ryūkyūan people bear the closest resemblance to the Japanese of Kagoshima Prefecture at the southern end of the island of Kyūshū, which tends to support the theory that the majority of the Ryūkyūan population migrated from mainland Japan to the islands during the Jōmon Era (14,000–400 BC). The fact that this genetic dominance was sustained over the course of many centuries suggests that mainland Japanese and Ryūkyūans maintained ongoing interaction throughout this entire period. The Ryūkyū Islands also served as a refuge for defeated samurai fleeing the numerous wars on mainland Japan. A prime example of this is Minamoto no Tametomo, who, following the Hōgen Rebellion of 1156, was banished from mainland Japan. It is widely believed (though also disputed by some scholars) that sometime prior to 1170, Minamoto no Tametomo fathered Shunten, the first recorded king of Chūzan. Regardless of the ancestry of King Shunten, it is almost certain that the combat arts of the mainland Japanese samurai were among the significant influences on the development of combat arts in the Ryūkyū Islands, particularly Okinawa, even before the Satsuma Invasion of 1609.

The largest island in the Ryūkyū archipelago is Okinawa, which became the most powerful and prosperous of these kingdoms. By the twelfth century, Okinawa and the twenty nearest islands had consolidated into three kingdoms, known as Hokuzan (Northern Mountains), Chūzan (Central Mountains), and Nanzan (Southern Mountains). In 1373, China established formal diplomatic relations with the Ryūkyūan kingdoms, with emissaries in permanent residence. According to oral tradition, this event, and the arrival of the renowned Thirty-Six Families from China in 1393, began a period of integration of native Okinawan ti with Chinese chuan fa ("kung fu"). However, historical records in China document trade, diplomacy, and conflicts between China and the Ryūkyū Islands at least as early as the Sui Dynasty (AD 581–618). Recent scholarly research into the similarities between White Crane Fist from the Fujian region and some styles of Okinawan karate leave little doubt that Chinese chuan fa had a substantial influence on Okinawan ti—especially prior to 1600—just as the legends of karate's origins have long asserted. What is far less certain is which other styles and types of Chinese fighting arts also had substantial influence, and whether Shaolin chuan fa had as great an influence on karate as many legends claim it had. Debate on these issues has been extensive in the latter twentieth and early twenty-first centuries, and the issues and questions may never be fully resolved. This period of strong Chinese influence in Ryūkyū lasted for nearly the entire Ming Dynasty (1368–1644), during which Ryūkyū maintained an embassy in Fujian, but it is likely that many of the scholars, artisans, and advisers also came from the Ming capital of Nanjing and would have brought different styles of chuan fa. It is also probable that the term *kempō* (拳法, the Japanese reading of *chuan fa*) was introduced to Okinawa during this period.

In 1429, the three Ryūkyūan kingdoms were united by King Shō Hashi into a single kingdom with its capitol at Shuri, Okinawa. Oral tradition holds that a ban on swords was imposed shortly after this unification by his son, King Shō Shin, giving rise to increased interest in methods of unarmed combat. And while this is a logical consequence of such a ban, no other evidence has yet been found to support this legend. It would be nearly two hundred years after the unification before the first legendary masters of karate appear in Okinawan folklore.

In 1609, Shimazu Tadatsune, the *daimyō* of Satsuma-Han, invaded and conquered Okinawa with a force of 2,500 samurai. If it had not already been the case beforehand, mainland Japanese combat arts certainly influenced the development and practice of Ryūkyūan fighting arts from that time forward. In 1629, Shimazu issued a ban on the possession of all bladed weapons by the Ryūkyūan people. This act, more than any other, served to elevate karate to prominence in Okinawan folklore and traditions, even though the word *karate* did not come into usage until at least the mid-eighteenth century.

Few documents have survived to establish how and when the various terms for unarmed combat in Okinawa, such as *te* (also pronounced "ti," "de," and "di"), Okinawa-te (or Uchinaa-di), *kempō (kenpō)*, *tegumi*, and *karate* (or *tōde*), actually came into use.

Most references to these terms came from late-nineteenth- and early-twentieth-century sources.

It was in the aftermath of the weapons ban that the first of the karate masters whose identities are still renowned today arose from the ranks of Ryūkyūan *peichin* (the equivalent of samurai). Men like Takahara Peichin, Chatan Yara, and Sakugawa Kanga, whose names are associated with kata still practiced today, were royal bodyguards or other government officials. These men had to be capable of much more than just knocking an opponent senseless with a punch or a kick. They had to be able to defend against a sword or a spear bare-handed in mortal combat.

These pioneers taught their art to a generation of younger disciples whose names have been immortalized in the annals of karate, like Matsumura Sōkon, Matsumora Kōsaku, Oyadomari Kōkan, and Aragaki Seishō, who in turn passed it on to those who ushered karate into the twentieth century, including Itosu Ankō, Higaonna Kanryō, Motobu Chōshin, and Yabu Kentsū. These were the last generation of karateka to live in the late Tokugawa Era—the waning years of samurai rule—and to be adult citizens of the Kingdom of Ryūkyū before it was fully annexed into the Empire of Japan in 1879. Their disciples, most of whom were born shortly after the samurai were officially abolished and the Ryūkyū Islands became Okinawa-ken, grew up and lived in the transitional period in which Okinawa continued its assimilation of Japanese culture. These included many who are still highly revered today, such as Funakoshi Gichin, Mabuni Kenwa, Miyagi Chōjun, Ōtsuka Hironori, Kyan Chōtoku, Aragaki Ankichi, Motobu Chōki, Chibana Chōshin, Yabiku Moden, and Hanashiro Chōmo. They were also the generation that witnessed Japan's transformation from an isolated island nation to a militarist empire seeking conquest of many of its Asian neighbors, culminating in its invasion of China in 1931 and subsequent entry into World War II.

The first major shift in the training emphasis of karate since the Satsuma Invasion was precipitated by the Meiji Restoration in 1868 and the abolition of the samurai class. Armored samurai no longer walked the streets of Okinawa, and Ryūkyū was no longer a nominally independent kingdom under Japanese occupation. Okinawa was now a *ken* (prefecture), Okinawans were Japanese citizens, and order was maintained by local constables. The primary enemy against whom karateka had trained for nearly three centuries no longer existed. If karate was to survive as an art and lifestyle, it would have to find a new raison d'être. And it did.

The First Sino-Japanese War (1894–1895) created a need for healthy military conscripts and a renewed interest in samurai traditions and spirit. Kendō (fencing with bamboo swords) became a popular sport and was introduced into Japanese schools. Around 1902, Itosu Ankō began teaching karate at Shuri Jinjo Shōgakkō (Shuri Public Elementary School) as a method of improving the physical fitness and mental and spiritual well-being of the students. Soon, several of his contemporaries were teaching karate in schools and recreation centers, and to police departments in Okinawa. By 1905, three changes in karate were already evident. Karateka were training in large groups, as seen in figure 1.1, rather than individually or in groups of less than ten. Itosu sensei had created five simplified kata (practice patterns) to facilitate instruction to large groups of school children. And training emphasized general physical, mental, and spiritual fitness, safety, and the philosophical aspects of karate over its combative uses.

In October 1908, Itosu sensei wrote a letter to the Japanese Ministry of Education urging the adoption of karate in Japanese schools. His introduction includes this revealing statement: "In the past the Shōrin-Ryū school and the Shōrei-Ryū school were brought to Okinawa from China. Both of these schools have strong points, which I will now mention before there are too many changes." It is clear from this comment that changes to the way karate was being taught were already occurring by 1908, and it was sufficiently different from the way it had been taught during the samurai era that it warranted explanation. Although Itosu sensei did mention self-defense as one of the reasons for training in karate, he also included the following:

- ◆ "Karate is not merely practiced for your own benefit; it can be used to protect one's family or master. It is not intended to be used against a single assailant but instead as a way of avoiding a fight should one be confronted by a villain or ruffian."

- ◆ "If children were to begin training in karate while in elementary school, then they will be well suited for military service."

- ◆ "You must decide if karate is for your health or to aid your duty."

- ◆ "In the past, masters of karate have enjoyed long lives. Karate aids in developing the bones and muscles. It helps the digestion as well as the circulation."

Figure 1.1   Mass instruction at Shuri Castle circa 1938.

It is clear from these statements that Itosu sensei considered karate training in the post-samurai era to be as much for developing general health and fitness as combat.

Over the next twenty years, karate adopted the training uniform (*gi*) and belt system of the sport of jūdō. Several of Itosu's students, notably Funakoshi Gichin, Mabuni Kenwa, Tōyama Kanken, and the founder of Gōjū-Ryū, Miyagi Chōjun, moved permanently from Okinawa to mainland Japan and established public dōjō or karate clubs at major universities. In the early 1930s a few university karate clubs began holding intervarsity tournaments, and collegiate karate programs began emphasizing karate as a sport, following the example of intercollegiate jūdō and kendō competitions. Efforts to establish rules and tournaments for karate increased after jūdō was presented as a demonstration sport at the 1932 Olympic Games.

In 1933 or 1934, the Dai Nippon Butoku-Kai first recognized karate as a form of traditional Japanese budō. This, coupled with Japan's conquest of Manchuria in 1931–1932, as well as several provinces of northern China in 1933–1935, precipitated several more significant changes to karate. Once considered the epitome of sophistication, all things Chinese came to be viewed as inferior, so the kanji for *karate* were changed from 唐手 ("Tang [Chinese] hands") to 空手 ("empty hands"), as we know it today. The Butoku-Kai insisted that the curriculum for karate instruction be formalized and systematized, including the award of ranking and titles in a manner similar to the curricula and rankings of other forms of classical Japanese budō, like kenjutsu, iaidō, and the martial sports of jūdō and kendō. With the outbreak of the Second Sino-Japanese War in 1937, the Butoku-Kai received increasing demands by the Ministries of the Army and Navy to train citizens for military service. By the time of Japan's entry into World War II in 1940, the Butoku-Kai was effectively under the control of Japan's armed forces ministries. This increasing militarism further altered the nature and purpose of karate training, with greater emphasis on physical fitness, stamina, nationalism, and samurai spirit.

Defeat in World War II changed the psyche of the Japanese and Okinawan people. They became deeply repentant, convinced that their own government's wartime aggression had brought ruin upon their once great nation. They collectively repudiated war and violence, proclaiming in the preamble to their new 1947 Constitution:

> We, the Japanese people, acting through our duly elected representatives in the National Diet, determined that we shall secure for ourselves and our posterity the fruits of peaceful cooperation with all nations and the blessings of liberty throughout this land, and resolved that never again shall we be visited with the horrors of war through the action of government …

[Article 9] Aspiring sincerely to an international peace based on justice and order, the Japanese people forever renounce war as a sovereign right of the nation and the threat or use of force as means of settling international disputes.

This dramatic shift in the cultural paradigm drastically altered their view of karate and other forms of budō. Nevertheless, sensei throughout Japan recognized the value of karate training to reaffirm the dignity of a defeated people and inspire them to rebuild their war-ravaged nation. After all, in addition to physical strength, stamina, and prowess, karate had long served as a means to develop strength of character, determination, respect, and purposefulness—traits that were now desperately needed to give their nation the physical, emotional, and spiritual resolve to rebuild and quickly rise to become an industrial leader of the postwar world. So, despite the nation's conscientious refutation of war and aggression, karate rapidly gained in popularity throughout both Okinawa and mainland Japan in the postwar era—but with a dramatically altered emphasis and underlying purpose.

No longer was the primary focus of karate on combat by royal bodyguards or the constabulary against criminals, assassins, and the once oppressive samurai. Postwar karate was instead viewed chiefly as a method of fitness, character development, and self-improvement. *Ti (te)*, *karate*, and even *karate-jutsu* were no longer considered appropriate terms for the art. In postwar Japan and throughout the world to which it rapidly spread, the art was now almost universally and quite emphatically called karate-dō—the karate way of life—to emphasize training in the art as a holistic lifestyle, not merely a combat system. Although much of this transformation occurred in the first half of the twentieth century, the postwar era brought it to full fruition. By the mid-1950s, karate-dō was practiced chiefly as a sport that emphasized the cultivation of personal discipline, respect, and strength of character rather than a system of life-or-death combat.

Karate also became extremely popular among members of the U.S. occupation forces, who took this exotic fighting art back to their homeland, where it caught on rapidly. By the 1960s what had been an obscure fighting system unique to the island of Okinawa prior to the 1920s had grown into a global phenomenon. With this unprecedented proliferation of karate came the worldwide development of karate tournaments, and concern for the safety of competitors contributed substantially to the reduction of the practical effectiveness of karate techniques. Immediately, the most damaging techniques, such as eye gouges, joint dislocations, neck-breaking, and strikes to the groin, throat, spine, and other lethal and debilitating targets, were banned from tournament sparring. All joint locks, throws, and pins, other than foot-sweeps, were also banned. Soon, acceptable scoring techniques were limited to punches directed at the front and sides of the body and head as well as kicks targeting the body and head. Kicks and strikes below the belt, as well as to the spine or back of the head, which are among the most effective for self-defense, were forbidden. In addition, penalties were imposed for excessive contact force or deliberately injuring an opponent. In other words, the most useful and effective karate techniques were all forbidden in competition.

One result of imposing these stringent safety rules on kumite (sparring) competition is that competitors spent most of their training time practicing the very techniques that were the least effective in actual combat. In the nineteenth century, kumite was considered to be so dangerous that it was outlawed in Okinawa, and kata were the primary method of karate training. Other training methods were employed to strengthen the body and harden its striking surfaces. In combination, those two methods alone were deadly, and many karateka of that era, like Yabu Kentsū and Aragaki Ankichi, who never practiced kumite in the dōjō but rigorously trained in kata, were known (or at least reputed) to have killed men barehanded in street fights.

Further illustrating the lethality of karate as taught prior to the twentieth century is that in order to be accepted for training by some sensei, a student would have to demonstrate their sincerity and strength of commitment—often by performing mundane tasks, like working for months in the sensei's garden. This wasn't simply to weed out those who weren't dedicated; it also gave the sensei time and opportunities to evaluate the character and attitudes of the prospective student by observing how they behaved when they thought no one was watching. But even that wasn't always enough. Some sensei required new students to be vouched for by a *hoshōnin*—a person of high standing in the community, such as a constable, teacher, or government official, who served as a personal sponsor and guarantor that the student would not misuse the skills the sensei would impart. In those times, karate was considered so lethal that it could not be entrusted to anyone other than those of high moral character. And it could not have been mere myth or superstition that brought this about, but rather centuries of practical experience.

As any athletic trainer will attest, whatever you practice most is what you will perform when put to the test, so karateka who devoted most of their training to preparing for kumite competition were inadvertently training to be incapable of inflicting serious harm to an opponent.

Training to perform tournament kata produced similar outcomes. Emphasis shifted from training to improve the combat effectiveness of the techniques in kata to practicing to be judged primarily on the aesthetics and athleticism of kata performance. Instead of training to deliver a killing blow, kata practice became an exercise in graceful movement, balance and poise, symmetry and correctness of standardized stances, artistic tempo, good posture, and precise posing at the completion of each technique to elicit the notice of tournament judges and garner a high score. In other words, tournament kata training literally became a matter of form over substance.

Many believe that karate was deliberately "watered down" for instruction to foreigners, like American servicemen. While it is consistent with the Japanese tradition of teaching some of the most effective and lethal techniques of classical budō only to advanced students of long standing whom the teacher considers physically, emotionally, spiritually, and morally ready to be entrusted with them, the authors believe this is an oversimplification. Instead, we are convinced that it is primarily an unintended consequence of excessive emphasis on the sporting applications of karate in the latter half of the twentieth century.

Regardless of the underlying causes, counteracting this trend toward practicing karate as a harmless sport is the purpose of this book. We seek to restore for our readers a sense of awe and respect for karate as the deadly art it was created and intended to be—karate as true bujutsu. In pursuing this goal, we are not disparaging or discouraging competitive karate—only recognizing that tournament karate is not true budō and that karate is far more comprehensive than the limited selection of techniques permitted in tournaments. Competition can serve a useful role in training, as we will describe later, but to be true to its origins, we believe karate must be understood and practiced as the art of killing.

In one sense, karate is obsolete. People are no longer attacked with swords and spears by samurai encased in *yoroi* (bamboo armor). Firearms have replaced the weapons wielded by the criminals, assassins, and invaders faced by the legendary karateka of the seventeenth through nineteenth centuries. Even interest in sports karate has waned significantly in the twenty-first century because the growing popularity of MMA ("mixed martial arts") competition has made it appear ineffective for street fighting or practical self-defense. We believe that the best way to overcome this misperception of karate is to restore the lethal essence of koryū budō to karate training so that it can accomplish its full and true purpose in the lives of modern karateka.

In that regard, the question now becomes, What is the appropriate method and focus of training to practice karate as true budō?

The answer to that question is what we endeavor to address in the remainder of this book. We hope to present a framework for training in karate as koryū budō—a framework that does not denigrate or diminish the benefits of tournament competition or training in the aesthetic aspects of karate, but instead encourages training that puts all aspects of karate practice in unified and balanced context that is consistent with the spirit of true budō.

Chapter Two

空手道の目的

Karate-dō no Mokuteki

The Purpose of Karate-dō

If karate is the art of killing, then a natural assumption would be that the purpose of training is to become a killer. Nothing could be further from the truth.

Ten thousand years of human history have demonstrated one unassailable fact: the only way to stop someone who is determined to injure, capture, or kill another person is to overpower the attacker with an even greater force. Kind words will not dissuade them, nor will compromise or conciliation. Only defeat will stop them. As we explain in detail in chapter 4, the need to protect the property and lives of farmers—the source of life itself in ancient Japan—was the impetus for the rise of the bushi in Japan, and eventually led to them being merged into the samurai class. To fully understand this in both its historical and philosophical context is so important to how we should be practicing karate today that we have devoted an entire chapter to it.

The abridged version is that there must be people who are willing, trained, and equipped to risk their own lives to preserve and protect the lives of others. This role was filled by the bushi of ancient Japan, the earliest knights of medieval Europe, the militias of early America, the posses of the Wild West, and others around the world before police departments were established to perform this function. It has only been in the past 150 years that professional police have usurped the role of protector from private citizens. However, in most countries, the role of police has become primarily to investigate crimes after they have been committed, rather than to prevent or stop crimes in progress. As the saying goes, "When seconds mean the difference between life and death, the police are only minutes away." Pragmatically, it is the right and responsibility of every person to defend their own life and property. Therefore, one purpose of training in karate is to become a preserver and protector of life.

An argument could be made that devoting a lifetime to training in karate is unnecessary to become a guardian of life when one can simply purchase a firearm, taser, pepper spray, or similar weapon and spend a few hours learning how to use it. We believe this is an inadequate and potentially dangerous idea. Without a conceptual, philosophical, emotional, and moral framework and sufficient training to make sound judgment, justice, compassion, and to restrain instinctive reactions under stress, possessing the capacity to kill or disable can lead to abuse, vigilantism, and vengeance. This is why we believe karate must be practiced as karate-dō—a way of life, not merely a skill.

As historian John Dalberg-Acton so famously stated, "Power tends to corrupt, and absolute power corrupts absolutely. Great men are almost always bad men." It is also true that a person who is not dangerous—not capable of harming others, if necessary—is all but useless. Power of one kind or another, whether it is physical strength, intellectual power, political or authoritative power, or the power of persuasion, is essential to accomplishing anything worthwhile.

There is no more absolute power a person can have than the power of life or death over others. The greater the power, the greater the restraining forces must be to prevent that power from corrupting those who possess it. This is why we are convinced that a lifetime of training in budō is essential to karateka. Frequent and consistent training that emphasizes and continually reinforces the principles and core values of bushidō serves as the restraining force to prevent the corruption of karateka.

However, as we detail in chapter 5, karate-dō as a way of life involves more than protecting others. Bushidō is not a product of the bushi alone, but is a fusion of the bushi and samurai traditions. The samurai of mainland Japan had a significant influence on the culture of Okinawa well before the Satsuma Invasion of 1609, and certainly a primary influence after that. Most of the famous karate masters of the nineteenth century either reputedly or proudly claimed to be *shizoku* (士族)—descendants of bushi or samurai. The bushi and *oyakata* (aristocrats) from whom these masters were descended, and whose values they emulated, clearly perceived themselves as servants of both their kings and the people, similar to the way the mainland samurai perceived their roles and duties. This attitude of servanthood is therefore as essential to a karateka as the role of protector. So, a second purpose of karate training is to become a servant-leader.

Psychologists and sociologists have many terms for it, but everyone has an emotional need for significance. Psychologist Abraham Maslow called it "self-actualization." It is the need to feel that your life has meaning and purpose, that you are important. People either fulfill this need in a healthy and constructive way by accomplishing things that are beneficial to others, or they fulfill it in an unhealthy and detrimental way, such as narcissism or dominating others. Living life as a servant and protector of others, whether professionally or as an avocation, fulfills this need in a beneficial and healthy way. Karate training that instills the attitudes, character traits, and behavior of bushidō is an effective means of ensuring that karateka meet this need in uplifting and meaningful ways.

We devote chapter 5 to a more thorough presentation of the major precepts of bushidō, but at a minimum the following traits should be cultivated by a karateka: respect, benevolence, righteousness, sincerity, faithfulness, reputation, courage, and self-discipline. Respect entails recognizing and protecting the basic human rights of every person. Benevolence is doing what is best for others. Righteousness is doing what is right and just. Sincerity is speaking and acting honestly, not merely to please others or for personal gain. Faithfulness is being trustworthy, dependable, and responsible. Reputation is acting in a manner that evokes admiration from others. Courage is doing what you know to be right or necessary in spite of personal fears. And self-discipline is both restraining yourself from acting impulsively and compelling yourself to act responsibly.

Not only does following the principles of bushidō constrain karateka from abusing or misusing their skills, but it equips karateka to lead meaningful, accomplished, and fulfilling lives. Those eight character traits are the foundation of crucial life skills. Accomplishing anything of significance requires courage, discipline, sincerity, and faithfulness. Respect, benevolence, and reputation will rally others to support your efforts. And righteousness affords a clear conscience to pursue your goals without inhibition or doubts. It is, quite simply, a blueprint for success. A sincere, highly principled person driven by a worthwhile goal, unwavering dedication to honorable core values, and following a disciplined course of action is practically unstoppable. Thus, a third purpose of training in karate-dō is to develop the skills and attitudes to live a more meaningful and fulfilling life.

A vital way in which karate training develops and reinforces the attitudes and behavior of bushidō is membership and regular training in a dōjō. The word *dōjō* (道場) means "place of the ways." For karateka, these ways are karate-dō and bushidō. As we will explain later, a dōjō is much more than just a building in which people go to train. It is a community of like-minded people who share a commitment to developing character, moral values, and living a productive and meaningful life. The members of a dōjō hold one another accountable for living in accordance with the principles of bushidō and adhering to the *dōjō kun* (道場訓).

In chapter 11 we explain the function and purpose of the dōjō kun ("code of the dōjō") in greater detail, and provide some examples. Nearly every traditional karate dōjō has a dōjō kun that states a number of training objectives that the karateka pledges to seek. These objectives typically include such traits and behaviors as respect, self-control, personal discipline, perseverance, compassion, and ethical conduct. Each training session in the dōjō begins and ends with the participants reciting the dōjō kun. This frequent recitation of the dōjō kun imprints the mind with these goals and reminds the karateka of the true purpose of training.

The founder of Shitō-Ryū, Mabuni Kenwa, famously said that karate-dō is *kunshi no ken* (君子の拳): "the fists of a gentleman." Taken literally, *kunshi* means "offspring of a leader," so one implication of kunshi no ken is that every karateka is—or is striving to become—a person of nobility, strong character, wisdom, and sophistication worthy to lead others. The characteristics and behavior of a kunshi are therefore essentially those of a samurai.

Another purpose of karate training is character development. Any and all forms of budō afford budōka the training and character traits of bushidō to live an exemplary and extraordinary life. A feature that makes karate-dō particularly well suited for this is found in the name we use for the art. Karate, pronounced *tōdi* or *tōde* in the Okinawan dialect, was originally written 唐手 in kanji. The *tō* or *kara* (唐) referred to the Tang Dynasty (AD 618–907), which was the time in which China first established trade and cultural exchange with Okinawa. 唐手 is therefore taken to mean "Chinese hands." As early as 1905, Hanashiro Chōmo, a senior student of Itosu Ankō, was already writing karate as 空手 ("empty hands") in his personal notes. When karate was first introduced on mainland Japan in the early 1920s, many people considered it odd that an Okinawan art would be called "Chinese hands," so "empty hands" soon became the favored term on the Japanese mainland. Most Okinawans, however, resisted this change to the traditional name for the art.

The outbreak of the Second Sino-Japanese War in 1931 resulted in widespread anti-Chinese sentiment and intense nationalism throughout Japan. This, coupled with the Dai Nippon Butoku-Kai establishing a branch in Okinawa in the mid-1930s, created pressure on Okinawan karateka to adopt the mainland's term for karate. After more than a decade of discussion, a meeting sponsored by the Ryūkyū Shimpō newspaper was held at the Showa Kaikan in Naha, Okinawa, on October 25, 1936—the day now celebrated as Karate Day worldwide. Most of the leading Okinawan sensei were present, including Miyagi Chōjun (Gōjū-Ryū), Chibana Chōshin (Shōrin-Ryū), Hanashiro Chōmo (Shōrin), Kyan Chōtoku (Tomari-te), Kyōda

Juhatsu (Tōon-Ryū), Motobu Chōki (Motobu-Ryū), and noted karate scholar and author Nakasone Genwa. Two significant decisions resulted from this historic meeting: adoption of the kanji 空手 for karate, and treating karate as a way of life (道) rather than just a physical skill set.

Although they might appear to be little more than insignificant changes in spelling and semantics, these decisions have had substantial and lasting consequences.

Consider first the implications of karate being a way of life. This elevated karate from being merely a sport or pastime to a comprehensive lifestyle equivalent to the way bushidō served as the template for the life of a samurai in pre-Meiji times. In effect, it brought karate full circle, restoring its role in the lives of karateka to what it had been during the Tokugawa Era. Karate-dō is not merely a method of unarmed self-defense but an allegory for life itself. When viewed as an allegory, the concept of "empty hands" takes on a meaning of far greater impact and value than just unarmed combat.

The typical view of "empty hands" karate is that of defending oneself without using weapons. But, to be empty-handed is not only to be without weapons; it is to be without any physical resources at all. As an allegory for life, empty-handed means dealing with all of life's challenges relying entirely on one's mind, body, and spirit. Approaching life empty-handed strips the karateka of all excuses and the false sense of security people derive from money and possessions. In the same way a karateka must prevail empty-handed over an attacker armed with a sword, spear, knife, or cudgel, a karateka must also prevail over any difficulty or obstacle life presents without money, equipment, status, credentials, or other resources. No excuses—only victory or defeat.

One of the purposes of karate training is to develop greater ingenuity and self-reliance to meet life's challenges. The "empty hand" kanji for karate reveal the means by which a karateka can achieve this level of self-reliance. The *kara* (空) of karate has a deeply nuanced meaning beyond just "empty" or "void." It also means "vast," "expansive," or "limitless." So, the hands of a karateka may be empty, but they are full of boundless possibilities and potential. The only real limit faced by a karateka is their skill, training, effort, ingenuity, or spirit.

The *te* (手) in karate is both singular and plural, so besides referring to the hands in a purely physical sense, it also implies the fusion of the mind and body to produce the techniques, methods, and strategy of karate.

Hands that are empty are more versatile than hands that are clutching a tool or weapon. They need not release one thing in order to hold another. They are free to push, pull, grasp, swing, sweep, strike, or perform any task the mind can conceive without impediment or delay. Similarly, as a metaphor for life, the empty hands of a karateka can achieve more than the hands of one who is burdened by the need to hold the things they rely on for security and support. Being empty-handed is freedom and opportunity—a life without limits.

Another key purpose of karate training is to increase awareness of life's boundless possibilities and potential. To live the empty-handed life of a karateka requires several character traits, however. Courage is among the foremost of these in order to face the countless adversaries and adversities that come into our lives without any weapons other than our skills, attitudes, and ingenuity. Self-control, discipline, and perseverance are vital to prevent ourselves from being distracted, deterred, or diverted from our objectives. Righteousness and benevolence are essential to ensure that we don't use unethical or illegal methods to achieve our goals or abuse others in the pursuit of our ambitions. For these reasons, karate-dō training emphasizes philosophical, spiritual, emotional, and moral development as much or more than skill development.

The limitless nature of karate also applies to the art itself. When it was written as "Chinese hands," karate techniques were limited to those originating with, or derived from, Chinese combative arts. After several centuries of evolution, adaptation, and refinement, karate as "empty hands" has no limits to the techniques, tactics, strategies, and applications for which it may be used. The ultimate purpose of karate training is to become the best human being you can become, and to live victoriously.

Budō no Arikata
PURPOSE OF BUDŌ

To understand the purpose of budō training, we need only understand that the goal of budō is to win. It really is that simple. At the same time, it is far more complex: obviously, we train in budō in order to prevail in an encounter. We certainly don't spend years training in order to be defeated. However, budō training involves much more than merely learning how to injure or kill another person in battle.

A Japanese legend relates that, centuries ago, there were two samurai who were closer than brothers. As they matured and prepared to embark on their *musha shugyō*—the customary travels to perfect their skills—it was apparent that their paths would separate for many years. So, before departing, they met by a quiet stream and vowed to meet again on that very spot twelve years later to share tales of their training and heroic exploits. Just as they had vowed, they both returned to the bank of the stream on the very day twelve years later, but found that a recent storm had swollen the gentle stream into a raging torrent, barring their way to the exact spot of their last meeting.

Determined to live up to the letter and spirit of his vow, and to demonstrate the incredible skills he had mastered during their twelve-year separation, one samurai dashed to the river and made a spectacular leap that carried him over the deadly current and safely to the other side. The jump exceeded today's Olympic records, and should have amazed his friend. Instead, the other samurai calmly strolled about fifty yards upstream and walked across the bridge to the other side.

The skills one man spent a lifetime of sacrifice and dedication to develop had only accomplished what anyone could achieve with minimal effort and only an extra minute or two of time. Similarly, if our goal in karate training, or any form of budō, is merely to kill people, we can simply purchase a gun or build a bomb rather than invest years in training. So, a vital factor in karate-dō is to be certain that your training goals are worthwhile.

Next, we must realize that "winning" is not merely defeating an opponent; it is perfecting yourself—your personal character as well as your skills—to the degree that an opponent cannot prevail against you. Yet, winning is still more than this.

The samurai considered *saya no naka ni kachi* ("victory while the sword is [still] in the scabbard") to be the ultimate victory. There is no equivalent statement like "win without striking a blow" in karate, but the principle of saya no naka ni kachi applies equally. It is implied by the "empty hands" of karate. The karateka has no sword to draw in the first place, so the best victory is one in which no blow is struck, no swords are drawn, no blood is shed. This is the concept behind the *bu* (武) in budō—to prevent violence from starting in the first place, and only to use violent means of defense if nonviolent means fail.

Another layer of meaning in saya no naka ni kachi derives from the fact that fighting skills alone, no matter how highly perfected, are not always sufficient. There is always someone more skillful, or someone with a dirty trick for which you are unprepared. But attitude is more important than aptitude in real combat. We have all seen encounters reminiscent of that between David and Goliath, where the underdog defeated a far mightier opponent through sheer determination and faith. If you have already visualized yourself as victorious while your sword is still in its scabbard or your hands are still at your sides, and you have trained diligently enough to have supreme confidence in your ability to be assured of victory, then you are more likely to prevail if swords are drawn or blows are struck.

Only a fool or a lunatic would engage in a life-or-death battle without wholeheartedly believing they will win.

Therefore, a key purpose of karate-dō is to develop courage, confidence, and an indomitable spirit through consistent and diligent training. Without them, a high degree of skill is useless. It would be like painting a great masterpiece, then storing it away where no one can ever see it. This is not only a waste of time, talent, and effort, but a loss of something valuable to humankind.

Ultimately, the purpose of karate-dō is to develop the mind and spirit of a bushi, an attitude and strength of character that wins any battle before it begins. This is no simple matter to achieve. It takes years of daily training to cultivate these attributes and to rid oneself of attitudes and reactions, such as anger, fear, selfishness, jealousy, and hate, that are counterproductive or self-destructive.

Furthermore, winning must be accomplished without trying to win. Once again, this concept at first seems self-contradictory. After all, how can you be victorious if you don't even try to win? The answer is that the key to winning a battle is a steadfast determination to not lose. This is more than just a semantic difference; it requires a fundamental shift of focus and commitment. When you are trying to win, you will be inclined to take unnecessary risks in your determination to defeat your opponent. But when you are instead resolved not to be defeated, you have the luxury of waiting for your opponent to make a mistake or expose a vulnerability that you can then exploit to achieve victory.

Lastly, the empty and unlimited hands of a karateka are not merely for fighting. Although a recent study stated that 73 percent of females and 89 percent of males are assaulted at least once during their adult lifetime, only one in every seventy adults is assaulted in a given year. The average adult is therefore likely to have only one or two fights in a lifetime. Even the average professional boxer now has fewer than twenty fights in a career, and the average MMA fighter has under forty—and those are sports, not life-threatening attacks on the street. The truth is that most budōka never have to use the fighting skills they develop more than two or three times in an entire lifetime. If self-defense or protecting others was the sole or even primary purpose of karate-dō training, it would be a waste of time and effort.

Fortunately, fighting has never been the primary purpose of karate or any other form of budō. Its purpose, as we hope you already realize, is to make budōka better people.

Our hope and objective in *Karate As the Art of Killing* is to encourage karateka to train at a deeper level, to pursue karate as more than just a pastime, an exercise program, or a sport, and to recognize the terrifying potential of this art and devote themselves to becoming people capable and worthy of wielding its power as a force for good in society.

Chapter Three

糸東流の特徴

Shitō-Ryū no Tokuchō

Characteristics of Shitō-Ryū

Every karateka is convinced that the style of karate they practice is authentic and effective, if not simply the best of all available styles. In truth, the quality of instruction is far more important than the style being taught. We believe that what karateka should seek is not the "best" style, per se, but the style best suited to them as an individual, and a sensei who will guide them to getting the most benefit out of training in that style. Having said that, there are several characteristics of Shitō-Ryū that karateka should consider when evaluating the suitability of a style and potential sensei.

Shitō-Ryū is the style of karate founded by Mabuni Kenwa around 1931 in Ōsaka, Japan. It is the second most popular and considered one of the four major styles of Japanese karate, the other three being Shōtō-kan, Wadō-Ryū, and Gōjū-Ryū. Mabuni Kenwa was born on November 14, 1889, in Shuri, the capital city of Okinawa, ten years after the nominally independent Kingdom of Ryūkyū was annexed into the Empire of Japan as Okinawa-ken. An important factor in understanding the nature of Shitō-Ryū is that Okinawa was already assimilating mainland Japanese culture when Mabuni was born, and during his entire lifetime that culture and Japanese nationalism dominated Okinawa.

Mabuni was a seventeenth-generation descendant of the renowned Okinawan bushi Ufugushuku Kenyū, known as "Oni" ("Demon") Ufugushuku. Perhaps because his frail and sickly nature contrasted with the image of his famed ancestor, Mabuni's parents sought to improve his health and stamina. In 1902, at the age of thirteen, he began training under famed karate master Itosu Ankō, probably at one of the Okinawan schools in which Itosu sensei taught at the time. Mabuni's closest friend was Miyagi Chōjun, who would become a famous karateka in his own right. In 1908, Miyagi introduced Mabuni to his sensei, Higaonna Kanryō, and Mabuni began training with him as well.

Itosu Ankō (1831–1915) was the single most influential person in the transition of karate from its origins as a pragmatic and lethal form of combat prior to the Meiji Restoration of 1868 into karate-dō as a lifestyle of physical, mental, and spiritual development as it is practiced today. He was considered the foremost exponent of the style known as Shuri-te (also known as Shōrin-Ryū at the time) in the early twentieth century. Higaonna Kanryō (1853–1915) was the leading proponent of Naha-te (also known as Shōrei-Ryū) in the early twentieth century. These were the two major forms of karate practiced in the late nineteenth and early twentieth centuries, so Mabuni developed a deep understanding of both styles.

A third style, Tomari-te, existed in the nineteenth century. Its two best-known sensei were Oyadomari Kōkan (1827–1905) and Matsumora Kōsaku (1829–1898), and it was generally considered to be a branch or variant of Shōrin-Ryū, since it shared several kata with Shuri-te, but none with Naha-te. Their two most prominent students were Kyan Chōtoku, who studied under both, and Motobu Chōki, who was a student of Matsumora and others.

Higaonna and Itosu both died in 1915. The last of the major nineteenth-centuries masters, Aragaki Seishō, died in 1918. Their sensei had died between 1890 and 1905. Bridging the gap between Itosu's generation and Mabuni's were men like Hanashiro Chōmo (1869–1945), Kyan Chōtoku (1870–1945), Yabu Kentsū (1866–1937), and Motobu Chōki (1870–1944), highly accomplished karateka who made significant contributions to the art but were not acknowledged as the successors to their sensei and did not acquire the large followings that several of their kōhai (juniors) later garnered. The lack of recognized successors to Itosu, Higaonna, Matsumora, and Oyadomari left a vacuum in the leadership of karate from the time of their deaths until the mid-1920s.

It was Mabuni Kenwa who led the efforts to establish the Karate Kenkyū-Kai ("Karate Research Association") in 1918. Members included all the prominent Okinawan karateka of the time, who met regularly to exchange theories and techniques. The association did not have a building in which to train, so in 1925 Mabuni opened the garden of his home for its use as a meeting location and training facility. In this way, Mabuni developed a comprehensive knowledge of all three major factions of karate, Shuri-te, Naha-te, and Tomari-te, from their foremost practitioners—a knowledge considered unequaled by his peers.

In 1928 or 1929 Mabuni relocated to Ōsaka and established a dōjō there. To honor his primary teachers, he named his combined style of karate by concatenating the first kanji of each of their names, taking the *ito* (糸) from Itosu and the *higa*

Figure 3.1 Karate Kenkyū-Kai in Mabuni Kenwa's garden.

(東) from Higaonna, which together (糸東) are pronounced "shitō." Thus, Shitō-Ryū contains the combined teachings, or style, flowing primarily from Itosu and Higaonna. In addition to the karate of his direct teachers, Mabuni also incorporated what he learned of Tomari-te from Kyan Chōtoku and others in the Karate Kenkyū-Kai, as well as aspects of White Crane kung fu he learned from his friend Wu Xianhui (known in Okinawa as Gō Kenki).

In effect, Shitō-Ryū combines all three of the major nineteenth-century karate factions—Shuri-te, Naha-te, and Tomari-te—into a single, comprehensive, and unified curriculum.

Following the death of Mabuni Kenwa on May 23, 1952, each of his sons, Mabuni Kenei (1918–2015) and Mabuni Kenzō (1927–2005), claimed succession to Shitō-Ryū. Mabuni Kenei was the elder of the two, and by tradition would be considered the rightful successor, but he had not trained significantly in the art, so one of Mabuni Kenwa's most senior students, Iwata Manzō, served as the chief instructor and technical adviser for Mabuni Kenei until he had trained sufficiently to fill that role himself. Conversely, the younger son, Mabuni Kenzō, had trained consistently with his father and accompanied him on most of his travels, so his mother ensured that he assumed leadership of the hombu dōjō in Ōsaka and his father's complete syllabus of Shitō-Ryū. Although considerable rivalry ensued for decades between dōjō affiliated with each of the two brothers, in recent years both factions have come to acknowledge and respect the legitimacy of each other as successors to the Shitō-Ryū legacy.

Students of either lineage can be assured that they are members of a ryū and are inheritors of the authentic legacy and teachings of Mabuni Kenwa and his forebears.

Just as a dōjō is more than merely a building, a ryū is more than just a curriculum. Or a style. Or a lineage. Or a school of thought. Or a social organization. It is all of these and more. It is, as the word *ryū* implies, a flow. A continuum. An aggregation. A ryū is not just the teachings of its founder or founders; it is the accumulated knowledge, research, analysis, wisdom, and experience of all its past and present sensei and members. It is the DNA of an art, to which each generation contributes something new and unique, giving it life and causing it to evolve and adapt to its changing environment. Every karateka has a unique personality, unique talents, and a unique perspective of the art, and each of us leaves an imprint of those unique characteristics on the other members of our ryū.

This concept is readily apparent in Shitō-Ryū. Itosu Ankō and Higaonna Kanryō each represented a different approach to karate. Mabuni Kenwa was the "child" produced by combining the karate "DNA" of Itosu and Higaonna. Mabuni then combined their "DNA" with principles and techniques he learned from Gō Kenki, Aragaki Seishō, and members of the Karate Kenkyū-Kai. To that, he added the lessons from his personal research and passed on to his sons that accumulated and expanded knowledge, which they in turn imprinted with their own research and personality and passed on to their students.

This book is a product of a similar process. Shimabukuro Hanshi first trained for thirty years with Hayashi Teruō, who was a student of Kokuba Kōsei, one of

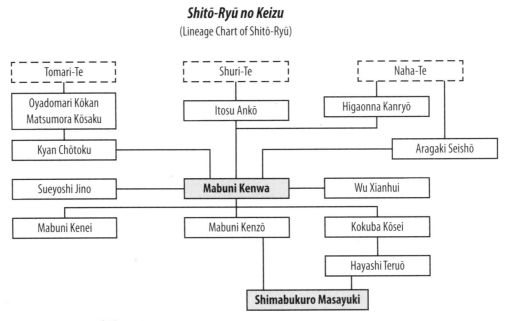

Shitō-Ryū no Keizu
(Lineage Chart of Shitō-Ryū)

Figure 3.2 Keizu of Shitō-Ryū.

Mabuni Kenwa's early pupils. Hayashi also trained with Nakaima Kenkō of Ryūei-Ryū, and incorporated much of the Ryūei-Ryū curriculum into Hayashi-Ha Shitō-Ryū. Beginning in 1996, Shimabukuro Hanshi trained with Mabuni Kenzō until the latter's death in June 2005. As a result, the Shitō-Ryū that Shimabukuro Hanshi imparted to his students is a blend of the "DNA" of Hayashi-Ha Shitō-Ryū and Mabuni Kenzō's Seitō Shitō-Ryū, to which he added his own research and experience.

Figure 3.2 is a *keizu* (lineage chart) providing a visual representation of the flow of teaching and tradition in our ryū.

Shugyō no Mokuteki
TRAINING OBJECTIVES

Shugyō is often translated as "ascetic training." This is an apt term for karate training, provided it is correctly understood. For some, the word *ascetic* may evoke images of a monk sitting beneath a mountain waterfall, or a hermit living a life of deprivation and isolation. That is not what shugyō is really about. The austerity involved in karate training is not so much about self-deprivation or abstaining from all of life's pleasures; it should instead be understood as intense focus on the primary objectives of one's training. Such focus is, of course, self-discipline, but it is not deprivation. It is merely using discipline and self-control to avoid distractions, procrastination, and laziness. Shugyō is serious, diligent, and purposeful training, but that does not mean it cannot also be enjoyable.

We believe that every karateka's training objectives should include:

- physical fitness and endurance
- healthy lifestyle choices
- mental and spiritual well-being
- moral and ethical behavior
- practical application of karate techniques
- personal discipline and self-control
- strategic and tactical thinking
- a purpose-driven lifestyle

All of these objectives can be accomplished through karate training, and those who devote themselves to shugyō that addresses these goals will enjoy more successful, meaningful, and fulfilling lives.

Chapter Four

武士道の起源

Bushidō no Kigen

The Origins of *Bushidō*

The first half of the seventh century AD was a desperate time for Japan. Since 620 the country had been ravaged by battles between the rival Soga and Fujiwara clans vying for military power and influence over the emperor. Heavy taxes were being imposed on farmers to pay the costs of this conflict, and not enough rice and other crops were being produced to feed the entire populace. The peasants—even many farmers—were starving.

Following the assassination of the leader of the Soga faction and a coup d'état, the Empress Kōgyoku and her eldest son both abdicated the throne, and her younger son, Kōtoku, became emperor on July 12, 645. One of his first official actions was directed at increasing food production. It is known today as the Taika Land Reform, and it set in motion a series of events that over a period of centuries produced the samurai as we typically think of them today.

The samurai of the seventh century bore almost no resemblance to such legendary figures as Miyamoto Musashi, after whom the modern image of the samurai is modeled. They were exactly what the literal meaning of *samurai* suggests: servants. They carried out the wishes of the imperial family and the nobility. For the most part, they were clerks and stewards. But the Taika Land Reform would eventually change that.

Prior to the reform, all land in Japan was technically owned by the emperor, but actual control over most of the land was exercised by members of the imperial family who served as governors or by the heads of competing clans, called daimyō. It was the daimyō who actually determined the distribution of the crops raised in the lands under their control. The reform first reinstated control by the emperor along with a specified system of distribution. In an effort to stimulate production, private ownership of land was also introduced. Called the Handen Shūju Sei (班田収受制), "Group Field

Allotment System," it entitled each male *ryōmin* (良民)—citizens in good standing (literally "good people")—aged six or older to a parcel of land a little over twenty acres in size, and each female about fifteen acres. The production from these lands was taxed at 3 percent, and a census was taken every six years, with lands reapportioned accordingly. Upon death of a landholder, their parcel reverted to imperial control.

This reform proved so successful in increasing farm production and improving the nation's prosperity in the first seventy-five years that it was modified in AD 723 to permit retention of lands by two generations of a landholder's descendants after their death, and in 743 it was further amended so that ownership remained in a family permanently. In addition, any land that had previously stood fallow would be granted to any ryōmin who would farm it. These amendments not only further increased food production, but also allowed large families to amass significant tracts of land. And as a side effect, it created a prosperous middle class for the first time in Japan's history. However, it also brought an unintended consequence that led to the rise of some of the most formidable combatants the world has ever seen. That unintended consequence was greed.

When individuals were forbidden to own land and received the same share of what they produced as those who did not produce it, there was little reason for farmers to maximize their efforts or production. But now that farmers could keep 97 percent of what they produced, fertile land was of great value—particularly to those with large families or strong ambitions. Motivated families reclaimed larger tracts of land, and through marriages with other aspiring families, grew into wealthy and powerful local clans. As their holdings grew beyond the capacity of their own families to manage, they hired members of the *senmin* (賤民) class of "despised people" to help with the work. Those holding large tracts of land thus became known as *jinushi* (地主), or landlords.

At the same time, land was being privatized under the Taika Land Reform, a related policy change that led to the development of *shōen* (荘園) or manor estates. Lands that had been granted to Buddhist temples and Shintō shrines were tax-exempt, but one of the land reform policies provided that any such lands that had been allowed to go fallow could be reclaimed by ryōmin and would remain tax exempt. This policy fomented disputes, not only between opposing jinushi over available tracts, but also between jinushi and the temples and shrines that were not eager to have their excess lands taken away, even if those lands were not in use. The results of these various disputes were often violent, so to protect their lands, families, and hired workers, jinushi soon either had to become skilled in combat or hire trained guardians to protect their property and the people tending it.

Fortunately for the emerging jinushi, an imperial edict implemented back in AD 703 made men with military training and equipment available to them. That edict was the Taihō Code, which, among other things, established Japan's first standing imperial army. To provide sufficient equipment and labor for this army, one in every three males was required to enter military service and to supply his own weapons. This led to a large number of men who were both equipped and trained for armed combat throughout Japan—men who, after returning to civilian life, were capable of helping to defend disputed property and who were motivated to do so as members of the families they were protecting. By the early ninth century, these protectors were a recognized profession apart from farmers or jinushi, so a new term was coined for them: bushi (武士).

As a reminder, the kanji 武 (*bu*) means to "stop or prevent violence," and 士 (*shi*) means "gentleman," "scholar," or "wise person." So a bushi is a wise protector or guardian, one who stops or prevents violent conflict—a peacemaker and strategist who defends those who are unable to defend themselves.

The bushi were not initially samurai. This came as a much later development. During the Nara and early Heian eras, samurai were bureaucrats and other servants of the imperial family and aristocrats. The imperial army that had been established in AD 702 was disbanded by Emperor Kammu at the beginning of the Heian Era, around 794, after which the imperial government had only two armed forces available: the *ōryōshi* (押領使) "territorial control emissaries," who were stationed in the provinces to suppress rebellion, and the *tsuihoshi* (追捕使) "pursuit-and-capture emissaries," who served the imperial court in the apprehension of criminals.

The bushi serving the jinushi and those temples and shrines whose monks were not trained in combative arts soon outnumbered the troops under imperial jurisdiction. Within the next hundred years, the bushi had gained importance to society and influence lesser only to that of the aristocracy, jinushi, and high-ranking samurai, yet they lacked the equivalent social status. Meanwhile, the Fujiwara clan, which had long controlled the imperial family, were gradually waning in power, and the Taira and Minamoto clans were growing in wealth and influence. By the mid-tenth century the three clans—all of which were related to the imperial family—were engaged in frequent battles for control of lands, which created additional opportunities for bushi to be employed.

A concurrent development that provided bushi an opportunity to serve as merce-naries was the feuding that began between rival temples in the mid-tenth century. The first known violent skirmish occurred in AD 949, when fifty-six armed *sōhei* ("monk soldiers") from Tōdaiji attacked the home of a Kyōto official who had made a ruling unfavorable to that temple. Many battles subsequently occurred between Tōdaiji, Kōfukuji, Enryakuji, and Miidera sōhei. Temples and shrines also used sōhei and mercenaries to protect their lands from encroachment by jinushi. All of these factors combined to spur the growth in number and power of the bushi well into the twelfth century.

At the end of the Hōgen Rebellion of 1156, the bushi took control of the imperial court, extending their power and prestige even further. In 1160 the Heiji Rebellion resulted in the Taira clan gaining supremacy over the Fujiwara and effective control over the emperor. After another twenty years of sporadic warfare, the Minamoto overthrew the Taira in 1183, although fighting in the Gempei War continued until 1185. In 1192, Minamoto Yoritomo had himself proclaimed Sei-i Tai-Shōgun (征夷 大将軍), or "Barbarian-Conquering Great Army Commander" of Japan. Although it was not the first time the title had been granted to a military leader, it was the first time the *shōgun* held greater power than the emperor or empress.

Due to their key role in the Minamoto victory over the Taira, the bushi had grown powerful enough to demand such recognition and were finally granted offi-cial standing as samurai within the Japanese caste system. From this point until the close of the Tokugawa Era, the terms *bushi* and *samurai* would be nearly synonymous, even though many of the samurai class continued to hold positions that were chiefly administrative in nature, and would be essential to the *bakufu* (幕府) "curtain-office" government that ruled Japan for the next 666 years.

The *gunki monogatari* ("war tales") of the thirteenth and fourteenth centuries, such as the *Heike Monogatari* and *Genji Monogatari*, described many noble ideals, acts, and personal sacrifices of the bushi, but did not yet use the term *bushidō* to denote those ideals. Nevertheless, themes common to bushidō began to emerge in the gunki monogatari literature, such as loyalty, duty, honor, courage, self-sacrifice, compassion (to a degree), wisdom, morality, and scholarly pursuits. For the most part, however, the ideals of bushidō expressed in the early literature focused primarily on battlefield behavior rather than cultural and philosophical refinement.

It wasn't until the mid-sixteenth century, at the height of the Sengoku (Warring Provinces) Era, that the term *bushidō* came into common usage to describe the prac-tices and ideals of the samurai. It appears in the writings of such men as daimyō Katō

Kiyomasa (1562–1611) and chief retainer Nabeshima Naoshige (1538–1618) when setting forth the duties and expectations of the samurai under their commands. The Sengoku Era lasted about 150 years, from 1467 until 1603, and was marked by a combination of nonstop warfare among the daimyō and tremendous social upheaval. The Ashikaga shogunate had been severely weakened and could no longer control the daimyō whose domains were distant from the capital city of Kyōto. The increasing wealth of the jinushi had stimulated increased trade with China, resulting in the emergence of a merchant class in Japan, and with it, a degree of social mobility never before available.

At the time the term *bushidō* began appearing in Japanese literature and taking root among the samurai, daimyō Oda Nobunaga had conquered and controlled roughly half the land area of Japan and was intent on conquering the remainder of Honshū, Shikoku, and Kyūshū. He was opposed in this effort by Takeda Shingen, Uesugi Kenshin, Saitō Tatsuoki, and several other daimyō. Among Oda's chief retainers were Hashiba Hideyoshi and Tokugawa Ieyasu, men who epitomized the two extremes among samurai of that time due to the social upheaval of the previous hundred years. Tokugawa was the son of daimyō Matsudaira Hirotada and had been born and bred into the position of samurai, with the formal education and cultural sophistication expected of a future daimyō. In contrast, Hashiba had begun life as a nameless farmer and had been elevated to samurai status due to his battlefield prowess. By 1575 he was Oda's highest-ranking general and daimyō of three provinces, and had given himself the surname Hashiba.

In 1582, another of Oda's generals, Akechi Mitsuhide, staged a successful coup d'état by surrounding Oda's small entourage at Honnōji in Kyōto while Hashiba was away besieging Takamatsu Castle in Shikoku. Facing overwhelming forces and a certain overthrow, Oda committed *seppuku*. Hashiba returned immediately from Shikoku, and just eleven days later killed Akechi at the Battle of Yamazaki. Already the daimyō of the majority of provinces under Oda's control, Hashiba quickly established his leadership over the remainder of Oda's domain.

Hashiba was installed as *kampaku* (imperial regent) in 1585, and the next year was given a new family name: Toyotomi. Ironically, it was Toyotomi—the man who had risen from a lowly peasant without a surname to become the ruler of more than half of Japan and chief adviser to the emperor—who issued an edict in 1586 establishing the samurai as a hereditary caste, prohibiting members of lower castes from rising to samurai status and requiring all samurai to take up residence in castle towns. In 1588 he issued a ban on peasants owning weapons and initiated the Taikō no Katanagari

("Retired Regent's Sword Hunt") to confiscate all arms in possession of non-samurai throughout Japan. This left the farmers without bushi or arms of their own to protect their lands, but by this time most land ownership had consolidated in the hands of daimyō, who already lived in the castle towns.

Toyotomi died September 18, 1598, while a significant portion of his armed forces were engaged in an attempt to invade Korea in preparation for a later invasion of China. His five-year-old son, Toyotomi Hideyori, became titular head of the Toyotomi domain. A council of five elders, the *go-tairō* (五大老), ruled as coregents in his stead. The most powerful of these elders was Tokugawa Ieyasu, who had grown increasingly independent since the death of Oda Nobunaga. Tokugawa spent the next two years secretly forging alliances with daimyō who opposed Toyotomi rule, and in October 1600 Tokugawa defeated the greatly weakened forces of Toyotomi at the Battle of Sekigahara. Although skirmishes with factions loyal to Toyotomi continued until the Siege of Ōsaka Castle in 1615, Tokugawa effectively became the supreme ruler of all Japan upon his appointment as Sei-I Tai-Shōgun on March 24, 1603, and the islands of Honshū, Kyūshū, and Shikoku were truly unified as a single nation for the first time in history.

The unification of Japan precipitated the most significant development in bushidō as a philosophy and way of life. With the peasants stripped of weapons with which to revolt and all armed forces under a single command, Japan enjoyed an unprecedented level of peace for the next 250 years. The role of the samurai once again became exclusively that of the bushi in the truest sense—as peacemakers—and bushidō took on its fullest and deepest meaning. After 150 years of continual civil war, the role of the samurai became primarily that of diplomacy and politics, rather than strategy and battlefield tactics.

Thus, it wasn't until the early Tokugawa Era (1603–1868) that bushidō began being expressed in the terms with which budōka are familiar today. Earlier writings about bushidō focused on the behavioral aspects of samurai life—constant wariness, vigilance, and preparedness for battle on a moment's notice—rather than the ideology and character by which a samurai should conduct the affairs of state and only occasionally be involved in combat to quell a minor uprising or apprehend a criminal.

As part of unifying all of Japan under the rule of a single Sei-I Tai-Shōgun, the island of Okinawa was brought under the jurisdiction of the Satsuma Han of southern Kyushu in 1609 by what is called the Satsuma Invasion. The event is called an invasion because some three thousand Japanese troops landed in Naha Harbor, but King Sho Nei of Okinawa had ordered his diplomats to negotiate a peaceful surrender prior to their arrival, so although a few skirmishes with casualties had occurred on other Ryūkyū islands, the invasion of Okinawa was a bloodless one, and the surrender of King Sho Nei occurred with only minor incidents. By most surviving accounts, the Okinawan people—particularly the aristocracy who were allowed to remain in office under Japanese oversight—quickly embraced Japanese culture and customs, including the Japanese language and, of course, bushidō.

It was several decades after Okinawa came under direct Japanese rule that the earliest known karateka arose, among them Chatan Yara (1668–1756), who was the primary sensei of Takahara Peichin (1683–1760), who in turn taught Sakugawa Kanga (1733–1815). By the time Chatan Yara began instructing Takahara, bushidō was already well established among the samurai of mainland Japan and the bushi and shizoku of Okinawa. It is said that Sakugawa was thirteen years old when he began training under Takahara, which would have been roughly the midpoint of the Tokugawa Era and the philosophical peak of bushidō. It was Sakugawa who coined the term *karate* (then written as 唐手 and pronounced "tōdi" or "tōde" in the Okinawan dialect) for the art he passed on to Matsumura Sōkon (1803–1899), which is why Sakugawa is generally considered the father of karate-dō. Sakugawa is also said to have given Matsumura the nickname "Bushi" because of his ferocity and spirit. It is noteworthy that Sakugawa, and later the students of Matsumura, would consider "Bushi" an appropriate and complimentary nickname, unless the concepts of the bushi and bushidō were not already familiar to, and accepted by, Okinawans by the early nineteenth century.

This is further reinforced by the fact that Matsumura traveled to Kyūshū to learn Jigen-Ryū kenjutsu, the sword style used by the Satsuma samurai, and taught it to some of his students. Certainly, if the major concepts of bushidō had not already been infused into karate beforehand, they were in the teachings of Matsumura Sōkon. Among Matsumura's students was Itosu Ankō (1831–1915), who introduced karate into the Okinawan school system and encouraged the Ministry of Education to do likewise in mainland Japan. It was principally Itosu, his contemporaries Higaonna Kanryō and Aragaki Seishō, and their direct students who ushered karate into the twentieth century and created the foundation for karate-dō as it is practiced today. Men like Funakoshi Gichin, Mabuni Kenwa, Miyagi Chōjun, Hanashiro Chōmo, Kyan Chōtoku, Chibana Chōshin, and Nagamine Shōshin were the ones who adopted the *karate-gi*, *dan* and *kyū* ranking systems, identifying rank with belt colors, rules of competition, and organized instruction methods. They were also the ones who changed the writing of karate from 唐手 ("Chinese Hands") to 空手 ("Empty

Hands" or "Limitless Hands"). Perhaps most importantly, they were the ones who promulgated karate as karate-dō (空手道)—a way of life.

What specifically is the dō (道) that makes karate-dō more than just a sport, a pastime, or a fighting method? Bushidō. Karate-dō was never a peasant's method of self-defense, as many incorrectly believe. Perhaps in its most primitive stages, a thousand or more years ago, te was used by farmers and fishers in the Ryūkyū Islands to fend off thieves and marauding pirates, but since no later than the unification of Okinawa in 1429, it was almost exclusively an art practiced by the aristocracy and military. Every karateka known by name, from Takahara Peichin in the late seventeenth century to Itosu Ankō and Higaonna Kanryō in the early twentieth century, was either a member of the Okinawan nobility, held a position of significance in the Okinawan government, or was a shizoku (descendant of bushi). The fact is that it has only been since the 1920s that karate has been taught to the general public. Therefore, it is bushidō that provides the moral and philosophical framework for karate training, and serves as the *dō* in karate-dō.

Chapter Five

武士道の概念

Bushidō no Gainen

Principles of *Bushidō*

To be a karateka—a person who trains in karate-dō—one must follow the way of life called bushidō.

By this time it should be evident that karate-dō is not just a fighting skill, a sport, a form of entertainment, or a pastime. It is a lifestyle—a lifestyle based upon the way of life of the ancient bushi of Okinawa and Japan. It is a lifestyle driven by purpose (serving others), personal discipline, and a set of core principles that guide every word and deed. The word we use for that set of guiding principles is *bushidō*.

Volumes have been written on the subject of bushidō, and a single chapter is not sufficient to explain it fully. All we can hope to accomplish here is to provide an outline of the major concepts of bushidō, knowing that to fully understand and apply those concepts is a lifelong endeavor. The eight major principles or precepts of bushidō are:

- 礼 (*rei*) respect
- 誠 (*makoto*) sincerity
- 義 (*gi*) righteousness
- 勇 (*yū*) courage
- 自制 (*jisei*) self-restraint
- 仁 (*jin*) benevolence
- 忠義 (*chūgi*) faithfulness
- 名誉 (*meiyo*) reputation (honor)

Over the centuries, several additional traits have been associated with bushidō, but the eight characteristics listed above are those most widely considered to be the core principles of bushidō, so they are the essential ones all karateka should strive to develop from the outset of their training.

Rei
RESPECT

In many ways, *rei* (礼, "respect") is the cornerstone of bushidō. It can be argued that all other attributes of bushidō are by-products of respect, which is why we allotted an entire chapter to respect and ways to develop it. Perhaps the simplest way to describe respect is treating other people the way you want to be treated. Of course, *rei* has deeper and more nuanced meaning than that, but it succinctly states the behavior that results from cultivating an attitude of respect. In order to be respectful, one must understand people and why they behave as they do, and have compassion for them.

Respect is far more than courtesy and the rituals of proper etiquette. It must become an attitude that pervades every aspect of our character. In simplest terms, it is caring about people and things, treating them as you want to be treated, and preserving their basic humanity and dignity. Even the most loathsome criminals can be treated with respect by not abusing them, ensuring that their rights are not infringed, and giving them a fair trial presided over by an impartial judge, based on factual evidence, and decided by an impartial jury. Respect does not require admiration, agreement, or acceptance of misbehavior; it merely demands humane and considerate treatment of others, regardless of their attitude or conduct.

Respect also has two sides, like a coin: respect for the benefit and value of someone or something, and respect for the potential danger that person or object presents. In karate-dō we speak of katsujinken and satsujinken. The same hands that preserve and protect life can murder. A tool designed to improve life, if mishandled, can injure or kill its owner. An enemy should be respected as a human being, and also for the danger they represent.

Viewed in this context, every aspect of our training derives from respect. The care we take in *sahō* shows our respect for the dōjō, our equipment, sensei, and colleagues. The courtesies we offer in *reihō* likewise demonstrate our respect. But also, the diligence and perseverance we exercise in perfecting our skills are derived from respect for our potential opponents. Respect for the skill and potential danger of an opponent is exemplified in our posture and bearing (*shisei*), in correct structure (*kamae*) that optimizes the effectiveness of our techniques, in maintaining eye contact (*chakugan*), controlling the distance between oneself and opponents (*maai*), the intensity of our spirit (*kihaku*), and maintaining a constant state of alertness and vigilance (*zanshin*).

Respect is not merely a matter of courtesy and politeness; it is a matter of life and death. You will also find that the time you spend cultivating respect through the depth and sincerity of your reihō will reap great rewards by improving your personal relationships. As you learn to take the time to demonstrate your respect and appreciation, these attributes will carry over from the dōjō into your personal life. There it will reveal itself in your desire and ability to invest time in the people you care about, the way you treat customers and coworkers, and it will help solidify those relationships you hold most dear.

Makoto
SINCERITY

If rei is the cornerstone of bushidō, *makoto* (誠, "sincerity") is its foundation. In some ways it is the most important aspect of bushidō, because pretending to be righteous, courageous, benevolent, respectful, dependable, or honorable is a fraud that is worse than not having those qualities at all.

Sincerity takes many forms. Most of them are already familiar to us. Say what you mean and mean what you say. Keep your word, or don't give your word in the first place. Be honest—kind, but honest. Be yourself, not what you think others expect you to be. Behave the same way around others that you behave when you are alone.

Sincerity is the highest expression of a pure heart, because it requires speaking or acting with no ulterior motives, hidden agendas, or pretenses.

Gi
RIGHTEOUSNESS

Gi (義) means "righteousness." As the protector and servant of those who are unable to protect themselves, a bushi must always do what they believe is right, even at great personal sacrifice. Simply stated, righteousness is thinking, saying, and doing what is right. So, the task of the budōka is to know what is right in order to do what is right. Not what you feel is right, what you think is right, or what is right for you, but what you are certain is objectively and immutably right.

In a world of conflicting ideals, to know what is objectively right might sound like an impossible task. It is. We can never be absolutely certain that an action is objectively right unless we are omniscient. But we must constantly strive to understand what is right, to seek perfection of our motives and the principles we live by, or we cannot hope even to approach righteousness in our thoughts, words, and conduct. Righteousness therefore demands that we engage in continual self-examination to ensure that we are seeking perfection of our character, motives, ideals, and ambitions. We must search for sources of truth and develop a code of moral conduct and ethics. We must seek justice, not vengeance, for ourselves and others. And we must do good without any expectation of reward or recognition.

Philosophers, monks, and scholars across the ages have sought to definitively determine what is right. Whether we find the answer in religion, philosophy, science, great literature, personal reflection, or a combination of these, we must do likewise. No one can do it for us.

Budōka are aided in this endeavor by being members of a dōjō, where we are surrounded and supported by like-minded people who are engaged in the same struggle for perfection and will hold each other accountable for progress toward it.

Yū
COURAGE

Yū (勇) means "courage." Courage is not merely bravery in battle or facing an enemy. Courage is also needed to admit our faults and failings, to seek forgiveness, to strive for self-improvement, to take risks in order to achieve our goals, and to make amends for any wrong we have done others. Often, our greatest need for courage is not in facing danger, but in facing the truth about ourselves in order to grow and mature. Do not mistake courage for the absence of fear. Courage is the act of overcoming fear and doing what is right despite still being afraid.

True courage is rarely selfish. Acting in our own self-interest requires little courage, but to take physical or emotional risks solely for the benefit of others often does. One of the most courageous acts a person can perform is to risk or let go of all they have attained to this point in order to pursue something even more worthwhile. And courage is willingly accepting the consequences of our faults, failures, and mistakes without complaint. Then, after learning what lessons we can from that experience, trying again.

Jisei
SELF-RESTRAINT

Jisei (自制), "self-restraint," has two closely related components: self-control and discipline. Jisei is the combination of those two. In simple terms, self-control is stopping yourself from doing things you should not do, and discipline is forcing yourself to do things you should do. A simple example of self-control is resisting the temptation to have a second helping of dessert when we know it is bad for us. An example of discipline is having an extra helping of broccoli, even though we dislike its flavor, instead of dessert.

Together, self-control and discipline form jisei as practiced in bushidō. If there is a secret to a meaningful and highly accomplished life, it is jisei. True jisei is a rare trait. We all struggle greatly against losing our temper, overindulgence, acts of selfishness, jealousy, and envy that greater self-control would eliminate from our lives. And we all struggle equally against procrastination, lethargy, distractions, and inconsistency that more discipline would overcome.

Jisei is also a vital counterpart to *chikara* (power). As mentioned in chapter 2, power tends to corrupt, so the power to do great harm must be restrained if karateka are not to become monsters. There is no great virtue in lacking the power to harm others, but there is tremendous morality in possessing that power and keeping it under restraint.

One of the most noticeable and immediate benefits that karate training offers is improved jisei.

Jin
BENEVOLENCE

Jin (仁) means "benevolence." Benevolence is doing—not merely thinking or wishing—what is best for other people. Benevolence is not the same as generosity because simply giving people things is not always what is best for them. Sometimes true benevolence can seem cruel, since the most helpful thing we can often do for someone is to let them suffer the consequences of their actions and learn from their suffering.

Benevolence requires *chikara to jihi*, power and compassion in balance. Power without compassion to constrain it can lead to tyrannical, abusive actions. Compassion without power results in impotence—the desire to help without the means to do so. Jin can only result from power and compassion (chikara to jihi) being developed in balance and harmony, guided by gi (righteousness) and compelled by yū (courage) into action.

Chūgi
FAITHFULNESS

Most commentators translate *chūgi* (忠義) as "duty" or "loyalty," but we believe those terms can be too easily misconstrued. Better English equivalents would be "faithfulness" or "devotion to duty." Chūgi is more akin to dependability and steadfastness than to steadfastly following a cause or a leader. Loyalty can sometimes be blind to right and wrong, but the word *chūgi* is derived from gi (righteousness). The *chū* in *chūgi* means "fidelity," so chūgi should be understood as a commitment to doing what is right. In practice, that commitment supersedes friendships or personal loyalties.

There are many ways chūgi is manifested in our lives: dependability, keeping our commitments and promises, remaining steadfast in pursuit of our objectives, and remaining true to our calling or cause in the face of opposition or criticism.

Meiyo
REPUTATION

We mention *meiyo* (名誉) last, not because it is any less important than other aspects of bushidō but because in many respects it is the result of applying the other seven principles. Meiyo can mean both "honor" and "reputation." We think *reputation* is the preferable term, since a reputation must be earned from others as a result of one's actions, while honor can sometimes be little more than self-righteous posturing. Meiyo is not about acquiring honors and awards but about living honorably—meaning living in accordance with bushidō.

Honor is too easily motivated by selfishness or conceit—the desire to receive accolades for one's achievements, rather than the personal satisfaction of having done something that is beneficial to others. A reputation, on the other hand, is usually bestowed voluntarily in recognition of worthwhile accomplishments or benevolence. The difference may seem small, even chiefly semantic, but a person's perspective can often make a drastic difference in their motivation.

Paradoxically, by living a life of respect (rei), sincerity (makoto), righteousness (gi), courage (yū), self-control and discipline (jisei), benevolence (jin), and faithfulness (chūgi) while maintaining the humility not to seek or expect honors or recognition in return, the inevitable outcome will be a reputation as a person of honor.

Bushidō is an inherent and essential part of budō. It is the philosophy, character traits, and mindset that put the *bu* (peacemaking) in budō, but the two terms are not synonymous. Budō is more comprehensive. It includes all of the physical, mental, emotional, and spiritual aspects of karate training, while bushidō is limited to the character traits and behavior that results from budō training.

Chapter Six

武士の目

Bushi no Me

Eyes of a Bushi

A bushi does not see things in an ordinary way. Years of training cause a bushi's mind and spirit to process the impulses from the optic nerves in a highly refined manner.

Just as in Western culture, for the bushi the concepts of "eye" and "sight" include both physical vision (to see an object) and insight (to "see" someone's point of view). In fact, to the bushi, there is probably less distinction between these two concepts than in the West. For many Westerners, vision seldom rises above the first or second levels described below, but the bushi recognizes five distinct levels of eyesight and tries to "see" at the highest of these levels in a way that combines physical sight with deep insight.

Nikugen
"NAKED EYES"

Nikugen is nothing more than the plain image received on the retina, devoid of any mental or emotional process or filter. Obviously, it is the lowest of the five levels of vision, and it has three major limitations. First, nikugen is completely superficial. A person using nikugen sees nothing beyond the existence of the objects within their field of vision. Nikugen does not involve any deeper comprehension of these objects, such as how they came to be where they are, how they might interact, what direction they might be heading, what risks or opportunities they might present, how they might affect the observer or others, or any other implications.

Secondly, nikugen is limited by the observer's point of view. Someone using nikugen can see only that side of things that is facing their direction. In this sense, nikugen is almost two-dimensional. Staring at a circular object, a person using nikugen would not know if it is just a circle, or the bottom of a cone, the bottom of a cylinder, or the visible outline of a sphere. Thirdly, nikugen is easily obstructed. Simply placing something between the observer's eyes and the object renders it effectively invisible.

These qualities not only apply to physical sight but also to the "insight" sense of nikugen. People trying to "see" a problem using only nikugen can see only its superficial aspects. They also see the problem only from their own point of view, and their vision is easily obscured by circumstances, preconceived ideas, or even emotions. For example, using only nikugen, a person with no money might see their situation as hopeless poverty. With this two-dimensional view, the person is blind to other possibilities, such as bartering, borrowing, or selling some possession to raise money, or searching out sources that might provide what they need for free.

Tengen
"HEAVEN EYES"

The next developmental step in vision is *tengen*, translated literally as "heaven eyes." This does not mean heaven in any divine sense, but in terms of the observer's point of view—as if looking down from a high altitude that provides a much wider perspective.

With tengen, the observer is no longer bound by their own point of view, but has a neutral perspective in which they are better able to see the relationships between the objects or problems being observed, as well as more of the environment in which they exist. Quite literally, tengen is being able to "see the forest for the trees." In this way, not only can one clearly see the true nature and shape of objects, as in the first example of nikugen, but also all aspects of a problem from a broader and more detached perspective. With the less self-centered perspective of tengen, the observer's viewpoint is not as susceptible to the distortions of their own preconceived ideas, emotional reactions, or living conditions as it would be with nikugen. In addition, tengen cannot easily be obstructed, because the view of the situation is less dependent on the observer's point of view.

Using the previous examples, a person with tengen is more likely to perceive what one or more of the unseen surfaces of the circular object are. Similarly, someone with tengen will have the ability to "see" more sides to a problem and more possible solutions to it. Rather than narrowly perceiving a lack of money as utter poverty, a person with tengen might be able to see that they have other resources or options available.

However, even with this elevated perspective, the observer's emotions, preconceptions, and life circumstances can interfere to some degree with their perception, and their view is still limited to what the eyes alone can see.

Egen
"KNOWING EYES"

Egen (literally "thinking eyes") is a more useful level of sight, at which the image received by the brain is enhanced by knowledge or experience about the implications of the things being observed. It is important, however, not to confuse egen with analytical thought. Egen is not the product of consciously thinking about what you see; it is an automatic, subconscious process in which the eye and mind work together to interpret the images received by the brain, thus producing a deeper level of vision than mere physical eyesight. It is the product of knowledge and experience enhancing and informing what the eyes behold.

To use a simple example that many of us may have experienced, a person observing two cars approaching a blind intersection at right angles sees a collision about to occur. Most people would not have to stop and think to realize this. By experience, realizing that neither driver can see the other's oncoming vehicle, we automatically and subconsciously know they are about to collide. With only nikugen or tengen, and no past experience of traffic accidents, we would only see two cars in motion. Where nikugen and tengen are akin to the perspective of a child who has never witnessed a traffic accident, egen is enhanced by the insights from our cumulative knowledge and experiences.

Unfortunately, while most mature adults have egen with respect to common physical events, many lack the same insight with respect to emotional interactions or human motives. But with true egen, we would recognize when a clash of personalities or wills was about to occur just as readily as we can see an accident about to happen. Egen is the ability to comprehend an event not just in its immediately visible form, but also the forces and actions leading up to the present moment and the likely consequences of what we are observing.

Thus, the main benefit of egen is that the observer now naturally and subconsciously perceives and understands the cause-and-effect relationship of the things they witness. Egen is not limited by the observer's point of view, nor is their vision or insight clouded by emotions, preconceptions, or life circumstances. However, egen remains impaired in a crucial way.

Shingen / Hōgen
"COMPASSIONATE EYES"

For all its benefits, egen is still limited. Although the observer receives a complete, unobstructed, and undistorted view of situations and their causes and effects—including the reasons and motives underlying people's behavior—the egen perspective is detached and dispassionate.

The next level of vision, *shingen*, adds the most vital ingredient of all: compassion. Compassion is the spark that motivates the bushi to take beneficial action in a situation. With shingen, a bushi sees an event not merely from their own perspective and how it may affect them personally, but how the event will likely affect the lives of everyone involved—including society as a whole. Furthermore, with vision enhanced by understanding and compassion for all those affected, a bushi's action will not be motivated solely on what is best for themselves, but what will be the best for all involved.

The bushi with shingen does not view the feelings, actions, or desires of others in an adversarial way, such as "I'm right, so you must be wrong," or "I'm important, but you're not." Therefore, a bushi's judgment is not clouded by a need to prove themselves right, win an argument, or do what's best only for themselves. Instead, the bushi is only concerned with what has greater value or benefit. Thus, in a disagreement, the bushi sees the opinions of others only as alternatives, and they are able to use shingen to see which of these alternatives has the most value to those affected, whether it is their own preference or not. With this approach, it is far easier to persuade others to accept the best choice as well.

A bushi's viewpoint also takes into account the immutable laws of nature. A bushi understands the principles of cause and effect and that even wrongful actions are produced by these cause-and-effect forces. Because of this, shingen is often referred to as *hōgen*. Hōgen translates literally as "law eyes," but it does not refer to the laws of people. Instead, it means "law" in the sense of laws of nature, laws of science, or the law of cause and effect. It might be best understood as "universal perspective" in the sense of having equal compassion and concern for each person in a world operating under a natural order that never changes, but in which a person can choose to intervene. It is from this neutral, compassionate point of view that the bushi tries to observe the world and take the most beneficial action.

Thus, as shown in figure 6.1, a bushi is trained to "see from the heart." Training in the life-or-death art of karate-dō develops a deep, abiding compassion for people, and the experiences of life teach an understanding of the unchanging forces that shape both people and events. As their training and experience continue, their sight evolves through these stages from nikugen to shingen.

The easiest way to compare the differences—and the effects of those differences—between nikugen, tengen, egen, and shingen may be an example from everyday life: You are running late for a very important business meeting, and when you get onto the freeway, the traffic is heavily congested and moving at a crawl.

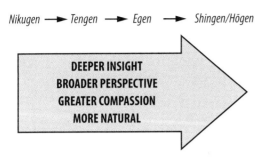

Nikugen ⟶ *Tengen* ⟶ *Egen* ⟶ *Shingen/Hōgen*

DEEPER INSIGHT
BROADER PERSPECTIVE
GREATER COMPASSION
MORE NATURAL

Figure 6.1 Progression from nikugen to shingen/hōgen.

With nikugen, all you can see is that you are going to be extremely late for the meeting and make a terrible impression. As a result, you will probably speed frantically through the traffic, swerving wildly from lane to lane, trying to gain a few precious minutes.

A person with tengen, however, can see that wild driving might earn them a traffic ticket. They might slow down a little, but more likely they will just be more vigilant in watching in the mirror for police cars, since they still want to save as much time as possible getting to the meeting.

The person with egen, on the other hand, does not allow their desire to make a good impression make them act rashly. Based on experience, they know that driving recklessly not only could earn them a traffic ticket and an additional delay, but also endangers them and other people on the road—people who have just as much right to safe use of the highway as they do. Furthermore, they are also aware that their business associates will probably be delayed by the same traffic jam, and that the minor consequences of being late do not justify the risks of driving negligently. Without having to think about it, they will understand the futility of speeding to make up lost time.

The bushi is already at the meeting, waiting for the others to arrive, relaxed, well prepared, and thinking of the best strategy to obtain the desired outcome. With the benefit of hōgen, the bushi understood that the freeways would be packed at rush hour and traffic jams were likely, so they got up earlier than usual to be sure traffic would not be a problem. In this way, if traffic was terrible, they would still be on time; if traffic was not congested, they would arrive early. The bushi also understood that by being early, the others would feel obligated to make up for their tardiness in some way or be frustrated over being late, so they would gain a psychological advantage at the meeting and be better prepared.

A true-life historical example of shingen comes from the exploits of one of Japan's greatest military leaders, Takeda Shingen, whose life exemplifies many of the training goals of iaijutsu. In Takeda's time, there was a brilliant tactician and warrior named

Yamamoto Kansuke. Yamamoto's prowess, however, was not apparent to the naked eye (nikugen), but his ugliness most certainly was. His battlefield experience left him with only one eye, a maimed leg, and a disfigured finger, in addition to his generally unattractive appearance. One of Takeda's rivals, Imagawa Yoshimoto, took one look at Yamamoto and turned him down flatly for a command position.

Takeda, possessed of shingen, quickly saw past the scarred and unpleasant surface appearance of Yamamoto to his strength of character and tactical knowledge. Takeda at once selected Yamamoto as one of his twenty-four *taishō* (generals). Not only did Yamamoto produce numerous victories for Takeda, but as a man who overcame severe physical handicaps, especially for his day, he was a tremendous inspiration to Takeda's other commanders and warriors, and thus doubly valuable.

Bushi no Me no Renshū
TRAINING TO DEVELOP EYES OF A *BUSHI*

Understanding *bushi no me* is a good start, but developing bushi no me is another matter. This is especially true if you intend to develop the eyes of a bushi in both its literal and figurative sense.

Karate training does not significantly change the core of your personality. The essence of your personality was formed by the time you were five years old. Instead, budō training enhances your existing character strengths and suppresses or compensates for your weaknesses. Since "the eyes are the mirror of the soul," developing bushi no me also allows you to see yourself clearly so you can make the greatest improvement possible in your attitude and character.

To develop bushi no me in the literal sense, gradually developing eyesight that is all-encompassing, compassionate, and deeply understanding requires concentrated effort in the dōjō. Your objective should be to both broaden and deepen your sight as well as your insight. Broadening your sight means enhancing your use of peripheral vision and combining sight with your other senses to provide awareness of things and events your eyes alone cannot see. Deepening your sight involves developing an understanding that delves far below the surface. A simplified example is being able to see past the frown on a person's face (the surface) to the emotion or problem that produced that frown. Of course, shingen is far more subtle, deep, and complex than this simplistic example, but it serves to convey the concept.

Whether you are training literally or figuratively to develop bushi no me, the first step, obviously, is to open your eyes. Of course, this means more than simply looking around—that would merely be nikugen. It means to practice being aware, to consciously observe the "big picture" without missing the details, to be cognizant of the causes and effects of the events you witness, to strive to understand other people's point of view and why they hold to it, to notice the subtleties of people's behavior, and to refrain from being judgmental toward them. It equally implies making an effort to "stop and smell the roses," to realize that there are always positive influences in your life—even when you are beset by what appear to be insurmountable difficulties—and to give at least equal attention to them.

To train in the figurative sense of bushi no me and reach a point where you are naturally using shingen most of the time is a difficult, lifelong process. So it helps to find a good starting point, such as *shin • ku • i,* as a means to begin developing bushi no me.

Shin • Ku • I
BODY • MOUTH • MIND

Like many training concepts in karate-dō, *shin • ku • i* will seem a bit paradoxical at first. Literally "body • mouth • mind," shin • ku • i refers to action, speech, and thought. This order is stated in the reverse of causation, but it is the proper order of training.

It is practically self-evident that the mind controls speech and action (with the exception, perhaps, of reflexive reactions), yet budōka through the centuries have found that in training it is more effective to begin at the surface and work back toward the source.

This approach may also recognize the fact that people readily notice our actions and immediately judge us by them. People also listen to our words, but in doing so they usually weigh them against our actions to test for hypocrisy. Our thoughts, of course, remain forever hidden from others. It doesn't matter to others what our thoughts or intentions are if our actions are harmful or disrespectful. Similarly, if we speak negatively, no amount of good thoughts and intentions will alter the impression left by our words.

Therefore, when we train to improve our character, we begin with the outward manifestation—our behavior. We act with respect toward ourselves and others. We train with discipline and diligence. As we train with this focus, our actions begin to be reflected in the way we speak. The more we consciously act in a respectful and disciplined manner, the more our language becomes respectful and disciplined as well. Thus, by learning to exercise control over our actions, we also develop control over our speech.

Of course, the conscious effort to control our actions and speech requires that our mind exert that control, and this conscious effort eventually becomes habitual and unconscious, thereby reshaping and controlling our thought processes. Once we have developed thoughts and emotions reflective of our improving character, then our words and deeds will continue to demonstrate our increasing maturity. In this way, the process naturally reverses, so that at higher levels of training, the mental discipline produces change in our actions and speech.

Shin • ku • i is a vital part of training for a bushi, for whom the slightest misstatement or misdeed could result in instantaneous lethal combat. It is therefore essential that a bushi exercise discretion in both words and actions. This can only be accomplished if their mind is thoroughly in control.

Even in modern Western cultures, shin • ku • i remains a valuable asset. Read the biographies of highly successful, inspirational people and you will uniformly find that their lives are guided by principles (the mind), which find their way into every word they utter and every action they take. Those aspiring to any measure of greatness in life must follow this model, and shin • ku • i is an effective means of developing such a lifestyle.

Ken Shin Ichi Nyo
BODY AND MIND AS ONE

The next stage of training to achieve bushi no me is known as *ken shin ichi nyo* ("body and mind as one"). In shin • ku • i, we train our bodies to respond to our minds, so that our actions become the result of our guiding principles and character. Ken shin ichi nyo takes that process a step further and makes our mind and body act in unison. Karate-dō is an excellent training method to accomplish this unity of body and mind.

In the sword arts of kenjutsu and iaijutsu, ken shin ichi nyo is normally written as 剣心一如, meaning "sword and mind as one," but by substituting 拳 ("fist") for 剣 ("sword"), which are both pronounced "ken," it can be written like this:

Figure 6.2 Kanji for ken shin ichi nyo.

This variation has the meaning "fist and mind as one," which is a core training objective in karate—to reach the point at which no conscious thought is necessary for the body to act, but instead the body acts the moment the mind perceives a stimulus. As we approach mastery of karate, we eventually reach a stage at which, rather than the mind instructing our body to take the appropriate kamae, then use our legs and hips to propel the arm and hand to strike, our fist simply strikes the instant our mind becomes aware of the need to do so because our mind and body are acting in unison.

An interesting paradox to consider while you are progressing through shin • ku • i to achieve ken shin ichi nyo is the Japanese proverb *Kokoro no shito wa narutomo, kokoro o shito sezare:* "Your mind can't be your master; you must master your mind." How are we to understand this axiom when we are training so that our mind controls our speech and action (shin • ku • i), and our body and mind act as one (ken shin ichi nyo)?

The answer is found in the fact that your mind is a complex mechanism in which your intellect, emotions, character, ideals, and motivations continually interact to produce your speech and actions. Each of these areas of your mind has both strengths and weaknesses. And each of these elements is also constantly evolving, influenced not only by external forces and circumstances but by the development of the other parts of your mind and personality as well.

Not only are these elements continuously struggling to control your conduct, but you are relentlessly besieged by outside influences trying to shape your behavior. The most overt of these are advertising, peer pressure, laws, social forces, financial pressures, and a variety of temptations. As if these were not enough, your own character adds stresses to this complex equation. For example, you might have a tendency toward laziness that is in constant conflict with your desire to succeed, or perhaps it is a sweet tooth at odds with your plans to go on a diet right after you finish the next doughnut. Our internal conflicts are different for each of us, both in nature and severity, but they plague every human being.

The point made by the proverb is that the sum total of all these forces will control your mind unless you make a conscious determination that they will not. Your mind will either react in some way to the inundation of these influences, or you must instead take proactive steps to ensure that it will stand against the combined effect of this bombardment. The force that will enable you to withstand these pressures and master your mind is the combination of your character, ideals, principles, and highest aspirations. These are the "you" that control your mind, and are the aspects of yourself that are most essential to develop through training in karate and bushidō.

Hen Doku I Yaku
CHANGE POISON TO MEDICINE

Another way in which bushi no me serves to improve both your character and your quality of life is found in the adage *hen doku i yaku* ("Change poison to medicine"). This is a deeper approach to adversity than simply learning to recognize that "Every cloud has a silver lining." It is more akin to the notion that "When life deals you a lemon, make lemonade."

Many of the medicines we use to cure illnesses are quite toxic. They work by killing bacteria, viruses, or even our own cells in a small enough dosage that they do not severely harm us. However, taken in greater quantity, many medicines can be lethal to humans. Recognizing this, the bushi have long known that, like certain poisons, adversities often have a medicinal effect if taken in the right dosage. Once again, the proverb suggests a proactive approach by the bushi; not merely looking for the good that might come out of a negative event, but deliberately creating a positive outcome from it.

The comparison of difficulties to medicine is also apropos in other respects. Most of the time we do not like the taste of medicine, but we take it to cure a malady that is even worse than the unpleasant flavor. Some medicines even produce adverse side effects, but we still take them because the disease is worse than the cure. Likewise, we seldom enjoy adversity, but we can use it as a means for self-improvement. With insight and effort, we can use life's setbacks to develop and improve such character traits as patience, endurance, determination, winning spirit, moral and mental fortitude, and perseverance.

Medicines are used to cure disease. Often, if we reflect honestly on the causes of our adversities, we find that they either resulted from, or were worsened by, our own shortcomings. By making a forthright self-analysis when we encounter a challenge, we can identify the area of our personality or character that requires a dose of "medicine." And, as we develop greater understanding of ourselves, we can learn to recognize the need to change our attitude and behavior before they create or worsen adversities in our lives, and thereby become less dependent on "medicine" to provoke those changes.

By learning to be more proactive in improving our character and the behavior that stems from it, we practice "preventive medicine." We cause ourselves and others less harm if we take our "medicine" when any symptoms first appear, rather than waiting until those symptoms are severe and require stronger doses. Over time, we will find fewer and fewer instances in which "medicine" it is needed. By maturing in our character and improving our bushi no me, both the frequency and severity of our difficulties will be reduced.

Takeda Shingen knew how to apply the lesson of hen doku i yaku in dire circumstances. Itagaki Nobukata, one of his generals, plunged his troops into a battle that Takeda's twenty-three other generals had strongly advised against and was soundly defeated. Upon Itagaki's return, he was harshly criticized by his peers, and he fully expected Takeda to strip him of all rank and honor—or possibly worse.

Takeda could have ordered Itagaki to commit suicide and made an example of him to impress on his other generals the importance of taking sound advice and never losing. Instead, Takeda wisely chose hen doku i yaku, so instead of chastising Itagaki, he praised him as a brilliant commander for having minimized his losses under such a crushing defeat, and saying that he doubted any other general could have done so well under the same circumstances.

Instead of being shamed and disheartened by his overwhelming defeat, Itagaki's attitude was strengthened with a renewed determination to merit Takeda's lavish praise and faith in him. As a result, he went on to lead several victorious campaigns for Takeda. Instead of lessening the effectiveness or losing a good general, Takeda created a great general by applying the principle of hen doku i yaku.

Yūdan Nashi
NEVER OFF GUARD

The last—and broadest—aspect of bushi no me is *yūdan*, being "off guard." The fighting skills of a well-trained bushi were so great that the best chance to defeat one was to catch them off guard. A famous story about Miyamoto Musashi illustrates this point well.

According to the legend, one of Musashi's enemies brought a force of several men to his bathhouse while he was bathing. They heavily stoked the fire under his bathwater, lit the bathhouse on fire, then waited in ambush outside the tiny shed. They intended to leave him only three choices: to be boiled alive, burned to death, or run out naked and defenseless to be slaughtered by their superior forces. With the benefit of bushi no me, Musashi had anticipated the possibility of such an attack, and taken his swords with him to the bathhouse. As the treachery unfolded, Musashi broke out through a side of the shed weakened by the flames and killed the enemies who were lying in wait for him.

Even when relaxing in his bath, when a sense of fair play should have placed him off-limits to attack by any but the most craven coward, Musashi never permitted yūdan. His mind and senses were always alert to danger, almost in the fashion of an animal subject to predation. By virtue of hōgen and without any conscious effort, his eyes were continually evaluating the cause and effect of all they surveyed, so that he could never be caught unaware.

An example of training to avoid yūdan is found in the story of a karate master and a young pupil who had requested to join his dōjō. As was common at the time, the sensei did not immediately accept the student for training, but instead asked him to tend his garden for an indefinite time to gauge the pupil's dedication to training. As the young man went about raking leaves, pulling weeds, and trimming plants, the sensei would approach quietly and slap him on the back of the head at every opportunity. This was, of course, extremely annoying to the young trainee. With each passing week he became more wary of the sensei's approach, and as his perception improved, he received fewer and fewer slaps. As months passed, the sensei had to become increasingly treacherous and inventive to catch the young man off guard, until at last he was no longer able to do so. At that point the sensei accepted the pupil for formal instruction and, with only minimal training in the fundamentals, the disciple quickly developed into a karate master, since no opponent was able to find an opening to attack him.

If you have hōgen and remain constantly vigilant, you will never be caught off-guard. Nothing in life will catch you by surprise. This is not to say that your life will never be beset by adversity or trials, but that you will be prepared and capable of meeting these challenges when they arise. Thus, true bushi no me—the combination of hōgen with the complete avoidance of yūdan—is essential to achieving heijōshin (see chapter 7).

You should be aware that the most vulnerable time for yūdan to overtake you is during your happiest times. In ancient days, it was well known that one of the best times to attack was when the enemy was celebrating a victory. When you are happy, you tend to relax and grow serenely oblivious to the events transpiring around you. It is also a state in which it seems pressing problems can be temporarily ignored. Typically, when you are unusually happy, your customary inhibitions are lessened, and it is easier for various pitfalls and temptations to slip unnoticed into your life.

On his deathbed, Takeda Shingen counseled his son Katsuyori to wait three years before leading an attack against any of his enemies. This period of engaging only in defensive battles would allow time for Takeda's army to adjust to Katsuyori's leadership, and for Katsuyori to mature and gain experience and credibility as their commander. Ignoring his father's advice, immediately after the mourning period for his father's death had ended, Katsuyori led his forces into a decisive battle against Oda

Nobunaga at Nagashino, relying on the legacy of his father's reputation and countless past victories to motivate the troops and intimidate the opponents. Instead, because of the yūdan of his overconfidence, Takeda's army was decimated. Soon thereafter, they were attacked again and utterly destroyed, forcing Katsuyori to commit seppuku. In a single act of yūdan, Takeda Katsuyori lost everything his father had spent a lifetime building.

Shinnen
UNSHAKABLE CONVICTION

As we have seen throughout this chapter, the mind is the focal point of all budō training. The mind working in concert with the eyes is shingen or hōgen. The mind controlling words and actions is shin • ku • i. The mind working in inseparable harmony with the body is ken shin ichi nyo. The mind never dropping its guard is yūdan nashi. The constant factor throughout these concepts—the hub around which they all revolve and the source of their fulfillment—is the mind.

The mind is the key to all of life, so the conclusion to be drawn is: Make up your mind! All other training will be pointless unless you do. You will never achieve shingen, you will never progress through shin • ku • i, you will never develop heijōshin without first having made up your mind. Once you have set your mind to something, and you believe in yourself strongly enough, nothing can prevent you from accomplishing that goal.

But this is not simply saying to yourself that you will do it. Nor is it merely writing some goals on paper. It means making an unshakable, steadfast determination that nothing short of death itself will stop you. This is the type of resolve that leads you to train even when you don't feel up to it—when you are bruised and blistered and aching and bone-weary, and you can't bear the thought of going back to the dōjō—but you go anyway because that is what you made up your mind to do.

The Japanese call this kind of strong spirit *shinnen*, meaning "unshakable faith" or "resolute conviction." But shinnen is more than simply iron-willed determination or merely believing strongly in yourself. It implies a belief that you are part of something greater than just yourself, that you have a moral right and responsibility to do what you are doing. The moral imperative of shinnen was a powerful stimulus for self-discipline and noble deeds to the bushi, who were only able to devote their full mind, body, and spirit to prevailing over their adversaries because of their unshakable conviction that they were fighting for a just cause.

Shinnen is impossible to achieve without the certainty that your goals and ambitions, or the cause that you are pursuing, and the methods you employ in pursuit of those goals are righteous. With that certainty, you have a moral imperative to do your utmost to prevail, and you can devote your entire mind, body, and spirit to achieving your goal, unhindered by doubts, fears, or conscience, and unleash the full power of shinnen.

Chapter Seven

心

Kokoro

Heart

Kokoro ("heart") is a core concept of budō and of Japanese life in general, so it is worth exploring the role of heart in karate training. Japanese use the word *kokoro* almost identically to the way *heart* is used in English. When used literally, it refers to the internal organ that pumps blood through the body. Figuratively, it has a wide variety of closely related nuances, including courage, fortitude, strength, spirit, personal character, compassion, and more. In budō, *kokoro* is generally used in reference to the combination of intellect, emotions, character, and spirit—the entire inner essence of a person.

When coauthor Leonard Pellman was in Japan training as an *uchideshi* (live-in student) in 1973, he spent three weeks living in Kōchi, Shikoku, with shōdō (calligraphy) master Sōnō Yoshiō, who was a *ningen kokuhō* (Living National Treasure), to learn the art of Japanese calligraphy. For several hours a day during those entire three weeks, Sōnō sensei had Pellman shihan practice writing only one kanji: 心 (kokoro). He told Pellman shihan, "In shōdō, we don't write with the hand; we write with the heart. So I want you to write *kokoro* until I can see *your* heart on the paper, not just a kanji." As Pellman shihan was preparing to leave on the final day of his stay, Sōnō sensei held up one of the hundreds of pages of *kokoro* from those weeks of training and said, "Len san, this is a good heart."

It is important to note that Pellman shihan's rendition of *kokoro* had none of the artistic merits present in the same kanji written by Sōnō sensei. It was amateurish and lacked the correct proportions and brushstroke characteristics Pellman shihan had been trying to imitate for three weeks. It was "good" only because it

Figure 7.1 Kanji for kokoro.

had been written with genuine feeling, rather than an effort to copy proper form and style, and some of that emotion had been transferred to the paper. To a calligraphy master, shōdō isn't an art form as much as it is a revelation of the soul and spirit of the writer.

The point of this illustration is that kokoro is central to nearly every aspect of Japanese life, and particularly to budō.

That is why we find kokoro or *shin* (two ways of pronouncing 心) at the heart of nearly every significant principle of budō and bushidō, including such terms as *heijōshin, jikishin, seishin ryoku, zanshin, ken shin ichi nyo, mushin, shin • ku • i*, and many more. Several of these aspects of kokoro, such as zanshin, seishin ryoku, ken shin ichi nyo, and shin • ku • i, are presented in other chapters in connection with topics to which they specifically relate. In this chapter, we will examine some of the additional ways kokoro is essential to karate-dō training and life in general.

Busshin
HEART OF A SAINT

A familiar saying in karate-dō is *kisshū busshin*, which is commonly translated as "demon's hands, saint's heart." This axiom may have been borrowed from the medical profession, where it is also widely used. It admonishes anyone who has great power, particularly the power of life or death, to exercise that power with compassion and morality. In this sense, it is an essential concept for karate-dō as the art of killing.

We also view kisshū busshin as more than a reminder to maintain balance in our karate training, as encouragement to strive for perfection in every aspect of our training. To be worthy to be called "demon's hands," our karate skills must be beyond what most would consider possible for humans. Likewise, to be perceived as having the heart of a saint, our compassion, morality, service to others, self-sacrifice, and demeanor must epitomize those qualities. Neither of these goals can be achieved through mediocrity. They require diligence, persistence, and unflagging determination to become the best we can possibly be.

Heijōshin
PEACE OF MIND

Heijōshin is perhaps the most vital aspect of any form of budō training, yet it remains widely misunderstood and rarely a subject of conscious training effort. When we consider that karate is an art of ichi geki hissatsu, and a single blow struck in anger can destroy someone's life, including your own, heijōshin becomes supremely important.

Heijōshin is typically translated as "peace of mind," and this is probably as good a translation into English as any. No two- or three-word English translation can do *heijōshin* justice because it is a concept borne of a figurative language.

The word *heijōshin* is composed of three kanji: 平 *(hei)* has numerous related meanings in Japanese: "peaceful," "calm," "steady," and so on. The closest English equivalent is probably "level" or "even," particularly as those words are used in such ways as "level-headed" and "even-handed." 常 *(jō)* has a more singular meaning, at least in terms of its English translations: "always," "constant," or "continually." 心 (shin) translates both literally and figuratively as "heart," with all the same nuances in both languages.

A basic, literal translation of heijōshin would be "constantly steady heart," and in a purely physical sense it would suggest not letting your heart race, which is not a bad way to begin thinking about the broader meaning of heijōshin. By extending that concept to the mind and spirit, heijōshin becomes the state in which the whole inner being of a person is continually at peace or composed. While we will call it "peace of mind" for the sake of simplicity, the fullness of heijōshin warrants a more detailed explanation.

Normally, when faced with danger, we exhibit acute stress reaction (the fight-or-flight response), in which a sudden flood of adrenaline in the bloodstream makes the heart begin to race and our field of vision narrow. This provides a burst of energy to allow us to flee from danger or to focus intently on the threat and fight ferociously if escape is not possible. The acute stress reaction was essential in prehistoric times, when human survival was based solely on hunting, gathering, and marauding for food. But since the dawn of civilization the flight-or-fight response has become increasingly detrimental to people because it also clouds the thinking, diminishes hearing, causes tunnel vision, and rapidly saps the body of energy. Complex thought, acute hearing, and panoramic vision are unnecessary when fighting or escaping a predatory carnivore or a human attacker armed only with primitive weapons, but they became indispensable once humans formed more complex social structures and developed more advanced combat tactics.

Now the fight-or-flight response can actually prove detrimental in all but the most extreme circumstances. It is what causes stage-fright in actors or public speakers. It obscures peripheral vision and increases muscle tension, making you less aware of your surroundings and more likely to flinch at sudden movements or sounds—a state that can easily be exploited by an opponent who is not experiencing acute stress response. By learning to overcome the acute stress response—in other words, maintaining a constantly steady heart—you become far less susceptible to mistakes, flinching, being faked out, getting winded, or tiring too quickly, are far more aware of your environment and your opponents' actions, and are better able to perceive your opponents' intentions and tactics.

In addition, any number of normal workaday situations can trigger the acute stress reaction: a layoff or transfer notice, a remark in a business meeting, heavy freeway traffic, a scathing comment by a friend or loved one, or any other situation that threatens our immediate sense of security. These are not circumstances in which it is beneficial to have the mind closed off and the senses dulled by an overload of adrenaline. Even in a physical confrontation, because the attacker's weapons and tactics are more sophisticated and cannot be simply outrun with a brief burst of muscle energy, clear thinking and awareness of the environment are critical to survival. This is why heijōshin has been a fundamental principle of classical martial arts training for many centuries now.

However, heijōshin is far more than simply keeping one's heart from racing when under intense pressure. Perhaps it can best be understood not as a single attribute but as a combination—or rather the culmination—of several character traits. Each of the aspects that together create heijōshin may take years of effort, experience, and disappointment to develop, making heijōshin the product of a lifetime of patient training. To achieve genuine peace of mind requires a high degree of mental development in three key areas: (1) the intellect, (2) the emotions, and (3) that indefinable element we usually call "character" or "integrity." And these three areas must be developed in balance.

As we age, our physical prowess, no matter how great, will eventually lessen. This is especially evident in professional sports, where few athletes enjoy a career longer than ten years. And we can never be certain that ill health or a serious accident might not leave us with drastically impaired physical ability. With diligence, on the other hand, we can constantly improve our character and our mental prowess. The key to lifelong fruitfulness and happiness, then, is not in our development of physical strength or skills, but in our mental development.

Cultivating heijōshin is far more important to the martial artist than merely perfecting one's fighting skills. Heijōshin is an unlimited quality, as there is always room for more knowledge, greater compassion, stronger love, and a higher level of character development.

Heijōshin is not only difficult to attain, but there is no simple, precise method to develop it. This is a stumbling block to many Westerners, especially in the United States, where people have become culturally conditioned to a quick-fix or "fast-food" approach to nearly everything. Americans in particular have become conditioned to believe that if something cannot be achieved with a wonder drug, an overnight miracle, in three easy steps or a five-day program, it is too difficult and time-consuming to attempt.

So, right from the outset, budōka need to understand that heijōshin demands a lifestyle change: a life of discipline, effort, sacrifice, and commitment. The reward for this commitment, however, is that a lifestyle devoted to developing excellence of character sets the karateka apart from most people in a confused and generally unhappy society.

Not only is there no easy way to develop heijōshin, but for each of us the path will be different because of our different personalities, experiences, and circumstances. To further complicate matters, heijōshin is rife with paradoxes. The first of these is the nature of heijōshin itself: it is the product of diligent training and continual effort to reshape the mind, yet in the end it must be completely natural and unforced. So how do we practice something that must occur spontaneously?

If heijōshin was merely a single attribute, it could be practiced and learned, like multiplication tables. But heijōshin is itself the by-product of a person's complete inner being. It can only be achieved by refining that whole inner essence. And this can only be accomplished if one's intellect, emotions, and character are developed in balance.

When a person realizes the true nature of karate training, and practices accordingly, it leads to a fuller understanding of the nature of life itself. At its essence, karate is concerned with life and death. Although they need not always be applied with lethal effect, every karate technique has the potential to maim or kill an opponent, and the art was developed not to settle schoolyard brawls but to defend against life-threatening armed attacks.

So if the karate student is serious about their training, each kata represents far more than simply performing punches, kicks, and blocks in a prescribed sequence. It is a symbolic battle—fought with full force and lethal intentionality in the imagination—in which your opponent will most certainly die. Will you end their life without just cause? Will you throw their family into turmoil and perhaps ruin over some trivial insult or mistake? When you have developed true compassion for others, then conduct your training in a life-or-death context, you gain a whole new appreciation of life—both your own and the lives of others.

The irony of a comfortable life is that few people, other than the best-trained martial artists, truly understand how tenuous life is. The samurai understood this, because they were trained and conditioned to realize that each new day might bring death. But in our age of relative comfort, security, and ease, we seem to have become oblivious to the precariousness of our existence. Even when we read of a major celebrity succumbing to cancer or a terrible accident, most of us believe that "it won't happen to me."

The life-or-death awareness of karate training allows us to see clearly that death is, quite literally, only one heartbeat away. Part of heijōshin is coming to grips with our own mortality and the inevitability of death—the fact that it will ultimately claim the high and low alike—movie stars, drug addicts, sports heroes, bank robbers, politicians, janitors, business executives, and even us.

Once we understand how fragile our lives are, we have a vital choice to make. We can either live in seclusion or we can determine to live each moment we are given to the fullest and die with no regrets. Yet it is only after deciding to live life to its fullest that we have the most difficult choices to make. It is then that we must come to grips with what brings true and lasting happiness and fulfillment to life.

If you were given only one week to live, what would you do? Would you live out your final days in a wild uninhibited bacchanalia of sensual pleasures? Many would. Would you sell all that you had accumulated and spend your last week donating to every worthy cause you could think of? That would be more noble. Would you feverishly attend to every detail of settling your estate so your loved ones would be provided for after your death? That would demonstrate a high degree of responsibility and integrity. Would you spend every moment possible with your family and closest friends? That would probably give your final hours the greatest comfort. Or would you do nothing differently than you had done the previous week or the week before that, because you were living every day in the way that expresses your highest principles, priorities, and values? That would indicate that your lifestyle has instilled you with heijōshin.

This brings us to another paradox: if you have achieved heijōshin, you will live every day as if it were your last. But just because you live every day as if it were your last does not mean you have attained heijōshin. It is not simply "living like there's no tomorrow" that demonstrates heijōshin, but how you live your last day that is the barometer of your character. It is the quality and purpose of your life that gives it value.

The highest principle of heijōshin is to develop your mind (the combination of intellect, emotions, and character) to such an elevated state that you are unaffected by your environment. How often do you encounter people who are miserable because they are out of work, had an argument with a loved one, feel deprived of something they think will make them happy, are bored or lonely, or because something didn't go the way they wanted? With heijōshin, no adverse circumstances can dictate your emotions, nor can your emotions cloud your judgment.

If your happiness and security are based primarily on your financial status, you will only be comfortable when things seem to be going well. If you lose your job and begin to have difficulty paying your bills, soon you will find yourself constantly under stress, doubting your own abilities and value, and angered by the loss of the material freedom you once had. In the end, you will likely find yourself taking a job that is not right for you, just to regain your self-esteem and recover your lost financial status. This is an example of your circumstances controlling your emotions, and your emotions in turn confusing your judgment.

If your contentment is instead derived from knowing the type of person that you are inside, then you will more readily understand that life has its ups and downs. You will realize that the sun rises on the evil and the good and the rain falls upon the righteous and the unrighteous alike. Everyone experiences an occasional windfall, and no one is exempt from times of hardship, so it is foolish to allow these circumstances to dictate your emotions. What is more, the rich and famous are often the unhappiest people in the world, while the so-called "lowly," like Mother Teresa, enjoy a rich and fulfilling life. Once you understand that it is what you are, not what you have, that is important, you are able to rise above your circumstances.

The second key tenet of heijōshin is to understand that you are part of your environment, that what you are and what you do has an effect on other people. Even your emotions affect others. If you are discouraged, you will drop a cloud of gloom on the people with whom you come in contact. If you are joyful, just the sight of you will gladden them. If you behave rudely, you will anger people or hurt their feelings. If you are pleasant and respectful, you will brighten their day. People who look up to you will follow your example, whether it is good or bad.

This presents another of heijōshin's paradoxes: How can we be unaffected by our environment when we are part of our environment?

Obviously, our environment will affect us to some degree. The state of the economy will affect us, our health will affect us, the actions of friends and loved ones will affect us. Heijōshin is not a condition in which we insulate ourselves from our surroundings, nor deny that our problems exist, nor deaden our minds and senses to our feelings. Heijōshin is not a means of escape, like drugs, which allows you to ignore or be unaware of your emotions. Quite the opposite: to possess heijōshin demands that you be deeply in touch with your emotions. It is perfectly natural to feel anger, joy, disappointment, love, and the full range of emotions. Heijōshin, however, allows us not to be controlled by these emotions so that our actions are not determined by a fleeting impulse, but are the product of a consistent, balanced, and focused mind.

The idea of experiencing your emotions fully without allowing them to affect your outlook or actions may seem like another paradox of heijōshin, but this apparent ambiguity is resolved by developing two essential character traits: understanding and compassion.

First, you must understand yourself, understand why you feel the way you do, why certain events or situations evoke certain emotions in you. Then you must have compassion for yourself. Accept yourself for what you are, and why you are what you are. You cannot change who you are now. You have already become that person. You can only change who you will be in the future. The present has already been determined and cannot be undone, so if you condemn yourself for your present faults and failures—or your past actions that led to them—it is only a waste of your emotional energy and destructive to your self-esteem. But, if you can compassionately accept yourself as you are now, then you have a positive starting point from which to resolve to change into the person you want to become.

Second, you must have the same understanding and compassion for others. Once you have thoroughly understood yourself, you can appreciate that other people have also become who they are for a reason. There have been influences and circumstances that have shaped them into the people they have become. By compassionately accepting others with both their strengths and weaknesses, you will be able to distinguish between your feelings toward the person and your feelings about their behavior. This separation is vital to human relationships.

If someone behaves rudely, for example, I can either become offended at the person or at the person's behavior. If I become offended at the person, my natural reaction will be to avoid or detest that offensive person. If, instead, I look beyond the person and see the behavior as offensive, then my natural reaction will be to try to understand what caused it because I can now view the situation as an offensive action committed by an acceptable person. And rather than detesting the person, I will try to communicate with them, and my reaction will be motivated by concern rather than anger or resentment.

Heijōshin is not something you turn on and off like a politician's smile. Once heijōshin is rooted in you, it is with you at all times everywhere you go, from the time you wake up to the time you go to bed—even while you are sleeping. It becomes your natural state of mind, not something you summon only when you "need" it.

By developing a constant, peaceful state of mind, you, as an individual, will lead a happier, more serene life, liberated from the emotional roller coaster of forces beyond your control. But the benefits of heijōshin cannot remain exclusively personal. By its nature, heijōshin cannot exist in a vacuum, so its benefits will spread from you to society as a whole.

Society is simply a collection of individuals. Social ills, like crime and drug abuse, are merely the reflection of the combined failings of the individuals who make up society. Laws cannot reform society and cure its ills; they can only punish violators. Society is like our collective shadow. If the shadow is bent and twisted, no amount of effort can straighten it alone. Only by straightening myself can my shadow be straightened, and then it does so effortlessly and automatically. So it is that social reform must start with individuals and spread through society. It cannot be dictated by our leaders but can only be a grassroots process in which each of us is either part of the disease or part of the cure. And if we can cure our social ills, we cannot wait for a leader to inspire us or for others to start the process; we must begin with ourselves, regardless of what others do.

If our behavior is controlled by our circumstances and emotions, rather than by our strength of character and ideals, then we are only part of the disease. If, instead, we develop sufficient heijōshin to lift ourselves above our circumstances and help us live with greater purpose and meaning, our example will inspire others to become part of the cure.

Thus, the ultimate objective of heijōshin is the same as the ultimate objective of martial arts: to help each individual reach their full potential, and thereby improve society as a whole.

Kōjōshin
CONSTANTLY RISING SPIRITS

Kōjōshin can be written two ways in Japanese, and the meaning of both spellings is applicable to karate-dō. One version of kōjōshin, 高常心, is closely related to heijōshin in concept, but instead of its literal translation being "constantly steady heart," this kōjōshin means "constantly high heart." The implication of kōjōshin should already be apparent: it is of greater benefit to you and to society if your heart is steadily joyful than if it is steadily miserable, anxious, or depressed. If we wish to live truly victorious lives, we must choose to maintain positive attitudes and demeanor.

One concept that can elevate our attitude is *rakkan shugi* (optimism). Human life has no more inherent value than a blade of grass. It is as fleeting, common, aimless, easily extinguished, and destined to pass equally unnoticed. The only real value of your life is the value you create, both for yourself and for others. You must decide to live a life worth living. You must decide to find the joy and fulfillment in life. It will not happen by itself, and it will not come without effort.

The way karate-dō helps accomplish this is by providing training that develops those attributes found at the integrity level: self-control, determination to succeed, saya no naka ni kachi (victory with the sword still in the scabbard), positive attitude, *onore ni katsu* (conquering yourself), and so forth. As these aspects become increasingly habitual, you remain at the higher stages of life—integrity and elation—for longer periods of time and spend less and less time in states of intolerance, impulsiveness, discontent, and mental anguish.

Optimism is the prerequisite for nearly every concept we have presented. Take as an example the principle of hen doku i yaku (changing poison to medicine) from chapter 6. It can only be effective if you maintain your optimism. Without hope, you cannot envision the possibility of a positive outcome to adverse circumstances, so you will be unable to find or create that outcome. This is especially important to understand because one of the most vital truths of changing poison to medicine is that the more powerful the poison, the more potent the medicine. You gain the most benefit from the worst problems, but without optimism you will never be able to conceive that something positive can result from your direst circumstances. Maintaining hope and optimism is one of the keys to maintaining a consistently positive attitude.

The other way of writing *kōjōshin* is 向上心, which means "aspiring to improve." We speak constantly throughout this book about training diligently to improve our character and attitudes. To some it may seem inordinate. However, character and attitudes are the wellspring of a productive and meaningful life, so their role and importance cannot be overemphasized. And the foundation upon which karate training rests is the aspiration to improve.

We have all heard the tales of the sensei who refused to accept new students unless they first performed months or years of menial tasks to prove they were devoted to learning the art. These legends exemplify the concept of aspiring to improve. The menial tasks are used to demonstrate that the prospective student has true *shidō* (志道)—the desire and willingness to follow the way before being accepted into the dōjō. Since the overarching purpose of karate-dō is self-improvement, having shidō and kōjōshin (向上心) are absolutely essential.

In the context of the first meaning of kōjōshin (constantly high spirits), possessing the aspiration to improve is vital. Furthermore, the acts of striving for improvement, of rising above your circumstances, of being optimistic about achieving your goals, and similar aspects of your training that provide assurance you will be a better person tomorrow than you are today should cause your spirits to rise. And if your self-esteem is derived from your character, compassion, and service to others, rather than your outward appearance or material possessions, then you have excellent reasons to be in high spirits.

Thus, the implication of kōjōshin (高常心) is that your spirits are not merely at a constant high level, but they are instead constantly rising. If your character is improving every day, then you have every reason to be more fulfilled and joyful tomorrow than you are today.

Mushin
NO MIND

Mushin (無心) is a widely misunderstood term whose literal meaning is "without heart" or "without mind." It is an abbreviation of the term *mushin no shin*, which is often stated as "mind of no mind." Many explanations of mushin translate it as "empty mind," but it appears that this term confuses people into believing that a state of mushin is achieved by emptying the mind of all conscious thought and emotion. This is not our understanding of mushin. We instead view mushin as expanding the mind. If the mind is not closed to new ideas, new stimuli, new experiences, and more knowledge, then, regardless of how much it currently contains, its capacity is as limitless as if it were empty.

The famous monk Takuan Sōhō used the example of the Senju Kannon, a bodhisattva with a thousand arms displayed in many temples in Japan, to describe his understanding of mushin. He said if the Kannon focuses her attention on the hand holding a spear in order to strike with it, she effectively loses the use of her other 999 arms. We believe this is another appropriate concept of mushin for budō. Our goal should not be emptying the mind, but rather not allowing the mind to fixate on anything: freeing it. A mind freed in this way is capable of instantly responding to any need and acting in any manner required. Rather than the attention being fixed on what may appear to be the most immediate condition or problem, it can flow freely and be more fully aware of circumstances.

Another common misunderstanding is the notion that mushin involves emptying the mind of conscious thought so that reactions are subconscious or instinctive.

We believe this interpretation allows equal possibility for those reactions to be detrimental to oneself and others. Our subconscious minds are filled with fears, doubts, uncertainty, and prejudice, all of which can produce negative reactions to our circumstances. Animals react by instinct. Humans should respond out of character, compassion, and conviction. Our belief is that mushin should be the product of hōgen—eyes that see with compassion and understanding—and respond naturally and without conscious thought, but by training and not by instinct, to what is observed out of our innate desire to do what is right.

Suishin
MIND LIKE WATER

A closely related state of mind to mushin is *suishin* (水心) or "mind like water." Suishin is another expression of freedom of mind, based in part on the idea that flowing water seeks the path of least resistance, so its course winds around obstacles and does not allow those obstacles to prevent it from completing its journey. In addition, flowing water is persistent and will eventually erode away any obstacle it cannot flow around. The power of water is determined by the pressure exerted upon it. Water given sufficient pressure can cut through concrete or steel, and the human mind given enough force of will can likewise overcome any problem or obstacle.

Danketsu Shin
SPIRIT OF UNITY

The Japanese term *danketsu shin* loosely translates as "unity of ideals." The great sixteenth-century field general Takeda Shingen understood the power of diversity within a unified group. He carefully selected subordinate generals who had vastly different abilities, opinions, and experiences and united them under the banner in figure 7.2, the symbols on which read: *fū* ("wind"), *rin* ("forest"), *ka* ("fire"), and *zan* ("mountain"). This banner was emblematic of the diversity of Takeda's soldiers and generals. Because Takeda had commanders with differing ideas and talents, yet who were all committed to the same goal, the divisions of his army could take on the characteristics of each of the elements depicted on their banner.

Arrows launched by his archers came like the wind (fū), fast and unpredictable, whistling in from any direction. His spearmen were like a forest (rin), a dense and impenetrable mass, bristling with danger. His cavalry swept across battlefields like fire (ka), consuming an enemy with raging intensity and impossible to contain. And his foot-soldiers were as rock-solid and immovable as a mountain (zan), massive and unassailable. The diverse talents and strategies of Takeda's commanders allowed him to combine these four distinct qualities into a single, unified army—an army which never suffered a defeat during Takeda's lifetime.

People draw *ki* (energy) from each other, so groups create excitement and enthusiasm. They become a wellspring of creativity and ideas as their members stimulate each other's imagination and enthusiasm. There is also strength to be gained if the members of a group continually encourage one another. In these ways individuals can multiply, not merely add, to their energy and power by forming a group. Such a group's greatest power results from the combined strength of each member's determination.

Figure 7.2 Fu-Rin-Ka-Zan banner.

To be a true karate practitioner requires that one recognize and harness the power of unity. On a small scale, this can be as simple as the encouragement of fellow karateka to achieve training goals, or the support of family and friends in meeting the challenges of daily life. On a larger scale, the advantage of unity is to be found in achieving the greater goals of karate-dō by combining with those of like purpose to promote the ideals of karate-dō in schools, businesses, and social settings. Broad purposes of this nature are the value of a dōjō, in which the members encourage and strengthen one another in applying the true ideals of karate-dō to daily life, and to provide a platform for a concerted effort to improve our society and our world. In like manner, dōjō can join organizations like the Jikishin-Kai to add even greater numbers and reach a broader audience.

Despite its great strength, unity has one tremendous weakness. As Abraham Lincoln stated in his 1838 address to the Young Men's Lyceum, "If destruction be our lot, we must ourselves be its author and finisher." A cohesive group can withstand almost any attack from the outside, but no organization can long prevent its own disintegration if it loses its sense of unity.

Maintaining unity requires both a shared purpose and goals, combined with the same character traits that are the foundation of karate-dō: respect, compassion, humility, and determination. The seeds of destruction are the attributes a karateka seeks to conquer: greed, jealousy, selfish ambition, and pride. Karateka must recognize that titles, ranks, and belt colors are no more than indications of levels of training and development, not entitlements to special honors or privileges. Even such titles and positions as *kaichō*, shihan, sensei, sempai, and kōhai are merely descriptions of responsibilities for supervision and instruction; not positions of power and prestige to be flaunted over those who have not yet attained them.

Jikishin
PURE HEART

The Jikishin-Kai gets its name from an ancient Japanese proverb: *Jikishin kore dōjō nari*—A pure heart produces a dōjō. A dōjō isn't merely a building; it is the hearts of those who train in the building. Its strength doesn't lie in the strength of its floor, walls, and ceiling but in the hearts of karateka.

This adage implies two important concepts. First, that in order to benefit from training, and to be a benefit to other members of the dōjō, your heart must be pure. You must be dedicated to your training and sincere in your desire for self-improvement and the improvement of your fellow karateka. Second, that wherever you are at the moment, you are in the dōjō. Karate-dō was never intended to remain inside a building. Its purpose is to serve the people in the world outside the dōjō, not the people you train with. The building in which you develop those skills and attitudes is merely the laboratory in which you experiment, but your everyday life is your true dōjō—the place where you apply the lessons learned and the skills developed in your training.

Shoshin
BEGINNER'S SPIRIT

Every form of būdō shares a common adage: *Shoshin wasuru bekarazu*: "Never forget [your] beginner's spirit." Scrolls containing this admonition can be found in dōjō all over Japan. In a very real sense, the secret to becoming a master is to remain a beginner.

Each time you step inside the dōjō, it should feel like your first time. You should be eager to learn, determined to exert yourself fully in your training, willing to accept instruction and correction without objection, willing to try new things, willing to push yourself beyond your perceived limits, and prepared to fail more times than you succeed. You must abandon your ego at the door and expect everyone else to be more knowledgeable and skilled than you are, so you have nothing to show off.

One of the simplest ways to develop a pure heart (jikishin) is to maintain a beginner's heart (shoshin), a mind with the purity and openness of a child's.

Seishin Ryoku

Power of the Spirit

When many people think of karate, the first image that comes to mind is probably that of a wizened old karate master, like Mr. Miyagi in *The Karate Kid*, speaking in riddles. "What is the sound of one hand clapping?" or "A blind man does not need a lantern to see in the darkness." For others it may bring to mind the sayings of Confucius, burning incense sticks, or perhaps bowing reverently before an altar or statue honoring an ancient sage. In short, they expect karate-dō to be something mystical and arcane.

If you are reading this book expecting to learn how to levitate or to move objects with your mind, you will be greatly disappointed. In real karate we do not use "the force" from *Star Wars* to fling our opponents across a room or jolt them with energy bolts. Nor are we air benders. We don't shoot energy balls from our hands. We do use ki (energy) and seishin ryoku (spiritual power), but not in any mystical sense. Karate is science. It is physics, biomechanics, and structural engineering, aided by psychology and sociology.

Intellect, emotions, and spirit are all real. While we may not be able to fully understand or measure them, they are nonetheless real. Applying our mind and spirit to maximize the power and effectiveness of our body movements is a vital part of karate training, so an understanding of the spiritual aspects of life provides greater insight into karate-dō and the ways the art can enhance every aspect of your life.

Before we can examine the fundamental issues concerning karate and mysticism, it is important to understand the true essence of karate-dō.

What people normally see of karate training are only its visible, external aspects—punching, kicking, blocking, grappling, and mock battles. On the surface, karate-dō training involves fighting and defeating opponents, breaking boards, winning tournaments, and other physical skills and challenges. These, however, should not be the ultimate goals of a karateka, but merely methods of training to achieve deeper objectives. While these physical activities serve useful and important purposes, the real value of karate training occurs internally—the mind, senses, emotions, ideals, and spirit—all of which are invisible. Yet these are the aspects of karate training that are the most beneficial and life-enriching. Only under the tutelage of a knowledgeable teacher and in a healthy environment (dōjō) can one appreciate that karate is an exploration of the very roots and nature of human behavior. And human behavior is controlled by the mind, emotions, and spirit, so an understanding of seishin ryoku is essential for every karateka.

Seishin (精神) refers to the mind, but it connotes a mind composed of the spirit, the soul, and morality. And *ryoku* (力) means "strength" or "power." Thus, when we speak of seishin ryoku, we really mean the power of your intellect, spirit, soul, and morality combined. For brevity, we will refer to seishin ryoku as "spiritual power," but a more complete translation might be "the consolidated power of a clear, completely focused mind." However, even such a practical definition gives little clue to how seishin ryoku can be achieved, or how it can benefit you.

Seishin ryoku is more than just strong willpower. Its vitality lies less in the intensity of the will, which is little more than ardent desire, than in the clarity or purity of the mind. The kind of purity we mean is as much a matter of remaining unwaveringly focused on your goals as purity in the moral sense. Both are equally essential to seishin ryoku since both mental clutter and immorality are distractions that can readily divert your concentration away from your objectives. So, one crucial element is freeing the mind of all unnecessary distractions and remaining intently centered on your principal objectives. In this way, the problems of everyday life will be less likely to steer you off course.

To visualize this concept, think of life as the ocean. The up-and-down motion of the waves represents life's peaks and valleys. At the same time, the steady, forward movement of the waves is like life's obstacles and setbacks, because they pour in endlessly, broken only by brief interludes of calm. One after another the waves of adversity crash in, some much bigger than others, sometimes with a strong undertow, sometimes slow and rolling, and occasionally in overwhelming sets that give almost no respite. If you simply try to stand against the driving waves or swim into them, you will be buffeted from side to side, beaten down, and driven off course. But, developing seishin ryoku is like learning to surf. By riding the waves, rather than struggling against them, you can control your speed and direction as the waves carry you forward in life. Once you are adept and comfortable with your skill, you will find that the biggest waves are the ones that give you the best ride and the greatest joy.

More than just a pure and intently controlled mind, seishin ryoku draws its real power from the mind (conscious thought) and spirit (unconscious motivation) working in union. Electricity is a close analogy to mind and spirit, since it comprises both voltage and amperage. Voltage is the amount of electricity flowing through a circuit, and amperage is the pressure driving it through the wires. Similarly, the mind is the capacity and will, while the spirit is its driving force or pressure. When the mind and spirit are harnessed together, the outcome is far greater than the sum of the two. Just as wattage (electrical power) is the result of voltage multiplied by amperage, seishin ryoku is the power of the mind multiplied by the force of the spirit.

But, the question remains, how does one develop and maintain this powerful state of mind we call seishin ryoku? The answer again is karate-dō. By its systematic disciplining of the mind, by developing kihaku, *kime*, shinnen, and similar mental aspects of karate, employing the mind and spirit in unison against the physical challenges of training, karate-dō trains you to fuse your mind and spirit together to produce seishin ryoku.

Only with a clear, strong, and pure mind can you see the opportunities to make something positive out of an adversity. But it is important to remember that in the face of serious problems, there is a fine line between maintaining this clarity of mind and succumbing to bewilderment and despair. That line is *kami hito-e*, as the Japanese say—as thin as a sheet of paper. In many respects, composure and bewilderment are merely opposite sides of the same page. Regular, continual training of the mind and spirit is therefore essential to developing and maintaining seishin ryoku, just as regular exercise is necessary to keeping your body fit and healthy, and karate training is one of the best sources of such training.

Karate techniques are more powerful and effective when performed in a natural, relaxed state, and they will work for self-defense only when they are spontaneous and flow from mushin. The same is true of seishin ryoku. It must be natural, not something you think about or force yourself to do. To ensure that your spiritual power becomes a natural, integral part of your life, it is important to develop heijōshin, as discussed in detail in the previous chapter.

As your karate training produces in you the permanent state of tranquility we call heijōshin, your clear, relaxed mind will be able to better unleash the full potential of seishin ryoku when faced with even the most severe problems. By strengthening both mind and body in balance, and providing frequent opportunities to apply your training in realistic, yet controlled, conditions of attack and defense, karate-dō provides an ideal venue in which to develop heijōshin.

By then combining heijōshin with seishin ryoku, your karate training will produce a strong body, mind, and spirit. This threefold strength is essential to living a fulfilling and joyful life because weakness—and the fear, uncertainty, doubt, anxiety, and hopelessness that weakness produces—is the root source of all human misery.

Emotional and spiritual strength is the source of generosity, mercy, forgiveness, humility, gratitude, kindness, and love. Such attributes as these can only be genuinely and unconsciously ingrained in those who have the courage, confidence, and fortitude to place the interests of others on a plane at least equal to their own. And it is these qualities that enrich and elevate both ourselves and society at large.

Seishin ryoku and heijōshin will also provide you with the spiritual might and mental clarity to empower you to prevail over any problem that might confront you, along with the assurance and inner peace to do no more than you are able. To force yourself to do more than you are capable of doing is unnatural, and in most cases an inept effort only worsens the situation you are facing. A sign of true spiritual strength is the serenity to be comfortable with your limitations while employing all your genuine capabilities to overcome the adversities of life.

Only through years of training can both heijōshin and seishin ryoku become completely assimilated into your life, so that they are natural and perpetually functioning. When fully mastered, they operate together like the guidance system of a cruise missile, so you will never lose track of your target while making continual subtle adjustments to your terrain and environment, calmly veering around any obstacles you may encounter. Sustained by the strength and serenity of seishin ryoku and heijōshin, your flight through life will be neither completely mechanical nor fully mystical, but a natural manifestation of your character and ideals.

These mental and spiritual benefits, the results of training which are most profoundly and substantively life-enhancing, are not merely by-products; they are the very essence and purpose of karate-dō.

Karate practice can enhance both the understanding and practical application of a person's individual spiritual beliefs. The intense mental discipline and profound introspection of karate training will produce a deeper and more sincere desire for peace and reconciliation, genuine humility, and a high level of authentic respect and compassion for people. At the same time, a rich spirituality can help you establish noble and worthwhile goals for your life and solidify and strengthen the personal convictions that motivate you toward perfection of character. Your faith will fortify your seishin ryoku with added spiritual resolve and bolster the serenity and steadfastness of your heijōshin through confidence in a power higher than your own.

Thus, karate-dō and the spiritual life can be viewed as the two legs of a person—the solid foundation supporting the rest of the body. Although most people can readily stand on just one leg, it is much more comfortable to use both. You tire less easily, and the strength and stability of two legs allows you to carry a much heavier load and move through life with greater freedom. If you are a person of religious faith, coupling it with karate-dō can reward you with a more fulfilling and joyful life, and a life that is of greater value to society as a whole.

You are therefore the foundation for a better world. Society is merely a collection of individuals, so society can only improve if each person improves. Great speeches by world leaders have no impact on society whatsoever unless people make up their minds to improve themselves. And you cannot change someone else against their will; you only have control over yourself. So it is up to you.

When other people see the joy and maturity manifested in your life, many will be motivated to seek the same for themselves, and a chain reaction will begin. Most people in the world feel lost and frightened. They are just waiting for someone like you to show them the way to a better life. Using the heijōshin and seishin ryoku you develop in your karate training, you can lead the way. That is what it means to truly be a karateka.

Kofuku
FULFILLMENT

Kofuku is often translated as "happiness," but the meaning of the English word *happiness* has changed significantly in the past two hundred years. It originally meant fortunate, successful, or prosperous—the opposite of hapless. In the twentieth and twenty-first centuries *happiness* has come to mean "joyful" or "delighted." The kanji for *kofuku*, 鼓腹, is literally "drum belly," with a belly as tightly full as a drum being a metaphor for complete fulfillment or contentment. So, for purposes of discussing "happiness," we have chosen to use the word "blissful" instead, to distinguish the emotional state of bliss from the physical reality of success or prosperity in connection with the concept of kofuku.

Everyone wants to be blissful. They want to go through life in a permanent state of joy. No one wants to be miserable or even just indifferent. Nevertheless, most choose not to be blissful. That's right: bliss is a choice. It may sound simplistic or trite, but it truly is as simple as that. Blissfulness is a willful decision, not an emotion that inevitably occurs when good things happen, conditions are right, people treat us well, we accomplish something worthwhile, or we acquire enough possessions. Nor does our brain invariably switch bliss off and turn on sorrow, grief, anger, resentment, or sullenness when bad things happen, conditions worsen, people treat us poorly, we fail at something, or we lack possessions. We choose to react in those ways. It may be the result of conditioning, but it is still a choice, other than in cases of a chemical imbalance in the brain.

While choosing blissfulness may sound simple, it is far from easy. Our minds are saturated daily with depressing news, emotional hurts, distractions, setbacks, and hardships. Our natural response to these obstacles is anxiety, anger, frustration, impatience, envy, fear, and other emotions that rob us of contentment. But remember from chapter 2: the true purpose of karate-dō is conquering one's self. We train ourselves to face life's challenges empty-handed—with no weapon other than our bodies, minds, and hearts. Thus, karate-dō trains the mind to avoid or clear away these self-destructive, self-repressing emotions so that the blissfulness we all desire remains undiminished, regardless of our circumstances. Each time a hardship arises, each time we suffer a setback, each time an obstacle inhibits our progress, each time we fail, each time we are treated badly, each time we receive heartbreaking news, we must remind ourselves to remain blissful, despite those conditions.

It helps to understand the source of true fulfillment. Fulfillment results from who you are. Once again, the apparent simplicity of this statement is deceptive. Our materialistic culture tends to condition us to perceive fulfillment as the outcome of achieving something we consider worthwhile, whether it is acquiring wealth or fame, having a challenging and satisfying career, raising a wholesome family, or doing something noble, heroic, or charitable for others. But these are fleeting accomplishments, and the emotional uplift they provide is only temporary. That sense of fulfillment fades quickly when fame dwindles, financial reversals occur, the career takes a downturn, family members do not live up to your expectations, or your noble deeds are finished or go unrecognized. In order to have lasting fulfillment, the source of your fulfillment must be permanent.

Permanent fulfillment is internal—a matter of character, not deeds. Lasting fulfillment can only be found in knowing that you are the best person you can be at this moment. By continually honing your character, striving for perfection in your ideals and persona, karate-dō is an excellent way to attain genuine fulfillment in life. And with that lasting fulfillment comes lasting bliss.

Renshū Hōhō

Training Methods

Hopefully, we have set the stage for you to embark on your training. We have presented the background, meaning, and purpose of karate-dō. We have explained the training objectives of developing your mind, body, and spirit in unison and the ability to apply your knowledge, skills, character, and attitudes to living a victorious and fulfilling life. In this chapter we will present a training program designed to accomplish all that. It is not a program of our own creation but the product of centuries of instruction by the karate masters who preceded us.

Training in karate-dō has several components. In this chapter, we will briefly explain each of those components, how they relate to each other, and how to establish a training regimen that will incorporate all of them to optimize your results. In subsequent chapters, we will address these components in greater detail. These major components are:

- *sahō to reihō*
- *jumbi taisō*
- *kihon*
- *idō kihon*
- *jūhō*
- *kata*
- *bunkai to ōyō*
- *kumite*
- *hojo undō*
- *kitae*
- *bunbu ryōdō*

Sahō to Reihō
PREPARATION AND ETIQUETTE

Sahō is preparation and reihō is etiquette. They are usually lumped together because it is impossible to draw a clear line of separation between the two. Much of sahō is also reihō, and much of reihō is sahō. Sahō includes such things as:

- personal hygiene, cleanliness, trimming fingernails and toenails to avoid injuring others
- maintaining a clean and neat karate-gi (training uniform) and *obi* (belt)
- changing before and after training
- meditation at the beginning and end of class sessions (*mokusō*)
- recitation of the dōjō kun at the beginning and end of each session
- properly folding and storing the karate-gi after training
- cleaning up the dōjō after training (*sōji*)

The etiquette followed in the dōjō is called reihō, which includes:

- bowing when entering and leaving the dōjō
- bowing to sensei and other students upon meeting them
- bowing when entering and exiting the training area of the dōjō
- formal bowing at the beginning and end of each class session
- bowing to each training partner
- bowing to sensei and other students when leaving

It is important not to treat sahō and reihō as tasks or duties that are unrelated to your training. They are a vital part of karate training and should be performed with the same diligence and seriousness as any other aspect of training.

Jumbi Taisō
WARM-UP EXERCISES

After the opening formalities of class, the first activity is typically *jumbi taisō* (warm-up exercises) to loosen up the muscles and joints. These include a variety of stretching exercises and movements intended to increase the heart rate and circulation in preparation for a vigorous workout. Each dōjō has its own routine, but we recommend a systematic approach that makes it easier to remember what to do next. Our suggestion is to perform loosening-up movements from head to toe, beginning with loosening the neck muscles by tilting the head slowly forward and backward several times, side to side several times, then circling the head clockwise several times and counterclockwise several times. Next, loosen the shoulders by rotating them forward and backward several times and swinging the arms across the body several times. After that, use one hand to flex the wrists of the other hand forward and backward several times, and circle both wrists clockwise and counterclockwise several times. Loosen the waist following the same pattern used for the neck: leaning forward and backward, side to side, then rotating clockwise and counterclockwise, each several times. Next bend the knees and swivel them in circles several times, which also loosens the ankles. Following that, rise on tiptoe and lower again several times. In the foregoing descriptions, we say "several times" rather than prescribing a specific number of repetitions. Everyone's physiology is different, so some will require more repetitions than others to warm up fully. As a general rule, each of the exercises described should be done no fewer than ten times, and fifty repetitions should be sufficient for nearly all participants.

Once all the major joints are loosened up, bounce up and down for about fifteen seconds, using your ankles to spring upward two to three inches, followed by a minimum of ten jumping jacks. Then perform a minimum of ten full squats and rises. Next, perform at least ten jumps as if trying to touch your knees to your chest. Finally, either trot in a circle around the perimeter of the dōjō or run in place for at least thirty seconds, preferably a full minute.

With the body fully warmed up, perform a few mild stretching exercises for the legs. The best time to stretch to increase flexibility is at the conclusion of the training period when the muscles and tendons have been exercised thoroughly and are least susceptible to tearing. As warm-ups, we recommend only mild stretching for the purpose of reducing the chances of injury. These preliminary stretches should only push the limb an inch or two beyond the point you initially feel resistance or tightness.

A minimum of ten minutes should be devoted to jumbi taisō to properly prepare for training and minimize the potential for injury.

Kihon
FUNDAMENTALS

Once the body is fully warmed up, immediately begin performing kihon (fundamentals). In most dōjō the sensei or a sempai will lead this activity, but it should also be performed if you are training at home. As we have repeatedly said, mastery of kihon is the key to mastery of karate-dō, so your focus, diligence, and effort to perfect your technique should actually be stronger during kihon than when performing kata. If your kihon is excellent, every other aspect of your karate will be excellent.

The specific techniques to perform during kihon training depend on your rank and experience. As a guideline, you should perform all of the kihon that are contained in the kata that you already know, plus those you are currently learning. During kihon training, your emphasis should be on improving the mechanics of your technique as well as power. There is a progression that should be followed in order to perfect kihon: *dai* (big), *kyō* (powerful), *soku* (fast), *kei* (light).

Dai (大): big. This is the first stage of kihon training. Focus is on the big: big movements and the major actions involved. Little emphasis need be placed on the fine points of a technique until a student can perform the large actions without having to think about them.

Kyō (強): powerful. Most beginners try to develop power too early in their training. Big actions are already reasonably powerful. As students become more adept at the large motions, power usually develops as a by-product. In addition, by learning to engage the entire body—not just the arms and hands—greater power is produced, so repetition alone usually results in achieving power.

Soku (速): fast. Speed also tends to steadily improve without conscious effort. As the movements become more natural, and more of the body—particularly the hips and core—are utilized in kihon, speed follows.

Kei (軽): light. "Light" in this case means effortless. Again, light technique is the natural outcome of learning to fully engage the hips, legs, and abdominal muscles in movements. Those muscles are so much larger and stronger than the arm muscles that extremely powerful techniques can be performed without clenching the arm and shoulder muscles, making them appear effortless.

Once you have gained proficiency, and your kihon consistently exhibit kei, appearing effortless—which usually occurs around the rank of *yondan* (4th dan) or *godan* (5th dan)—your emphasis in kihon training will begin to reverse the foregoing characteristics, and you will develop *shō* (small), *jū* (soft), *kan* (slow), and *chō* (heavy).

Shō (小): small. Another effect of utilizing the hips, legs, and core to impart power into your techniques is that larger movements are no longer required to deliver enormous power to the target. This results in movements becoming more compact—smaller. Again, this is mostly the result of years of repetition, rather than conscious effort.

Jū (柔): soft. In this case, "relaxed and flexible" is what is meant by soft. Beginners tense up and are stiff when trying to use muscle power alone to perform techniques. As you learn to strike with your entire body, and transfer power from your legs and hips, the muscles of the arms and shoulders lose that rigidity, and many techniques are performed with more of a whipping action of the body.

Kan (緩): slow. Better words might be "unhurried," "delayed," and "lagging." A natural tendency of beginners is always to try to move faster than their opponents. Masters use timing to create openings for counterattack, sometimes delaying a movement to throw off the opponent's rhythm. Beginners tend to initiate movement with the arm that is striking, while masters initiate movement with their *tanden* (lower abdomen) and hips, so that their arms often seem to be lagging behind the rest of their body when striking or blocking.

Chō (重): heavy. As used here, "heavy" refers to the ability to transfer greater body weight and energy into a technique with less effort, making a blow feel much heavier to the recipient than its effortless delivery would appear. The effect is like being struck by a piece of lead when expecting a ping-pong ball.

The purpose of performing kihon while standing in place is to allow karateka to focus exclusively on the biomechanics of the specific technique without the distraction of trying to maintain balance and body structure at the same time. Therefore, karateka should resist the temptation to move on to *idō kihon* before devoting sufficient time and effort to static kihon.

Idō Kihon
BASIC MOVEMENTS

Idō kihon is simply kihon performed with *tai sabaki* (movement), striking, blocking, or kicking while moving forward, backward, sideways, at angles, and turning rapidly. It serves as the next building block by linking footwork with a variety of offensive and defensive techniques. As with kihon, much of the time spent in idō kihon should be devoted to training in the footwork and turns in the kata in which you are training. A few minutes to perform a score of repetitions of a sequence from a kata, especially movements that you are having difficulty with, will advance your proficiency much faster than the same amount of time spent performing the kata in its entirety.

About ten minutes of a one-hour training session should be devoted to kihon and idō kihon in preparation for kata and kumite.

Kata
TEMPLATES

Kata are the primary means by which karate has been transmitted from sensei to seito for some three hundred years or more. We know from the names and oral traditions that kata like Seisan, Kūshankū, and Naifanchi were being performed and taught by the masters who lived in the early eighteenth century. The word *kata* is usually translated as "form" or "pattern," but we prefer to consider kata as templates, models, or examples. The difference may seem chiefly semantic, but our reason for the distinction is to help people see kata for what they were originally designed to be, rather than what they became as a result of kata competition in tournaments.

A form or pattern is merely a diagram you follow by rote. Thousands of karateka perform kata in tournaments with only the vaguest idea what the movements in the kata are actually for. They place their feet in the right positions, their hands sway and sweep in the air, and they pose for the judges at the completion of every move. Their movements are quick and powerful, athletic, and beautiful to watch. They display poise and grace, and occasionally scream like a maniac, but they are doing little more than a dance without music. Most could not use the movements they just performed to stop a teenager from knocking them down and stealing their lunch money.

When Sakugawa Kanga or Matsumura Sōkon or Itosu Ankō performed a kata, they were imprinting their minds with a template that trained them to kill or disable an attacker assaulting them with a sword, a spear, a club, or a similar weapon. And if they were attacked on the way home after performing a kata, without having to think they would have used some of the movements in that kata to disable or kill their assailant. That's the difference between a form and a kata.

Ideally, kata should be performed under the observation and guidance of a sensei or sempai so that any errors can be immediately identified and necessary corrections made in the next repetition. It is counterproductive to perform a kata repeatedly making the same mistakes. If no observer is available, then it is best to either watch your performance in a mirror or make a video to watch immediately afterward and attempt to identify your own errors and deficiencies.

Roughly ten minutes or one-fifth of your total training time should be spent working to perfect your kata performance.

Jūhō
GRAPPLING

At least 50 percent of all the techniques in karate are jūhō ("soft methods"), so called because they involve little or no striking. Jūhō consists of throws, foot and leg sweeps, joint dislocations, strangulation techniques, pins and holds, pressure point techniques, and escapes from grappling techniques. The majority of these techniques were ignored in the postwar era, most likely because they were not included in tournament events due to the high risk of injury. It has only been since the growing popularity of MMA that there has been a resurgence of interest in the grappling techniques of karate-dō.

Jūhō training with a partner should consume about ten minutes or one-fifth of your training time in each session.

Bunkai to Ōyō
ANALYSIS AND PRACTICAL APPLICATION

The purpose of kata training is to learn and practice the movements and kamae (structure) to defend against life-threatening attacks. The kata teach the movements, but they do not explicitly demonstrate how those movements can be used. In addition, many of the movements in kata have the potential to be used as a block, strike, throw, or joint dislocation by simply applying them in slightly different ways. The process of examining the movements in kata in order to determine their potential uses is called *bunkai*.

Bunkai literally means to disassemble and inspect, so the process of bunkai is to carefully analyze each individual movement in a kata and consider the various ways it can be used to defend against a variety of attacks, including attacks using weapons, bare-handed strikes, or grappling techniques. Traditionally, the uses of the techniques in kata have not been revealed by sensei to their students, other than perhaps a few examples to stimulate their thinking. The purpose of bunkai training is to compel students to think tactically and strategically, rather than simply memorize what they have been told. This process is an essential part of the mental training in karate-dō.

In other words, instead of telling students, "If you are attacked in this way, use this technique," in karate-dō we tell students, "Here are all the techniques you will need to defend yourself; now figure out the best ways to use them." The first way is much easier for the students, but they end up only knowing one or two ways to defend against a specific attack, and they only know how to defend against those attacks that have been explained to them. Using bunkai, the karateka learns an unlimited number of ways to defend against a specific attack and develops the ingenuity to find a way to defend against any attack. It may be more time-consuming, but it is more thorough and comprehensive training.

Once you have performed bunkai, and determined uses for the techniques in kata, you must train in their practical application, called ōyō. Working with a partner to make techniques work under realistic conditions is done during kumite training, so ōyō is usually not a separate training activity.

Kumite
SPARRING

The literal meaning of *kumite* is "crossed hands" or "woven hands," so it implies a similar situation to "crossing swords." It means combat with the bare hands or, more simply, sparring. There are two basic kinds of kumite: *yakusoku kumite* and *jiyū kumite*. Yakusoku kumite is "prearranged" or choreographed sparring in which both participants know in advance what the other will do. Jiyū kumite is "free" sparring in which neither participant knows in advance what the other will do.

Yakusoku kumite typically takes three forms: *ippon kumite, sambon kumite, and yakusoku kumite*. In ippon kumite, the attacker makes a single attack, usually by taking one step forward while doing so. Sambon kumite is slightly more aggressive. The attacker makes three attacks in quick succession, taking a step forward with each. In yakusoku kumite, any number of attacking scenarios can be choreographed, and they are often as complicated as movie and television fight scenes. Jiyū kumite has no predetermined attacker or defender, nor any predetermined techniques, although rules or limitations are usually imposed for the safety of the participants.

Students typically begin with ippon kumite, so they can learn the basics of maai (distance control) and gain experience in attack and defense under highly controlled conditions. They then move on to sambon kumite and jiyū kumite. Yakusoku kumite is often used for practicing ōyō and *goshinjutsu* (self-defense techniques), as well as to train to defend against combination attacks.

About ten minutes or one-fifth of total training time should be committed to kumite to ensure that you can use the techniques you are learning.

Hojo Undō
AUXILIARY EXERCISES

Hojo undō is primarily used to develop general strength and fitness. Traditionally it employs several devices for exercises to strengthen the muscles of nearly every part of the body, and the muscles used in karate techniques in particular. The most common of these devices are: *chi ishi* (weighted handles), *nigiri game* (gripping jars), *ishi sashi* (stone padlocks), and *tetsu geta* (iron shoes). Barbells, kettle bells, ankle weights, and wrist weights are also frequently used in addition to, or in place of, the more ancient devices.

We recommend that at least five minutes be used for hojo undō at the end of each training session. Some stretching exercises are also recommended.

Kitae
HARDENING

The practice of hardening various parts of the body, either to minimize pain and injury from striking or to develop the ability to withstand strikes, is called *kitae* (hardening). Common kitae activities include striking a *makiwara* (striking post) with the hands, elbows, and feet; striking into a *sune bako* (sand box) or *jari bako* (gravel box) with *nukite tsuki*; striking the shins, forearms, and tops of the feet (*sokkō*) with a wooden pole or paddle; or striking a large smooth rock with the hands and feet. A more recent form of kitae is striking a hanging heavy bag with the hands, elbows, knees, shins, and feet.

Karateka who are serious about being prepared for some form of full-contact fighting should devote at least five minutes per day to kitae.

Bunbu Ryōdō
SOPHISTICATION

"The pen is mightier than the sword" is a concept far older than this famous quote from Edward Bulwer-Lytton's *Richelieu*. The earliest traditions of the samurai and the Okinawan bushi placed great emphasis on these budōka developing an understanding of art and culture at least equal to their skill in battle. This balanced training has long been referred to in Japanese as *bunbu ryōdō* ("the dual way of culture and peace-making"). For brevity, we have used the word *sophistication* ("refined character, ideas, tastes, or demeanor as the result of education, training, and worldly experience") to summarize the concept—or, in Mabuni Kenwa's parlance, a *junshi*.

To merit their high social station and power, the bushi and samurai were arduously trained to be a master of several forms of bujutsu as well as being thoroughly versed in history, literature, philosophy, calligraphy, politics, statesmanship, and fine arts. The well-trained samurai was the archetype of what Europeans called a "Renaissance man," and the reasons for adhering to such a high standard were as much pragmatic as they were an outgrowth of the sense of nobility and chivalry of the bushi.

The bushi, like Gandhi and Martin Luther King Jr. of more recent times, understood that the strength of ideas could overcome any army. To this day, it is for these same practical reasons that true karateka strive to follow bunbu ryōdō. A vital part of honing both your mind and character, therefore, is devoting at least an equal portion of your training time to deepening your knowledge of history, philosophy, ethics, religion, politics, fine arts, and culture. In the practical aspects of training, the discipline of karate-dō results in a more serious and purposeful approach to these studies, while the mental exercise of intellectual pursuits develops a mind able to learn and apply budō concepts more readily.

The purpose of bunbu ryōdō is to help provide karateka with unlimited avenues of learning and expression for their individual aesthetic and cultural tastes, and to cultivate in them a level of intellectual and artistic development at least equal to their advancements in physical training. The secret of bunbu ryōdō is that it better prepares a person to assume the appropriate role of a karateka and as a leader of society, and to apply their power—both mental and physical—and compassion for the benefit of their community and society.

Bunbu ryōdō is rarely practiced as a distinct activity in the dōjō, other than sensei perhaps sharing a few thoughts during class about the meaning and life application of a topic, like *ken shin ichi nyo* or *karate ni sente nashi*. It is therefore up to each individual karateka to immerse themselves in the study of literature, art, music, philosophy, and other expressions of human thought and emotion. A person training three hours per week in the dōjō should spend at least three hours a week in the pursuit of bunbu ryōdō. The authors spend at least twice as much of their training time on bunbu ryōdō as they do honing their combative skills.

Shugyō no Junjō
PROGRESSION OF TRAINING

As you train in karate-dō, you will pass through several stages of development in your progression from beginner to expert to master of the art. You may also reach physical and emotional plateaus, at which your progress may appear to slow or stop—or even decline. Understanding that such plateaus are a normal part of the training process will help you avoid allowing a setback or plateau to discourage you. Remember that shugyō is "ascetic" training in the sense that it is highly focused and requires elimination of habits and activities that distract or detract from your training.

Ketsui o Suru
MAKE UP YOUR MIND

The first step in your journey is to make up your mind. You must decide to make your training a high priority in your life, not merely something you do for entertainment or a diversion whenever you lack something more interesting to do. A closely related concept mentioned earlier is kōjōshin—aspiring to improve. Without a deep-seated desire to improve yourself, you will be constantly plagued with excuses not to train.

Budō training is a lifestyle, not just a pastime, hobby, or extracurricular activity. As you progress, the discipline and dedication of your training will set you apart. You will begin to approach all of life with the outlook of a budōka. Over time, your entire attitude and personality will evolve. But this kind of fundamental improvement of your character cannot occur without a strong determination to train, even when you don't feel like it. No, *especially* when you don't feel like it.

Kihon o Manabu
EMPHASIZE THE BASICS

There is always a great temptation, particularly for beginners, to learn the flashy, complex, or difficult techniques of any art. It is natural for you to feel this way, especially if you have a desire to excel at karate and truly master it. However, your primary emphasis must be on the fundamentals, which are described in chapter 12.

It is true with any form of budō that a practitioner who has truly mastered the basics will handily defeat one who has trained in advanced techniques after having only a cursory knowledge of the fundamentals. A single basic powerful punch that lands squarely on target is far more effective than three flashy, off-target spinning kicks. If you understand the nature of basic techniques, it is easy to see why this is universally true.

Basics are no more or less than the ideal technique as it would be performed under optimal circumstances. Fundamentals demonstrate the perfect method of maximizing power, balance, self-protection, and effectiveness of technique. It is only after you have mastered performing under such ideal conditions that you can learn how to best adapt basic techniques to the less-than-ideal circumstances of real life.

It is also a mistake to assume that basics are only for beginners. Emphasis on fundamentals must be a lifelong habit. Anyone who has studied the lives of the renowned budō masters has observed that, without exception, they have shared a continuing passion for improving their kihon.

In the final analysis, there really are no "advanced" techniques; only fundamentals that have been adapted and applied to less-than-ideal circumstances. Everything is fundamentals, and the fundamentals are everything.

Riron o Shiru
UNDERSTAND THE PRINCIPLES

As you study the fundamentals, it is not sufficient merely to master the body mechanics necessary to perform them with precision, speed, and power. To progress beyond the basics, you must understand the underlying principles that make them effective—as well as the exigencies that can make them fail. This is the reason we have devoted so much of this book to the principles of karate, and far less to specific techniques.

With such an understanding, you will then be able to apply the basics to intermediate and advanced techniques and make these techniques as effective and natural as your basics. Furthermore, with a deep understanding of the principles that make techniques effective, you can readily apply those same principles to the decisions, challenges, and conflicts you face in everyday life.

Kaisū o Kasaneru
DEVELOP THROUGH REPETITION

The objective of training is to make the techniques natural—to make them a product of mushin, simply an extension of your mind. Nothing becomes this natural without practice, which is another reason for kihon o manabu: emphasizing the basics. You must be certain you are developing good habits in your training: that you are reinforcing correct technique, not errors or sloppiness, through your countless repetitions.

It can truly be said that the only difference between a novice and an expert is the number of repetitions of technique. A master is simply a novice who has practiced the techniques literally thousands, or in some cases millions, of times. Their depth of character and their knowledge of the art came in the same fashion—endless repetition.

There is a well-known saying among Japanese budōka from many disciplines: *Manabu no tame ni hyakkai, jukuren no tame ni senkai, satori no tame ni manga okonau.* This adage translates as "One hundred repetitions to learn, a thousand repetitions for proficiency, ten thousand repetitions for enlightenment." To truly master the fundamentals requires countless repetitions—and not just mindless repetitions, but repetitions performed with conscious effort to improve your technique with each one. Consider this: if you attend class three times a week and repeat a technique ten times in each class, then it will take only a little over three weeks to learn the technique. However, to become proficient—meaning to be able to perform the technique correctly almost every time—will take seven and a half months of training. And to be able to execute the technique flawlessly and with complete understanding of all its intricacies, principles, and applications will take over six years. Just for one technique!

Repeated practice not only develops the physical skills of the art, but also develops the mental attributes needed for mastery. You simply will not be able to train frequently and regularly for a prolonged period without developing both the physical skills and the mental attitudes—patience, persistence, fighting spirit, bushi no me, compassion, and heijōshin—of a budō master.

Tairyoku ni Ōjite Okonau
DIFFERENT STRENGTHS, DIFFERENT PEOPLE

Different people have different strengths and weaknesses. Some people learn faster or slower than others, have more or less innate athletic ability, and are in different stages of physical condition. All these things must be taken into account because they can significantly affect the pace at which one is able to learn new skills.

The only fair and true measure of progress is your own progress. It is not fair, either to yourself or to them, to compare yourself to others. Your body structure, learning ability, athletic prowess, age, maturity, and motivation are all vastly different from anyone else's, and your comparative rate of progress in learning karate will likewise be different.

In the 1990s Pellman shihan had a student with seven severe neuromuscular disorders. When he first began training, he literally could not cross the dōjō floor without stumbling over his own feet at least once. His progress was excruciatingly slow, and he left the dōjō in tears most days out of frustration. But he returned. Day after day, six days per week and often two classes per day, struggling more against his own body than against his training partners. It took him three years to achieve the rank of *rokkyu* (6th kyu, the first level of green belt). In that time, every other student who had started around the same time had reached *sankyu* (3rd kyu, the first level of brown belt). But he was a superior karateka to those brown belts in every respect except the rank he held because he had kokoro. Heart. More courage, more determination, greater discipline, and stronger character.

Twenty years later, those brown belts who had natural athleticism and had not struggled to learn new skills were struggling with life. Two had already had divorces, another was unable to hold a job more than a few months, and one was an alcoholic living in a cardboard box. But the green belt had a strong marriage, a good job as a research scientist, a close-knit family, was active in several community and charitable organizations, and had received several community service awards. The struggles he endured had made him the strongest of the group. He had learned to overcome adversity and to apply suishin to life's problems.

His progress had appeared slow because it took him so much longer to acquire new skills, but his advances in character and maturity—the things that mattered most and made the greatest difference in his life—had far outpaced his peers. *Tairyoku ni ōjite okonau.* You will progress in some ways much faster and farther than most people realize. Don't let appearances or comparisons discourage you.

You must also keep in mind that there are karate techniques that appear simple but are in fact incredibly complex and difficult to master, even with years of training. Paradoxically, while karate stresses the natural posture and movement of the body, it feels extremely unnatural for the first several months of training. It is important to train with realistic expectations, and not expect overnight successes. All budō training is a process of minute improvements over a long period of time to reach proficiency and full understanding.

Jishin ni Tsuite
CONFIDENCE

Just as there will be times during your training that you reach plateaus or encounter disappointments, there will also be times in which your performance excels or you achieve significant triumphs. And, just as there is danger in allowing disappointment to cloud your perception of your progress, there is equal danger in becoming overconfident when your progress seems exceptional.

Confidence is an important strength to possess. A bushi had to be confident, not only to face life-or-death battles but to achieve saya no naka ni kachi (victory before the sword is drawn) in all areas of life. But confidence must also be realistic, balanced, and tempered with humility.

One of ancient Japan's most famous leaders was Takeda Shingen, who was not only a great general but a great philosopher. He firmly believed that the best fight was no fight, and very seldom provoked a conflict. However, between 1553 and 1564, one of his most tenacious adversaries, Uesugi Kenshin, engaged his army in no less than five major battles. Takeda's forces were always victorious and could easily have crushed Uesugi's army on several occasions. But Takeda carefully engineered his victories so that they appeared to come by only a narrow margin, because he understood the danger of overconfidence.

In Takeda's view, the best victory was by a sixty to forty margin—wide enough to allow for unexpected events yet narrow enough to keep his troops aware of the possibility of defeat and therefore intensely focused. He felt that the closer to an absolute hundred-to-zero victory he achieved, the more likely his warriors would become overconfident, leading to recklessness, lack of discipline, and yūdan. For his first forty years, Takeda's goal in battle was to win, but as he matured as a commander, his perspective shifted to not losing, as we explain in detail in "Budō no Arikata" in chapter 2.

The same reasoning applies to overconfidence at the personal level. If we allow ourselves to become overconfident because of a few triumphs, we are likely to lose our strength of concentration and self-discipline and we will begin to decline rather than progress in our training.

Jiga ni Tsuite
CONTROL YOUR EGO

It was consistent with Takeda Shingen's philosophy that he selected a wide variety of trees to grow in his garden. He had cherry trees so he could admire their blossoms in the spring, weeping willows to provide spreading shade in the heat of summer, maples to set his garden ablaze with color in the fall, and pines to add bright spots of greenery to the stark winter landscape.

He selected his twenty-four subordinate generals (taishō) in a similar manner. These men not only reported to him and controlled his troops in battle but acted as his trusted advisers. Having risen to such positions of power and prestige, many men would surround themselves with sniveling yes-men, but Takeda instead chose men of varied backgrounds, perspectives, and ideas in order to get the very best and most creative advice possible. In addition to their having the courage to speak their minds frankly even if they felt he would not like to hear it, Takeda had five key criteria for selecting each of his generals: (1) they had to be good budōka, (2) they had to possess deep compassion and understanding for people, (3) they had to exhibit extreme *reigi* (politeness and self-discipline), (4) they had to evidence heijōshin in their behavior, and (5) they had to have a resolute sense of loyalty.

In order to receive the best possible advice from this diverse group of leaders, Takeda had to be willing to accept blunt criticism of his own plans and ideas, even of his goals and motives. Furthermore, he was willing to listen to their suggestions because of their wisdom and sincerity, not necessarily because they were his friends or agreed with him. Few of us are truly willing to subject ourselves to this sort of scrutiny, especially when our egos have been enlarged by holding a position of any consequence or power. But to achieve our highest potential, we must set our egotism aside and willingly listen to the voice of sincere constructive criticism, whether it be from our sensei in the dōjō or our close family members and friends.

In fact, one of the best ways to make significant improvement in areas of personal character is to surround yourself with loving, compassionate friends or family members who are willing to examine your actions and hold you unflaggingly accountable for your personal growth. While this is often a painful ordeal, for most of us it is the only way we can build the resolve needed to tackle the really deep-rooted integrity issues in our lives. This is one of the most valuable benefits of membership in a dōjō.

Like Takeda Shingen, you must be extremely careful in your selection of the people who will hold you accountable. They do not all have to be budōka, but they should all possess the compassion, discipline, heijōshin, and loyalty exemplified by Takeda's generals. And they must all love you enough to be willing to face you honestly, boldly, and respectfully and reveal your worst faults and failings, even though to do so will usually be as painful for them as it is for you.

Shin • Ki • Ryoku
MIND • SPIRIT • TECHNIQUE

When we presented the concept of shin • ku • i earlier, we explained how the mind is the key to self-control. The first topic in this chapter was making up your mind. There can be no question that the mind is the pivotal aspect of all martial arts training—all human endeavor, in fact. Once again, the concept of *shin • ki • ryoku* points to mental focus as the core of karate technique.

Shin • ki • ryoku is used to signify that mind, spirit, and technique should be inseparable. But it is even more refined than the notion of the three simply working together in harmony; it is the recognition that technique is the product of the mind (conscious thoughts, strategy, mental focus) and spirit (emotions, attitudes, character, and subconscious) working together. For an analogy, think of your left hand as your mind and your right hand as your spirit. When the two hands slap together, the resulting clap is technique.

Thus, a goal of your training should be to so completely unite your mind and spirit that your body's movements are the instinctive and natural response to their combined workings.

Shu • Ha • Ri
OBEY • BREAK • SEPARATE

Shu • ha • ri is a term the Japanese use to describe the overall progression of budō training, as well as the lifelong relationship the student will enjoy with their instructor.

SHU (守)

Shu can mean either "to protect" or "to obey." The dual meaning of the term is aptly descriptive of the relationship between a budō student and teacher in the student's early stages, which can be likened to the relationship of a parent and child. At this level, the student should absorb all that the sensei imparts and be eager to learn and willing to accept all correction and constructive criticism. The teacher must guard the student in the sense of watching out for their interests and nurturing and encouraging their progress, much as parents guard their children during their growing years. Shu stresses kihon in an uncompromising fashion so the student has a solid foundation for future learning, and all students perform techniques in identical fashion, even though their personalities, body structure, age, and abilities all differ.

HA (破)

Ha is another term with an appropriate double meaning: "to break free" or "to frustrate." Shortly after the student reaches dan (black belt) level, they will begin to break free in two ways. In terms of technique, the student will break free of the fundamentals and begin to apply the principles acquired from the practice of basics in new, freer, and more imaginative ways. The student's individuality will begin to emerge in the way they perform techniques and kata. At a deeper level, they will also break free of the rigid instruction of the teacher and begin to question and discover more through personal experience. This can be a time of frustration for the teacher, as the student's journey of discovery leads to countless questions beginning with "Why …" At the ha stage, the relationship between student and teacher is similar to that of a parent and an adult child. The student is more independent but still relies on the teacher for advice and guidance. The teacher is a master of the art, and the student is now a sempai or even a sensei to others.

RI (離)

Ri is the stage at which the student, now a *kōdansha* (high-ranking black belt), separates from the instructor, having absorbed all that they can learn from them. This is not to say that the student and teacher are no longer associated. Actually, quite the opposite is usually true. They should now have a stronger bond than ever before, much as a grandparent does with their son or daughter who is now also a parent. Although the student is now fully independent, they treasure the wisdom and patient counsel of the teacher, and there is a richness to their relationship that comes through decades of shared experiences. But the student is now learning and progressing primarily through self-discovery and research, rather than by instruction, and can give outlet to their own creative impulses. The student's techniques will bear the imprint of their own personality, character, and decades of training. Ri also has a dual meaning, the second part of which is "to set free." As much as the student now seeks independence from the teacher, the instructor likewise must set the student free.

Shu ◆ ha ◆ ri is not a linear progression, as many people seem to think. A karateka does not progress systematically from shu to ha to ri as their formal rank increases, or in direct proportion to time spent training in the manner suggested by the diagram below.

Figure 9.1 Linear concept of shu ◆ ha ◆ ri.

Instead, shu • ha • ri is more akin to concentric circles, so that there is shu within ha and both shu and ha within ri. Thus, the fundamentals remain constant; only the application of them and the subtleties of their execution change as the student progresses and their own personality begins to flavor the techniques performed. Similarly, the student and teacher are always bound together by their close relationship and the knowledge, experience, culture, and tradition shared between them.

Ultimately, shu • ha • ri should result in the student surpassing the master, both in knowledge and skill. This is the source of improvement for the art as a whole. If the student never surpasses their master, then the art will stagnate at best. If the student never achieves the master's ability, the art will deteriorate. But if the student can assimilate all that the master can impart and then progress to even higher levels of advancement, the art will continually improve and flourish.

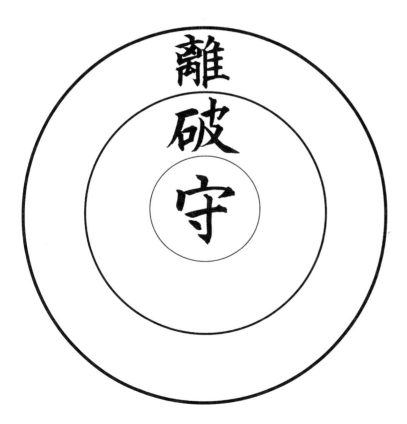

Figure 9.2 Correct concept of shu • ha • ri.

Shingi o Omonzuru
STAND FOR RIGHTEOUSNESS

True budō and true budōka are rooted in a tradition of righteousness. Budō are a means of preserving peace and overcoming ill intention. This foundation allows the budōka to develop shinnen, an unflagging strength of conviction that is a powerful motivation to prevail over adversity.

In battle, however, budōka will often find themselves pitted against *jadō* (literally, "the way of evil") embodied in those who hold to the belief that "all is fair in love and war." You may even encounter instructors whose teaching philosophy would condone underhanded tactics or inhumane acts for the sake of winning at any cost. While it is true that there are no rules on the battlefield, there is good and evil. To use the glare of the sun, kick sand in the face of the opponent, or use the terrain or obstacles to one's advantage are battle tactics, but they are not inherently evil. However, to threaten, harm, or kill innocent people in order to distract or coerce an opponent would indeed be jadō.

The true budōka also realizes that jadō is more than just unscrupulous fighting techniques. It inevitably degenerates into a perverse approach to life. In effect, this approach applies shin ∙ ku ∙ i in the negative: misdeeds influence one's speech and ideals, leading to increasingly hostile behavior and an amoral, utterly self-centered attitude.

In addition to its degenerative effects, jadō is also inherently weak. There are few people so depraved that their conscience does not inhibit them—at least slightly—when they utilize some underhanded method to gain advantage. This restraining influence, however small, prevents them from employing shinnen, so they cannot put their whole body, mind, and soul into their actions. On the other hand, the budōka who is acting justly can wholeheartedly pursue any endeavor. *Shingi* (righteousness) is therefore an empowering influence, creating a moral imperative that lends not only mental and spiritual strength, but—through ken shin ichi nyo (body and mind as one)—physical power as well.

Saigo Made Eizoku Suru
PERSIST TO THE END

We have repeatedly challenged you to make a strong commitment to training—to make up your mind to train in karate as a lifestyle—so we close this chapter with the admonition to persist until the end. Commitment and persistence are bookends, the beginning and end of all worthwhile human endeavors. To state it simply and directly: never quit!

To understand the importance of persistence, we need only to look at the common struggle to control bulging waistlines. The reason why diets fail and people almost always gain back the weight they lost (usually with a little extra thrown in for good measure), is that a diet—by definition—is only a short-term commitment. Diets are designed to accomplish only a singular goal—a specific amount of weight loss, a change in waistline, a change in appearance, and so on—and once that goal is achieved (or abandoned), the diet ends—by design.

The only weight-loss programs that ever succeed in the long run are nutritional lifestyle changes. This is more than a semantic distinction; it is a difference in purpose and objective. A diet is a temporary change made in order to achieve a specific goal, but a nutritional lifestyle is a change in how one lives life—a permanent change in one's overall behavior pattern with no objectively measurable goal.

Karate training is of little value if it is treated like a diet. One of the main reasons people stop training is that they started with the goal of reaching black belt *(shodan),* and when they do, they stop training, not unlike people who stop learning once they receive a high school or college diploma. For karate training to be of benefit to you and to society, you must make a lifelong commitment to continual growth and improvement. Budō training is not just for a certain time or until you achieve a certain goal; it is a lifestyle. Always remember that karate is a method for perfection of character, not a hobby or a fitness program. The day you stop maturing and improving your character is the day you begin dying.

If an accident, illness, or drastic change in your life makes an interruption of your training necessary or unavoidable, simply resolve that you will resume as soon as you are able. And then do it! Even if you stop training for five years due to some circumstance, you will not have quit if you hold to your commitment, continue bunbu ryōdō, and eventually resume your training.

Also remember that there is more to karate than just punching and kicking. If an injury leaves you temporarily or even permanently unable to practice your techniques, you can still continue your training by applying karate principles to other areas of your life. You will probably find that you recover faster if you apply karate principles to your recovery process, whether it is recovering from a physical, emotional, or even a financial setback.

Karate is training for life-or-death confrontation, so to quit means death. Once you have decided to be a karateka, you cannot quit.

Chapter Ten

一般原則

Ippan Gensoku

General Principles

INTRODUCTION

Mastery of karate-dō is not achieved by learning and practicing its advanced techniques. The true secret of mastering karate-dō is mastering its fundamentals or kihon. Masters perform advanced techniques, to be sure, but they devote the majority of their training to the continual perfection of fundamentals. This is a level of discipline that few karateka are capable of sustaining, and it probably accounts for the high percentage of those who quit karate training prior to reaching shodan (first level black belt), much less mastery of the art. Yet, if there is a "secret" to mastering the art of karate-dō, and in the process mastering oneself, it is the relentless effort to perfect the performance of the fundamentals.

The other hallmark of every genuine karate master is etiquette, as explained in chapter 11. Together, they are both the foundation and the epitome of karate-dō. For anyone who diligently trains in kihon and reihō, mastery is inevitable.

Underlying all fundamentals are several general principles:

- *chikara* (power)
- *tai sabaki* (whole-body movement)
- *shisei* (posture)
- *chakugan* (eye contact)
- *maai* (distance control)
- *seme* (pressure)
- *zanshin* (awareness)
- *machigai* (mistakes)

Chikara
POWER

As explained in the previous chapter, the human body serves as a multifaceted weapons system for the karateka. Nearly every surface of the hands, feet, arms, and legs can be used to strike an opponent or deflect an attack—even the hips, buttocks, and parts of the head can be used as weapons. All it takes is the correct and sufficient application of force.

Striking power is produced by combination of seishin ryoku (spiritual power), as described in chapter 8, and correctly applied biomechanics. Eight key elements of biomechanics that generate maximum striking power are:

- *kokyū* (breath control)
- *kamae* (structure)
- *koshi mawari* (hip rotation)
- *hikite* (pulling hand)
- *kihaku* (effort and intensity)
- *kiai* (unified spirit)
- *seido* (precision)
- *kime* (fixation)

When combined, these eight elements dramatically increase the amount of power delivered at the point of impact, and they make karate strikes devastating.

Kokyū
BREATH CONTROL

Breathing is life. To cease breathing is death. Breathing inefficiently robs the body of energy and strength. Reducing oxygen flow to the brain impairs the ability to think, reduces awareness of one's surroundings, slows reaction time, and diminishes willpower. So, breath control is vital to all karate techniques. It is the reason all styles of karate-dō place considerable emphasis on correct breathing methods.

The Japanese word for breathing, *kokyū* (呼吸), provides an important clue to the proper method. The kanji for kokyū literally mean "exhale, inhale," serving as a reminder that the correct cycle for breathing is to exhale first, then inhale. By exhaling first, carbon dioxide and impurities are expelled from the lungs before they are refilled, ensuring that oxygen intake is maximized when inhaling.

To begin each breath, you should therefore exhale as completely as possible to empty the lungs, which is the opposite of human instinct. Under duress, our natural response is either to hold our breath or to breathe rapidly and shallowly, almost panting. Performing kokyū trains the body to overcome this innate tendency, which not only provides the body with more energy for fight or flight, but also helps to suppress fear and panic when under attack.

The key to proper breathing is *fukushiki kokyū* (abdominal breathing), so called because the abdomen appears to swell or inflate as the breath is drawn in. This occurs because the diaphragm is pressed down into the abdominal cavity to fill the lungs more completely during fukushiki kokyū. It is the same breathing method taught to professional singers and musicians who play horns or woodwind instruments to maximize their breathing efficiency.

To perform fukushiki kokyū, begin by exhaling slowly and fully through the mouth to empty the lungs, then inhale slowly and steadily through the nose. The feeling should be as though the air is being drawn in through the nostrils, flowing up around the crown of the head, then down the spinal column to the tanden. It may help to visualize the air traveling in this fashion when you first begin practicing this technique. Even though the air does not actually follow this path, many karateka report feeling a cooling sensation on the inner surface of their skull when breathing and visualizing in this manner. When the lungs are completely full, exhale slowly with the feeling or visualization that the air is flowing directly up from the tanden and out through the mouth.

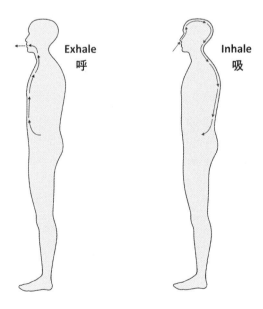

Figure 10.1 Fukushiki kokyū visualization.

Try to make the transition from exhaling to inhaling and from inhaling to exhaling unnoticeable to anyone watching you. Your shoulders should not rise and fall, nor should your chest contract and expand. Your mouth should not open and close but should remain only slightly open throughout. And, in most situations, there should be as little sound as possible.

During mokusō meditation at the beginning and end of each training session, fukushiki kokyū should be accompanied by visualizing all impure and negative thoughts and emotions being expelled from your mind and body as you exhale, and pure positive thoughts and emotions being drawn in as you inhale. Examples of negative thoughts and emotions are fear, anger, jealousy, envy, hatred, worry, doubt, anxiety, insecurity, arrogance, and guilt. Positive thoughts and emotions include courage, confidence, forgiveness, gratitude, love, contentment, humility, respect, faith, determination, hope, and compassion.

The process of performing fukushiki kokyū while ridding your mind and body of negativity and filling your mind and body with positivity is often called *kiyomeri kokyū* (cleansing breath) or *jaki o dasu* (expelling evil). Kiyomeri kokyū is as vital to karate-dō as correct technique and should be an integral part of every aspect of your training. Begin each training activity with a minimum of three cleansing breaths and concentrate on using fukushiki kokyū throughout the activity until it becomes so ingrained in your performance that you no longer have to think about it.

Kamae
STRUCTURE

The word kamae is most often translated as "stance" or "posture," but a more appropriate translation of the term is "structure." Kamae provides the stable platform upon which all karate techniques are built. Although the various ways of providing structure for techniques have names like Heikō Dachi (Parallel Stance), Zenkutsu Dachi (Front [Leg] Bent Stance), and Shiko Dachi (Forked Stance), there is far more to kamae than just the position of the legs and feet.

Kamae includes everything needed for stability, facilitating movement, protecting the body, and maximizing the power and effectiveness of a technique. Few forms in traditional Japanese budō have formal names for their stances and structure. Karate-dō and its closely related art of Okinawa kobudō are notable exceptions to this. In other arts, kamae is typically presented in terms of *shizentai* ("natural body"), meaning the position of the body that is best suited to the technique being used. This is a useful way of thinking of kamae in karate-dō as well, especially in connection with bunkai (analysis) and ōyō (practical application).

In most respects, kamae can be compared to the structure of a building. A building has a foundation (stance); a framework (skeleton); struts and supports (muscles, tendons, ligaments, and membranes); plumbing, ducting, and wiring (circulatory, nervous, and gastrointestinal systems); and walls and roof (skin). Both must be designed to withstand a static load—its own weight, including its contents—as well as dynamic forces of different kinds, such as wind, rain, snow, earthquakes, and even some foreseeable impacts.

Thus, when forming a particular stance in karate, not only must the feet and legs be in their proper positions, but the entire skeleton must be correctly aligned, and the muscles and sinews must provide the needed support for the entire structure. The whole body is involved in creating a stance or kamae. Any part of the anatomy that is misaligned or lacking the appropriate degree of tension-relaxation or rigidity-flexibility weakens the entire structure and creates a vulnerability to attack.

Figure 10.2 depicts Jiyū Kamae (Sparring Stance) as an example. The stance itself is Han-Zenkutsu Dachi, but the kamae involves more than just the position of the feet. Most of the weight is on the balls of the feet rather than evenly distributed along the soles. The knees, ankles, and hips are slightly flexed to facilitate immediate movement. The shoulders are aligned with the hips so that the upper body is angled relative to the opponent, presenting a smaller target area. The arms form a triangle with its apex directed at the opponent. Together, these factors make Jiyū Kamae stable, mobile, highly protective, and able to withstand a forceful attack.

Figure 10.2 Jiyū Kamae.

Nevertheless, kamae is neither stiff nor static. In actual combat, we don't hold these positions. We are in constant motion, maneuvering to preempt an attack, evade an attack, create an opportunity to counterattack, or perform a counterattack. It may therefore be helpful to think of the stances used in karate as merely freeze-frames taken at the moment of contact with the opponent from a video of the technique being applied. Kamae is therefore the optimal structure for maximizing the effectiveness of a technique, and the stances we describe are merely the optimal position of the body at a specific moment in time, such as the moment of impact of a strike or the completion of a throw.

A disadvantage of kata competition in sports karate is that judges can only evaluate the aesthetic qualities of the performer's kamae, not how effective the structure would be in lethal combat. The emphasis therefore becomes erect posture, joint flexibility, and the muscle strength needed to assume poses that are "picture perfect," rather than to develop the structure most effective for surviving or performing a violent attack. The corresponding advantage of kata competition is that it provides an ideal kamae to which karateka can aspire and serves as an incentive to train in order to come as close as possible to that ideal.

Koshi Mawari
HIP ROTATION

Most of the power in karate techniques is generated by the legs. Even punches and other hand strikes are chiefly powered by the much larger muscles of the legs, buttocks, and hips, not just the shoulders and arms. The hips therefore serve as the transmission by which this power in directed through the spine and into the shoulders, arms, and hands to the target.

As we are taught in elementary or middle school, $k = \frac{1}{2}mv^2$. Kinetic energy (k) or power is one-half the mass (m) times the square of the velocity (v) or speed that mass is traveling at the moment of impact. So if a mass of 10 is traveling at a speed of 3, it generates 45 units of kinetic energy. (One-half of 10 is 5, the square of 3 is 9, and 5 times 9 is 45.) If the speed of that mass is increased to 4, it then generates 80 units of kinetic energy, an increase of 78 percent in total power by increasing the speed only 33 percent. However, increasing the mass by 33 percent to 13.33 results in only a 33 percent increase in the resulting energy.

The primary role of the hips in karate, therefore, is to significantly increase the speed of a kick or hand strike by adding a whiplike action through swift and powerful rotation called *koshi mawari*. In addition, the hips increase the effective mass of the strike by propelling more of the body's mass into the striking surface.

The key to transmitting power through the hips is kamae (structure). It is not enough simply to "snap" the hips powerfully while striking. The hips must serve as the conduit by which energy travels from the legs up the spine through the shoulder and down the arm to the hand. For this to happen, a connection must be maintained between the leg, hips, spine, shoulder, and arm. If the hips move independently of the rest of the body, like the rapid hip-shaking of a belly dancer or in the Tahitian 'ōte'a, the speed, mass, and energy will not transfer to the striking surface.

To make koshi mawari effective, you must feel that connection during your training. A common mistake in koshi mawari is to engage only one hip in the movement— usually the hip on the side of the striking limb. For maximum speed and power, both hips must be utilized in unison, one pushing forward and the other pulling rearward with equal force.

Hikite
PULLING HAND

Another action that sets the striking and blocking techniques of karate-dō apart from those performed in other forms of combat is called *hikite*, or "pulling hand." Nearly every block or strike by one hand is accompanied by a retraction of the other hand with equal speed and force, an action called hikite. This hikite action accomplishes four valuable things: (1) it prepares the pulling hand to execute an immediate follow-up strike or block; (2) it assists in the timing and performance of koshi mawari; (3) it dramatically increases the power of the technique being employed; and (4) if the hikite hand is grasping the opponent, it yanks the opponent sharply off-balance, compounding the impact of the strike and minimizing the effect of any attempted countermeasure.

The most common hikite position is to bring the pulling hand to the side of the body about one fist width above the hip bone. In this position (fig. 10.3), the pulling hand (the left hand in the photo) is roughly parallel to the ground and about solar plexus height, which is the most advantageous position from which to initiate a punch or block. Many instructors refer to this position as the "chambered" or "cocked" position of the hand.

To reach this position, the pulling hand is drawn back at the same speed as the movement of the striking hand. If the pulling hand began in the punching position (palm down), it must be twisted palm-up as it is pulled back. This rotation does not occur at a continuous even pace during hikite, but rather as a sudden twist in the last few inches (about one fist length) of rearward movement, just as the twist when punching is done in the last few inches of motion, finishing in the position shown in figure 10.4.

Figure 10.3 Hikite (close-up).

Figure 10.4 Hikite with *seiken tsuki*.

A common error in hikite is to overtense the withdrawing arm, so that the shoulder rises as the hand reaches the fully retracted position. Notice that in figure 10.3, the shoulders remain level. When practicing hikite to perfect your technique, you may find it helpful to concentrate on pushing both shoulders slightly downward as you complete the punching motion. This conscious exaggeration for a few repetitions will help you develop the unconscious habit of keeping the shoulders relaxed and even.

When performing kihon, hikite is employed simultaneously with every punch, every striking technique, and every blocking technique. When performing *shutō uchi*, the hikite is normally drawn back only to a point adjacent to the solar plexus, palm-up and open in *nukite* formation. There are other intermediate and advanced techniques in which the fingers of the hikite hand are curled inward to approximate gripping a wrist. When formed in this manner, hikite is sometimes retracted adjacent to the solar plexus, while in other cases it is pulled all the way back to the hip, with the hand kept palm-down throughout the pulling action in both variations. Additional adaptations of hikite are found in several kata, so the importance of hikite in kihon is to develop the habit of hikite and understand its principles, so this knowledge can be applied to the numerous hikite variations as they are encountered during training.

Kihaku
EFFORT AND INTENSITY

Kihaku is written in Japanese as 気迫, and it is one of countless terms used in karate that has several nuances of meaning, including "intensity," "spirit," and "concentration." Taken literally, it means "to produce or exert ki."

Ki (気) is perhaps the most difficult to define concept used in karate. It is typically translated as either "energy" or "spirit." For some, ki has all the mystical properties of "the force" from the *Star Wars* movies. Although not a mystical or metaphysical force, ki does have physical, mental, and spiritual elements in its composition that make it more than the sum of its parts. It is more than merely physical effort, but it is not entirely mental or spiritual energy either. It might best be understood as the combination or concentration of physical, mental, and spiritual energies—body, mind, and spirit working in unity.

Kihaku requires physical effort and energy, but it is more than physical strength. Mental focus, determination, and willpower add intensity to the body's strength. And that ethereal quality we call "spirit" further amplifies the combined power of mind and body to produce what the Japanese call kihaku.

The English phrase that might best capture the concept of kihaku is "giving it all you have." Taken literally, when you put all the mental, physical, and spiritual energy you can muster into a technique, you are applying kihaku.

Kiai
UNIFIED SPIRIT

A concept closely related to kihaku is *kiai,* written as 気合 in kanji. As in kihaku, *ki* refers to "energy" and "spirit." *Ai* (合) means "to gather," "unite," "consolidate," "blend," or "join." So kiai is the process of gathering, consolidating, and unifying your physical, mental, and spiritual energy and focusing it on a single action or propelling it into a specific target. This often manifests itself as a loud shout during the execution of a technique and has led some people to wrongly believe that *kiai* means "to shout." *Donaru* (怒鳴る) means "to yell," so it might help to use *donaru* or its noun form, *dona,* to denote the vocalization to distinguish it from the more profound action of kiai. When a sensei instructs students to kiai, they certainly expect to hear them yell, but what they are really telling them to do is apply their utmost effort and spirit in the technique they are performing.

The vocalization that accompanies kiai should be a reflection of the act of kiai—compact, concentrated, ferocious, and driven from the tanden rather than the chest. It should be more of a roar than a scream. As you progress in your training, your dona will become natural, but we recommend that beginners use the sound, "ei" for the *dona*. Forcing the sound "ei" up from the tanden is easier than "hai" or "ya," which both tend to originate in the chest. Forming the sound in the tanden makes it easier to unite (*ai*, 合) the sound with the powerful action of the hips in the abdominal region and from there to drive their combined energy into the target.

Seido
PRECISION

Seido (精度) is usually translated as "precision" or "accuracy," and it is a vital aspect of karate training. Obviously, no technique is effective if it misses its target, and many of the most effective targets for karate strikes are relatively small, such as the temple, an eyeball, or the throat. Others, like the armpit or groin, are often obstructed, so striking them requires considerable accuracy. Very few karate techniques involve wild flailing.

Kime
FIXATION

Kime (決め) is one of the most difficult Japanese terms to translate into English because there isn't an equivalent word in the English language. "Fixation," the word we used here, is somewhat close but not a complete or adequate definition. *Kime* is also commonly translated as "focus" or "concentration." Both are also aspects of kime, as is "resolve" or "determination." We have even heard some mistakenly describe kime as being derived from the *ki* (気) in *kihaku* ("intensity") and focusing or concentrating that ki on the target. Although kime plays a vital role in directing energy into the target, it is not what is meant by the word. The best clue to the true nature of kime is probably found in its uses in everyday speech outside budō.

The verb form of kime, *kimeru*, is commonly used much like the English terms "to set" or "to lock in," as in setting a wedding date, setting a broken bone, or locking in the terms of a contract. It implies greater firmness and rigidity than "decide," since something that is "set" or "locked in" cannot easily be changed. It is fixed in time or space and held there with considerable force and intentionality—allegorically set in concrete.

In karate-dō, kime is thus the act of mentally, spiritually, and physically "locking in" on the target. It involves concentration, resolve, intensity, singularity of purpose, and maximum physical exertion all focused on the target at the moment of execution of a technique. The manifestation of kime occurs when the entire body "locks" for an instant in which the muscles, maintaining kamae and transmitting energy into the technique, are exerting their maximum power, and the mind and spirit are focused solely and with utmost intensity on the target.

Tai Sabaki
BODY MOVEMENT

Karate-dō is not a stationary art. A karateka must be able to move quickly and stably. The Japanese terms for the way a karateka moves is tai sabaki. Although tai sabaki means "body movement," in karate-dō it should be understood as whole-body movement, rather than just footwork *(ashi sabaki)*. Ashi sabaki—the different types of footwork employed by karateka—is just one aspect of tai sabaki. In essence, the karateka moves the entire body as a unified force, of which footwork is merely one component. In order to optimize stability by maintaining a low center of gravity, the *koshi* (hips) or *saika* (lower abdomen)—usually called the tanden in traditional Asian medicine—serves to initiate movement, rather than the legs or upper body.

Those without karate training typically either lean forward to initiate movement by shifting their weight, or begin pulling their body forward with their leading leg. Both these actions shift the center of gravity upward, making the person less stable. In karate, movement is initiated by pushing the tanden forward, which requires both knees to bend slightly and lowers the center of gravity. The feeling should be as if someone has grasped your belt and pulled you forward. In this way your posture remains erect and your body well balanced while moving.

To provide additional stability, the feet should slide across the floor, maintaining light contact, rather than being lifted. In this way, called *suri ashi* ("sliding feet"), both feet remain in constant contact with the floor, enabling the karateka to remain balanced if jostled. Specific methods of ashi sabaki (footwork) and *mawari-kata* (turning) are explained in detail in chapter 12.

Shisei
POSTURE

The basic rule of posture is to remain erect and natural. For most of us, this is already a contradiction in terms, since slouching or slumping has become "natural" to us. The body must be held erect and alert, but this carriage must not be rigid, forced, or artificial. The neck and back of the head should be in a straight line with the spinal column, but with the chin not tucked in. This is definitely a paradox, since the back of the head cannot truly be straight unless the chin is, in fact, tucked in somewhat. Again, what is meant by this admonition is that a happy medium must be found, so that the head is held high with the neck and back straightly aligned, yet the chin is not tucked so far in as to cause a double or triple chin.

In the simplest terms it means to sit straight when sitting and stand tall when standing. If you can do this and still remain relaxed, then you are on the right track. It is especially important for beginners to avoid muscle tension in the shoulders. In the awkwardness of trying to perform karate techniques the first several times, it is quite common to tense and raise the shoulders in an effort to better control the movement of the arms. This tension will usually throw off the balance and cause the arms to move stiffly and unnaturally, robbing the body of power and actually slowing the striking hand.

Until the basic movements of karate begin to feel natural and comfortable, it often helps to make a conscious effort at the beginning of every technique to relax and lower the shoulders. This upright yet relaxed bearing is maintained in every aspect of karate, from the time you assume a preparatory position for performing a technique until you rest after completing the technique.

Shisei is of greatest importance while you are moving. Much of your power and correct technique rely on proper posture, which connects your legs, hips, spine, and shoulders in order to transfer the full power of your body into the movement. Your balance also stems predominantly from correct posture.

Try to avoid training in shisei only while performing karate techniques. Instead, if practiced from the moment you enter the dōjō to the moment you leave, proper posture will more quickly become habitual. With sufficient time and training, it will simply become your natural state, no longer requiring any conscious effort. You will have correct posture whether you are practicing karate, driving your car, working, or relaxing at home.

Chakugan
EYE CONTACT

As you might imagine, chakugan (eye contact) is crucial to karate. If a karateka fails to notice an opponent's attack, they will lose the battle—and possibly their life. The result is the same if you are fooled by a feint. As soon as you face a training partner (aite) for the first time, you will find yourself wondering where to look: should you watch the partner's eyes? Their hands? Their feet? Should you stare at your target?

There are as many theories about eye contact as there are styles of karate, and each theory has much merit. Some say to watch the opponent's eyes, but the eyes can often be used to deceive with a fake glance. Others advocate watching the opponent's hands because the hands cannot lie. But the hands of an experienced karateka can move so swiftly that by the time you notice them moving, it may be too late for a parry. Another idea is to watch the opponent's hips, since aite cannot move without the hips revealing it. Still others believe the opponent's elbows should be the focal point for the same reason. How can we possibly know which theory is right?

We are not concerned with which of these theories is right, because we employ *enzan no metsuke* ("distant mountain sight"). By viewing the opponent with the same slightly out-of-focus eyesight we use when viewing a panorama of distant scenery, with the eyes directed at about the level of aite's solar plexus, our vision encompasses their entire body. In this way, we can watch our adversary's eyes, hands, elbows, hips, and feet all at the same time. This method also prevents us from being easily duped by an eye-fake or a distracting hand movement, because the positions of the hips, elbows, and feet will betray any deception attempted with another part of the body. The karateka only reacts when the whole body reveals aite's true intentions.

When practicing without a partner, as when performing kihon or kata, enzan no metsuke is accomplished by directing the line of sight toward a spot on the ground about fifteen to twenty feet away. This angle approximates the correct direction and focal length that would be used with a training partner or opponent.

Maai
DISTANCE CONTROL

Maai is the key to victory in karate. Whoever controls the distance between you and your opponent controls the outcome of the battle, so maai (distance control) is of supreme importance in karate training, and the primary emphasis of most forms of kumite.

There are two major aspects of maai: *mazakai* (safety distance) and *uchima* (striking distance). Mazakai is everywhere that is beyond an opponent's ability to strike by taking a single full stride from their current position. Uchima is any point within that range. Due to differences in body size, arm length, and speed of motion, correct maai varies for everyone.

To determine the closest point of mazakai, you simply work backward from the position you would be at the moment of contact when striking or being struck by your opponent. To understand how to identify mazakai, then, you must first understand how to strike. In most cases, the strike used to determine mazakai is *oizuki* (lunging punch) performed in Zenkutsu Dachi, as depicted in figure 10.5. By leaving your rear foot in place and drawing your leading foot back into Heikō Dachi, you arrive in *issoku ichi geki no maai* ("one step away from attack") or uchima (fig. 10.6).

Figure 10.5 Position at point of contact.

Figure 10.6 Uchima (leading foot withdrawn from contact position).

Everything behind uchima is considered mazakai, so uchima is the closest an opponent should ever be allowed to come without taking some form of defensive action—either moving away or counterattacking. As shown in figure 10.7, it is safest to remain an additional half-step or more behind uchima to ensure safety from attack. In a self-defense situation, the instant an adversary crosses the boundary between mazakai and uchima (fig. 10.6), they should be struck down.

Figure 10.7 Mazakai (6 inches farther than uchima).

During kumite training, the closest point of mazakai is usually the starting point for a technique. In this way, attacks are initiated from the edge of mazakai and reach uchima in one stride. This undoubtedly originated from early karateka training to defend against attacks with a *katana* (sword) or *yari* (spear).

It was essential to remain just out of reach of the sword or spear because a single cut or stab, even if not immediately fatal, could fester and eventually kill: ichi geki hissatsu (killing with one blow). A battle between a karateka and an armed attacker was essentially a chess game of maneuvering into a position in which the karateka remained just out of range until an opening could be created to move into uchima. The same tactic applies to kumite in which both opponents are unarmed karateka. Both must consider the other's hands and feet to be lethal weapons and maneuver accordingly. This is the essence of maai.

Figure 10.8 Mazakai against katana.   Figure 10.9 Mazakai against *bō* (staff) or yari.

Some of the tactics to apply maai include taking advantage of physical differences like length of stride and reach, using angles to reduce the opponent's effective reach while increasing your own, using speed and timing to move faster than the opponent can react, employing deceptive ways of closing distance without appearing to do so, and developing the ability to take longer strides than the opponent without sacrificing stability or mobility. Much of this is accomplished through tai sabaki and practicing various methods during kumite. It is achieved by developing improved perception as your experience grows.

For safety during kumite, we practice *sundome* ("inch stop"). Sundome is a form of maai that entails the use of your stance and length of stride to stop your strike one inch from its intended target. Critics say this trains karateka to miss their targets. We strongly disagree. Sundome trains a karateka to be extremely aware of, and precise in, tai sabaki (body movement), kamae (structure), and shisei (posture). Once a karateka can move with full speed, intensity, and power into a position that stops a blow an inch from the partner's body, they have the ability to control maai with tremendous accuracy.

Reversing sundome produces what the Japanese call *issun no maai o mikiru*, which means to ascertain a distance of one inch. In other words, it develops the ability to observe from an opponent's body, attitudes, skill level, and movement when they are in a position to strike within one inch. With that ability, you are able to stay an inch out of range of your opponent, allowing you to evade an adversary's strike by the slightest margin, then counterattack while the opponent is still within your uchima. Developing issun no maai o mikiru should be a major focus of kumite training.

Attaining skill in judging maai demands countless hours of training in the dōjō. By trial and error—often painful error—you will eventually be able to instinctively retreat just a hair's breadth beyond an attacker's reach, and in a single fluid motion, step in for a counterattack that is both too quick for your adversary to block and too close for them to avoid. The highest ideal of this maai is sometimes called kami hito-e—the thickness of a single sheet of paper—in which the opponent's strike touches the surface of your gi but does not compress the fabric enough to touch your skin. When you reach this level of skill, you have truly mastered maai.

Seme
PRESSURE

Seme is usually translated as "pressure," but an equally appropriate term might also be "intimidation." It is a term used frequently throughout this book, especially when explaining techniques and movement. The general concept of seme is to relentlessly maintain pressure against your opponent to suppress their ability to attack, to oppress their spirit, to force mistakes, and basically dominate their mind and spirit. Seme is accomplished by a combination of technique, strategy, and *bushi damashii* (bushi spirit).

Technique is used to create a credible threat to the opponent's safety. An example of this is Jiyū Kamae (Sparring Stance), in which the hands are positioned in a manner that both protects most of the target areas of our upper body and threatens the target areas of the opponent. Just the presence of the hands and arms in this position serves as a visible barrier preventing the opponent from moving into uchima, and it is thus an element of seme.

Similarly, strategy can be a form of seme. For instance, by moving diagonally instead of linearly, we may be able to limit an opponent's options for attack or defense, while at the same time presenting fewer possible target areas on ourselves and exposing potential target areas on the opponent. We can also use changes in stance and angle of attack to maneuver the opponent into a weakened position, such as backing them into a corner or against an obstacle. By maintaining superior position, we intimidate the opponent into a mistake borne of fear or desperation. The sheer ferocity of bushi damashii can undermine the opponent's confidence, causing them to hesitate to act or make a mistake at a crucial moment that allows us to prevail. The power of a confident posture and gaze cannot be overestimated as a form of seme.

By combining these three aspects of seme, it becomes one of our most potent weapons. As you progress in your training, you will find that seme is involved in practically every facet of karate, especially kumite, and is the key to prevailing in battle.

The driving force behind seme is *sen* ("initiative"). We describe sen in greater detail in chapter 19, but its role in seme bears explanation here. Sen can be viewed as the determination to deliver the first effective strike in battle. There are two closely related sayings in karate that relate this principle. One is *Sente hisshō* ("First attack is certain victory") and the other is *Katte utte* ("Striking is victory"). To be credible, and to be powerful enough to be sensed by your opponent, seme requires you to be steadily working toward striking a devastating blow. The imminence of a ferocious and potentially lethal attack is the pressure exerted by seme.

It may seem contradictory to say, on the one hand, Karate ni sente nashi ("In karate, never attack first"), and then to say, Sente hisshō or Katte utte. In our minds, however, these sayings do not actually contradict each other. They simply require deeper examination.

Karate ni sente nashi, long a fundamental adage of karate-dō, is both a philosophical admonition against being aggressive or hot-tempered and a practical warning that any attacking technique exposes your own body to debilitating counterattacks. By extending an arm to strike or a leg to kick, you expose the joints of that limb to dislocation and its bones, muscles, and blood vessels to injury. An attack also commits you to a course of action and a posture that, if perceived by your opponent, can be exploited. Thus, one implication of karate ni sente nashi is that if you attack first, a well-trained opponent will exploit a weakness or vulnerability inherent in that attack to defeat you.

In one respect, Sente hisshō merely states the obvious in an art based on ichi geki hissatsu: whoever strikes first, wins. So, while we never want to be the aggressor, we do want to be the first to deliver a fight-ending attack. Conceptually it is equivalent to the Western adage, "The best defense is a good offense."

At a deeper level, Sente hisshō describes the surest path victory: *sen no sen*—to seize the initiative and counterstrike before the opponent's attack is completed. In essence, it means beating your opponent to the punch. This does not make you the aggressor. Instead, it means that when you sense your opponent's intention and commitment to attack—perhaps a shift in stance, clenching a fist, setting the jaw, or drawing the shoulder back—you strike before the opponent does. Once sen no sen has been mastered, it is practically invincible.

In a similar way, Katte utte simply underscores the basic truth that you cannot win by merely blocking, evading, and retreating. Eventually you must counterattack, or your opponent's attacks will continue until you make a mistake and lose.

Another aspect of Sente hisshō is more subtle than beating the opponent to the punch: maai. Controlling the timing and distance of an encounter ensures that you will be the first to deliver a finishing blow. If you are unable to control the distance separating you from your opponent, you can flail around until you are worn out while your opponent is blocking or evading your efforts, and you will only provide your opponent with opportunities for counterattacks. Therefore, maai is a primary means of exerting seme.

Zanshin
AWARENESS

Zanshin is a term that appears to be unique to the Japanese language; there is certainly no single word in English equivalent to it. Taken literally, it means "remaining spirit," "leftover spirit," or "excess spirit," but it is usually explained as "leaving your spirit focused on the opponent." None of these terms does *zanshin* justice, however. Unfortunately, there is no easy way to define or explain zanshin. It is simply a state of mind that must be experienced to be truly understood. And once understood, it defies accurate description.

Zanshin is a complex state of mind that encompasses indomitable will—the will not to lose that we explained earlier—a projection of fighting spirit that should be almost palpable to the opponent, mental and physical readiness to respond to attack, and an intense state of alertness, all of which are tempered with a complete lack of fear, worry, excitement, or tension. Zanshin is almost a paradox in itself since it combines the fiercest possible fighting spirit (bushi damashii) with the serenity of heijōshin.

Some people have the mistaken belief that because zanshin is "leftover spirit," it is the spirit we cling to and exhibit after a fight has ended. We believe this is a misconception. Zanshin should be present in us before, during, and after a battle.

When practicing karate technique, zanshin should arise as you begin inhaling your kiyomeri kokyū purifying breaths. This corresponds to the moment a threat is first perceived. This intense state of mind then continues throughout the activity, whether it is kihon, kata, or kumite. It is especially important when performing kata.

It is natural for almost anyone to maintain fighting spirit while preparing for battle or engaged in battle, but one of the most vulnerable moments for a bushi was when the battle appears to be over. The best time for a wounded or hidden opponent to make a final effort to defeat you is when you let down your guard (yūdan) after an apparent victory. This may be the reason that people expect zanshin to be most apparent at the end of a kata or other activity.

Just as there is no simple way to describe its characteristics, there is no simple way to learn zanshin. It is a state of mind that can only be developed by dedicated training. It may have been easier for the bushi of old to develop zanshin because there was a much greater probability that their training would be put to the test with their life at stake than there is for modern karateka. In the twenty-first century it takes a bit of imagination to develop zanshin.

Visualization helps many people practice and develop their fighting spirit. By imagining that you are actually facing an opponent while performing kata or other training activities, you can more readily enter a mental state of alert concentration. By pretending that your life is at stake, you can imitate the fierce resolve and willpower necessary to win the imaginary battle. And if you finish each kata anticipating that your defeated foe might spring up for one final attack, or that another enemy might be lurking nearby just waiting for a lapse in your concentration to attack, you can more easily practice that state of calm yet wary preparedness that is zanshin.

Zanshin would hardly qualify as an aspect of budō if it did not have a somewhat paradoxical nature—fortunately, zanshin readily meets this criterion. As already mentioned, zanshin literally means "remaining spirit," and it is often associated with the warrior spirit remaining after combat, yet it is to be present at all times, before, during, and after the battle. On the other hand, the Japanese have a saying, *Meijin ni zanshin nashi* ("A true master has no zanshin"). This suggests that at the highest levels of training, you no longer exhibit zanshin.

This doesn't mean that zanshin is absent, or that you let down your guard, but that the highly advanced karateka has so much zanshin active every moment of their life—even during sleep—that to the untrained eye it appears that zanshin is absent. Instead, however, what is absent is not zanshin; it is the lack of zanshin, with no noticeable difference between being at rest or in the heat of mortal combat.

A final word about zanshin is that it permeates every other aspect of karate. It is the driving force behind all of the physical techniques. Its courage is manifest in the erect posture of shisei. It is the nearly palpable resolve-crushing spirit evident in kamae. It shines from the eyes to challenge the opponent in chakugan. It energizes every breath in kokyū. It emboldens the karateka to maintain correct, relentless maai. And it provides the ferocious single-minded focus of kihaku.

Heijutsu no Sambyō
THREE SICKNESSES OF MARTIAL ARTS

Shitō-Ryū founder Mabuni Kenwa identified three traits he called the *heijutsu no sambyō* ("three sicknesses of martial arts"):

一、疑慮 *hitotsu: giryo* (doubt)

一、懈怠 *hitotsu: ketai* (laziness)

一、慢心 *hitotsu: manshin* (conceit)

Giryo means doubt, mistrust, or misgivings. Like most aspects of budō, giryo applies on several levels. It refers to doubt in one's ability, mistrust of the instruction being received, or misgivings about the efficacy of techniques. Any of these can be detrimental to training and fatal in combat. To go into combat without resolute belief in your ability to prevail over the opponent is insanity and practically guarantees defeat.

Nearly every society and every warrior culture has a saying similar to "the more you sweat in peace, the less you bleed in war," which has been quoted by military leaders and sports coaches around the world. *Ketai* (laziness) is either the failure to exert sufficient effort in training or the temptation to slack off after achieving a level of proficiency, such as black-belt ranking. In any athletic endeavor, including combat, the person who devotes the most time and effort to honing their skills and maintaining their physical conditioning is usually the victor.

Conceit or overconfidence (*manshin*) is the opposite of giryo, but it is just as dangerous. It often manifests itself as ketai when karateka become so confident in their abilities that they either no longer train diligently or they fail to take their opponents' skills seriously and are taken by surprise. Misplaced pride sows the seeds of self-destruction.

Machigai
MISTAKES

In budō, a battle ends in the blink of an eye—the flash of a katana, the jab of a yari, or a single blow from the karateka—and one of the combatants lies helpless or dead on the ground. A bushi could not afford to make a mistake. In ancient times, mistakes, very simply, meant death.

On the other hand, the only way to learn an art as difficult and complex as karate-dō is to make mistakes. So, in one respect, you must train as if there is no room for mistakes—as if they would be fatal—while in another respect you must accept the fact that mistakes are both inevitable and a normal part of the learning process. In fact, mistakes are the source of most learning.

We learn little from success. Few people stop and think critically about what they did to achieve success. We usually expect to succeed, and when we do, we accept that success without question. It's an entirely different matter when we fail. "What did I do wrong?" is the first thing that comes to mind. Successful people effectively perform bunkai when they fail. They examine their decisions and actions piece by piece in minute detail, looking for clues that they can learn from. That's the value of failure.

Mistakes and failure are the keys to success and accomplishment. It is important, therefore, not to dwell on your mistakes, whether they are simply training errors in the dōjō or mistakes that have a serious impact in your life. If you allow errors in your past to discourage you from future attempts, at the very least you will find yourself losing confidence and going into a slump. At the worst, you can become so paralyzed by the fear of failure that you will no longer even try. Furthermore, your mind will inevitably try to achieve whatever you visualize. So if you keep visualizing yourself making that same mistake over and over, you are effectively programming your subconscious to repeat it.

Instead, analyze your mistakes without dwelling on them. Try to determine what caused the error and how it can be corrected or avoided in the future, then visualize yourself acting correctly. In this way, rather than being a setback or hindrance, each mistake becomes an investment in your future success. Remember too that it is far better to have tried and failed—and learned from the experience—than never to have tried, never to have learned, and never to have truly lived.

The dōjō should be viewed as the safe place to make mistakes and fail. If we fail on the battlefield, we die. If we fail in the dōjō, we just get up, dust ourselves off, massage a bruise or two, and try again. And in the process we learn valuable lessons that prevent us from failing on the battlefields of life. The dojo is our safety net or parachute, and the mistakes and failures that occur in the dōjō are our allegorical sweat that prevents us from bleeding outside the dōjō.

So, fail your way to greatness!

五道心
Go Dō Shin
FIVE PATHS OF THE SPIRIT

It seems fitting to conclude this chapter with principles passed down by the founder of Shitō-Ryū, Mabuni Kenwa. He called them Go Dō Shin (五道心), which is often translated as "The Five-Way Path" or "The Five-Fold Path" of karate-dō. Another possible translation, and one we find appropriate, is "The Five Paths (or Ways) of the Spirit," since the principles themselves are about the attitudes that should guide karateka in their training:

初心忘れる勿れ。
Shoshin wasureru nakare.
Don't forget your beginner's spirit (original intention).
礼儀怠る勿れ。
Reigi okotaru nakare.
Don't neglect etiquette (courtesy).
努力怠る勿れ。
Doryoku okotaru nakare.
Don't neglect your efforts.
常識欠ける勿れ。
Jōshiki kakeru nakare.
Don't lack sound judgment.
和乱す勿れ。
Wa midasu nakare.
Don't disrupt harmony.

Chapter Eleven

作法と礼法

Sahō to Reihō
Preparation and Etiquette

Anyone who has visited a traditional Japanese or Okinawan dōjō has witnessed the almost fanatical degree of care and attention that is paid to sahō (preparation) and reihō (etiquette) in classical budō. There is a prescribed, proper way to do nearly everything, from removing your shoes and stowing them away, folding your street clothes, handling your *dōgi*, and tying your obi to the way you greet and address your fellow students and instructors. This is a result of two major influences: the collective nature of Japanese and Okinawan society and culture, and the lethal nature of budō.

While their cultural origins ensure that sahō and reihō are inherent to traditional karate training, they should not be viewed as mere vestiges of a bygone age, nor as actions that must be performed in order to participate in training. They are an essential part of the training in and of themselves. Sahō and reihō help to instill personal discipline and respect.

THE ORIGINS OF ETIQUETTE

In a collectivist culture, the group is more important than the individual, and adhering to social customs and attitudes is essential to harmonious living and prosperity. Japanese and Okinawan cultures are basically collectivist in nature, as evidenced by the popular Japanese saying *Deru kugi wa utareru* ("The nail that sticks up gets beaten down"). Those who stand out, who fail or refuse to conform to traditional customs and behavior, become social outcasts and are prevented from attaining roles of importance. Respect and deference to the social hierarchy is therefore an essential element of life for Japanese and Okinawans, and this was even more the case during the feudal era.

More specifically with respect to budō, respect—especially respect for those in authority—was a matter of life or death in Japanese and Okinawan feudal society.

As described in greater detail in chapter 5, respect (reihō) was a core principle of bushidō, and the slightest infraction could result in lethal combat or a demand to commit ritual suicide by seppuku. Reihō is thus a central element in all forms of budō, including karate-dō.

THE INSEPARABILITY OF SAHŌ AND REIHŌ

It is impossible to identify a specific line of demarcation between sahō and reihō. Much of what we typically consider sahō—personal hygiene and cleanliness, removing our shoes before entering the dōjō, neat appearance, properly tied obi, cleaning the dōjō after training (sōji), and more—is done for reasons that combine pragmatism and respect.

For instance, we bathe and wash our garments both because it promotes our own health and eliminates odors that might offend others. We remove our shoes as we enter the dōjō because it keeps the floor clean, prevents injuring partners during training, and reduces the cleaning we and others must do later. We tie our obi correctly because it prevents it coming loose during training, which could endanger both ourselves and others. These reasons are essentially pragmatic, but they have more profound ramifications. By caring for our own health and safety, we are performing acts of self-respect and making self-respect a habit—an essential part of our lifestyle. Similarly, by caring for the health and safety of others, we demonstrate our respect for them and develop the habit and lifestyle of respecting others and considering the effects even the simplest of our actions have on them. Sahō is a form of reihō, and reihō is a key reason for sahō.

THE BEGINNING AND END

A well-known Japanese axiom is *Rei ni hajimari, rei ni owaru*. This is usually translated as "Everything begins and ends with respect." We must therefore consider what constitutes the beginning and end of any activity. The beginning point seems obvious: it is when we start the preparations (sahō) for it. So, not only are the preparations themselves pragmatically an act of respect, but in a purely philosophical sense, sahō is an act of reihō.

But at what point does an activity end? In Western cultures we tend to think of the aftermath of an activity as separate from the activity itself. If we have been playing a sport, for example, we consider the game over when the final whistle blows and we leave the field. Showering, changing our clothes, cleaning the equipment, and putting it away are all separate activities from the sport itself. But Japanese and Okinawan cultures view these as essential parts of the sport. After all, you can't play the sport if you don't get the equipment ready and set it up, so you're not finished with the sport until you've cleaned the equipment and put it away.

Thus, sōji and changing back into street clothes are integral parts of budō training, not something separate from it or merely appended to it. Just as sahō is the beginning of budō training, sōji is the end.

Or is it?

Consider what is actually accomplished by sōji. It prepares the dōjō for its next use. Therefore, sōji is actually sahō. The two are inseparable. If sōji had not been performed after the last use of the dōjō, it would have to be performed as sahō prior to the next use. The only difference is the lapse of time involved. Sahō and sōji are simply arbitrarily defined points on a continuum or endless cycle.

NO BEGINNING OR END

In reality, there is no beginning or ending point. Our training doesn't begin when we get in the shower, put on our clothes, get in the car, arrive at the dōjō, change into our gi, or step on the training floor. And it doesn't end when we step off the training floor, put away the equipment, put on our street clothes, walk out of the dōjō, or drive away. Once we take on the mantle of a budōka or karateka, we are training every moment of every day.

As you have probably guessed by now, Rei ni hajimari, rei ni owaru does not mean "Everything begins and ends with respect." Its deeper meaning is "Respect from beginning to end." The fact that we show respect by bowing as we enter the dōjō and again when leaving, and bow to our sensei and our fellow students when we first see them, and again when we are parting, is chiefly a symbolic gesture to remind us of the adage Rei ni hajimari, rei ni owaru.

Since there is no beginning or end, we must exhibit respect at all times and all places. That is the deeper meaning of Rei ni hajimari, rei ni owaru. It doesn't mean merely to make an outward show of respect, such as bowing, at the start and finish of a training session; it means to maintain an attitude of respect at all times. In that way, every person you encounter experiences your respect from the beginning of their interaction with you to the end, because you were conducting yourself with respect long before that encounter until long afterward.

ETIQUETTE IN KARATE-DŌ

Etiquette (reihō) generally refers to your manners and how you behave. It is the way of showing your compassion and respect for people and the world around you. We have already seen that reihō is inseparable from sahō, and eventually becomes a part of every waking moment for a karateka. Now we shall examine some of the outward expressions of reihō in the dōjō and in everyday life.

Etiquette is required for the budōka of any age to apply to their everyday life and should be practiced by both the student and the teacher. It may seem that many people in the world today do not practice etiquette and do not even care about what it means. However, as a karateka, more is expected of you. You are learning traditions and techniques that go back hundreds of years, and part of that tradition is the practice of reihō.

Fortunately, etiquette is easy to learn and develop. It is easy to learn, very simple to use, and can also be a very effective defensive weapon. Although you will practice etiquette in your dōjō, you will find that etiquette is one aspect of karate-dō that you will eventually apply more in the real world than in the dōjō. It is the only element of karate technique that you will use every day for the rest of your life, and if used well, it will certainly make your life easier and more fulfilling, and even serve as a form of self-protection.

We are now living in an age in which it is very easy to be lazy and rude. For rapidly growing numbers of people, most of their social contacts are remote and made through social media or electronic communications rather than face-to-face. People now even text one another when in the same room. Our computers and smart phones have become our window to the world, and it is easy to think we are insulated from the consequences of disrespect and rudeness.

Many people also do most of their shopping remotely, using their computers or phone apps to order products, groceries, even meals to be delivered. By doing so we can become accustomed to having anonymous interaction with people serving our needs but little or no direct contact with them. It is easy to take them for granted and to become oblivious to their importance in our lives and their status as fellow human beings.

As budōka, we have an obligation to make the world a better place by going against this trend of personal isolation, indifference, and rudeness. By showing people respect through our etiquette, we make them aware that we care about them and the world, which in turn gives them a greater sense of personal significance. When each of us shows just one other person a little respect and compassion it truly does help make the world a better place. We cannot, nor should we try to, force other people to be more respectful of themselves, others, and their world, but we can both serve as an example of that respect and demonstrate the ripple effect that respect has on our community and society.

WHAT ETIQUETTE IS NOT

Before examining specific principles and practices of dōjō etiquette, it may be helpful to understand what etiquette is not. Etiquette is not a set of rules or ancient customs to follow by rote. You don't have to follow a set of rules to understand and practice reihō, nor memorize strange terms, customs, or ideas. Although a person who is practicing etiquette will want to obey rules and laws out of respect for the people that rules and laws protect, etiquette is not made from those rules and laws. True reihō results in obeying the rules because you are committed to an even higher standard of conduct than the rules dictate.

Etiquette is not about flattery or kissing up to people. Pretending to respect someone or giving them false praise is hypocritical and deeply disrespectful. So is showing deference to people you don't sincerely respect in order to curry favor with them. Etiquette must be the product of your genuine respect for others.

Respect, and the courtesy and etiquette that outwardly manifest respect, must not be confused with admiration. A budōka even respects, and therefore follows proper etiquette toward, their worst enemies. Genuine respect is merely acknowledging and according other people their basic human rights and dignity. Even criminals or enemies on the battlefield have a right to be treated humanely. If we fail to do so, then we have lost our own humanity.

COMPASSION AND RESPECT: THE FOUNDATION OF ETIQUETTE

The etiquette we practice inside and outside the dōjō all stems from two fundamental attributes: respect (rei) and compassion (jihi). These two attributes serve as the counterbalance to the power (chikara) and lethality of karate-dō, which is why the formalities of etiquette are such an integral and repetitive aspect of karate training. Without the restraining influence of reihō, karate-dō has the potential to create monsters of us.

The entirety of chapter 4 is devoted to explaining how the bushi as people, bushidō as their way of life, and budō as their methodology all arose from the need and desire to protect the innocent and those who sustain the lives of others. The use of lethal force against those who would unjustifiably harm others is katsujinken, the life-giving fist. But even when defending the innocent or striking down evil, we must use lethal force with the restraint of compassion and respect.

The use of lethal force for any self-serving reason is satsujinken, or death-inducing fist. This is perhaps the most compelling reason that we must maintain respect for all people, even our mortal enemies. Even when acting in defense of the innocent, if our use of lethal force is driven by selfish emotions like anger, hatred, outrage, or vengeance, rather than by pure compassion and justice, then we are committing satsujinken.

Katsujinken not only gives life to those we protect from harm, it can give life to our own spirit and emotions, knowing that we have thwarted evil and benefited others as well as society as a whole. Conversely, satsujinken not only unjustly destroys the lives of other human beings, but in doing so without justification, we bring death to our own soul and spirit. Even those acting justly sometimes suffer post–traumatic stress from taking a human life. The damage we do our own psyche by unjustly using karate-dō is immeasurably worse.

KEY PRINCIPLES OF ETIQUETTE

The following principles and examples are derived from compassion and respect, so each of the principles presented is related to the others in much the same way that a child is related to their parents and siblings.

DISTANCE AND FAMILIARITY.   Whether we realize it or not, we all have different levels of distance and familiarity between ourselves and other people. We wouldn't dream of walking into a stranger's house without knocking and eating food out of their refrigerator without asking permission. But most of us have close friends or family members with whom this is perfectly acceptable.

Part of good etiquette is understanding these different levels of distance and familiarity between you and different people. You relate differently to your best friend than you do with your mother or father, complete strangers, your teachers or boss, your spouse or intimate companions. Even in relatively egalitarian societies, we treat high ranking officials and dignitaries with greater formality than we do our peers.

EMPATHY.   Empathy is sensing the emotions and needs of other people and showing them consideration. An example of empathy is muting your mobile phone's ringer and not talking at the cinema, the library, or a similar setting in which it would be an unwelcome distraction because you know it will disturb others as much as it would disturb you if the situation was reversed. So, another aspect of etiquette is remaining conscious of the people around you and their right to be free of unnecessary disturbances or interference in their activities.

At a deeper level, empathy is being aware of the effects your actions may have on other people's emotions, not just their physical comfort. Causing someone who cares about you to worry unnecessarily or embarrassing them by your behavior is just as inconsiderate as spoiling their enjoyment of a movie. As karateka we must not only be aware of how our actions affect the physical environment of others, but their emotional and spiritual environment as well.

DEPENDABILITY.   Doing what you say you will do, following through on your commitments, and keeping your promises are fundamental aspects of reihō. Whether those promises are big or small, spoken or implied, they must be kept. Failing to do so is a clear sign of disrespect for those who are depending on you and a major breach of etiquette.

SINCERITY.   The most respectful thing you can do is to be sincere in your expressions of etiquette. Insincerity is hypocrisy and dishonesty. Acting courteously or deferentially toward someone you don't truly respect is worse than being rude to them. At least if you are rude, you are being honest. This is why, as karateka and practitioners of bushidō, we must train ourselves to have sincere respect, even for those whose behavior or actions we despise.

Sahō
PREPARATION

Preparation to participate in karate-dō training can be thought of as taking place in two locations and corresponding time frames: prearrival preparation and in-dōjō preparation. As we previously stated, many aspects of sahō and reihō cannot be clearly separated because some actions serve both purposes.

Prior to arrival at the dōjō for training, personal hygiene is generally considered sahō, yet it is also a reflection of respect for the dōjō, sensei, and fellow students. Bathing, oral hygiene, trimming the fingernails, and keeping the hair and beard well groomed and trimmed are done chiefly for the comfort and safety of others. Eliminating body odor and bad breath prevents offending other participants. Clean and well-trimmed hair prevents bacteria, body oils, and lice from accumulating and transferring to others during training. Trimmed fingernails are less likely to scratch other students. So, hygiene and grooming are essential parts of sahō. For the same reasons, keeping your karate-gi clean and neat serves the purposes of both reihō and sahō.

One task involved in maintaining a karate-gi is properly folding and storing it between uses. While this is usually considered an aspect of sahō, it might more accurately be considered reihō. We carefully fold the gi, smoothing out any wrinkles as we do so, not merely to prepare it for storage, but to accord it a measure of respect. A karate-gi has only one use and purpose: to clothe us while we engage in training. It is therefore a unique garment in our wardrobe, and the act of folding treats it with a degree of reverence that acknowledges its special place in our lives and its role in our growth and maturation. Once properly folded, the gi isn't tossed in a corner; it is placed in a drawer or on a shelf where it will be protected from soiling and dust. Again, this is as much out of respect as it is the practicality of preparation for its next use.

On arriving at the dōjō, our first act is to remove our shoes and place them either in the *getabako* (shoe rack) or to the side in the *genkan* (entryway). Once again, this is both practical—keeping the floor clean—and respectful. We then go to the changing area and change into our karate-gi. As described in the "Reihō" section below, we bow on entering the training area, where sahō continues.

Ideally, students should be ready and waiting for class to begin rather than straggling onto the dōjō floor when sensei appears. The time between donning your gi and class starting should not be wasted, but instead used for additional preparation by warming up, practicing techniques learned from a previous lesson, and mentally preparing. By the time sensei or a sempai calls the class to order, your mind should already be focused, free of distractions, and attentive.

When the formal class has ended, sahō resumes, beginning with sōji ("sweep away"), cleaning the dōjō. To many Westerners, sōji would be considered the conclusion or aftermath of training, but to the karateka it is the beginning of preparation for the next training session. When viewed in this way, it is easier to understand that the interval between class sessions is a continuation of one's training—the time when lessons from the dōjō are put to practical use in daily life and effort is devoted to bunbu ryōdō. Sōji must therefore be undertaken with the seriousness and purposefulness of all other training activities.

Reihō
DŌJŌ ETIQUETTE

In karate-dō, the most common outward manifestation of respect is the bow. It is worth noting that the Japanese word most commonly used for bowing in the dōjō is *rei*. But *rei* doesn't mean "bow"; it means "respect." The term for the physical act of bowing is *ojigi*. So, when your sensei or sempai says "Rei," they really mean, "Show respect." The bow we perform in response is therefore a visible expression of our heartfelt respect.

Thus, when we bow, it must involve more than merely a physical movement in which we lean forward at the waist. It must be initiated and accompanied by an inner feeling of genuine respect for the persons or objects to which the bow is directed. It must not be perfunctory or a mindless ritual. It must be given as much attention and effort as any other aspect of karate training. For that reason, the formal etiquette in a traditional dōjō is extensive, and great emphasis is placed on performing it correctly and with sincerity.

However, the informal etiquette is of at least equal importance to the formal etiquette, since the informal etiquette is often a better barometer of a karateka's true state of mind, since it reveals their attitudes and behavior when not under sensei's observation. Informal etiquette are those courtesies performed voluntarily before and after a training session. It includes things like bowing upon entering the dōjō, greeting fellow karateka, assisting with preparation for class, and bowing when leaving the dōjō after training.

Formal etiquette is typically guided by the sensei or a sempai. It typically begins with the students being instructed to assemble with the command *"Seiretsu"* ("Straight line"). This class leader will then normally have the students face the dōjō emblem or founder's portrait, which is considered the "true front" (*shōmen*) of the dōjō, and bow. The command for this is *"Shōmen ni rei."* Then it is typical for the class to be seated in *seiza* ("true sitting," sitting on the knees) for a period of meditation (mokusō). At the completion of meditation, the class will normally perform *shirei* (bow to instructor) before rising. It is common for both students and sensei to say *"O-negai shimasu"* ("I request a favor") as they perform shirei.

During class activities in which students practice with each other, such as ippon kumite, goshinjutsu (self-defense techniques), jūhō (grappling and throwing), or jiyū kumite (free sparring), students will perform *tachi-rei* (standing bow) each time they begin a new activity or face a new training partner. Again, it is common for the students to say "O-negai shimasu" to each new partner during this bow. At the completion of each activity, they should also perform tachi-rei to their training partner. This concluding bow is commonly accompanied by the words *"Arigatō gozaimashita"* ("Thank you very much"). While these formalities should be automatic between students, some instructors give the command *"Otagai ni rei"* ("Bow to each other") before and after each training exercise to be certain it is done. Similarly, if the instructor selects a student with whom to demonstrate a technique, the instructor and student will bow (tachi-rei) to each other before and after each such demonstration. These actions serve as repeated reminders of Rei ni hajimari, rei ni owaru, of course, but they have another meaning as well.

It is important to note that when we say "these formalities should be automatic between students," we do not mean that etiquette should be perfunctory—something that is done thoughtlessly simply because it is supposed to be done. Quite the opposite: etiquette must be sincere and with consideration. We don't bow because it is a time-honored tradition. We bow because we are genuinely grateful for the opportunity to train, for the instruction provided by our sensei, for the assistance of a training partner and the care for our safety and well-being that partner accords us. We bow because we truly mean it. We bow to ensure that genuine respect (rei) and sincerity (makoto) become permanently instilled in our attitude, character, and actions as a way of life. It becomes a reflexive or "automatic" expression of our true feelings.

Each of these formal bows—to the dōjō, to the sensei, and to each other before practicing techniques together—seals a tacit understanding. Bowing to the dōjō acknowledges that the students have come for the purpose of serious training. Shirei acknowledges a mutual pact: that the students will be diligent to learn, and that the sensei will be diligent to teach. Similarly, the bow preceding and following each training exercise is a way of the students saying to each other, "I will help you train. Please help me train in return." When accompanied by the words "O-negai shimasu," this covenant becomes even more explicit. The bow that follows each training exercise, especially when it includes "Arigatō gozaimashita," expresses mutual appreciation for the assistance given.

Finally, at the conclusion of each class, it is customary to have the class line up once more facing the instructor. Then the class will be instructed to sit in seiza position for a closing period of meditation (mokusō). This is often followed by a recitation of the dōjō kun (code of the dōjō) and possibly a brief lesson from the sensei or a sempai in application of a karate principle to daily life. The class will then be instructed to perform shirei while in seiza.

BOWING METHODS

Bowing from a standing position is the most frequently performed demonstration of respect. Tachi-rei is performed from Musubi Dachi (fig. 11.1) by bending forward at the hips about 30 degrees, keeping your hands at your sides, as shown in figure 11.2. The back and neck should be kept straight, as if a pole ran from the top of your head to the base of your spine. This means you should neither tilt your face up toward the person to whom you are bowing, nor pull your chin inward as you bow. Although there is no prescribed duration of a bow, this position is typically held for about two full seconds before rising.

Figure 11.1–2 Tachi-rei (standing bow), front view.

From a side view (fig. 11.3), the angle of the bow and the alignment of the spine and head can be better seen.

Figure 11.3 Tachi-rei (standing bow), side view.

Some sensei occasionally tell students never to take their eyes off the other person when they bow, to avoid exposure to a sneak attack. As a result, they tilt their face upward while bowing. To your sensei or sempai such an obvious expression of distrust is a serious affront. Instead, since the other person's hands also remain at their sides, it is more polite—and just as safe—to simply keep their hands and feet in view while bowing. From a normal bowing distance of two to three paces, no one can attack without moving their hands or feet and thereby alerting you to their intentions.

The *za-rei* (seated bow) is performed from seiza and is consider more formal and respectful than tachi-rei. To sit in seiza from a standing position, begin in Musubi Dachi, as shown in figure 11.4. Keeping the back straight, bend both knees until your rump nearly touches your heels (fig. 11.5), then place your left knee on the floor (fig. 11.6), followed by your right knee (fig. 11.7). Flatten your feet with the big toes nearly touching, and then sit on your heels. Once seated in seiza, your back and neck should remain straight, shoulders and arms relaxed, with your hands resting naturally atop your thighs, fingers pointing inward, aligned with the crease between your thighs and groin, as shown in figure 11.8.

Erect, but not stiff, posture should be maintained when seated in seiza, as depicted from a side view in figure 11.9.

Figures 11.4-8 Assuming the seiza position.

When bowing to someone other than the instructor or a kōdansha (person of high rank), it is customary to perform za-rei in the following manner: keeping the back and neck perfectly straight, reach forward and place the left hand flat on the floor (fig. 11.11), followed by the right hand (fig. 11.12), with the hands centered and just less than a forearm's length in front of the knees. Your thumbs should be bent inward toward your index fingers, with the index fingers touching, so an arrowhead-shaped opening is formed between the hands. As soon as your hands are in position, bow forward until your back is parallel to the floor and your nose is pointing down at the center of the opening between the hands. At this point your face will be about two fist widths above the floor, as shown in figure 11.12. Avoid pulling your chin inward while performing za-rei or touching your forehead to the floor. Hold the bow in this position for about three full seconds before rising.

Figure 11.9 Seiza posture (side view).

Figures 11.10-13 Za-rei (seated bow).

The side view in figure 11.14 shows that the spine and neck remain as straightly aligned as possible during zarei, and the buttocks do not lift away from the heels.

Rising from za-rei follows exactly the reverse order (fig. 11.15). Keep the back and neck straight as they return to vertical, allowing your rising motion to pull your hands from the floor, with the right hand withdrawing first, followed by the left hand, and place them once again on your thighs.

Figure 11.14 Za-rei (side view).

Figure 11.15 Rising from za-rei.

To perform shirei in seiza involves only one slight modification that demonstrates a degree of additional trust and respect for one's sensei or kōdansha. In za-rei, the left hand is extended first because it is the defensive and weaker hand for a right-handed bushi. The stronger offensive hand is extended a moment later. In shirei, as a gesture of absolute and implicit trust, both hands are extended—and thus vulnerable to attack—simultaneously, as shown in figure 11.17. Shirei and rising to seiza are demonstrated in figures 11.16–20.

Figures 11.16-20 Shirei (bow to instructor).

Mokusō
MEDITATION

While still in seiza, most traditional dōjō will have a period of mokusō. There are many forms of meditation, which is probably why there is also much confusion about the role of meditation in budō. Different styles and different sensei take differing approaches to meditation. Although some styles and instructors have embraced the Zen tradition, we have not. The Zen approach, in simplified terms, is to willfully empty the mind of all conscious thought to achieve mushin. Our preference, as explained in chapter 10, is instead to use meditation to focus the mind intently on reality and a powerful positive thought—victory, success, courage, perfection of technique, improvement of character, and so forth—to the exclusion of all else, and to simultaneously expel from the mind all negative and distracting thoughts. This method is also considered mushin, because a mind focused on a single thought to the exclusion of everything else is empty of all that is not beneficial, and it retains its unlimited capacity for learning, growth, and action. This latter concept is the one followed by the traditions taught by the Jikishin-Kai and the Seishin-Kan. Thus, to the budōka, mokusō is not a religious act but is instead an act of preparation (sahō) for training, performance, combat, or the daily activities of life.

Thus, the true purpose of mokusō for a budōka is to simultaneously rid the mind of any thoughts or emotions that would be a distraction from training and fill the mind with a single objective (*ichinen*) to achieve while training.

Mokusō usually commences with a command from the sensei or a sempai: "Mokusō!"

The mechanics of mokusō begin with good posture in seiza. Begin by breathing slowly out, using your lower abdominal muscles to push the air out, letting it escape through your mouth. As you breathe out, imagine any negative thought you've been clinging to—anger, worry, spite, fear, resentment, sorrow, jealousy, doubt—being expelled from your mind along with the stale air that is leaving your lungs. At the same time, while maintaining good posture, try to feel your body relax as you exhale, especially your neck and shoulders.

When your lungs are empty, breathe slowly in through the nose, trying to draw the air down into your lower abdomen, and imagine that you are drawing in that one thought you are focusing on. For this example, let's use self-control. Visualize yourself accomplishing that one thought: remaining focused and under control despite distractions, provocation, or the urge to fidget. This method of breathing deeply using the lower abdominal muscles is called fukushiki kokyū, and it is the same method used by opera singers to improve breath control and maximize the efficiency and capacity of the lungs.

If a negative thought invades that image—you see yourself fidgeting during class, or an irritating incident from earlier in the day comes to mind—visualize that thought being forced out the next time you exhale and yourself becoming even more resolute and more controlled the next time you inhale. Continue this pattern of breathing and meditation until you are given the command to stop: "*Mokusō yame!*"

With your meditation complete, open your eyes, but continue fukushiki kokyū. You should now feel alert, attentive, and ready for action, but relaxed and confident. Because seiza is usually uncomfortable for Westerners, you will be told to stand: "*Kiritsu.*" Once standing, you will be told to recite the dōjō kun.

Kiritsu
STANDING UP

To rise from seiza (fig. 11.21) following za-rei or shirei, push your rump upward, keeping your back straight, and place the balls of your feet on the floor. Place your left foot forward so that the back of its heel is about even with your right knee (fig. 11.22) and push upward with both legs simultaneously until you are nearly standing erect (fig. 11.23), then draw your right foot into Musubi Dachi (fig. 11.24) as you come fully upright.

When you have risen to a standing position in Musubi Dachi, you will be instructed to recite the dōjō kun.

Figures 11.21-24 Kiritsu (stand up), front view.

Dōjō Kun
CODE OF THE DŌJŌ

According to tradition, the first dōjō kun (dōjō code of conduct) for karate-dō was created sometime in the mid-eighteenth century by Sakugawa Kanga, the man who first called the Okinawan unarmed fighting system "karate." Reciting the dōjō kun at the beginning and end of each training session serves to remind us of the major goals of our training. One common misconception is that the behavior and attitudes of the dōjō kun are to be followed during training. The behavior and attitudes of the dōjō kun are to be practiced during training and followed in everyday life. They are not limited to the dōjō.

The examples of dōjō kun we present below are those used at the Jikishin-Kai and the Nippon Budō Seishin-Kan.

Jikishin-Kai Dōjō Kun for Adults

One. Seek perfection of character.

One. Live with politeness and discipline.

One. Honor a code of ethical behavior.

One. Strive for excellence through effort.

One. Act with dignity and compassion.

JKI Dōjō Kun for Youth

One. I respect myself and others.

One. I challenge myself to overcome obstacles.

One. I live with a positive and healthy attitude.

One. I have true compassion for others.

One. I am committed to doing my best.

Seishin-Kan Dōjō Kun

一、人格の完成に喫すること。

Hitotsu: Jinkaku no kansei ni kissuru koto.

One: Relentlessly strive for perfection of character.

一、礼と節に終始すること。

Hitotsu: Rei to setsu ni shūshi suru koto.

One: Always behave with respect and discipline.

一、信義を重んずること。

Hitotsu: Shingi o omonzuru koto.

One: Exemplify righteousness.

一、千鍛万錬に徹すること。

Hitotsu: Sentan banren ni tessuru koto.

One: Persevere through all adversities.

一、血気の湯に早るべからざること。

Hitotsu: Kekki no yu ni hayaru bekarazaru koto.

One: Always exercise self-control.

Every traditional dōjō has its own dōjō kun, but their content is almost always a variation on the themes contained in those shown above. Those presented here can be used as guidelines for those wishing to create a dōjō kun for their own dōjō or personal use.

Once you have completed the formal etiquette and meditation, and recited the dōjō kun, you are fully prepared—mentally and spiritually—to begin your training session, which usually begins with several minutes of kihon (fundamentals).

Kihon

Fundamentals

Kihon, or fundamentals, are those attributes that form the foundation for all karate techniques. They are the basic movements used to create the wide variety of offensive and defensive techniques found in kata. Mastery of kihon is the key to becoming proficient in karate-dō. The more time you spend improving your kihon, the less time it will take to acquire more advanced skills and the less frustration you will experience in doing so. The importance of kihon cannot be overemphasized. Without sound fundamentals—all working together flawlessly—you will not be able to perform karate techniques or kata with sufficient effectiveness to apply them to actual combat.

Generally, kihon are grouped into categories of related items, but since their functions are all interrelated, it is impossible to completely separate them from each other. Most of the movements we consider kihon can be used both offensively and defensively. *Gedan barai*, for example, can be used to sweep aside a strike; perform a strike to the lower abdomen, groin, thigh, or knee joint; dislocate an elbow; as a pinning method; or to throw and opponent to the ground. The names assigned to the techniques, which have been derived from their most obvious use, have resulted in each being classified as either offensive *(kōgeki waza)* or defensive *(bōgyō waza)*, but it is more beneficial to think of them as movements that can be applied in a variety of ways.

In chapter 10 we described the overarching principles that maximize the power and effectiveness of kihon, so those principles—such as shisei (posture), kamae (structure), kokyū (breath control), chakugan (eye contact), maai (distance control), and kihaku (effort and intensity)—must be borne in mind as you train in kihon.

There is a tendency to want to learn the more spectacular-looking and athletic techniques—the ones featured in cinematic fight scenes—as soon as possible. But mastery of karate-dō is not achieved by learning its most advanced and difficult techniques. Karate is mastered by mastering its fundamentals. Masters do perform and practice advanced techniques, to be sure, but they devote the majority of their training to the continual improvement of fundamentals. A karateka who can perform only a handful of techniques with near perfection can easily defeat one who can perform countless advanced techniques poorly.

Gō to Jū Ryōhō
BOTH HARD AND SOFT

A critical point to bear in mind is that karate is not limited to striking with the hands and feet. In a section of the *Bubishi* titled "Kempō Hakku," there is a famous line that reads 法は剛柔呑吐 (*Hō wa gōjū donto*). A literal translation of this stanza would be "The method is hard-soft imbibe-vomit," but it is more commonly translated along the lines of "The method is hard and soft, receive and repel." This quotation is the source for the name Gōjū-Ryū, chosen by Miyagi Chōjun for his style of karate. The inference karateka have drawn from this for generations is that karate is a balance of hard (striking) and soft (nonstriking) techniques, and of receiving (blocking and deflections) and repelling (pushing, striking, throwing, pinning) techniques. Many also interpret *donto* to mean "inhale and exhale" in reference to the importance of breath control, but the word for breathing, *kokyū*, addresses breathing specifically, so we suggest that the broader interpretation is preferable.

Regardless of the interpretation you prefer, the message of the *Bubishi* and the application followed for centuries is that karate is a blend of hard (gōhō) and soft (jūhō) techniques. For this reason, our training in kihon must place equal emphasis on developing skill and knowledge of both aspects of the art. This becomes particularly clear as one closely examines (bunkai) the techniques in kata when viewed as templates for the art of killing. There are more killing and disabling techniques in jūhō than in gōhō.

Karada no Buki
WEAPONS OF THE BODY

In karate-dō, as the name implies, the body itself is used as both weapon and shield. Although *karate* means "empty hands," nearly every part of the body can be used in some way for defense or counterattack. The parts of the body most commonly used in kata and training exercises are:

- hands
- elbows
- forearms
- knees

- feet
- hips
- shins
- head

Although other areas are not featured in kata or typical training activities, karateka should be prepared to use any available part of the body in actual combat, such as the teeth to bite an opponent, a shoulder to push an opponent off balance, or the armpit to trap an opponent's limb when grappling.

Most of the major body parts listed above have more than one surface that can be used in striking, deflecting, or grappling. The most frequently used of these are described below.

Te no Meishō
STRIKING SURFACES OF THE HAND

The hands are the most versatile and frequently used weapons in the body's arsenal, with more than fifteen striking surfaces routinely used. Described below are the major contact areas of the hand and fist. In each illustration the specific striking surface is indicated by the shaded portion of the photograph. In most cases, the same striking surface is used whether as a block or a strike, and most techniques can have either a defensive or offensive application.

DAIKENTŌ: *FORE-FIST*

The striking surface for *seiken* is only the frontal area of the two largest knuckles, as shown in the shaded portion of figure 12.1, not the flat of the fist. In this way the impact is absorbed in a straight line from those two knuckles through the bones of the hand and into the forearm, helping to prevent the wrist from buckling upon impact and providing a direct conduit for the power generated by the legs, hips, shoulders, and arms.

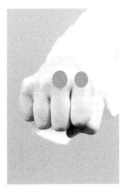

Figure 12.1 Daikentō: fore-fist (shaded area).

KOBUSHI NO NIGIRI KATA: *MAKING A FIST*

Many martial arts researchers believe that the major distinction between the native-born art of Okinawa-te and the Chinese chuan fa (kung fu) with which it was combined to formulate karate-dō was that Okinawa-te almost exclusively used the closed fist to deliver devastatingly destructive blows, rather than the open-handed techniques more common to chuan fa. The punch is still the mainstay of karate-dō, and the correct formation of the fist is essential to delivering an effective punch as well as to many basic blocking techniques.

Proper formation of the fist is crucial in two respects: (1) to ensure maximum effectiveness against the opponent, and (2) to minimize the chances of injury to the striking hand. To properly form a fist, begin with the hand open, then curl the fingers inward as shown in figure 12.3, and continue winding the fingers inward until the fingertips are pressed firmly against the palm of the hand and the longest segments of the fingers form a flat plane, as shown in figure 12.4. Finally, wrap the thumb over the middle section of the index and middle fingers (fig. 12.5). Never enclose the thumb within the fist or injury to the thumb will almost certainly result. Keeping the thumb tight against the fist protects it against snagging on the opponent's clothing or being injured by an opponent's attempt to block.

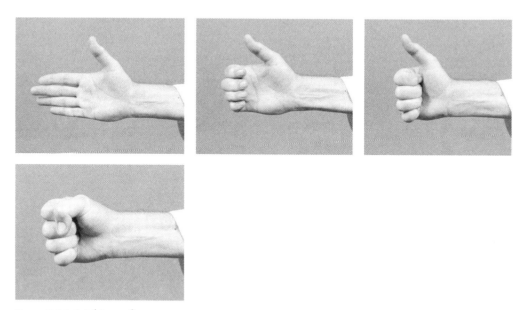

Figures 12.2-5 Making a fist.

As shown in the side view (fig. 12.6), the top of the fist should be aligned flat with the top of the forearm to prevent the wrist from bending when the fist strikes its target, reducing the likelihood of injury to the wrist. The fist is formed in this fashion for *seiken tsuki* as well as *kentsui uchi, ura-ken uchi, gedan barai, age uke, uchi uke, wa uke,* and *yoko uke,* even though different striking surfaces on the fist are used for these techniques, as described later in this chapter.

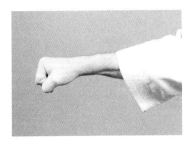

Figure 12.6 Alignment of the fist and the forearm.

In a philosophical sense, the Japanese recognize two broad categories of fist: *seiken* and *jaken,* "righteous fist" and "evil fist." These terms do not describe the shape of the fist itself but rather the mental state in which the fist is used. *Seiken tsuki* is a punch made in self-defense or in the act of protecting someone else from unwarranted attack. It is a punch thrown when peaceful alternatives are not available. It is a punch made with pure motives and intentions, noble ideals, and delivered with compassion. It is *katsujin-ken* ("life-giving fist").

Jaken tsuki is just the opposite. It is a punch hurled in anger, or without considering nonviolent options. It is a punch intended for selfish gain. It is aggression and destruction. It is *satsujin-ken* ("murdering fist"). Jaken tsuki can never be as powerful as seiken tsuki. When a person knows it is morally wrong to strike, there will always be that small twinge of conscience that makes them hold something back. Conversely, when you have the assurance that you are acting with pure intentions and a moral imperative, there is nothing to impede your physical strength or kihaku (emission of ki energy; see chapter 10). Furthermore, because you know it is wrong, every time you utilize jaken, you damage your own character and psyche, so ultimately jaken becomes self-destructive.

KENTSUI: *HAMMER-FIST*

The *kentsui* (sometimes called *kentsuchi*) is the bottom of the fist, especially the muscled area shaded in figure 12.7, that swells and hardens when the fist is tightened.

Kentsui uchi ("hammer-fist strike") is an extremely versatile technique that can be employed in a number of ways. Figure 12.8 shows the fist being swung inward to strike the opponent's jawline. In figure 12.9 it is swinging laterally outward to strike the base of the skull. It can also be swung down to either strike or block, as shown in figure 12.10.

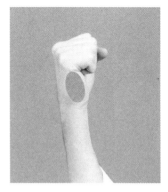

Figure 12.7 Kentsui: hammer fist (shaded area).

Figure 12.8 Kentsui uchi striking inward.

Figure 12.9 Kentsui uchi striking laterally.

Figure 12.10 Kentsui uchi striking downward.

URA-KEN: *BACK-FIST*

Ura-ken uses the back side of the two largest knuckles as the striking surface (fig. 12.11), not the entire back of the hand, to concentrate the impact in a small area for greatest effect.

Additional striking power is generated by allowing the wrist to snap forward at the point of impact for a whiplike effect as the knuckles strike their target. Figures 12.12–15 show this flexing of the wrist during ura-ken uchi. Arm movement stops at figure 12.13; impact occurs as the wrist whips forward in figure 12.14; and the fist returns to the position shown in figure 12.15 after striking the target.

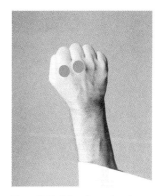

Figure 12.11 Ura-ken: back-fist (shaded area).

Figure 12.12 Beginning of ura-ken uchi.

Figure 12.13 Ura-ken uchi before whipping action of wrist.

Figure 12.14 Ura-ken uchi during whipping action of wrist.

Figure 12.15 Ura-ken uchi after whipping action of wrist.

HITOSASHI IPPON-KEN: *FORE-KNUCKLE*

In *hitosashi ippon-ken,* the index finger is made to jut forward by straightening only its main knuckle and wedging the thumb against the fingernail to reinforce it, as depicted from a side view in figure 12.17. This concentrates the impact in less than half the surface area. The striking area is the middle knuckle of the index finger, as shaded in figure 12.16.

Figure 12.16 Striking surface (shaded area) of hitosashi ippon-ken.

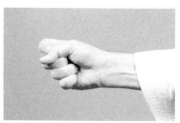

Figure 12.17 Formation of hitosashi ippon-ken (side view).

NAKADAKA IPPON-KEN: *MIDDLE KNUCKLE*

In *nakadaka ippon-ken*, the middle knuckle of the middle finger is extended to form the striking surface, as indicated by the shaded area in figure 12.18. The fist is tightened so that the index and ring fingers wedge against the middle finger to reinforce it, strengthened by the thumb wrapping tightly against the underside of the fist.

Figure 12.18 Nakadaka ippon-ken: middle-knuckle fist (shaded area).

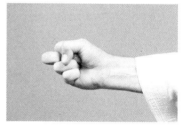

Figure 12.19 Nakadaka ippon-ken: middle-knuckle fist (side view).

SHUTŌ: *KNIFE-HAND*

The striking area of *shutō* (fig. 12.20) is the "meaty" edge of the open hand just below the base knuckle of the little finger—the same area used for kentsui, except that the hand is open. The fingers should be extended and tensed, but curved slightly inward, and the thumb "cocked" like the hammer of a pistol to keep the striking surface rigid. Striking motions with shutō are identical to those of kentsui.

Figure 12.20 Shutō: knife-hand (shaded area).

YONHON NUKITE: *FOUR-FINGER SPEAR-HAND*

Yonhon nukite (usually abridged to *nukite*) is formed identically to shutō, but its contact surface is the fingertips. In order to avoid injury to the fingers (fig. 12.21), it is imperative that they be curved slightly inward and kept rigid, and that strong ki be directed through the fingers into the target (fig. 12.22).

 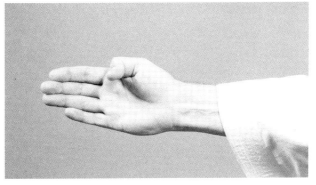

Figure 12.21 Yonhon nukite: spear-hand (shaded area).

Figure 12.22 Formation of yonhon nukite: spear-hand (side view).

IPPON NUKITE: *ONE-FINGER SPEAR-HAND*

The contact point of *ippon nukite* is the tip of the index finger only (fig. 12.23). The remaining fingers are curled fully inward at the middle knuckle. Figure 12.24 shows the formation of ippon nukite. Ippon nukite tsuki is usually used to strike soft tissues, such as the eyes, throat, armpit, or pressure points.

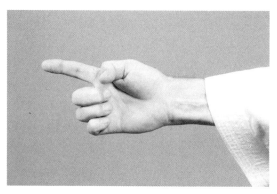

Figure 12.23 Ippon nukite: one-finger spear-hand contact surface.

Figure 12.24 Ippon nukite: one-finger spear-hand (side view).

NIHON NUKITE: *TWO-FINGER SPEAR-HAND*

Nihon nukite uses the tips of the index and middle fingers (fig. 12.25). In side view, the separation of the fingers to facilitate striking to the eyes is clearly shown (fig. 12.26).

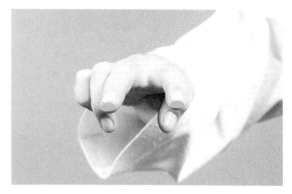
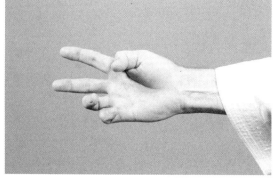

Figure 12.25 Nihon nukite: two-finger spear-hand contact points.

Figure 12.26 Striking with nihon nukite: two-finger spear-hand (side view).

HIRA-KEN (SHŌ KENTŌ): *MIDDLE-KNUCKLE SPEAR-HAND*

Hira-ken is similar to yonhon nukite, except that the striking surface is the ridge of the middle knuckles (*shō kentō*) formed by folding the fingers inward at their middle joint, as shown in figure 12.27. This allows for a more powerful thrusting strike (tsuki) without risking injury to the fingers (fig. 12.28). Hira-ken is also used for a back-hand strike (fig. 12.29) in a manner identical to ura-ken uchi.

Figure 12.27 Hira-ken: middle-knuckle spear-hand contact surface.

Figure 12.28 Hira-ken tsuki: middle-knuckle spear-hand thrust.

Figure 12.29 Hira-ken uchi: middle-knuckle spear-hand back-hand strike.

URA-SHUTŌ (HAITŌ): *REVERSE KNIFE-HAND (RIDGE-HAND)*

For *ura-shutō*, the hand is shaped similarly to shutō, except that the thumb is folded inward (fig. 12.30) so that the striking area is the soft tissue running from the main knuckle of the forefinger down to the base of the thumb and up to the bottom knuckle of the thumb (see shaded area in fig. 12.31).

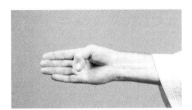

Figure 12.30 Formation of ura-shutō: reverse knife-hand.

Figure 12.31 Striking surface (shaded area) of ura-shutō: reverse knife-hand.

SHŌTEI (TEISHŌ): *PALM-HEEL*

The *shōtei* (sometimes called *teishō*) is the "heel" or "butt" of the palm, as shaded in figure 12.32. When striking with shōtei (fig. 12.33), it is important to bend the wrist back fully to extend the striking area toward the target because impact higher on the palm can injure the wrist. The fingers and thumb should also be pulled back as far as possible to avoid injury.

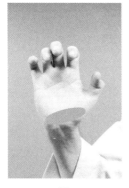

Figure 12.32 Formation and striking surface (shaded) of shōtei: palm-heel.

Figure 12.33 Striking with shōtei: palm-heel.

KOKEN: *WRIST-TOP*

The top of the wrist is called *ko* or *koken*. When blocking or striking with koken—the bony area shaded in figure 12.35—the wrist must be bent downward as far as possible with the fingers curled inward for maximum wrist flexibility. The tip of the thumb should be positioned between the index and middle fingers.

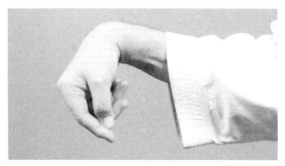

Figure 12.34 Formation of koken: wrist-top.

Figure 12.35 Contact surface (shaded) of koken: wrist-top.

Figure 12.36 Striking with koken: wrist-top.

Figure 12.37 Blocking with koken: wrist-top.

HIRA-BASAMI: *HAND SCISSORS*

Hira-basami uses the curvature from the thumb to the index finger (fig. 12.38) as the striking surface. It is most commonly used to strike the throat but can also be used to catch a downward striking arm just above the elbow.

Figure 12.38 Striking area (shaded) of hira-basami: hand scissors.

YUBI BASAMI: *FINGER SCISSORS*

The points of contact in *yubi basami* are the tips of the thumb and forefinger, plus the middle knuckle of the middle finger (fig. 12.39). Yubi basami is not usually employed as a strike but as a grappling technique, as shown in figure 12.40, in which the knuckle of the middle finger is pressed forcefully against the larynx or the windpipe just beneath the larynx while the thumb and index finger squeeze the upper portion of the throat.

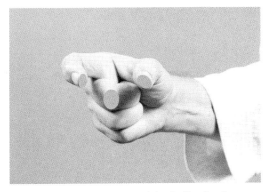

Figure 12.39 Contact points (shaded) of yubi basami: finger-scissors.

Figure 12.40 Applying yubi basami: finger-scissors.

KUMADE: *BEAR PAW*

Kumade is most commonly used for *metsubushi* (impairing the vision). As shown in figure 12.41, it is essentially yonhon nukite with the fingers spread apart. When thrust at an upward angle into the face, the spread fingers are likely to snag a lip or jab a nostril or eye. The technique nearly always causes the opponent to shut their eyes and flinch or turn away, creating momentary blindness.

Figure 12.41 Striking points (shaded) of kumade: bear paw.

The foregoing weapons formed with the hands are by no means an exhaustive list but are the most commonly used in kata and other training activities. The *teno* (back of the open hand) can be used effectively to deflect an incoming strike to deliver a back-hand slap. *Kaishu* (open hand) can be used for a forehand slap, making contact with the palm and fingers. The *koyubi no setsu* (knuckle of the little finger) can be used instead of kentsui in order to focus the impact on a pressure point or other small target. And many styles employ *washide* ("eagle hand"), in which the thumb and fingers are joined into a beak-like striking surface to deliver a whipping strike like the peck of an eagle.

Ude no Meishō
STRIKING SURFACES OF THE ARMS

As with the hands, many areas of the arms are also frequently used both offensively and defensively in karate.

HIJI (EMPI): *ELBOW*

The elbow has three contact locations: the point of the elbow (figs. 12.42–43) being primary when striking laterally, rearward, or downward; the ulnar edge (figs. 12.44–45) when striking forward or upward; and the back of the elbow (figs. 12.46–47) when striking rearward. The crook of the elbow (fig. 12.48) is frequently used to trap a limb, as demonstrated in figure 12.49. The elbow is also highly effective for a variety of blocking techniques, particularly during close-in fighting.

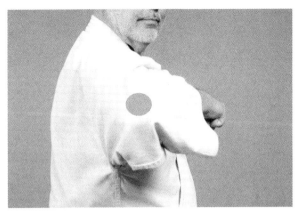

Figure 12.42 Hiji (point): elbow (shaded area).

Figure 12.43 Striking with the point of hiji.

Figure 12.44 Hiji (ulnar edge): elbow (shaded area).

Figure 12.45 Striking with the ulnar edge of hiji.

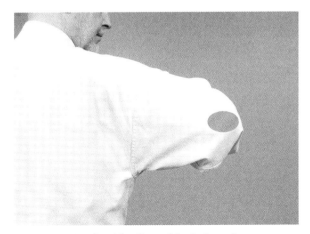

Figure 12.46 Hiji (back): elbow (shaded area).

Figure 12.47 Striking with the back of hiji.

Figure 12.48 Hiji (crook): elbow (shaded area).

Figure 12.49 Trapping the leg with hiji.

WANTŌ: *EDGE OF THE FOREARM*

The *wantō* (fig. 12.50) is a highly effective area for striking the jawline (fig. 12.51) as well as deflecting attacks to the face or head (fig. 12.52).

Figure 12.50 Wantō: edge of the forearm (shaded area).

Figure 12.51 Wantō uchi: upward forearm strike.

Figure 12.52 Age uke: upward forearm block.

UCHI UDE: *INNER FOREARM*

The *uchi ude*, the inner surface of the forearm (fig. 12.53), is extremely useful in deflecting and sweeping aside attacks.

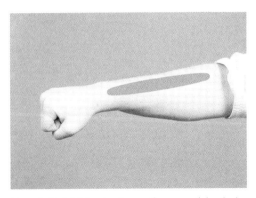

Figure 12.53 Uchi ude: inner forearm (shaded area).

Figure 12.54 Uchi ude: deflecting with the inner forearm.

SOTO UDE: *OUTER FOREARM*

The *soto ude*, outer surface of the forearm (fig. 12.55), is the flatter area of the forearm from the ulna to the radius. It is less effective for striking than the wantō but better suited for blocking and deflecting attacks due to its broader contact area and the added strength of two bones and the muscles between them.

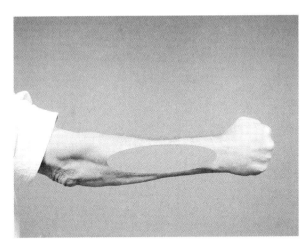

Figure 12.55 Soto ude: outer surface of the forearm (shaded area).

Figure 12.56 Soto ude: blocking with outer surface of the forearm.

TE KUBI: *WRIST*

By bending it outward, the back of the wrist (*te kubi*, fig. 12.57) is often used to deflect attacks.

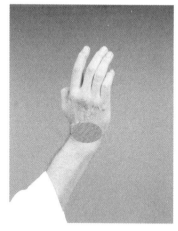

Figure 12.57 Te kubi: back of the wrist (shaded area).

Figure 12.58 Te kubi uke: wrist deflection.

KATA: *SHOULDER*

Although it may not be readily apparent when performing kata, the use of a shoulder (fig. 12.59) to drive an opponent off balance is implied in many grappling techniques found in karate, and it should be emphasized during ōyō (practical application) and jūhō training.

Figure 12.59 Kata: shoulder (shaded area).

Figure 12.60 Use of shoulder (kata) during takedown.

Figure 12.61 Use of shoulder (kata) during elbow dislocation or throw.

Ashi no Meishō
STRIKING SURFACES OF THE LEG AND FOOT

Like the hand and fist, various parts of the legs and feet are also used as contact surfaces in order to maximize the effectiveness of kicks to different target areas on the opponent's body. The most common of these striking areas are illustrated below.

HIZA (HIZAGASHIRA): *KNEE*

The striking area of the knee is primarily the top of the knee, as indicated in figure 12.62, not the front of the kneecap, which is more susceptible to injury. The knee is an effective weapon for striking the groin, inner thigh, lower abdomen, ribs, or solar plexus.

Figure 12.62 Hiza: knee (shaded area).

Figure 12.63 Striking with knee (*hiza ate*).

SUNE: *SHIN*

The shin (fig. 12.64), if properly conditioned (see "Kitae" in chapter 9), can be a devastating weapon for kicking in close quarters.

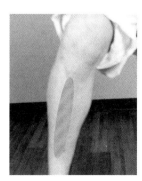

Figure 12.64 Sune: shin (shaded area).

Figure 12.65 Kick with the shin (sune).

JŌSOKUTEI: *BALL OF THE FOOT*

The ball of the foot (fig. 12.66) is used as the primary striking surface for *choku geri* (straight kick) and *mawashi geri* (roundhouse kick or turn kick). For maximum reach, the ankle should be angled forward to extend the foot as far as possible. At the same time, to avoid injury, the toes are pulled back as far as possible when kicking.

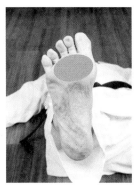

Figure 12.66 Jōsokutei: ball of the foot (shaded area).

SOKKŌ: *INSTEP*

The instep or top of the foot, illustrated in figure 12.67, is the secondary striking area used for choku geri or mawashi geri to target areas whose distance or angle of attack makes using jōsokutei impractical. The target areas can include the groin, side of the neck, thigh, or ribs. To reduce the chances of injury, the toes should be curled under. In addition, the brunt of the striking force should be taken at the upper portion of the striking area, close to the ankle, to avoid hyperextending the ankle on impact.

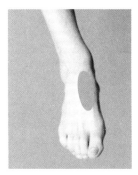

Figure 12.67 Sokkō: instep (shaded area).

KASOKUTEI: *BOTTOM OF THE HEEL*

The bottom of the heel, as shown in figure 12.68, is primarily used for *ushiro geri* (back kick) and for some *fumikomi* (stomping) techniques.

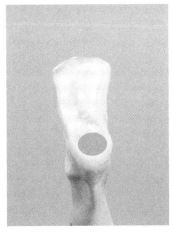

Figure 12.68 Kasokutei: bottom of the heel (shaded area).

KAKATO: *BACK OF THE HEEL*

The back of the heel (*kakato*, fig. 12.69) is sometimes called the "foot hammer" due to its powerful impact when used for a kick.

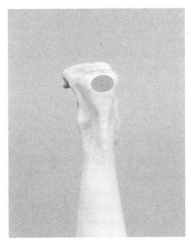

Figure 12.69 Kakato: back of the heel (shaded area).

SOKUTŌ: *BLADE OF THE FOOT*

The blade of the foot is the striking area used for *sokutō geri, gyaku mikazuki geri* (outward crescent kick), *kansetsu geri* (joint [knee] kick), and for some fumikomi (stomping) techniques. Only the lower one-third of the outer edge of the foot should be used, as shown in the shaded area of figure 12.70, so the impact is absorbed by the tibia and injury to the ankle is avoided.

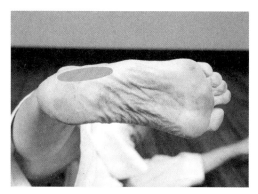

Figure 12.70 Sokutō: blade of the foot (shaded area).

CHŪSOKUTEI: *INSOLE*

The *chūsokutei* is the arched underside of the foot (fig. 12.71), typically used for *mikazuki geri* (crescent kick).

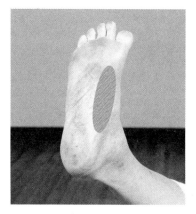

Figure 12.71 Chūsokutei: insole of the foot (shaded area).

Atama no Meishō
STRIKING SURFACES OF THE HEAD

GAKU: *FOREHEAD*

The forehead (*gaku* or *zengaku*, fig. 12.72) can be used with great effect to strike during close-in fighting, or to apply pressure during grappling.

Figure 12.72 Gaku: forehead (shaded area).

KŌTŌ: *BACK OF THE HEAD*

The back of the head (*kōtō* or *kōtōbu*, fig. 12.73) can be used to strike an opponent attempting to seize you from behind, or to apply pressure when grappling.

Figure 12.73 Kōtō: back of the head (shaded area).

AGO: *CHIN OR JAW*

The *ago* (chin or jaw, fig. 12.74) can be used in some grappling situations to apply pressure to joints or other sensitive areas, like the eyes.

Figure 12.74   Ago: chin or jaw
(shaded area).

The preceding contact areas are by no means an exhaustive listing. As with our treatment of stances, we have included only those striking surfaces most commonly used, and particularly those that would be considered basic. As you study advanced kata and their ōyō, you will discover a myriad of additional striking areas and ways to employ them.

Always bear in mind that real karate combat was seldom a fistfight. It was often a life-or-death battle against one or more armed attackers wielding swords, spears, knives, clubs, and similar weapons. The karateka of old were also well versed in Okinawa kobujutsu, the use of weapons like the *bō*, *sai*, *tonfa*, *kama*, *nunchaku*, and *eku*. Their first priority was to use such a weapon if one was available. Karate was for situations in which weapons were either not permitted—inside houses, castles, palaces, or in the presence of nobles or foreign dignitaries—or unavailable because they had been damaged or the karateka had been disarmed in battle.

Under those conditions, the various surfaces of the body mentioned above became substitutes for the weapons the karateka was precluded from using, but the strategy and tactics did not change. Most karateka realize that their hands and feet are weapons and, with proper training, are the only weapons one needs. But if you fully develop the mental and spiritual aspects of karate-dō in addition to its physical actions, you will realize that *you* are the weapon.

Kamae
STRUCTURE

In chapter 10 we explained the purpose and importance of kamae (structure) in maximizing the effectiveness of karate techniques. The foundation that supports kamae is the stance (*tachi* or *dachi*), the position and interrelationships of the spine, hips, legs, and feet. In the same way that the weight of a building and the forces acting upon it, like wind and snow, are transferred through its structure to the foundation and are ultimately borne by the earth itself, stances are the means by which the forces acting upon the human body are borne. Although stances are typically described in terms of correct posture, alignment of the hips and legs, and positioning of the feet, it is imperative to treat them as complete body structures and consider the purpose for which they are being used.

A dam restraining millions of tons of water requires a different structure than a house, a grain silo, or a skyscraper. Each must be designed with its purpose and use in mind. The same is true of karate stances. Unlike many other forms of traditional budō that lump all stances under the conceptual umbrella of shizentai (natural body position) and expect students to gradually learn—chiefly by trial and error—how to create kamae that is best suited for the techniques they employ, karate has a variety of named stances that are taught to students as part of kihon.

A famous action movie star once remarked that "stances are for beginners," and in a certain sense he was absolutely right. Highly advanced budōka understand the principles of kamae so thoroughly that they can create an infinite variety of kamae to adapt to any situation or condition. They appear not to use stances because they are in shizentai at all times. Conversely, beginners usually only utilize stances when they think they need the additional supporting structure stances provide, which is why it is obvious when they are in a stance and when they are not. The value of *tachi-kata* (stances) is that they provide karateka with a set of templates that allow them to learn the principles of kamae more quickly, and from those principles derive countless variations and adaptations for themselves as their skills increase.

Described below are the most common stances used to create proper structure. When utilizing these stances, it is imperative to treat them as complete body structures rather than merely correct posture and positioning of the hips, legs, and feet shown in the illustrations.

Figure 12.75　Heisoku Dachi: Closed-Feet Stance.

Figure 12.76　Musubi Dachi: Linked Stance.

Figure 12.77　Heikō Dachi: Parallel Stance.

HEISOKU DACHI: *CLOSED-FEET STANCE*

In Heisoku Dachi (Closed-Feet Stance), depicted in figure 12.75, the body is erect but should not be held stiffly, like a soldier at attention. Instead, it should feel as though your head is being pulled upward by a string, so your spine is straight but not tense. Also, be sure your knees are not locked but slightly flexed—just as they would be if you stood up without thinking about it. The feet are placed together so they are in contact nearly the full length from heel to toe. The center of gravity should be in the middle of the feet, with your weight evenly distributed along the full length of both feet. You should not feel more pressure on your heels than on the balls of your feet, or vice versa.

MUSUBI DACHI: *LINKED STANCE*

In Musubi Dachi (Linked Stance), depicted in figure 12.76, the body is held in the same position as in Heisoku Dachi. The only difference between Musubi Dachi and Heisoku Dachi is the angle at which the feet are placed, and many beginners confuse the two stances early in their training. The feet are placed with the heels together, but with the toes pointing outward at about 30 degrees from center, separating the feet by a total of roughly 60 degrees and forming a V shape. As with Heisoku Dachi, the weight distribution should be equal, with your center of gravity midway between the two insoles. Musubi Dachi is the stance in which you stand at attention (*"Ki o tsuke"*) and perform tachi-rei (standing bow) and *yōi* (preparation).

HEIKŌ DACHI: *PARALLEL STANCE*

Figure 12.77 shows Heikō Dachi (Parallel Stance), one of the most common karate stances. As shown, this stance is frequently called *nami* ("normal") Heikō Dachi to distinguish it from various parallel stances in which one foot is ahead of the other or the feet are turned to one side. Heikō Dachi is usually the stance taken for *kamaete* (ready position) in most kata and in kumite (sparring).

Like Heisoku Dachi and Musubi Dachi, Heikō Dachi is a knee-natural stance. The proper foot position for this stance is with the feet at shoulder width center-to-center, and the weight evenly distributed between the two feet. The outside edges of the feet should be parallel so that the natural curvature of the feet causes the big toes to point slightly inward. With the knees slightly flexed, the body's weight is borne more on the balls of the feet than on the heels, which allows for faster movement. Due to its stability and similarity to normal standing posture, Heikō Dachi is used frequently in kata for both striking and joint-locking techniques.

A common variation of Heikō Dachi is to place one foot slightly ahead of the other. This is often called Ashi Mae Heikō Dachi (Foot-Forward Parallel Stance), but most often it is simply called Heikō Dachi. The example in figure 12.78 is Hidari ("left") Ashi Mae Heikō Dachi, because the left foot is leading. When the right foot is forward, it would be Migi Ashi Mae Heikō Dachi. The feet are still shoulder width center-to-center with the weight evenly distributed and the outside edges of the feet parallel. The heel of the leading foot is even with the toes of the trailing foot. This variation of Heikō Dachi is used in several kata to perform oizuki.

Figure 12.78 Hidari Ashi Mae Heikō Dachi: Left-Foot-Forward Parallel Stance.

Figure 12.79 Migi Ashi Mae Heikō Dachi: Right-Foot-Forward Parallel Stance.

Another major variation of Heikō Dachi is with both feet turned 45 degrees to one side or the other. This is generally referred to as Naname Heikō Dachi (Angled Parallel Stance). With both feet angled to the left it is called Hidari ("left") Heikō Dachi, and with both feet angled to the right it is Migi Heikō Dachi. The feet remain shoulder width center-to-center with the weight evenly distributed and the outside edges of the feet parallel. The shoulders are perpendicular to the direction of the feet. This variation of Heikō Dachi is most often used in kata when deflecting or evading an incoming strike.

Figure 12.80 Hidari Heikō Dachi: Left Angled Parallel Stance.

Figure 12.81 Migi Heikō Dachi: Right Angled Parallel Stance.

HACHI-JI DACHI: *HACHI-SHAPED STANCE*

Hachi-ji Dachi (Hachi-Shaped Stance) is named for the kanji 八 (*hachi*), because of its resemblance to the position of the feet. There are two common varieties of Hachi-ji Dachi: Soto ("outward") Hachi-ji Dachi (fig. 12.82) and Uchi ("inward") Hachi-ji Dachi (fig. 12.83). In these cases, "outward" and "inward" refer to the direction in which the toes are pointing. Hachi-ji Dachi is identical to Nami Heikō Dachi in every respect, except that the toes of both feet are turned either inward or outward about 20 degrees. Like all of the preceding stances, the knees are kept naturally flexed and the back straight, but not stiff or tensed. The center of each heel is at shoulder width. Soto Hachi-ji Dachi (fig. 12.82) is the stance that most closely approximates

Figure 12.82 Soto Hachi-ji Dachi: Outward Hachi-Shaped Stance.

Figure 12.83 Uchi Hachi-ji Dachi: Inward Hachi-Shaped Stance.

that of a person's normal standing posture, since the 20-degree angle at which the feet are turned out is the angle at which most people's feet are positioned when they stand without giving conscious attention to their foot position. It is also the variant of Hachi-ji Dachi most commonly used in training, so it is typical to simply call it Hachi-ji Dachi and refer to Uchi Hachi-ji Dachi by its full name to distinguish the two. As depicted in figure 12.83, Uchi Hachi-ji Dachi differs only in that the toes are turned about 20 degrees inward rather than outward.

KIBA DACHI: *HORSE-RIDING STANCE*

Kiba Dachi is often called Naifanchi Dachi (or sometimes Naihanchi Dachi), probably because the three Naifanchi kata are the only Shitō-Ryū kata in which it is used. In Kiba Dachi (fig. 12.84), the knees are bent so that the kneecaps are in line with the toes. The buttocks are kept tight, pulling the hips slightly forward, and the knees are pushed outward, creating pressure against the floor from the outside edges of the feet. Weight is evenly distributed between the left and right feet. The spacing of the feet in Kiba Dachi is only slightly wider than that of Heikō Dachi or Hachi-ji Dachi. In fact, Kiba Dachi looks very similar to Uchi (inward) Hachi-ji Dachi, except that in Kiba Dachi the knees are bent slightly more and pushed outward, while the hips are pulled forward. To determine the proper width of Kiba Dachi for any body type, pivot 90 degrees to the left as you kneel on the right leg, and place the ball of the left foot half the length of one foot ahead of the right knee, then rise and pivot 90 degrees to the right into Kiba Dachi. For the correct angle of the feet, pivot both heels slightly outward until each insole is slanted inward about 20 degrees from parallel. The result is a bow-legged stance that closely resembles the position of the hips and legs when riding a horse.

Figure 12.84 Kiba Dachi: Horse-Riding Stance.

SHIKO DACHI: *FOUR-PLY STANCE*

Figure 12.85 depicts Shiko Dachi (Four-Ply Stance), another frequently used basic stance found in a wide variety of kata of both Shuri-te and Naha-te origins. Shiko Dachi probably derives its name from its appearance when viewed from the front. With the shins perpendicular and the thighs nearly parallel to the floor, the legs appear to be four equal-length segments. The knees are sharply bent and the hips pulled slightly back, making the buttocks appear to jut out. Weight is distributed evenly between the feet. The correctly proportioned width for Shiko Dachi is determined by pivoting 90 degrees to the left while kneeling on the right knee, and placing the left heel the full length of one foot ahead of the right knee, then pivoting right 90 degrees while rising into the stance. Turn the toes outward until the insole of each foot is pointed outward at about a 50-degree angle, and bend the knees until the shins are perpendicular to the floor to achieve the position depicted in figure 12.85.

Since Shiko Dachi is an extremely versatile and powerful stance with numerous applications in kata and self-defense, it should be practiced until it feels comfortable and natural. Shiko Dachi is sometimes confused with Kiba Dachi. The key structural differences are that in Kiba Dachi, the feet are turned slightly inward, while the feet point outward in Shiko Dachi; and Shiko Dachi is both a wider and lower stance than Kiba Dachi. These differences are not merely visual, however, but are the result of the two stances having entirely difference purposes and uses.

Figure 12.85 Shiko Dachi: Four-Ply Stance.

ZENKUTSU DACHI: *FRONT-BENT STANCE*

Zenkutsu Dachi (Front-Bent Stance, figs. 12.86–87) is one of the most common stances used in karate-dō, and several closely related stances are based on its general structure. The key elements of Zenkutsu Dachi are: (1) keep the back straight, not leaning forward; (2) keep the weight evenly distributed between the front and rear feet, not mainly on the front leg; (3) the front kneecap should be directly over the big toe of the front foot; and (4) the back leg should be locked straight. The center of each heel should be shoulder width. The length of Zenkutsu Dachi should be proportional to the individual's height and body structure, and can be determined by kneeling on the right leg and placing the left foot the full length of one foot ahead of the right knee, then standing. The outer edge of the front foot should point straight ahead so that the natural curvature of the foot will make it appear that the big toe is pointing slightly inward. The rear foot should point outward about 20 degrees along the insole.

The hips and shoulders should be aligned parallel with each other, thus placing the torso at roughly a 45-degree angle called *hanmi* ("half-body" or "half-visible," depending on the kanji used), reducing the size of the torso as a target area from the front. The width of Zenkutsu Dachi is also determined by individual body proportions. The distance between the center of each heel should be the same as the width of the shoulders in hanmi. Slight forward pressure should be maintained with the lead foot and slight rearward pressure with the trailing foot, as if trying to keep a carpet stretched taut on the floor.

Figure 12.86 Zenkutsu Dachi: Front-Bent Stance (front view).

Figure 12.87 Zenkutsu Dachi: Front-Bent Stance (side view).

It is important not to push or lean forward to align the front knee over the toes, but to sink directly downward so that a 50-50 front-to-rear weight distribution is always maintained to avoid fatigue of the front leg. A crucial factor for self-defense in Zenkutsu Dachi is ensuring that the knee of the front leg remains bent forward of vertical. If the shin is vertical or angled rearward, the front knee becomes highly susceptible to dislocation by a kick, but if the knee is bent forward of the vertical plane, it can withstand even a powerful kick. The other advantage of this forward-leaning position of the knee is that it shifts the body's weight onto the balls of the feet and flexes the ankles—much like the position of a sprinter in the starting blocks—in preparation for sudden, powerful movement.

The general principles underlying the structure of Zenkutsu Dachi apply to the closely related stances Han-Zenkutsu Dachi, Kōkutsu Dachi, and Han-Kōkutsu Dachi, described below, as well as the less commonly used Su Dachi and Moto Dachi, which we have not described. The major variable in each of these related stances is the length of the stance, with the angle of the rear foot also changing as a by-product of the differences in distances between the feet.

HAN-ZENKUTSU DACHI: *HALF FRONT-BENT STANCE*

The most common derivative of Zenkutsu Dachi is Han-Zenkutsu Dachi (Half Front-Bent Stance, figs. 12.88–89), which is widely used in attacking techniques as well as many defensive techniques. It is nearly identical to Zenkutsu Dachi, except that it is slightly shorter, affording greater mobility. As with Zenkutsu Dachi, the key factors of Han-Zenkutsu Dachi are: (1) a straight back, (2) even weight distribution between

Figure 12.88 Han-Zenkutsu Dachi: Half Front-Bent Stance (front view).

Figure 12.89 Han-Zenkutsu Dachi: Half Front-Bent Stance (side view).

the front and rear feet, (3) the back leg locked straight, (4) feet at shoulder width, (5) weight primarily on the balls of the feet, and (6) the front kneecap forward of vertical.

The width of Han-Zenkutsu Dachi is again measured with the center of each heel at shoulder width, but its length is established by kneeling on the right leg and placing the heel of the left foot directly even with the right knee, making the stance roughly the length of a normal walking stride. The rear foot should point outward about 10 to 15 degrees along the insole. The front knee will not be directly over the toes as in Zenkutsu Dachi, but roughly over the base of the toes. A 50-50 front-to-rear weight distribution should also be maintained in Han-Zenkutsu Dachi as well as the opposing pressure of the front and rear foot.

KŌKUTSU DACHI: *REAR-BENT STANCE*

Some form of Kōkutsu Dachi (Rear-Bent Stance) is used in nearly every karate style today. The original configuration of Kōkutsu Dachi involves facing toward the rear leg, with the body angled nearly a half-turn away from the direction of the opponent, almost like a reversed Zenkutsu Dachi. This stance, shown in figures 12.90–91, is the form of Kōkutsu Dachi used in Shitō-Ryū and several other Shuri-te and Naha-te styles. The body position is basically the same as in Zenkutsu Dachi, except that the upper body is turned to face toward the rear leg instead of the front leg. The key points are identical: (1) a straight back, (2) even weight distribution between the front and rear feet, (3) the back leg locked straight, (4) feet at shoulder width, (5) weight primarily on the balls of the feet, (6) slight opposing pressure of the feet, and (7) the rear kneecap directly above the big toe.

Figure 12.90 Kōkutsu Dachi: Rear-Bent Stance (front view).

Figure 12.91 Kōkutsu Dachi: Rear-Bent Stance (side view).

Kōkutsu Dachi is identical in width (shoulder width) and length (measured by placing the front foot one foot-length beyond the knee of the rear leg when kneeling) to Zenkutsu Dachi. As illustrated below, the line of sight diverges about 20 degrees from the alignment of the feet.

Note that some karate styles employ a different configuration for Kōkutsu Dachi in which the body is turned only about 45 degrees from the opponent's position and both knees are bent. We refer to that variation (figs. 12.92–93) as Hanmi (Half-Turned) Kōkutsu Dachi.

Figure 12.92 Hanmi Kōkutsu Dachi: Half-Turned Rear-Bent Stance (front view).

Figure 12.93 Hanmi Kōkutsu Dachi: Half-Turned Rear-Bent Stance (side view).

HAN-KŌKUTSU DACHI: *HALF REAR-BENT STANCE*

A slight variation of Kōkutsu Dachi that is more commonly used in Okinawa kobujutsu—ancient Okinawan weapons arts, like the bō, sai, and tonfa—is Han-Kōkutsu Dachi (Half Rear-Bent Stance). Han-Kōkutsu Dachi is the equiv-alent of Han-Zenkutsu Dachi, except that it is rear-facing rather than forward-facing. As depicted in figures 12.94–95, Han-Kōkutsu Dachi is identical to Kōkutsu Dachi in every respect, except that the feet are separated by only the length of one shin rather than a shin plus a foot-length, and the kneecap of the rear leg aligns with the base of the big toe instead of directly above it. The key points are identical: (1) a straight back, (2) even weight distribution between the front and rear feet, (3) the back leg locked straight, (4) feet at shoulder width, (5) weight primarily on the balls of the feet, (6) slight opposing pressure of the feet, and (7) the rear kneecap inclined beyond vertical.

Figure 12.94 Han-Kōkutsu Dachi: Half Rear-Bent Stance (front view).

Figure 12.95 Han-Kōkutsu Dachi: Half Rear-Bent Stance (side view).

SANCHIN DACHI: *THREE BATTLES STANCE*

A stance similar to the Zenkutsu Dachi family in its structural principles and applications is Sanchin Dachi (fig. 12.96), named for the kata Sanchin, in which it is the only stance used. Sanchin Dachi is the fundamental Naha-te stance, but it is used occasionally in Shuri-te as well. The critical points of Sanchin Dachi are: (1) a straight back, (2) chin slightly tucked in, (3) buttocks tight and hips pushed slightly forward, (4) 50-50 weight distribution between the feet, (5) inward gripping tension with both feet, and (6) both kneecaps over the big toes. Sanchin Dachi is also a shoulder-width stance, measured between the centers of each heel. The heel of the front foot should be aligned with the tips of the toes of the rear foot. The front foot is turned

Figure 12.96 Sanchin Dachi: Three Battles Stance (front view).

Figure 12.97 Sanchin Dachi: Three Battles Stance (side view).

inward about 30 degrees, aligned along the insole, and the outside edge of the rear foot points directly forward. Both knees are bent. Muscle contraction in the lower abdomen should produce the feeling that the navel and anus are being drawn toward each other.

When employing muscle tension in Sanchin Dachi, it is important to avoid the common mistake of curving the back and hunching the shoulders inward, which collapses the chest cavity.

In some kata, such as Sanchin, Sanchin Dachi is utilized with continuous muscle tension throughout the body, while in other kata the only continual tension is in the buttocks and legs to produce a strong inward pull of the feet to grip the floor with the insoles, as if trying to keep the ground from splitting apart. This muscle tension makes Sanchin Dachi considerably more stable than it at first appears, perhaps explaining why it is employed to some extent in nearly every kata of Naha-te origins.

NEKO-ASHI DACHI: *CAT-FOOT STANCE*

Neko-Ashi Dachi (Cat-Foot Stance or simply Cat Stance) is another of the most popular stances found in nearly every style of karate-dō. Its primary functions are protection of the groin and front knee, and positioning to launch an instantaneous front-foot kick. Named for the similarity of the front foot position to the rear leg of a cat, as seen in figure 12.98, Neko-Ashi Dachi has these key points: (1) the back is kept straight; (2) both knees are bent, so the buttocks appear pushed outward; (3) weight distribution is 70 percent on the rear leg and 30 percent on the front leg; (4) the entire ball of the front foot stays in contact with the floor; and (5) the front shin is vertical. The angle of the shoulders in Neko-Ashi Dachi depends on the technique being employed. For instance, in *shutō uke* (knife-hand block) or *junzuki* (straight punch), the hips and shoulders are in parallel alignment, but for *gyakuzuki* (reverse punch) the shoulders are perpendicular to the orientation of the stance, and for *yoko uke* (lateral block) the shoulders are aligned about halfway between those two positions. This is a prime example of the concept of shizentai: matching structure to function and purpose.

To find the correct length and foot positions for Neko-Ashi Dachi, begin in Heisoku Dachi, with the feet together. Move one foot forward until its heel is one-half the length of your foot ahead of the toes of your rear foot, keeping the inside edges of your feet aligned. Pivot your back foot on the heel until the line of the insole is about 30 degrees outward. Raise the front heel until the shin is vertical, keeping the entire ball of the foot on the floor, then bend both knees as much as possible without your rear heel beginning to lift. Your weight should remain even over the entire bottom of the back foot.

Figure 12.98 Neko-Ashi Dachi: Cat-Foot Stance (front view).

Figure 12.99 Neko-Ashi Dachi: Cat-Foot Stance (side view).

UKI-ASHI DACHI: *FLOATING-FOOT STANCE*

Basically a more erect version of Neko-Ashi Dachi, Uki-Ashi Dachi (fig. 12.100) employs the identical positioning of the feet, proportions, and weight distribution. The principal difference is that the knees are not bent as deeply as in Neko-Ashi Dachi and the heel of the front foot is only slightly elevated—no more than two inches above the floor. The knee of the rear leg is only slightly flexed, which results in the front knee also being only slightly bent and not completely vertical, as can clearly be seen in figure 12.101.

Figure 12.100 Uki-Ashi Dachi: Floating-Foot Stance (front view).

Figure 12.101 Uki-Ashi Dachi: Floating-Foot Stance (side view).

RE-NO-JI DACHI: *RE-SHAPED STANCE*

Named for the *katakana* (Japanese syllabary) character レ *(re)*, Re-no-Ji Dachi (figs. 12.102–103) is nearly identical to Uki-Ashi Dachi in the placement of the feet, but in all other respects it is more similar to Han-Zenkutsu Dachi. The entire front foot remains in contact with the floor, rather than the heel being raised, and the front-to-rear weight distribution in Re-no-Ji Dachi is 50-50, instead of 30-70 as in Neko-Ashi Dachi and Uki-Ashi Dachi. The rear leg is locked straight, and the front knee is bent forward of vertical as in Han-Zenkutsu Dachi.

Figure 12.102 Re-no-Ji Dachi: Re-Shaped Stance (front view).

Figure 12.103 Re-no-Ji Dachi: Re-Shaped Stance (side view).

KŌSA DACHI: *CROSSED STANCE*

Kōsa Dachi (figs. 12.104–105) is formed differently in Shitō-Ryū than in most other styles. The knee of the front leg is bent so that its kneecap is directly above the big toe. The knee of the rear leg is tucked into the hollow at the back of the front knee,

Figure 12.104 Kōsa Dachi: Crossed Stance (front view).

Figure 12.105 Kōsa Dachi: Crossed Stance (side view).

Figure 12.106 Close-up of the foot position for Kōsa Dachi.

serving as support for the front leg. The outside edge of the rear foot is aligned with the outside edge of the front foot and placed one and a half foot-lengths behind the front heel. The front foot is flat on the floor. The rear foot heel is raised, so the weight is borne entirely on the ball of the foot. Front-to-rear weight distribution is 50-50.

SAGI-ASHI DACHI: *CRANE-FOOT STANCE*

There are three ways to form Sagi-Ashi Dachi, which differ only in the placement of the raised foot. In the most commonly used variation, illustrated in figures 12.107–108, the top (sokkō) of the raised foot is tucked into the hollow of the knee of the base leg. Figure 12.109 is a close-up of this foot position. The base leg is flexed at both the knee and the hip and bears the full body weight. In another variation of Sagi-Ashi Dachi, the raised foot is held parallel to the base leg at knee level, as shown in figure 12.110. In the third variation (fig. 12.111), the raised foot is placed against the shin just beneath the kneecap.

Figure 12.107 Sagi-Ashi Dachi: Crane-Foot Stance (front view).

Figure 12.108 Sagi-Ashi Dachi: Crane-Foot Stance (side view).

Figure 12.109 Close-up of the basic foot position for Sagi-Ashi Dachi.

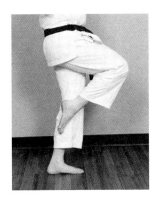 

Figure 12.110 Close-up of the side foot position for Sagi-Ashi Dachi.

Figure 12.111 Close-up of the frontal foot position for Sagi-Ashi Dachi.

OTHER STANCES

There are a number of other common stances and variations of stances that we have not described here. Some include Moto Dachi (Foundation Stance), Fudō Dachi (Immovable Stance), Katahiza Dachi (One-Knee Stance), and many others, most of which are rarely, if ever, used in Shitō-Ryū kata. Once you have developed familiarity with the basic stances we have described in this chapter, you can readily learn other stances or variations found in other styles, in a specific kata, or preferred by a particular sensei.

The crucial factor is understanding the purpose and structure (kamae) of each stance, meaning how the skeleton, muscles, and sinews align and connect to provide support in order to deliver maximum power to the target on contact. This requires more than just knowing how to stand correctly. Training must also include transitioning from one stance to another while maintaining stable and powerful structure. The timing of techniques with the movement into a stance is also a key factor. Through bunkai (analysis) and the trial and error of training in various forms of kumite and jūhō, karateka develop the ability to feel when a stance is effective, and which stances are best suited for a particular technique under specific circumstances.

In short, kamae cannot be learned solely from a book. It must be experienced—not only as kihon (fundamentals) or kata (solo examples), but most importantly with a training partner who is attempting to destabilize you. As your knowledge and experience grow, you will eventually reach the point at which kamae is instinctive and can be adapted to any situation.

Tai Sabaki
MOVEMENT

Tachi (stances) appear to be static in photographs like those presented in this book. In practice, however, stances represent only one moment in time—usually the moment in which maximum force or resistance is being applied against an opponent. Centuries of analysis have resulted in identifying the structures best suited to those moments of contact with the opponent and creating the templates for those structures that we call stances or kamae, but in actual use a stance is only held for that instant and the body continues moving. We don't actually *stand* in stances, as photographs might make it seem. We move constantly, so any given stance should be viewed as a freeze-frame from a movie, not as a posture to be maintained indefinitely.

Moving with proper structure to maintain speed, stability, and fluidity is as important as having the optimal structure and stance at the moment of executing a technique. Moving in a manner that affords optimal protection while delivering maximum force is called tai sabaki ("body movement") in Japanese. The concept of tai sabaki is that movement in karate engages the entire body, not just the feet and legs. As with stances, unified structure (kamae) of the body is utilized in all karate movement. Two major aspects of tai sabaki are the footwork (ashi sabaki) involved in moving forward, backward, sideways, and angularly, as well as turning (mawari-kata).

ASHI SABAKI: *FOOTWORK*

Over a period of centuries, karate has developed several specific methods of moving forward, backward, sideways, and angularly while maintaining kamae for the optimal blend of speed, stability, and transmission of power. The possible directions of movement are usually referred to as *happō* ("eight directions") in Japanese, depicted in figure 12.112. Although there are theoretically an unlimited number of directions in which a person can move, the eight shown in the diagram are a pragmatic summary, since the difference between moving 26 degrees to the front-right and moving 57 degrees to the front right is insignificant.

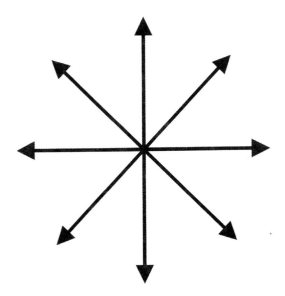

Figure 12.112 Diagram of happō (eight directions of movement).

SURI ASHI: *SLIDING FEET*

Most of the footwork in karate involves suri ashi, in which the balls of the feet remain in light contact with the floor, grazing the surface as they move, rather than being raised completely off the floor. Naturally, exceptions are frequently made in order to avoid obstacles, foot sweeps, or attempted strikes, but suri ashi is the default method for moving in any direction, since it affords greater stability, is less easily detected by the opponent, and provides the karateka with information—texture, slope, stability, and so forth—about the surface on which they are moving.

AYUMI ASHI: *WALKING FEET*

The simplest form of karate footwork is called *ayumi ashi* ("walking feet"), in which the lead foot changes with every stride in the manner of normal walking—left, right, left, right—as shown in figure 12.113. Ayumi ashi may look similar to normal walking, but it is not. When walking normally, most people push off primarily with the rear foot. In ayumi ashi, the front knee should bend and the weight shift onto the ball of the front foot, then both feet kick the floor simultaneously to drive the body forward with greater speed and power.

Figure 12.113 Ayumi ashi (walking feet).

Ayumi ashi is ordinarily performed using suri ashi, unless avoiding an obstacle, while maintaining internal structure and body alignment (kamae) with the opponent. The body should not bob up and down when moving in ayumi ashi. Instead, the head, shoulders, and hips should remain level as if balancing an object on the top of the head.

YORI ASHI: *SENDING FEET*

The karate footwork used to advance, retreat, or sidestep quickly is called either *yori ashi* or *okuri ashi*, both of which essentially mean "sending feet." To advance in yori ashi, the lead foot is driven ahead by the rear foot, then the rear foot is pulled forward—not dragged—using the hips. To move backward, this process is reversed. When moving sideways, the right foot leads to shift to the right, and the left foot leads to shift to the left. In yori ashi, the lead foot remains in front after each step, as shown in figure 12.114.

Figure 12.114   Yori ashi (sending feet).

Yori ashi is commonly used to advance suddenly or preemptively, since it moves the entire body immediately. For short or medium-range movements, it employs suri ashi, but to cover longer distances the moving foot is lifted so that it resembles a leaping or pouncing movement. Either way, the head and body should not rise when moving in yori ashi, but instead remain level.

TSUGI ASHI: *FOLLOWING FEET*

To move forward with *tsugi ashi* ("following feet"), the rear foot is drawn even with or slightly behind the front foot, then used to drive the lead foot forward. As with yori ashi, the leg should not be dragged forward but be pulled with the hips. To move backward, reverse this sequence. When moving sideways, the left foot leads to shift to the right, and the right foot leads to shift to the left. The lead foot remains in front after each step in tsugi ashi, as shown in figure 12.115.

Figure 12.115 Tsugi ashi (following feet).

Suri ashi is used when moving the trailing foot in tsugi ashi to maintain internal structure and body alignment (kamae) with the opponent. The body should not bob up or down when moving in tsugi ashi. This not only maintains structure and stability but makes it more difficult for the opponent to see and anticipate the movement. Tsugi ashi is particularly useful when moving rearward to evade a foot sweep or kick to the front leg.

Mawari-kata
TURNING METHODS

A key aspect of ashi sabaki is mawari-kata (turning methods). A karateka must be capable of engaging opponents in any of the eight potential directions. Thus, turning is as fundamental as stances or footwork. There are two major theories of turning: one applies the principles of Shuri-te and is sometimes called a "Shuri turn," while the other is chiefly employed in Naha-te and is frequently called a "Naha turn." Neither of these turning methods is more correct than the other. Each has advantages for a particular type of situation and anticipated attack by the opponent, so it is important that karateka learn to apply both turning methods with equal skill.

SHURI-TE NO MAWARI-KATA:
SHURI-TE TURNING METHOD

When performing kihon in Shitō-Ryū, we usually use what could be described as a Shuri-te method when changing directions, unless otherwise specified. In nearly all

Shuri-te kata and applications, the foot nearest the direction of the turn is moved into position to pivot. For example, to turn to the left, the left foot is moved into position for the stance in which the turn will finish. Similarly, to turn to the rear, the rear foot is shifted to the side, and then the turn is made by pivoting on the balls of both feet, as shown in figure 12.116.

Figure 12.116 Shuri-te turning method.

NAHA-TE NO MAWARI-KATA: *NAHA-TE TURNING METHOD*

In the Naha-te turning variation, primarily used in Naha-te kata and training activities associated with them, the foot opposite the turning direction is moved into position for the stance that will be assumed upon turning. For instance, to turn to the left, the right foot would shift into position first; to turn to the right, the left foot shifts first; and for a turn to the rear, the front foot steps across before pivoting on both feet. A Naha-style turn is depicted in figure 12.117.

Figure 12.117 Naha-te turning method.

Hikite
PULLING HAND

An action that sets the striking and blocking techniques of karate-dō apart from most of those performed in other forms of pugilism is called hikite, or "pulling hand." Nearly every block or strike by one hand is accompanied by a retraction of the other hand with equal speed and force, called hikite. This hikite action provides three benefits: (1) it prepares the pulling hand to execute an immediate follow-up strike or block; (2) it significantly increases the body's torque powering the technique being employed; and (3) if the hikite is grasping the opponent, it pulls the opponent sharply off-balance, compounding the impact of the strike and minimizing the effect of any attempted countermeasure.

The most common hikite position is to bring the pulling hand to the side of the body about one fist-width above the hip bone. In this position, the right hand (fig. 12.118) is roughly parallel to the ground and about solar plexus height, which is the most advantageous position from which to initiate a punch or block. Many instructors refer to this position as the "chambered" or "cocked" position of the hand.

Figure 12.118 Hikite position.

To reach this position, the pulling hand is drawn back with the same speed and timing as the movement of the striking hand, as shown in figures 12.119–122. If the pulling hand began in the punching position (palm down, fig. 12.119), it must be twisted palm-up as it is pulled back. This rotation does not occur at a continuous even pace during hikite, but rather as a sudden twist in the last few inches (about one fist length) of rearward movement, just as the twist when punching is done in the last few inches of motion.

Figures 12.119-122 Hikite sequence (side view).

A common error in hikite is to overtense the withdrawing arm so that the shoulder rises as the hand reaches the fully retracted position. Notice that in the front view (fig. 12.123), the shoulders remain level during hikite. When practicing hikite to perfect your technique, you may find it helpful to concentrate on pushing both shoulders slightly downward as you complete the punching motion. This conscious exaggeration for a few repetitions will help you develop the unconscious habit of keeping the shoulders relaxed and even.

Figure 12.123 Hikite sequence (front view).

When performing kihon, hikite is employed simultaneously with every punch, every striking technique, and every blocking technique. When performing shutō uchi or shutō uke, however, the hikite is normally drawn back only to a point adjacent to the solar plexus, palm-up and open in nukite formation (fig. 12.124). There are other

Figure 12.124 Hikite position for shutō uke (side view).

Figure 12.125 Hikite position for gedan shutō barai (side view).

intermediate and advanced techniques in which the fingers of the hikite hand are curled inward to approximate gripping a wrist. When formed in this manner, hikite is sometimes retracted adjacent to the solar plexus, while in other cases it is pulled all the way back to the hip, with the hand kept palm-down throughout the pulling action in both variations. Additional adaptations of hikite are found in several kata, so the emphasis of hikite in kihon should be to develop the habit of hikite and understand its principles so that this knowledge can be applied to the numerous hikite variations as they are encountered during training.

Hojo Undō
AUXILIARY EXERCISES

Hojo undō (auxiliary exercises) are not typically emphasized in Shitō-Ryū as much as we believe they should be. In many Gōjū-Ryū dōjō, particularly those in Okinawa, hojo undō consumes nearly half the total training time to ensure that students of that style develop muscle strength and physical fitness. Traditionally the kinds of devices used for hojo undō include chi ishi (weighted handles), nigiri game (gripping jars), ishi sashi (stone padlocks), and tetsu geta (iron shoes), shown in the illustrations that follow.

Figure 12.126 Chi ishi.

Chi ishi (weighted handles, fig. 12.126) are gripped near the end of the handle and are primarily used to strengthen the wrists and forearms by bending the wrists up and down and side to side while holding the chi ishi. Heavy chi ishi are wielded with both hands, while lighter chi ishi can be used in pairs, with one in each hand to add coordination to the exercise.

Figure 12.127 Nigiri game.

Nigiri game (gripping jars, fig. 12.127) are gripped around their rims with the fingers and thumbs. The arms are then raised and lowered and swung side to side and back and forth while holding the jars to increase finger strength and gripping power. Another common exercise with nigiri game is to walk back and forth while holding them, either swinging them or holding them steady. The weight of nigiri game can be varied by adding or removing sand or gravel inside them.

Figure 12.128 Ishi sashi.

Ishi sashi (stone padlocks, fig. 12.128) are grasped by the cylindrical crossbar. They are another tool used to strengthen the wrists, arms, and shoulders. They can be used like one-hand kettle bells and are often used to perform *chokuzuki* (straight punches) in slow motion to simultaneously work the wrists, arms, shoulders, and grip.

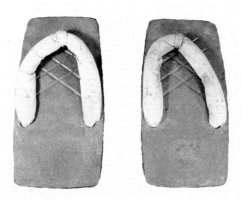

Figure 12.129 Tetsu geta.

Tetsu geta (iron shoes, fig. 12.129) are worn like regular wooden geta while either walking, doing knee and leg raises, or kicking in slow motion to strengthen leg muscles.

In recent times, barbells, kettle bells, ankle weights, and wrist weights have also been incorporated for use in hojo undō, either in addition to, or in place of, the more ancient devices from Okinawan tradition.

Danryoku
FLEXIBILITY

Another important aspect of hojo undō is stretching. While the muscles are still warm from training and hojo undō, a few minutes should be spent stretching the muscles and tendons of the hips and legs to gradually improve range of motion.

Many of the traditional methods of stretching followed during the postwar years were found to be damaging to the ligaments, so we recommend that you consult with your physician or a physical therapist to determine the most suitable stretching activities for you.

Kitae
HARDENING

Another component of training that receives less attention in most Shitō-Ryū dōjō than in Gōjū-Ryū dōjō is kitae (hardening). Kitae is a method of hardening various parts of the body, either to minimize pain and injury from striking or to develop the ability to withstand strikes. Customary kitae activities include striking a makiwara (striking post, fig. 12.130) with the hands, elbows, and feet; thrusting the fingers into a sune bako (sand box) or jari bako (gravel box, fig. 12.131) using nukite tsuki; striking the shins, forearms, and tops of the feet (sokkō) with a wooden post or paddle; and striking a large, smooth rock with the hands and feet.

Figure 12.130 Makiwara.

Figure 12.131 Jari bako.

These actions, while initially painful, gradually deaden the nerves in those areas to pain so that a karateka can strike with, or be struck on, those surfaces with minimal pain and reduced likelihood of injury. These activities tend to cause callouses to build on the surface or microfractures in the bones underneath that become denser than before and less susceptible to further damage.

Striking a hanging heavy bag (fig. 12.132) with the bare hands, elbows, knees, shins, and feet is a more recent form of kitae that allows karateka to derive some of the benefit of kitae with less pain and risk of deforming the striking areas.

Figure 12.132 Heavy bag.

We recommend that beginners train in this fashion for several months before using a makiwara or jari bako. The degree of kitae you seek should be determined by the use you expect to make of it. A military or law enforcement professional who can realistically expect to engage in hand-to-hand combat periodically in the course of their work will gain more benefit in kitae than an accountant, who may never have to actually strike another person.

Note that we strongly recommend that kitae not be performed by children. Their bones and growth plates are not fully developed, and kitae could be damaging to them.

CONCLUSION

Devoting oneself to the mastery of kihon is a level of discipline that few are capable of sustaining, yet it must be the goal of anyone seeking mastery of themselves or the art of karate-dō. A person who is able to master both the reihō and kihon of karate-dō is truly a master of the art.

Chapter Thirteen

防業技

Bōgyō Waza

Defensive Techniques

INTRODUCTION

There is a well-known Okinawan saying that is even inscribed on the gravestone of one of the best-known twentieth-century karate proponents, Gichin Funakoshi: *Karate ni sente nashi* ("In karate, there is no aggression"). Karate-dō is intended as an art of self-defense or the protection of others from unprovoked attack. Due to its lethality, it is a long-held conviction that karate should never be used for aggression, conquest, or personal gain. We wholeheartedly agree.

It is also widely believed that the spirit of karate ni sente nashi is manifest in the structure of kata, with the first movement of every kata being a defensive technique. We hold a slightly different view. It is our belief that there are no exclusively defensive techniques in karate—none. Instead, we are convinced that most techniques we describe in this chapter as bōgyō waza (defensive techniques) are in fact counter-attacking techniques. What differentiates bōgyō waza from kōgeki waza (attacking techniques) are that bōgyō waza initially deflect an incoming attack, but the purpose of bōgyō waza is to either simultaneously counterattack or to create the opening for an immediate counterattack that is impossible for the attacker to defend against. In that sense, bōgyō waza still embody the spirit of karate ni sente nashi, so we will present the basic defensive techniques before describing the counterattacking techniques.

In the dōjō, we try always to use the Japanese name for each technique. This not only establishes a universal nomenclature, so that a karateka can understand the sensei's instructions in any dōjō in the world, but it avoids confusion over the many variations in English names for the same technique. We have, however, tried to give the most commonly used English name for each technique described to assist readers in identifying it.

SHITŌ-RYŪ'S FIVE PRINCIPLES OF DEFENSE

Mabuni Kenwa, the founder of Shitō-Ryū, developed five general principles of defense (*uke no go gensoku*), which are: *rakka, ryūsui, kusshin, ten-i,* and *hangeki*. One or more of these principles applies to each of the bōgyō waza described in this chapter.

RAKKA: *FALLING FLOWER*

This principle of defense targets an act of aggression with such force that if one's single technique were applied to the trunk of a tree, its flowers would fall from its branches. In fact, one's block must be applied so decisively that the attack is not only halted in its tracks, but the aggressor is actually defeated with the single, forcefully applied waza.

RYŪSUI: *FLOWING WATER*

This principle of defense dictates that one actually "flows" with an attack, responding to it with fluid movement. For example, blocking an incoming left punch with a left knife-hand, then immediately blocking an incoming right punch with the same knife-hand, all the time moving the entire body like flowing water.

KUSSHIN: *FLEXIBILITY*

This third principle of defense deals with the control of an attack using body movement that originates in the knees. By maintaining an erect spine while utilizing vertical body movement, minimal effort is needed to counter even a vigorous onslaught.

TEN-I: *EVASION*

By understanding timing and direction of movement within an attack, one can simply avoid the assault.

HANGEKI: *COUNTERATTACK*

This last of the principles of defense dictates that an attack is met with a simultaneous block and counterattack, or a counterattack that itself also blocks the incoming strike.

Uke Kata
BLOCKING TECHNIQUES: THE FIVE MAJOR BLOCKS

HARAI UKE: *SWEEPING BLOCKS*

For most karate students, the first block learned is gedan barai (literally "low-level sweep"), commonly called "down-block" or "low block" in English. It is also usually the first block employed in beginner-level kata, especially in most Shuri-te styles. As its name suggests, this block sweeps across the region between the solar plexus and groin height. When performed in Heikō Dachi, this motion is sometimes called *chūdan barai* (mid-level sweep) or gedan barai Heikō Dachi. When performed in Zenkutsu Dachi, Han-Zenkutsu Dachi, or Shiko Dachi, it is usually called gedan barai (low-level sweep). The arm and hand movements are identical for each.

The arm and hand movements for *harai uke* begin with raising the blocking hand to the opposite shoulder with the base of the fist pointing toward the body. The other arm should generally remain in its previous position while the blocking hand moves to this preparatory position. Both hands then move simultaneously: the blocking hand sweeps down, stopping in line with the outside edge of the same-side hip, while the other hand—the hikite, or "pulling hand"—retracts into position, ready to punch as described in detail under "Hikite" in chapter 12. In the last few inches of movement (about the width of a fist) the wrist snaps sharply outward, as if striking with the bottom of the fist. Chūdan barai is typically performed as a warm-up exercise or kihon practice, while gedan barai is found in many kata. The sequence of movement for gedan barai is shown in figure 13.1.

In kata, gedan barai either begins from Heikō Dachi, as shown in figure 13.1, or from the kamae of the technique that preceded it, and it most often finishes in Zenkutsu Dachi (Front-Bent Stance). The arm movements are identical to those of chūdan barai, but the hand stops no more than a fist's distance above the same-side knee, and no farther to the side than the outer edge of the leg. This ensures complete coverage of the lower region of the body without wasted motion, as shown from the side in figure 13.2.

Figure 13.1 Gedan barai.

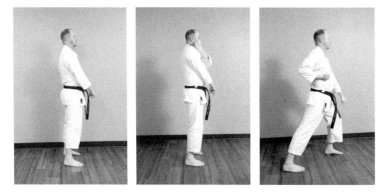

Figure 13.2 Gedan barai (side view).

AGE UKE: *RISING BLOCK*

Sometimes also called "high block" or "upper block" in English, age uke (rising block) is another of the first blocks taught to beginning karate students.

To perform age uke, the blocking hand begins in the retracted position, beside the floating ribs, with the fist clenched. At first the fist moves across the body at about a

45-degree angle, as if punching toward the face of an opponent in front of the opposite shoulder, while the hikite (withdrawing hand) begins retracting from its previous position. The blocking hand and hikite move at exactly the same speed. If the hikite is withdrawing from a position that will cause the two hands to cross each other, the blocking hand should pass on the inside of the hikite. When the blocking-hand fist passes in front of the solar plexus, it is driven more sharply upward. As the fist passes the face, the palm should still be inward. The fist snaps outward just as it clears the top of the head to finish the block, and the hikite should reach full retraction at exactly the same moment.

Figure 13.3 Age uke.

Figures 13.3–4 show the movements of age uke. The blocking hand must finish above and forward of the head, with the fist aligned with the opposite ear to cover the entire head. In this position, the blocking arm will be about 60 degrees above horizontal, with the elbow bent approximately 45 degrees inward, and the outer edge of the elbow roughly in line with the outer edge of the shoulder.

Figure 13.4 Age uke (side view).

YOKO UKE: *OUTER BLOCK*

Yoko uke ("lateral block," figs. 13.5–6) is a defense against a *chūdan* (mid-level) punch. There is a profusion of English names for yoko uke, including "outer block," "outer-forearm block," and "inside-to-outside block."

From the hikite position, yoko uke begins almost as if performing a sweeping twist-punch across the body toward a point in front of the opposite hip. During this portion of the block, the hips turn in the direction of the sweeping arm motion, and the fist moves across the body at about a 45-degree angle, with the wrist twisting inward until the palm is downward. Just before the blocking arm reaches full extension, the hips snap back toward the blocking-arm side, swinging the forearm in an outward semicircular motion as the wrist twists inward. If the hikite crosses the blocking hand, the blocking hand should pass on the outside of the hikite.

The block is completed with the blocking hand directly in front of the shoulder, palm inward, as shown, with the hikite fully retracted. The blocking-hand elbow is bent at a 90-degree angle the distance of one fist from the lower ribs. The shoulders are perpendicular to the direction of the stance.

Figure 13.5   Yoko uke (front view).

Figure 13.6   Yoko uke (side view).

Yoko uke requires considerable practice to perfect its timing. The blocking arm first makes contact with the opponent's attacking arm about midway down the forearm on the thumb side, which occurs while the blocking hand is making its inward-sweeping motion across the body. The opponent's attacking arm is then flung to the outside by the power of the twisting hips as the blocking arm makes the semicircular swing to complete the block.

Many beginners mistakenly believe that the blocking action of yoko uke occurs when the arm is moving outward. If attempted in this way from the hikite position, the block will be too slow to work against a full-speed punch. Compare yoko uke to nagashi uke later in this chapter to understand the difference.

UCHI UKE (YOKO UCHI UKE): *INNER BLOCK*

The inward forearm block, uchi uke ("strike block" or "inward block"), shown in figures 13.7–13.8, is one of the simplest basic blocks to perform. Like yoko uke, it is a defense against a chūdan (mid-level) punch.

From the hikite position, the blocking hand is raised to about shoulder level while the wrist is twisted so the palm faces away from the body. Using an inward snap of the hips, the blocking arm is swung across the body, with the wrist snapping around at the last moment, as if striking with the base of the fist, so the palm is turned inward at the completion of the block. The hikite retracts at the same speed as the movement of the blocking hand, and the blocking hand must swing to the outside of the hikite.

Figure 13.7 Uchi uke.

In the finished position, as shown, the blocking hand is at shoulder level, with the arm crossing the body at about a 45-degree angle. The elbow is bent at a 90-degree angle the distance of one fist from the stomach. The base of the blocking-arm fist will be roughly in line with the opposite shoulder, but it is important not to force the arm too far across the body, or improper stress will be placed on the shoulder joint.

Figure 13.8   Uchi uke (side view).

In application, the natural angle of the body in Zenkutsu Dachi or Han-Zenkutsu Dachi will align the outside hip with the blocking arm for complete protection of the body.

SHUTŌ UKE: *KNIFE-HAND BLOCK*

Shutō uke, the knife-hand block, is another defensive technique whose subtlety is often missed by beginners. While the block is named for the edge or "blade" of the hand being extended toward the opponent at its completion, this is not the portion of the hand that first contacts the attacker, as we point out.

Normally when we speak of shutō uke, we mean the version shown in figures 13.9–10, in which the ending position of the nonblocking hand is open-handed and palm-up in front of the solar plexus. Sometimes instructors call this *morote* ("both hands") shutō uke to differentiate it from the one-handed variant in which the nonblocking hand performs a normal hikite. Occasionally, you may hear the latter variation referred to as *katate* ("single-handed") shutō uke.

To execute shutō uke, raise the blocking hand (while opening it into shutō) in front of the opposite collar-bone with the thumb-side outward, then drive the hand straight forward as the other hand draws inward. In the last few inches of travel, twist the wrist of the blocking hand so the shutō striking surface turns outward while lowering two to three inches. The nonblocking hand retracts outside the blocking arm, stopping directly in front of the solar plexus—open to shutō and palm-up.

Figure 13.9 Shutō uke.

Shutō uke finishes in the position shown in figure 13.9, with the blocking hand aligned with the center of the body. The wrist of the blocking hand should be cocked back, so its striking edge is as vertical as possible, and the fingertips are at shoulder height. The wrist of the nonblocking hand should be straight and its forearm horizontal, just grazing the gi.

Figure 13.10 Shutō uke (side view).

The block actually takes place about three-quarters through the forward travel of the blocking hand, while the thumb is still on the leading edge. Contact is made at the wrist, just beneath the base of the thumb. As the block is completed, the back of the wrist rolls against the opponent's arm until the shutō edge wedges into the crook of the opponent's elbow at the base of the biceps. This movement foreshortens the opponent's punch, locking their arm open and creating a target for counterattack.

Contrary to what many beginners think, shutō uke does not strike with the knife-hand edge against the opponent's punching arm. A strike of that type would be considered a defensive shutō uchi (see chapter 14), rather than shutō uke, which is a more subtle deflecting and arresting technique.

URA UKE: *OUTER-RIDGE HAND BLOCK*

Ura uke (reverse block) is performed identically to yoko uke, except that the blocking hand opens into haitō (ridge-hand), rather than remaining closed in a fist. The hikite usually remains a fist when practicing kihon, but in some kata it is also opened in haitō fashion. The key to this block (figs. 13.11–12) is using a properly shaped haitō with the thumb tucked in against the palm to protect it from injury during contact with the opponent.

Figure 13.11 Ura uke (front view).

Figure 13.12 Ura uke (side view).

SHŌTEI UKE: *PALM-HEEL BLOCK*

There are numerous blocking techniques employing the heel of the palm (shōtei), with an inward motion reminiscent of the downward stroke of a windshield wiper, finishing at the forearm level with the hand open at about the level of the solar plexus.

Figures 13.13–14 show the basic inward shōtei uke, as it is normally practiced in the kata Tenshō. This form of shōtei uke is most often initiated from the ending point of a prior technique, rather than from the retracted hikite position.

Figure 13.13 Shōtei uke (front view).

Figure 13.14 Shōtei uke (side view).

KO UKE: *BACK-OF-THE-WRIST BLOCK*

The back, or top, of the wrist is called *koken* in Japanese. A block with this area of the hand is usually called *ko uke* (fig. 13.15), or sometimes *koken uke*. *Ko uke* is another block that is not usually performed from a prepared position. More often, it begins from a sparring stance with the hands on guard in front of the body or from the completion of a previous offensive or defensive technique.

Figure 13.15   Ko uke (front view).

Figure 13.16   Ko uke (side view).

From any neutral starting position, the blocking hand is snapped directly upward or sideways with the wrist sharply bent, striking the underside or inside of the attacking arm and deflecting. Figures 13.15–16 depict this block performed laterally (*yoko ko uke*), using a sideways movement of the arm to deflect a punch to the side. In either case, the nonblocking hand should perform hikite to be ready to strike. Both forms of ko uke, upward and lateral, are found in the Naha-te kata Tenshō.

NAGASHI UKE: *FLOWING BLOCK*

Nagashi uke (flowing block) looks quite similar to yoko uke in most respects; it is found in the kata Bassai Dai, among others. However, as explained in connection with yoko uke, nagashi uke is similar only in appearance. This block usually begins at the completion of a punch with the blocking hand. The blocking hand then retracts with a 180-degree outward twist of the wrist to the position shown in figure 13.17, "flowing" with the incoming punch and deflecting it. Nagashi uke is often used together with a 45-degree shift of stance away from the blocking-hand side.

Figure 13.17 Nagashi uke.

KAKETE UKE: *GRASPING BLOCK*

Kakete uke (figs. 13.18–22) can easily be mistaken for shutō uke with hikite, but the motion involved in kakete uke is vastly different from shutō uke. The blocking hand makes essentially the same motion as in ura uke, except that kakete uke reaches toward the opponent almost to arm's length before pulling inward to the final palm-down position shown in figure 13.22.

The hikite often retracts fully, so it is prepared to punch, but a common variation is for the hikite to draw inward until it is directly in front of the solar plexus with the hand open in a position similar to shutō, with the edge of the hand along the center-line of the body, as shown in figure 13.22.

As the blocking hand begins to pull inward, the wrist bends outward in order to help trap or "hook" the attacking arm at the wrist. Usually, when performing kakete uke in a kata, the ring and little fingers of the blocking hand are curled to represent grasping the opponent's wrist.

Figures 13.18-22 Kakete uke.

TSUKI DOME: *PUNCHING DEFLECTION*

The punching deflection, *tsuki dome*, is precisely what its name implies: a block performed in the process of counterpunching the attacker. As shown in figure 13.23, by counterpunching with a slight shift in body position to the opponent's outside, the midpoint of the punching forearm strikes the underside of the attacker's punching arm, driving it upward and off target as the counterpunch follows through to its mark.

Figure 13.23 Tsuki dome.

Tsuki dome is implied in the punches contained in numerous kata and is frequently used with devastating effect in kumite.

SUKUI DOME: *SCOOPING TRAP*

Sukui dome (figs. 13.24–28) is one of the most effective defensive techniques used against a kick. It begins in a manner similar to gedan barai, with the blocking arm swinging outward from the opposite shoulder while dropping into Shiko Dachi. Instead of twisting the wrist outward to block, however, the arm bends upward, hooking the opponent's leg, as shown in figure 13.27.

Figures 13.24-28 Sukui dome.

Once the opponent's kicking leg is scooped into the crook of the blocking arm, rise sharply to Heikō Dachi by pulling the foot on the blocking-arm side inward. At the same time, lift the blocking hand sharply until the upper arm is horizontal and the forearm is vertical, as depicted in figure 13.28. The combined lateral shift and upward movement will pull off balance or topple the opponent.

KŌSA UKE: *CROSSED-WRIST BLOCK*

Kōsa uke (crossed-wrist block) is sometimes also called *jū-ji uke* ("X block"). In some applications (as in the kata Heian Godan), kōsa uke begins with both hands drawn to one hip, wrists crossed, with the uppermost hand from the side to which the hands are drawn. The hands are then kept together as they are driven straight forward and down to groin level, finishing in the position shown in the last frame of figure 13.29.

Figure 13.29 Kōsa uke.

In other cases (like in the kata Chintō), kōsa uke begins with each hand pulled to its side in hikite position, as if prepared to double-punch (fig. 13.30). Both hands then drive simultaneously toward groin level, crossing with the right hand on top. Regardless of the starting position, the ending position is as depicted in figure 13.29.

Figure 13.30 Kōsa uke alternate method.

A common variation of kōsa uke is *jōdan kōsa uke* (fig. 13.31), in which the hands finish overhead, as if having performed age uke with both hands simultaneously. In most cases, the hands are open in the shutō position when jōdan kōsa uke is performed.

Figure 13.31 Jōdan kōsa uke.

WA UKE: *RING BLOCK*

Wa uke derives its name from the ending position shown in the last frame of figure 13.32, in which the arms form a ring *(wa)*. Wa uke is performed by simultaneously doing age uke with both hands, finishing with the forefinger knuckles nearly touching, centered above and forward of the forehead.

Figure 13.32 Wa uke.

KAKIWAKE UKE: *PUSHING ASIDE BLOCK*

To perform *kakiwake uke*, both arms simultaneously move as described for kakete uke, but the fists are kept closed and the wrists do not bend outward. The completed position, shown in the last frame of figure 13.33, is sometimes called *tazuna gamae* ("bridle-holding posture"), for its resemblance to a rider grasping the reins of a horse.

Figure 13.33   Kakiwake uke.

UCHI-OTOSHI UKE: *DOWNWARD-STRIKING BLOCK*

An example of a strike being used to deflect an incoming attack is found in *uchi-otoshi uke*. The hammer fist is slammed downward in a large circular motion onto the top of the attacking arm, as shown in figure 13.34.

Figure 13.34   Uchi-otoshi uke.

SOETE UKE: *SUPPORTED BLOCK*

In *soete uke* (fig. 13.35), both arms move in unison, with one performing yoko uke and the other stopping with its upturned fist lightly touching the forearm of the blocking arm just above the elbow. The name, soete uke, is somewhat of a misnomer, since the trailing arm doesn't actually support the blocking arm. Instead, the fist of the trailing hand is concealed by the elbow and forearm of the blocking hand to make it more difficult for the opponent to deflect.

Figure 13.35 Soete uke.

Soete uke is an example of a simultaneous block-and-counterattack technique since the fist of the trailing hand will continue forward to strike the opponent. There is a slight delay in the follow-up strike because its eventual target is determined by how the opponent reacts the moment after their attack is deflected, and thus soete uke is usually classified as a bōgyō waza, rather than a kōgeki waza like its similar counterpart *morotezuki.*

KEN-SASAE UKE: *REINFORCED-FIST BLOCK*

Ken-sasae uke (fist reinforced block) is performed exactly like soete uke but uses the open palm of the trailing hand to reinforce the blocking arm at the base of the palm, as shown in figure 13.36.

Figure 13.36 Ken-sasae uke.

HIJI-SASAE UKE: *REINFORCED-ELBOW BLOCK*

In nearly identical fashion to *ken-sasae uke*, *hiji-sasae uke* (elbow reinforced block) uses the open palm of the trailing hand to reinforce the blocking arm at the elbow, as illustrated in figure 13.37.

Figure 13.37 Hiji-sasae uke.

MAWARI UKE: *CIRCLING BLOCK*

Sometimes called *uzumaki uke* ("whirlpool block"), *kuri uke* ("rotating block"), and many other names, *mawari uke* involves circling both arms in front of the body. It is used to perform *karami nage* (tangling throw), an elbow or shoulder dislocation, or to pin the opponent's arms against their body.

For ease of illustration, the sequence of movements is shown in figure 13.38, beginning with one arm lowered and the other arm raised to roughly the ending position of yoko uke. The arms then cross in front of the body in a circular path, crossing when the lower hand has reached the opposite hip and the upper hand has reached the opposite shoulder, continuing until they are in the reverse of their starting positions, then drawing inward until the hand that began in the lowered position is pulled back to its hip and the hand that began in the raised position has retracted to the shoulder. From there, both hands push forward to complete mawari uke.

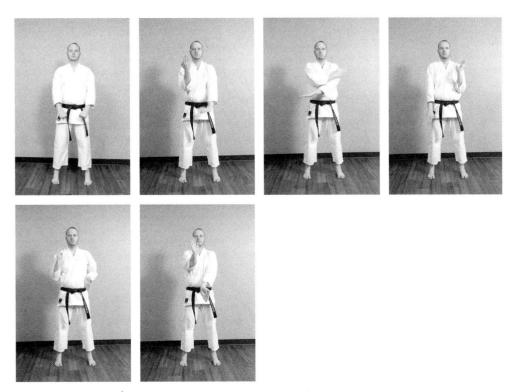

Figure 13.38 Mawari uke.

The forgoing bōgyō waza are the most common defensive techniques. There are at least a dozen more that are far less frequently found in kata and are used for specialized situations. An example of this is *sode-garami uke* (sleeve-tangling block), used to trap an opponent's hand if they grab the sleeve of your garment, or *furisute uke* (shaking-off block), which is actually a technique from jūhō for escaping when grasped by the wrist. The full spectrum of defensive techniques simply cannot be presented in a single chapter. It is better to discover them through bunkai (chapter 17) for reasons explained in that chapter.

TENSHIN: *BODY SHIFTING*

In traditional martial arts, a great deal of study has been applied to the subtleties of *tenshin* (body shifting), also called *ten-i*. If, when attacked, you stand in one place and simply block the incoming technique, your block must be perfectly timed and sufficiently powerful to deflect the attack. At its simplest level, tenshin adds a sideward or angular shift of the body to the blocking technique to help evade the opponent's attack or reduce its damage if it makes glancing contact.

In figure 13.39, for example, instead of simply blocking the opponent's attack, the defender makes a half-step to the side while performing gedan barai. This not only affords an extra degree of protection but adds greater hip-rotation power to the block and an angular line of counterattack that is more difficult for the attacker to block or avoid.

Figure 13.39 Application of tenshin.

Notice in figure 13.39 that the centerline (*seichūsen*) of the defender's body remains aligned with the centerline of the attacker's body during tenshin. Thus, when side-stepping the attack, the defender pivots in an arc rather than stepping directly to the side, so they remain facing directly at the opponent. This crucial aspect of tenshin ensures that the defender will not be off-balanced by the force of the attack and will be ideally positioned for a fast and powerful counterattack.

Although we do not usually call it tenshin, moving directly toward an attacker employs the same principle as tenshin in many cases. For example, *moving forward* while performing age uke allows the block to catch the attacker's technique before it has developed full power, making the block more effective. By driving into the opponent's technique before it is completed, the defender has also disrupted the attacker's balance and impelled the attacking arm upward, exposing an enormous target area for potential counterattack.

Tenshin is also a key factor in most *kansetsu waza* (joint-lock techniques) and many *nage waza* (throwing techniques). Correctly timed use of tenshin aids in the application of these techniques in two major respects. First, tenshin is often used to disrupt the opponent's balance during their attack. And second, it is used to upset the opponent's balance as well as to impart greater force to the technique while performing the kansetsu waza or nage waza counterattack. The first series of three movements in the kata Saifa are a prime example of this double use of tenshin. In each movement, the body first shifts to one side as the performer grasps the wrist of the attacker, then shifts again to the opposite side as a joint-lock technique is applied.

Another frequent application of tenshin occurs in kumite. As shown in greater detail in chapter 19, tenshin is often used as the primary defensive movement in kumite. In sen no sen (preemptive counterattack) techniques, especially, rather than blocking the opponent's attack, it is merely dodged by tenshin while simultaneously delivering a counterstrike.

Thus, for intermediate and advanced karateka, tenshin must be a subject of considerable study, and used during training in both bōgyō waza and kōgeki waza, so that it becomes a natural response to attack.

CONCLUSION

Whether blocking (uke kata), body-shifting (tenshin), or combining the two, defensive techniques are a reaction to an opponent's attack. As such, defensive techniques, or bōgyō waza, must be practiced consistently and rigorously in order to be effectively employed. Far more than offensive techniques, bōgyō waza rely on precise timing and execution to succeed. The slightest error will result in your being struck by your opponent. For purposes of self-defense, especially, far more training effort should be devoted to the timing and footwork of defensive techniques than any other element of karate-dō.

Furthermore, a great deal more effectiveness in kōgeki waza (offensive techniques) can be developed through solo practice than can be achieved for defensive techniques. The speed, power, and timing of strikes can be practiced against imaginary targets or stationary ones. But learning to evade or deflect a real, full-speed, full-power attack can only be accomplished by the experience of facing and reacting to realistic attacks in order to cultivate an instinct for anticipating the speed, power, angle, and timing of an attack. This is one of the vital skills developed by yakusoku kumite (choreographed sparring) and jiyū kumite (free sparring). We recommend that at least one-third of your total training time be devoted to activities with a training partner.

Chapter Fourteen

攻撃技

Kōgeki Waza

Offensive Techniques

In general, the counterattacking techniques of karate-dō can be divided into three broad categories:

tsuki kata (punching methods)

uchi kata (striking methods)

keri kata (kicking methods)

As you study the techniques portrayed in this chapter, refer to chapter 12 for detailed descriptions of the striking surfaces and basic principles of striking.

Tsuki Kata
PUNCHING METHODS

There are two key reasons why *tsuki* kata are somewhat of a hallmark of karate-dō. First, as we previously related, the Okinawan propensity for striking with a closed fist, rather than an open hand, is one of the key distinctions between karate-dō and other Asian martial arts. Secondly, the twist-punch unique to classical karate-dō distinguishes it from Western-style boxing as well as most other forms of pugilism.

Chūdan tsuki, either oizuki or gyakuzuki, is the most common striking technique found in the kata of Shitō-Ryū. There must be a reason for this; there are probably several. Unfortunately, the majority of kata were created by masters who died more than a century ago, and they did not record their reasons for posterity, so we can never know for certain. We can, however, make some informed guesses. One is that striking with the closed fist is a key distinction between most forms of Chinese chuan fa and

Okinawan karate, so it would have been only natural for the sensei of old to empha-size their belief in the superiority of the closed fist over the open hand. Another reason is that at the time karate was coming into its own under the direction of sensei like Sakugawa Kanga and Matsumura Sōkon, Okinawa was under occupation by the Japanese samurai who typically wore yoroi, armor made from strips of bamboo sewn together. A strike with a closed fist—especially a fist that had been thoroughly hard-ened on a makiwara—stood a better chance of bending or damaging those flexible bamboo strips than an open hand. Lastly, and perhaps most apropos, the occupying samurai had brought with them a core principle of kenjutsu: *ittō sunawachi bantō*— One sword [meaning "cut"] equates to ten thousand swords ["cuts"].

The meaning of this adage is that a samurai who fully understands what makes a cut effective can adapt those principles to any situation and make an unlimited variety of cuts with equal effectiveness. The same is true of karate-dō. Once you understand how to deliver a strike with lethal force and the full variety of *karada no buki* (body weapons) you possess, you can apply those principles to any and all strikes effectively. Therefore, kata do not have to contain every possible type of strike that can be used in a given situation; they only have to show where the strikes belong. Therefore a chūdan tsuki may represent any number of striking techniques and should not be understood to limit the possible techniques used at that point only to chūdan tsuki.

With that in mind, we believe an equivalent adage should be added to the lexicon of karate: *Itte sunawachi bante*—One hand [meaning "strike"] equates to ten thousand hands ["strikes"].

CHOKUZUKI: *STRAIGHT PUNCH*

Chokuzuki is the normal karate punch in two respects: it is a punch with the "true" fist (seiken tsuki), as discussed in chapter 12. The term *chokuzuki* is most often used for punches made while standing in Heikō Dachi. It begins with the striking hand in prepara-tory position (called "cocked" or "chambered" position in some dōjō). The fist is then driven straight forward, with the elbow directly in line with the fist. Just before the punch is completed—in its last fist-length of travel—the wrist snaps inward 180 degrees so that it finishes palm-down at the moment the elbow straightens, as shown in figures 12.118–125. A straight punch performed in a stance in which one foot is forward of the other is usually called one of the following: *junzuki, oizuki, kizamizuki,* and *gobuzuki.*

Junzuki ("regular punch") is a straight punch (chokuzuki) that is performed in place with the striking hand on the same side as the leading foot, as shown in figures 14.1 (front view) and 14.2 (side view).

Figure 14.1 Junzuki (front view).

Figure 14.2 Junzuki (side view).

A common mistake is to allow the elbow to swing outward during the punching motion. This robs the punch of structure (kamae) and much of its power, and exposes the elbow to severe damage if the punch is obstructed before it is completed. A simple exercise that can remedy this tendency is to consciously be sure your elbow brushes lightly against your side as you initiate each punch.

Another frequent error is to allow the shoulder of the punching arm to rise while punching. Often, this tendency is the result of excessive muscle tension, trying to make the punch faster or more powerful. Lifting the shoulder can also result in injury if the punch is jammed before completion. To prevent the shoulder from rising, consciously force the shoulder downward by tightening the latissimus dorsi muscle, as if trying to make the punching-side shoulder finish lower than the other shoulder.

A few hundred repetitions of either of these exercises will correct whichever of these erroneous tendencies you might experience, after which further conscious effort should be unnecessary in order to maintain a correct punching motion.

Generally, seiken tsuki is directed either to chūdan (mid-level, meaning solar plexus height) or jōdan (high-level, which is typically throat, jaw, or nose height). There are a few kata, however, that contain a seiken tsuki to gedan (low-level, either groin height or to an opponent on the ground). Figure 14.3 is a side view of chūdan seiken tsuki, and figure 14.4 shows jōdan seiken tsuki.

Typical terminology is to call a punch performed in Heikō Dachi either seiken tsuki or by its designated target level as jōdan, chūdan or gedan tsuki, and to refer to a straight punch executed with the same foot forward as the striking hand as junzuki.

Figure 14.3 Chūdan seiken tsuki (side view).

Figure 14.4 Jōdan seiken tsuki (side view).

OIZUKI: *LUNGE PUNCH*

The only difference between junzuki and oizuki (figs. 14.5–6) is that oizuki (literally, "pursuit punch") is performed in unison with a lunging step forward, while junzuki is performed standing in place.

Figure 14.5 Oizuki (front view).

Figure 14.6 Oizuki (side view).

GYAKUZUKI: *REVERSE PUNCH*

Gyakuzuki is a seiken tsuki performed with the hand opposite from the leading foot, as demonstrated in figures 14.7–8. This technique is considered gyakuzuki whether or not it is accompanied by a forward step—with no distinction in name between a stationary gyakuzuki and a lunging forward gyakuzuki.

Figure 14.7 Gyakuzuki (front view).

Figure 14.8 Gyakuzuki (side view).

TATEKENZUKI: *VERTICAL-FIST PUNCH*

Tatekenzuki is a tsuki kata performed with only half the wrist rotation of seiken tsuki, so that in the finished position the fist is vertical (thumb-side up) rather than horizontal. In figure 14.9 tatekenzuki is shown with the feet placement as in junzuki, but tatekenzuki can just as readily be performed as a variation of gyakuzuki.

Figure 14.9 Tatekenzuki (front view).   Figure 14.10 Tatek-enzuki (side view).

Kata contain a number of other interesting variations of seiken tsuki that need not be described in detail here but that you should recognize by name. *Morotezuki* (two-handed punch), for instance, is simply a simultaneous jōdan gyakuzuki and a palm-up chūdan oizuki, found in many traditional kata. Another two-handed punch is *heikōzuki* (parallel punch), in which the two hands simultaneously punch parallel to each other at chest level. *Agezuki* is an uppercut punch performed with an inverted (palm-up) fist. *Kizamizuki* is a leading-hand jab that begins with the punching hand extended in a guarding position in front of the body, as in Jiyū Kamae (Sparring Stance). A common variation found in many kata is *kagizuki*, a right-angle punch made across the front of the body, while *gobuzuki* is a foreshortened punch in which the elbow remains bent and tucked close to the body, found chiefly in the kata Naifanchi San-dan.

Other variations of seiken tsuki are solely in the formation of the fist used in striking. Nakadaka ippon-ken, for instance, is a fist with the middle knuckle of the middle finger extended to form the principle striking surface. *Hitosashi ippon-ken* uses the extended middle knuckle of the index finger as the striking point. A karateka who can correctly execute junzuki, oizuki, and gyakuzuki can readily perform any of these variations simply by changing the shape of the striking hand.

There are also several tsuki kata, or thrusting strikes, that do not employ the closed fist. Once again, in most respects these other tsuki kata are simply variations of oizkuki, junzuki, or gyakuzuki, each employing a different striking surface of the hand.

For instance, nukite tsuki is a spear-hand strike. When performed to solar plexus level (chūdan), the hand finishes in a vertical plane with the thumb topmost. Nukite tsuki even has three variations in striking surface: *yonhon nukite* (four-finger spear-hand), *nihon nukite* (two-finger spear-hand, using the index and middle fingers, usually spread apart), and *ippon nukite* (one-finger spear-hand). The choice of hand formation is usually determined by the target that is intended to be struck with the nukite technique. Nihon nukite, for instance, most often targets the eyes, while ippon nukite may be used to strike into the eye, throat, or any number of pressure points on the body.

Depicted in figures 14.11–12 is a basic yonhon nukite. The striking position shown is identical to that of junzuki, except that the striking hand is formed as nukite (spear-hand) rather than a fist. Nukite can also be performed with the feet reversed in a manner similar to gyakuzuki.

Figure 14.11 Yonhon nukite (front view).

Figure 14.12 Yonhon nukite (side view).

A common application of nihon nukite tsuki is depicted in figure 14.13. In this case the target is the opponent's eyes.

Figure 14.13 Nihon nukite (side view).

Another tsuki kata variation is *shōtei tsuki* (palm-heel strike), shown in figure 14.14, in which the base ("heel" or "butt") of the palm is the striking surface rather than the seiken fist. The most common form of shōtei is delivered to face level (jōdan), where the target is ordinarily the chin, jawline, or nose. Shōtei tsuki is performed exactly like a punch, except that in the last few inches of travel, the hand opens and the heel of the palm is extended toward the target.

Figure 14.14   Shōtei tsuki (side view).

Other, less common tsuki kata include *hira-basami*, a strike—usually to the throat—with the web between the thumb and index finger, and *yubi basami*, a method of grasping the throat in which the middle knuckle of the middle finger is extended beneath the outspread thumb and index finger so that it digs into the larynx while the thumb and index finger squeeze the esophagus.

Uchi Kata
STRIKING METHODS

Traditional karate-dō employs a seemingly endless variety of striking methods. In chapter 12 we reviewed roughly twenty striking areas of the hand and arm. Not only is there a striking technique utilizing each of these areas—such as kentsui uchi (hammer-fist strike), ura-ken uchi (back-fist strike), and so forth—but each of those striking techniques may have several methods and angles of application, depending on the target area to be struck.

KENTSUI UCHI: *HAMMER-FIST STRIKE*

Taking just the hammer-fist strike (kentsui uchi) as an example, there are at a minimum the following variations:

There is downward kentsui uchi, called uchi-otoshi (fig. 14.15), in which the hand swings downward to strike. This variation can either be executed from the striking-hand side by raising it overhead and swinging downward in a motion similar to that of a tennis serve, or by swinging it in an arc across to the opposite side of the body. Furthermore, the strike can either be made with a large powerful swing from the shoulder or a smaller, faster downward whipping motion of the elbow.

Figure 14.15 Uchi-otoshi.

For soto (outward) kentsui uchi, the arm is swung outward to strike laterally, as shown in figure 14.16. The ending position looks similar to that of junzuki, except that the striking hand is aligned with the shoulder, rather than centered on the opponent's solar plexus. This variation occurs in such kata as Heian Godan and Chintō, among others.

Figure 14.16 Soto kentsui uchi.

Inward kentsui uchi is performed by moving the striking hand in exactly the same manner as in uchi uke, but instead of deflecting a punch with the forearm, the hammer-fist is used to strike the opponent, as shown in figure 14.17, and as practiced in the kata Saifa.

Figure 14.17   Uchi kentsui uchi.

Rearward kentsui uchi uses a rearward swing of the arm to strike powerfully to the opponent's groin, usually while shifting the upper body away from the opponent's attack. Figure 14.18 shows this technique performed from Kokutsu Dachi, as it is found in such kata as Jion and Wanshū.

Figure 14.18   Gedan ushiro kentsui uchi.

Since the foregoing four examples are not even an exhaustive list of the frequently encountered versions of kentsui uchi, it is evident that an entire volume could be devoted just to descriptions of the major striking techniques and their most common variations. We do not believe it would be beneficial to undertake such an extensive review of striking techniques. Instead, we will present one example of each of the major striking techniques.

URA-KEN UCHI: *BACK-KNUCKLE STRIKE*

Not as powerful as kentsui uchi, but devastatingly painful when directed at targets like the temple, eye socket, or bridge of the nose, is ura-ken uchi. Much of the impact of ura-ken uchi is generated by the whipping action of the arm and wrist, as shown in figure 14.19.

Figure 14.19 Ura-ken uchi.

One of the best-known striking techniques of karate-dō must certainly be shutō uchi, the knife-hand or hand-edge strike, which laypeople so often refer to as the "karate chop."

Depicted in figure 14.20 is one of the most common forms of shutō uchi, performed with an inward striking motion almost identical to uchi uke, except with the striking hand open so the edge or "blade" of the hand contacts the target. Shutō uchi has as many variations—downward, sideways, backhand—as kentsui uchi and is one of the most versatile striking techniques found in karate-dō.

Figure 14.20 Shutō uchi.   Figure 14.21 Gyaku shutō uchi.

Some additional striking techniques found in karate-dō kata or occasionally employed in yakusoku kumite and other forms of practice are: *haishu uchi*, a strike with the flat back of the hand; *koken uchi*, a strike with the top or back of the bent wrist; *furi uchi*, an inward whipping strike with the fore knuckles of the fist; and *wantō uchi*, a strike with the outer edge of the forearm. Of these, koken uchi is the one most often found in kata, probably due to its versatility. Two examples of koken uchi are presented as a strike in figure 14.22 and a block in figure 14.23.

Figure 14.22 Koken uchi striking the jaw.

Figure 14.23 Koken uchi used as a block.

Keri Kata
KICKING METHODS

Although the art is called karate-dō—the way of empty hands—the world at large probably first thinks of spectacular and devastating kicks whenever the word *karate* is spoken. The arsenal of kicks is almost as vast as that of hand strikes, but the kicks that can devastate an opponent in a single blur of movement are the most basic ones. The kicks that dazzle movie audiences with their spectacular acrobatic leaps and spins are of little use in real combat. While we encourage karate practitioners to learn those kicks if they wish, we will focus here on those basic kicks that three hundred years of life-or-death combat have proved effective.

CHOKU GERI: *STRAIGHT KICK*

This is the most basic kick and the one most commonly found in traditional kata. A term often used for choku geri is *mae geri* (front kick). We try to avoid using this term because most karate kicks are to the front. Choku geri, sokuto geri, mawashi geri, mikazuki geri, gyaku mikazuki geri, and kakato geri are all routinely used to kick an opponent who is in front of the kicker, while few kicks are performed sideways or to the rear.

The basic form of choku geri is a true "snap" kick, meaning that the leg is "snapped" or "whipped" to the target and back almost like the crack of a whip. It is this fast snapping motion that makes a proper choku geri difficult to block or trap, and gives it its jarring destructive power.

The correct striking surface for choku geri is the jōsokutei (ball of the foot). To strike the target without self-inflicted injury, the toes must be drawn back as far as possible and the ankle fully extended forward so the jōsokutei projects toward the target, as described in chapter 12. From any forward-facing stance (Zenkutsu Dachi, Han-Zenkutsu Dachi, Sanchin Dachi, and others), raise the knee to hip level and pull the toes back, ready to strike. With a whipping action of the leg, combined with a forward thrust of the hips, drive the foot straight ahead into the target and snap it back immediately before returning it to the floor, as shown in figures 14.24–25.

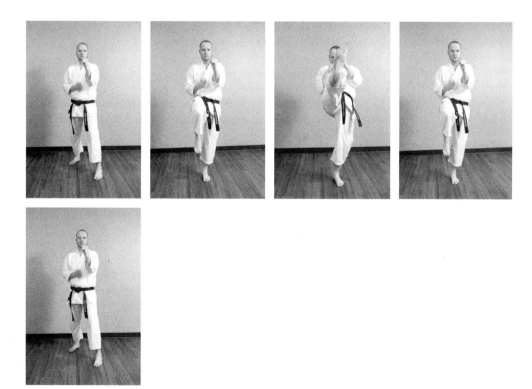

Figure 14.24 Choku geri (front view).

Figure 14.25 Choku geri (side view).

The two most common variations of choku geri are *mae keage* (front rising or swinging kick), in which the leg swings up in an arc and the top of the foot (sokkō) is used to strike the groin or similar target; and *choku kekomi* (front thrust kick), which has been popularized by styles that promote kicks to face level or above. As a general rule, the feet are best used to strike areas below the belt and hands to strike targets above the belt, so the less damaging kekomi is seldom used in traditional karate styles.

MAWASHI GERI: *ROUNDHOUSE KICK*

This kick is rarely found in kata but frequently used in kumite. The primary striking surface of mawashi geri is also the ball of the foot, but the top (sokkō) can also be used for striking fleshy parts of the body like the thigh. A well-executed mawashi geri is depicted in figures 14.26–27.

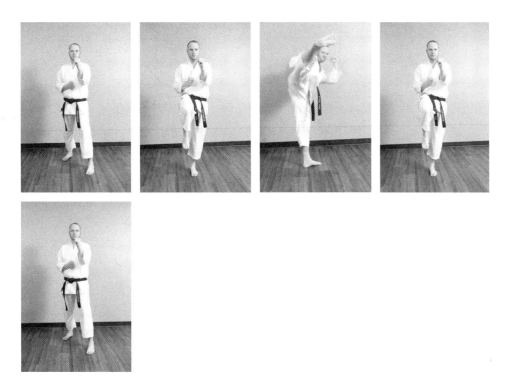

Figure 14.26 Mawashi geri (front view).

Figure 14.27 Mawashi geri (side view).

From almost any stance, mawashi geri can be performed by lifting the kicking foot until its knee is about hip level, and bending the knee until the kicking foot is close to the buttock. With a snap of the hips and pivoting sharply on the ball of the base foot, the kicking foot is whipped toward its target and immediately rebounds back. It is very important to keep the torso as upright as possible during the kick, avoiding the tendency to lean away from the kick to increase its height. Tilting the upper body drastically reduces the power of the kick and makes it easy for the opponent to throw you off balance.

Like choku geri, mawashi geri should be snapped out and back—returning as quickly as it strikes—so that it cannot be easily caught or trapped. A common mistake is to pause for a moment with the leg fully extended, making the foot appear to "stick" in the air at the point of contact. This may look impressive, but it makes the kick much easier to trap and defend against. A turning kick (mawashi geri) has slightly longer reach than choku geri, and when performed with sufficient hip rotation (koshi mawari), it can be devastatingly powerful.

SOKUTŌ GERI: *FOOT-EDGE KICK*

This is another kick not often found in traditional kata. When sokutō geri (figs. 14.28–37) does appear, it is usually in the form of kansetsu geri (joint kick) to the knee. In Shōtō-kan and some of the styles derived from it, some of the choku geri have been changed to sokutō geri, as in the kata Heian Yondan, Kōsōkun Dai (Kankū Dai), Chintō (Gankaku), and others.

The striking surface for sokutō geri is, of course, the sokutō, or outer "blade" of the foot. In particular, the strike should be concentrated on the portion of the blade of the foot directly in line with the ankle and shin, so that the energy from impact is transmitted straight into the bones of the lower leg. If the strike occurs closer to the toes, it can place damaging stress on the ankle joint on impact.

From a neutral stance, the foot is lifted until the thigh is parallel to the floor with the ankle bent inward to tilt the sokutō into position for striking. The hips are then driven sideways toward the target as the foot snaps outward. In figure 14.30, note that at full extension, the striking edge of the foot is parallel to the floor and the body leans only slightly. Excessive leaning away from the kick reduces its power and leaves you susceptible to being thrown off balance by the opponent.

Figures 14.28-32 Sokutō geri (front view)

Figures 14.33-37 Sokutō geri (side view).

As with choku geri and mawashi geri, the basic sokutō geri is a true snap-kick, with the leg striking and retracting at the same speed, providing substantial additional power through this whiplike action. In addition to kicking forward with sokutō geri to extend the reach of the kick, it can be used to kick sideways, as illustrated in figures 14.38–39. When performed in this manner it is sometimes called either *yoko geri* (side kick) or *yoko sokutō geri* to distinguish it from a frontward sokutō geri.

Figure 14.38   Yoko sokutō geri (front view).

Figure 14.39   Yoko sokutō geri (side view).

USHIRO GERI: *BACK KICK*

Found only in the traditional kata Unsū, the back kick is emphasized in many self-defense techniques involving attacks from the rear. The proper striking surface for ushiro geri (figs. 14.40–41) is the bottom of the heel (kasokutei) combined with the lower one-third of the sokutō. This focuses the strike on the portion of the foot directly in line with the bones of the lower leg for effective absorption of impact. If the strike involves the entire sole of the foot, the energy is dispersed over too large an area, reducing its effectiveness.

To prepare for ushiro geri, raise the kicking leg almost to hip height (only a few inches lower than if preparing for choku geri) and turn the head 90 degrees toward the kicking side to peer over the shoulder. From this point, drive the leg straight backward to the target. It is important not to allow the knee to swing to the side as the kick is delivered but to swing it beneath the body so that the foot and leg travel straight to the target. The leg must immediately be pulled back on full extension. As with all basic kicks, do not allow the upper body to lean excessively during ushiro geri.

Figure 14.40 Ushiro geri (rear view).

Figure 14.41 Ushiro geri (side view).

HIZA ATE: *KNEE STRIKE*

Since it involves the leg, hiza ate (knee strike) is considered a keri kata. It is not only an excellent technique in many self-defense situations, but it occurs in many traditional kata, such as Heian Yondan. Hiza ate is not permitted in sport kumite, however, because of its likelihood of causing serious injury. The top of the knee is the proper striking surface for hiza ate—not the kneecap itself.

Hiza ate can begin from almost any neutral or forward stance, such as Han-Zenkutsu Dachi. The knee is then driven forward and upward into the target, finishing about waist level. In most kata, hiza ate is usually accompanied by pulling both hands down and to the sides as shown in figures 14.42–43, simulating pulling the opponent's body or head down to meet the rising force of hiza ate.

Figure 14.42 Hiza ate (front view).

Figure 14.43 Hiza ate (side view).

MIKAZUKI GERI: *CRESCENT KICK (INWARD)*

Mikazuki geri (crescent kick), shown in figures 14.44–45, is featured in several kata and has numerous uses. The proper striking surface is the insole (inner edge) of the foot. It is performed by swinging the rear foot in an inward arc, making contact at the peak of its travel.

Figure 14.44 Mikazuki geri (front view).

Figure 14.45 Mikazuki geri (side view).

GYAKU MIKAZUKI GERI: *REVERSE (OUTWARD) CRESCENT KICK*

Gyaku mikazuki geri (reverse crescent kick), shown in figures 14.46–47, is not present in any Shitō-Ryū kata and is generally not used as frequently as mikazuki geri. The proper striking surface is the sokutō (outer edge or blade) of the foot. It is performed by swinging the rear foot across the body, then in an outward arc, making contact at the peak of its travel.

Figure 14.46 Gyaku mikazuki geri (front view).

Figure 14.47 Gyaku mikazuki geri (side view).

USHIRO MAWASHI GERI: *REAR SPINNING KICK*

This kick has been popularized by its frequent use in martial arts fight scenes in television and movies. It does not occur in traditional kata, but it can be effectively employed under certain conditions. The striking area for ushiro mawashi geri is the back of the heel (kakato). When swung forcefully, combining the spin of the body and upper leg with a whipping action of the lower leg, it can deliver a devastating blow. When attempting ushiro mawashi geri, great care must be exercised to maintain control of the kicking foot. This kick, if performed without looking over the shoulder at the target or without adequate restraint, can be dangerous to your training partner.

Ushiro mawashi geri (figs. 14.48–49) is typically begun from an upright mobile stance, such as Han-Zenkutsu Dachi. Before the kicking foot is lifted from the floor, the body should pivot nearly 180 degrees, and the target brought into clear view by looking over the shoulder of the kicking-foot side. The torsion of the hips and upper body should begin to pull the kicking foot from the floor as it is lifted, then whipped toward the target, locking the ankle in the foot position used for sokutō geri, so the back of the heel is swung at the target and the spinning momentum of the kick returns the body and foot to the original starting position.

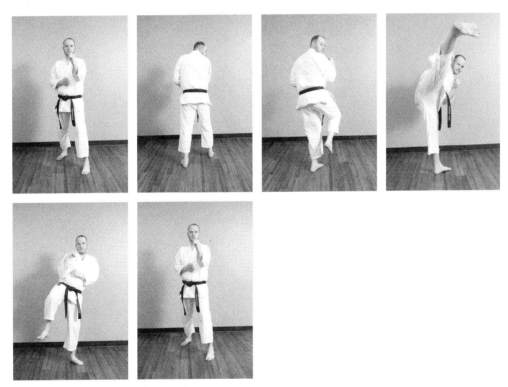

Figure 14.44 Ushiro mawashi geri (front view).

Each of the basic kicks profiled in this chapter has a number of variations. For instance, choku geri can be performed with the rear foot, as described, or with the front foot (*mae-ashi choku geri*). The same is true of mawashi geri and ushiro geri. Most often, the basic kick is considered the kick utilizing the rear foot, and the front-foot variety is considered a variation.

Figure 14.49   Ushiro mawashi geri (side view).

There are a great many leaping and spinning kicks that have been derived from these basic kicks. While we encourage students to learn many of the more flamboyant kicking techniques for their contribution to the student's balance, flexibility, and enjoyment of karate-dō, we are careful to emphasize that kata rarely deviate from the most fundamental kicks, meaning that it is the simple, basic kicks that are most effective for self-defense.

Similarly, in sport kumite, an occasional unexpected flashy kick can have a distracting effect on an opponent under the right conditions and may either score or set up a scoring technique. However, a difficult kick can also be more readily exploited by an opponent who is prepared for it, so there is an offsetting danger in attempting flashy kicks too often.

One of the hallmarks of authentic budō, as opposed to a sport, is that budō techniques are almost always direct, basic, and avoid any unnecessary motions that waste time or energy or that involve greater risk. Whether using a weapon or the bare hands, genuine martial arts do not employ purposeless flourishes, for they can only serve to bolster the ego at the risk of exposure to injury or death. True martial arts are about survival rather than showmanship: victory over vanity, humility over harassment, compassion rather than contempt, and last but not least, honor over arrogance.

Hiji Ate Gohō
FIVE WAYS OF ELBOW STRIKING

Mabuni Kenwa, the founder of Shitō-Ryū, created a simple exercise by which to practice the most common variations of *hiji ate*. We recommend that all Shitō-Ryū karateka memorize and practice this exercise, not only for its benefit in understanding how to create and apply effective variations of a basic technique, but also to honor the founder of our style. The sequence of movements is shown in figures 14.50–63.

Figure 14.50 Hiji ate gohō, starting from Heikō Dachi.

Figure 14.51 Ushiro hiji ate with gedan barai in Han-Zenkutsu Dachi.

Figure 14.52 Age hiji ate in Han-Zenkutsu Dachi.

Figure 14.53 Mae hiji ate or soto ude uke in Han-Zenkutsu Dachi.

Figure 14.54 Mae hiji ate in Shiko Dachi.

Figure 14.55 Otoshi hiji ate in Shiko Dachi.

Figure 14.56 Yoko hiji ate in Heikō Dachi.

Figure 14.57 Ushiro hiji ate with gedan barai in Han-Zenkutsu Dachi.

Figure 14.58 Age hiji ate in Han-Zenkutsu Dachi.

Figure 14.59 Mae hiji ate or soto ude uke in Han-Zenkutsu Dachi.

Figure 14.60 Mae hiji ate in Shiko Dachi.

Figure 14.61 Otoshi hiji ate in Shiko Dachi.

Figure 14.62 Yoko hiji ate in Heikō Dachi.

Figure 14.63 Hiji ate gohō in Heikō Dachi.

The sequence of movements for hiji ate gohō should be apparent from figures 14.50–63. The five types of hiji ate performed in this exercise are:

1. *ushiro* (rearward) with gedan barai in figures 14.51 and 14.57 and with *mae* (frontal) hiji ate or soto ude uke (forearm block) in figures 14.53 and 14.59

2. *age* (upward) in figures 14.52 and 14.58

3. *mae* (frontal) in figures 14.54 and 14.60

4. *otoshi* (downward) in figures 14.55 and 14.61

5. *yoko* (sideways) in figures 14.56 and 14.62

The stances used in the exercise are Heikō Dachi (figs. 14.50, 14.56, and 14.62–63), Shiko Dachi (figs. 14.50–51 and 14.56–57), and Han-Zenkutsu Dachi in all the others. It is important to note that most of these strikes can be made to either chūdan or jōdan targets. The elbows are also less susceptible to pain and injury than most other striking surfaces of the hand and arm, making hiji ate one of the most effective strikes for self-defense.

Jūhō

Soft Techniques

INTRODUCTION

Previously we stressed the adage from the "Kempō Hakku": *Hō wa gōjū donto*, meaning that karate contains a roughly equal balance of *gō* and *jū*—hard and soft. Our training, then, must devote as much time and effort to the development and understanding of jūhō as it does to gōhō.

The jūhō of karate have been long neglected, especially since the end of World War II. The reasons for this are probably manifold, but three seem readily apparent. One is that jūhō training requires considerably more floor space than does gōhō. The increasing instruction of large groups following the introduction of karate into the Okinawan school system, Japanese universities, and the Japanese armed forces was more conducive to gōhō training. In addition, jūhō instruction and training require much closer supervision and individual attention than mass gōhō training, meaning either more instructors or fewer students must be involved. Secondly, the increasing emphasis on the sport applications of karate and the growing popularity of tournament competition in the 1930s, and particularly in the latter half of the twentieth century, shifted attention to gōhō. A third factor may well have been that the sport of jūdō was already provided in Japanese schools, so karate sensei knew their students already had access to quality jūhō instruction.

There are some who believe that in the early postwar era, Japanese and Okinawan sensei did not want to teach foreigners, like American military personnel, all of the "secrets" of karate in order to preserve their superiority of knowledge and ability. We are reluctant to ascribe such ulterior motives, particularly in view of the considerable evidence that training in jūhō was already in decline among karateka prior to the war. It seems more likely that the near disappearance of jūhō from karate training was an evolutionary process, rather than a deliberate strategy.

Jūhō includes five broad categories of techniques: *kaihō waza* (escape techniques), *nage waza* (throwing techniques), *osaekomi waza* (grappling techniques), *ukemi* (breakfalls), and *tenshin* (body shifting). The key difference between the way jūhō is applied in karate and the way it is used in jūdō, wrestling, or MMA is that in karate we try to avoid going to ground. We want the opponent to hit the ground, while we remain on our feet or get back on our feet as quickly as possible, because we always assume we are beset by multiple attackers. Facing a lone opponent is a situation found primarily in sports, where rules of fair play apply. In real combat, there are no rules, and your opponent will always seek every possible advantage over you. As the old saying goes, "If you're in a fair fight, you've made a terrible strategic error." The reason for training in karate is to make sure you're never in a fair fight, but that you have every possible advantage to increase your chances of survival.

It would be impossible to provide pictorial instruction in all of the jūhō that are contained or implied in kata. That would require several volumes the size of this book, so in this chapter we have presented one representative example of each of the five types of jūhō.

Ukemi
BREAKFALLS

We recommend learning ukemi (breakfalls) as the first aspect of jūhō. *Ukemi* (受身) is usually translated as "falling" or "breakfalls," but the word actually means "body reception." Ukemi is what occurs when the floor or ground receives a falling body. The methods of ukemi are designed to minimize injuries resulting from the body falling to the ground, so they are the primary means of protection when being thrown. In addition, ukemi can be used to evade many types of attack, so it is a self-defense technique in its own right. Ukemi is therefore necessary both for practical self-defense and safety during jūhō practice in the dōjō, making it a logical starting point for jūhō training. The major types of ukemi:

- *ushiro-ukemi* (後ろ受身): backward breakfall
- *yoko-ukemi* (横受け身): sideways breakfall
- *mae-ukemi* (前受け身): forward breakfall
- *mae-mawari-ukemi* (前回り受身) or *zempō-kaiten-ukemi*: forward roll

The most frequently used form of ukemi in the dōjō is probably yoko-ukemi, the sideways breakfall. Beginners can learn yoko-ukemi by practicing from a kneeling position until they acquire the proper technique and timing, then progress to the standing position demonstrated here.

From a standing position (fig. 15.1), a basic yoko-ukemi can be performed by crossing one leg in front of the other to simulate it being swept aside by an opponent, as shown in figure 15.2. The body should be curved like a banana to shift the head away from the direction of the fall as the arm on the falling side swings across the body. Rather than falling like a tree, bend the knee of the supporting leg to reduce the height of the fall (fig. 15.3). As the hip contacts the floor or ground slap downward with the falling side arm to absorb as much of the impact as possible (fig. 15.4).

Figure 15.5 shows the position of the body at the completion of the fall. Note that the head is tilted away from the direction of the fall. The leg on the falling side is nearly straight, while the opposite leg is bent to prevent the knees or ankles from striking each other, and the slapping arm is straight alongside the body, not perpendicular or above the head.

Figures 15.1-5 Yoko-ukemi.

Kaihō Waza
ESCAPE TECHNIQUES

Once students can safety take ukemi, we generally believe that kaihō waza (解放技) are the most appropriate next stage of training in jūhō. Kaihō waza are techniques for freeing oneself from an opponent's grasp, utilizing *kamae* (structure), leverage, *tenshin* (body shifting), *kuzushi* (destabilizing), and other fundamental principles. The major escaping techniques include:

- 小手取り (*kote dori*): wrist grabs
  - 小手回り捻り (*kote mawari-hineri*): forearm rotate-and-twist
  - 抜き手押さえ (*nukite osae*): spear-hand downward press
  - 肘振り上げ (*hiji furiage*): elbow upswing
  - 手鏡小手返し (*tekagami kote-gaeshi*): hand-mirror wrist reversal
  - 外親指切り (*soto oyayubi-giri*): outward thumb-slice
  - 内親指切り (*uchi oyayubi-giri*): inward thumb-slice
  - 燕返し切り (*tsubame-gaeshi giri*): swallow-turn slice
- 袖取り (*sode dori*): sleeve grabs
  - 外袖絡み突き (*soto sode-garami agezuki*): outward sleeve-tangle uppercut
  - 内腕伸ばし (*uchi ude-nobashi*): inward forearm hyperextension
  - 肩車 (*kata guruma*): shoulder wheel
- 肩取り (*kata dori*): shoulder grabs
  - 内腕伸ばし (*ude-nobashi*): forearm hyperextension
  - 一本背負い投げ (*ippon seoinage*): one-armed shoulder throw
  - 腕絡み投げ (*ude-garami nage*): arm-tangle throw (a.k.a. *karami nage*)
  - 肩車 (*kata guruma*): shoulder wheel
- 胸取り (*mune dori*): lapel or chest grabs
  - 内腕伸ばし (*ude-nobashi*): forearm hyperextension
  - 一本背負い投げ (*ippon seoinage*): one-armed shoulder throw
  - 腕絡み投げ (*ude-garami nage*): arm-tangle throw (a.k.a. *karami nage*)

- 襟取り *(eri dori)*: collar grabs
  - 内腕伸ばし *(ude-nobashi)*: forearm hyperextension
  - 肘の脱臼 *(hiji no dakkyū)*: elbow dislocation
  - 一本背負い投げ *(ippon seoinage)*: one-armed shoulder throw
  - 腕絡み投げ *(ude-garami nage)*: arm-tangle throw (a.k.a. *karami nage*)
- 絞め技 *(shime waza)*: strangling techniques
  - 一本背負い投げ *(ippon seoinage)*: one-armed shoulder throw
  - 腕絡み投げ *(ude-garami nage)*: arm-tangle throw (a.k.a. *karami nage*)
  - 肩車 *(kata guruma)*: shoulder wheel
- 胴体抱擁 *(dōtai hōyō)*: body grabs (bear hugs)
  - 踵振り上げ投げ *(kakato furiage nage)*: heel upswing throw
  - おしのけ肘の脱臼 *(oshinoke hiji no dakkyū)*: push-away elbow dislocation
- 脚/足取り *(ashi dori)*: leg or foot grabs
  - 首捻り *(kubi hineri)*: neck twist
  - 足踏み込み *(ashi fumikomi)*: foot stomp
- 脚取り返し *(ashi-tori gaeshi)*: leg-grab reversal

One of the first kaihō waza typically taught to beginners is an escape from kote dori (forearm or wrist grab) called kote mawari-hineri (forearm rotate-and-twist), because it employs several key principles of jūhō in a single technique.

To learn this technique, uchikata (receiver of the technique) grabs the wrist of shikata (user of the technique), either right hand to left wrist or left hand grabbing the right wrist, as shown in figure 15.7. The strength of uchikata's grip should be commensurate with shikata's experience—moderate for a beginner to realistically strong for an experienced karateka. Shikata spreads their fingers to expand the muscles of their wrist and forearm and thrusts their hand toward uchikata's seichūsen (centerline), as depicted in figure 15.8, bending uchikata's wrist to weaken their grip and driving the thicker portion of shikata's forearm into uchikata's hand to spread their fingers slightly. Shikata continues moving forward, using their body weight and the strength of their legs to overpower uchikata's arm and grip while swinging their elbow rapidly inward as if to strike uchikata's forearm with hiji ate and simultaneously twisting their wrist sharply counterclockwise to tear free of uchikata's grasp, landing in Shiko Dachi with their foot positioned just behind the heel of uchikata's lead foot (fig. 15.9).

Figures 15.6-9 Kote mawari-hineri.

From the position in figure 15.9, shikata is poised to strike uchikata in the ribs with yoko hiji ate, to the face with ura-ken uchi (fig. 15.10), or to the throat with gyaku shutō uchi (fig. 15.11), as well as to drive their knee into the outside of uchikata's knee to off-balance them, then sweep their leading foot from underneath them. Once students can perform the kaihō waza alone with reasonable proficiency, they should always include practicing a follow-up technique of this kind.

Figure 15.10 Follow-up ura-ken uchi. Figure 15.11 Follow-up gyaku shutō uchi.

We recommend learning most of the kaihō waza listed in this chapter before proceeding to nage waza and osaekomi waza so that you fully understand their fundamental principles—leverage, angular movement, destabilization, and so forth—before attempting more advanced techniques based on those principles.

Nage Waza
THROWING TECHNIQUES

A wide variety of nage waza (投げ技) are presented or inferred in the kata of Shitō-Ryū. In effect, throwing techniques use the ground or floor as a weapon to inflict injury to an opponent while reducing the opponent's mobility. Some of the major throwing techniques are:

- 手技 (*te waza*): hand, arm, or shoulder throws
  - 一本背負い投げ (*ippon seoinage*): one-armed shoulder throw
  - 腕絡み投げ (*ude-garami nage*): arm-tangle throw (a.k.a. *karami nage*)
  - 肩車 (*kata guruma*): shoulder wheel
  - 踵返 (*kibisu gaeshi*): heel reversal (ankle-grab or heel-grab throw)
  - 双手刈 (*morote gari*): two-handed reap (both-leg frontal takedown)
  - 帯落 (*obi otoshi*): belt drop
  - 双手背負い投げ (*morote seoinage*): two-handed shoulder throw
  - 背負落 (*seoi otoshi*): *seoinage* by dropping to one or both knees
  - 掬投 (*sukui nage*): scoop throw ("*manji-uke*" throw)
  - 隅落 (*sumi otoshi*): corner drop (to *aite*'s rear corner)
  - 體落 (*tai otoshi*): body drop
  - 浮落 (*uki otoshi*): floating drop (corner drop to *aite*'s front corner)
  - 内股透 (*uchi mata sukashi*): inner thigh void throw (a counter to *uchi mata*)
  - 小内返 (*kouchi gaeshi*): small inner reap reversal
  - 朽木倒 (*kuchiki daoshi*): single-leg takedown
  - 入り身投 (*irimi nage*): "clothesline" throw (literally, "entering" throw)
  - 手車 (*te guruma*): "hand wheel" (lift and turn *aite* upside down)

- 腰技 *(koshi waza)*: hip throws
  - 抱上 *(daki age)*: hugging high lift (body slam)
  - 跳腰 *(hane goshi)*: spring hip throw
  - 払腰 *(harai goshi)*: sweeping hip throw
  - 山嵐 *(yama arashi)*: mountain storm (variant of *harai goshi*)
  - 腰車 *(koshi guruma)*: hip wheel
  - 大腰 *(ō goshi)*: large (full) hip throw
  - 袖釣込腰 *(sode tsurikomi goshi)*: sleeve lift-and-pull hip throw
  - 釣腰 *(tsuri goshi)*: lifting hip throw
  - 釣込腰 *(tsurikomi goshi)*: lifting and pulling hip throw
  - 浮腰 *(uki goshi)*: floating hip throw
  - 後腰 *(ushiro goshi)*: rear hip throw
  - 移腰 *(utsuri goshi)*: hip shift
  - 飛腰 *(tobi goshi)*: flying hip throw
  - 後車 *(ushiro guruma)*: rear wheel
- 足技 *(ashi waza)*: foot or leg throws
  - 足車 *(ashi guruma)*: leg wheel
  - 出足払 *(de-ashi barai)*: advancing-foot sweep
  - 跳腰返 *(hane goshi gaeshi)*: hip spring counterthrow
  - 払腰返 *(harai goshi gaeshi)*: hip sweep counterthrow
  - 払釣込足 *(harai tsurikomi ashi)*: lift-and-pull foot sweep
  - 膝車 *(hiza guruma)*: knee wheel
  - 小外掛 *(kosoto gake)*: small outer hook
  - 小外刈 *(kosoto gari)*: small outer reap
  - 小内刈 *(kouchi gari)*: small inner reap
  - 大車 *(ō guruma)*: large wheel
  - 送足払 *(okuri-ashi barai)*: sliding foot sweep
  - 大外返 *(ōsoto gaeshi)*: big outer reap counter

- 大外刈 (*ōsoto gari*): big outer reap
- 大外車 (*ōsoto guruma*): big outer wheel
- 大外落 (*ōsoto otoshi*): big outer drop
- 大内返 (*ōuchi gaeshi*): big inner reap counter
- 大内刈 (*ōuchi gari*): big inner reap
- 支釣込足 (*sasae tsurikomi ashi*): propping and drawing ankle throw
- 燕返 (*tsubame gaeshi*): swallow counter
- 内股 (*uchi mata*): inner thigh
- 内股返 (*uchi mata gaeshi*): inner-thigh counter
- 捨て身技 (*sutemi waza*): sacrifice throws
  - 引込返 (*hikikomi gaeshi*): pulling-in reversal
  - 隅返 (*sumi gaeshi*): corner reversal
  - 俵返 (*tawara gaeshi*): rice bag reversal throw
  - 巴投 (*tomoe nage*): circle ("comma") throw
  - 裏投 (*ura nage*): rear throw
  - 抱分 (*daki wakare*): high separation
  - 跳巻込 (*hane makikomi*): springing wraparound
  - 払巻込 (*harai makikomi*): hip sweep wraparound
  - 蟹挟 (*kani basami*): crab or scissors throw
  - 河津掛 (*kawazu gake*): one-leg entanglement
  - 大外巻込 (*ōsoto makikomi*): big outer wraparound
  - 外巻込 (*soto makikomi*): outer wraparound
  - 谷落 (*tani otoshi*): valley drop
  - 内巻込 (*uchi makikomi*): inner wraparound
  - 内股巻込 (*uchi mata makikomi*): inner-thigh wraparound
  - 浮技 (*uki waza*): floating technique
  - 横掛 (*yoko gake*): side prop
  - 横車 (*yoko guruma*): side wheel

- 横落 (*yoko otoshi*): side drop
- 横分 (*yoko wakare*): side separation
- 彈車 (*tama guruma*): jade wheel
- 腕返 (*ude gaeshi*): arm reversal
- 横巴投 (*yoko tomoe nage*): side circle ("comma") throw

Among the first nage waza typically taught to beginners is ōsoto gari, the large outer reaping throw. It is usually taught early in the curriculum because it not only employs the major fundamentals of nage waza and is one of the safest for beginners to perform ukemi, but it is also a throw that appears in many traditional kata.

Every nage waza has three major components or phases: *kuzushi* (destabilizing), *tsukuri* (setup), and *kake* (execution). An opponent who is not first destabilized will be able to resist or evade the setup and execution. Only after the opponent is destabilized can you get set up properly to perform the throw, and a throw can only succeed if the opponent has first been destabilized and set up. These facts become abundantly clear once you begin practicing with a training partner who resists your attempts to throw them.

In actual use, it is often difficult to distinguish where kuzushi ends and tsukuri begins. Usually, kuzushi flows so quickly into tsukuri that the two stages are almost inseparable. In many cases, they are a single motion that accomplishes both phases, but ōsoto gari provides a clear delineation between the three phases of a throw, which is another benefit of teaching it early in a beginner's training.

One way to practice ōsoto gari is for uchikata to begin in either Hidari Han-Zenkutsu Dachi or Heikō Dachi (fig. 15.12), take a step forward, and perform *jōdan oizuki*. From Heikō Dachi, shikata counters this attack by stepping into Han-Zenkutsu Dachi and simultaneously performing open-handed age uke and shutō uchi to the side of uchikata's neck, striking the carotid sheath containing the carotid artery, jugular vein, and vagus nerve, as shown in figure 15.13. In the dōjō, little or no contact is made with this strike due to the severity of injury that could result, but for self-defense, this strike, performed with sufficient power to stun the opponent, is the first step in kuzushi.

Following shutō uchi, shikata grasps uchikata's upper sleeve and collar (fig. 15.14) and pushes uchikata at a 45-degree angle to the rear corner to complete kuzushi, at which point uchikata should already be on the verge of falling. Being careful to maintain uchikata's off-balance condition, shikata then shifts into position in preparation (tsukuri) for the throw (fig. 15.15). Note that shikata presses their hip and side against uchikata's to prevent uchikata from evading the throw. To execute (kake) the throw, shikata sweeps uchikata's base leg away with the back of their own leg, as shown in figure 15.16.

Figures 15.12-17 Ōsoto gari.

During practice in the dōjō, shikata impedes the speed and force of uchikata's fall for safety by pulling upward on uchikata's sleeve and collar, as seen in figure 15.17. In actual combat, however, shikata would instead slam uchikata's head to the ground during ōsoto gari (fig. 15.18).

Figure 15.18 Self-defense use of ōsoto gari.

Another safety factor employed during practice in the dojo is little or no use of thumb pressure against uchikata's *dokko* (mastoid process) during kuzushi and tsukuri. For self-defense, either the point of the thumb or the thumb knuckle should be used first to sharply strike, then to maintain pressure on, the opponent's dokko, as shown in close-up in figure 15.19.

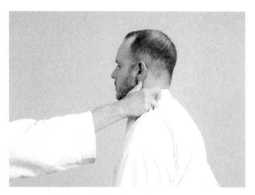

Figure 15.19   Use of the thumb in ōsoto gari.

Osaekomi Waza
GRAPPLING TECHNIQUES

The word *osaekomi* literally means "suppression," and the osaekomi waza (抑え込み技) or ne waza (寝技) in karate include many ways to grapple with, pin down, immobilize, and even strangle opponents. Among these are:

- 固め技 *(katame waza)*: holding and pinning techniques
  - 上四方固 *(kami-shiho-gatame)*: upper four quarter hold down
  - 肩固 *(kata-gatame)*: shoulder hold
  - 袈裟固 *(kesa-gatame)*: scarf hold
  - 崩上四方固 *(kuzure-kami-shiho-gatame)*: broken upper four quarter hold down
  - 崩袈裟固 *(kuzure-kesa-gatame)*: broken scarf hold
  - 縦四方固 *(tate-shiho-gatame)*: vertical four quarter hold
  - 横四方固 *(yoko-shiho-gatame)*: side four quarter hold
  - 裏固 *(ura-gatame)*: rear hold

- 浮固 (*uki-gatame*): floating hold
- 裏袈裟固 (*ura-kesa-gatame*): reverse scarf hold
- 後袈裟固 (*ushiro-kesa-gatame*): reverse scarf hold (another name for this technique is *kuzure-kesa-gatame*)
- 三角固 (*sangaku-gatame*): triangular hold
- 肘固 (*hiji gatame*): elbow pin
- 絞め技 (*shime waza*): strangulation techniques
  - 胴絞 (*do-jime*): torso strangle
  - 逆十字絞 (*gyaku jūji-jime*): reverse cross-strangle
  - 裸絞 (*hadaka-jime*): naked strangle
  - 片羽絞 (*kata-ha-jime*): single-wing strangle
  - 片十字絞 (*kata-jūji-jime*): half cross-strangle
  - 片手絞 (*katate-jime*): one-hand strangle
  - 並十字絞 (*nami-jūji-jime*): normal cross-strangle
  - 送襟絞 (*okuri-eri-jime*): sliding lapel strangle
  - 両手絞 (*morote-jime*): two-hand strangle
  - 三角絞 (*sankaku-jime*): triangular strangle, triangle choke
  - 袖車絞 (*sode-guruma-jime*): sleeve wheel strangle
  - 突込絞 (*tsukkomi-jime*): thrust choke
  - 地獄絞 (*jigoku-jime*): "hell" strangle
  - 裏十字絞 (*ura-jūji-jime*): reverse cross-strangle
- 関節技 (*kansetsu waza*): joint techniques
  - 腕押さえ (*ude osae*): arm lever
  - 手首曲げり (*tekubi mageri*): wrist bend (normal direction, to excess)
  - 小手回し (*kote mawashi*): forearm rotation
  - 小手捻り (*kote hineri*): forearm twist
  - 小手返し (*kote gaeshi*): forearm reversal
  - 手首押さえ (*tekubi osae*): wrist lever
  - 手首絞り (*tekubi shibori*): wrist double-torsion

- 腕延ばし (*ude nobashi*): forearm hyperextension
- 手首反り返り (*tekubi sorikaeri*): wrist flexion (bending wrist backward)
- 指反り返り (*yubi sorikaeri*): finger flexion (bending fingers backward)
- 腕絡み (*ude garami*): arm tangle
- 腕絡み固 (*ude-garami katame*): arm tangle hold or pin
- 脚絡み (*ashi garami*): leg tangle
- 腕挫膝固 (*ude-hishigi hiza gatame*): arm (elbow) dislocating knee hold or pin
- 腕挫十字固 (*ude-hishigi jūji gatame*): back-lying perpendicular arm bar
- 腕挫三角固 (*ude-hishigi sankaku gatame*): triangular arm bar
- 腕挫手固 (*ude-hishigi te gatame*): arm dislocating hand hold or pin
- 腕挫腕固 (*ude-hishigi ude gatame*): arm dislocating arm bar
- 腕挫腋固 (*ude-hishigi waki gatame*): arm dislocating side hold or pin
- 足取り絡み (*ashi-dori garami*): entangled leg dislocation
- 膝挫 (*hiza hishigi*): knee crush
- 足挫 (*ashi hishigi*): straight ankle lock
- 三角絡み (*sankaku-garami*): triangular entanglement

A basic osaekomi waza that employs several of the basic principles of leverage, angular momentum, and pressure on vulnerable joints, making it a good starting point for beginners, is ude osae.

There is more to ude osae than meets the eye. Practice begins with uchikata grasping shikata's collar or upper sleeve in preparation to strike (fig. 15.21). To ensure they learn to perform ude osae effectively, beginners allow uchikata to gain a secure hold on the sleeve or collar before acting. Intermediate and advanced karateka practice a more realistic approach to self-defense by reacting immediately after uchikata begins to reach for them. Shikata swings their arm in a motion like a hook-punch directed at uchikata's jaw to keep uchikata out of striking range, then steps back and bends their elbow sharply to grasp the back of uchikata's hand, as shown in figure 15.22.

With the body angled and the elbow in the position shown in figure 15.22, shikata is guarding their face from a strike and can use that arm to deflect an attempted strike to the body with *ukenagashi*. Having a secure grip on uchikata's hand is the key to ude osae. The thumb is inserted into the gap between uchikata's thumb and forefinger. The index finger is aligned with uchikata's knuckles on the back of their hand. The fingers are wrapped tightly around uchikata's shutō. This grip affords shikata complete control of uchikata's hand and wrist.

As soon as they have grasped uchikata's hand, shikata uses their other hand to strike downward on uchikata's elbow joint to bend their arm. Of course, in the dōjō this is done less injuriously by simply pulling the elbow down. Rather than trying to overpower uchikata with arm strength alone, shikata steps to the side while swinging uchikata's arm in an overhand rowing motion and twisting their wrist into the position depicted in figure 15.23. Having bent uchikata's arm provides additional leverage for this phase of the technique. Driving with the legs, using their body weight, and pulling rearward on uchikata's wrist while simultaneously pushing on their upper arm, shikata drives uchikata to the floor and pins their arm against their leg, as shown in figure 15.24.

Figures 15.20-24 Ude osae.

Uchikata's position in figure 15.24 is indefensible. By bearing down on uchikata's elbow, shikata can easily dislocate it and render uchikata helpless. In every osaekomi waza, uchikata is placed in a similarly untenable position, so it is vital that uchikata signal surrender to prevent serious injury by loudly slapping the mat or their side, striking the mat loudly with their foot, or saying *Maitta* ("I'm overwhelmed"). This also informs shikata that the technique has been performed effectively, so uchikata must not surrender prematurely, yet do so before any injury occurs.

Kyūsho Waza
VITAL (PAIN OR PRESSURE) POINT TECHNIQUES

Kyūsho (vital points) are areas of the body that are highly susceptible to pain from either direct pressure or a pinpoint strike. Most kyūsho are the same as the points identified on an acupuncture chart, so we will not list or describe them all here. Some of the kyūsho waza (急所技) most frequently used in karate techniques include:

- *tendo*: top of the head (bregma)
- *uto* or *miken*: between the eyes
- *kasumi*: temple
- *jinchu*: beneath the nose (philtrum)
- *zen-keibu*: front of the neck or throat
- *gakutō* or *kachikake* or *shita-ago*: point of the chin
- *dokko*: mastoid process
- *suigetsu* or *mizu-ochi*: solar plexus
- *denko*: right lowest floating rib
- *getsuei*: left lowest floating rib
- *myojo*: one inch below the belly button (hypogastrium)
- *tsuri-gane* or *kōkan*: testicles
- *shitsu* or *shita-kansetsu*: knee
- *ashi no ko* or *sokkō*: top surface of the foot

Kyūsho are used both as targets of strikes and as points to which pain-inducing pressure is applied during osaekomi waza to off-balance and distract the opponent, reducing the opponent's resistance to the technique. Although the use of kyūsho is implied in the majority of karate techniques, they are not usually taught to students until they have first gained proficiency and accuracy in both gōhō and jūhō, because they add considerable difficulty and complexity to the execution of techniques, as well as increased risk of injury to training partners.

Figure 15.25 depicts a nakadaka ippon-ken tsuki to uchikata's kasumi. In figure 15.26, thumb pressure is being applied to uchikata's dokko to assist with kuzushi. A hira-ken tsuki to uchikata's zen-keibu is shown in figure 15.27.

Figure 15.25 Nakadaka ippon-ken tsuki to the kasumi.

Figure 15.26 Thumb pressure to the dokko.

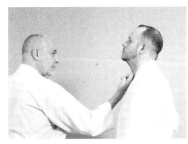

Figure 15.27 Hira-ken tsuki to the zen-keibu.

Tenshin
BODY SHIFTING

Although we also described tenshin as an element of bōgyō waza (defensive techniques), as nonstriking methods, tenshin also belong in the category of jūhō. As with kyūsho waza, tenshin is a key aspect of both gōhō and jūhō, and at least a slight degree of tenshin is implicit to nearly every karate technique.

The three major methods of tenshin waza (転身技) are:

- 転換 *(tenkan):* 180-degree spin (to the opponent's outside)
- 横歩み *(yoko ayumi):* sidestep
- 空受け *(kara uke):* empty "block" (twisting side-shift to 45 degrees)

The first tenshin waza customarily taught to beginners is kara uke, which is performed by turning the body and swinging the rear foot about 45 degrees outside uchikata's line of attack, as shown in figure 15.28. The key to successfully performing kara uke is timing. Moving too early allows uchikata to alter course mid-stride and still make contact, so shikata must wait until the last possible moment before moving.

Yoko ayumi (sidestepping) is a method closely related to kara uke. The primary difference between the two is that both feet step to the side in yoko ayumi, whereas in kara uke only the rear foot moves, or the front foot shifts only slightly. Both methods require precise timing. In the example in figure 15.29, shikata has moved just outside uchikata's line of attack, stepping first with the rear foot, then the front foot. Shikata's counterattack is again at a 45-degree angle.

Figure 15.28   Kara uke.

Figure 15.29   Yoko ayumi.

The most difficult of the tenshin waza is tenkan, which is a 180-degree turn as the attacker passes. In the example in figure 15.30, shikata has moved the leading foot just outside uchikata's leading foot during the attack, then used the rotation of the hips to pull the trailing foot to the side as shikata turned 180 degrees to deflect the attack. Tenkan places shikata at roughly a 90-degree angle at uchikata's side and facilitates moving behind uchikata for an indefensible counterattack.

Tenkan is implied by the 180-degree and 270-degree turns performed in many traditional kata.

Figure 15.30   Tenkan.

Kata

Templates

INTRODUCTION

For the first 250 years of karate-dō development, kata were the core of its training and discipline. Until the mid-twentieth century kumite was not a point-scoring contest but rather the Okinawan term for life-or-death combat. Yakusoku kumite and idō kihon were developments of the 1930s, when karate-dō was spreading through Japanese universities and the armed forces.

There are quite a few kata with origins that can be traced fairly accurately, such as the five Pinan (Heian) kata created by Itosu Ankō between 1902 and 1905; Chintō, originated by Matsumura Sōkon in the mid-nineteenth century; and Kōsōkun Dai (originally Kūshankū), created by Sakugawa Kanga sometime after he learned its techniques from its namesake in 1761. There are many more, including Gojūshihō, Wanshū, Niseishi, Naifanchi, and others that have been attributed to several different karate pioneers and whose complete pedigree we will probably never know.

Kata form a tangible link to the origins of karate-dō and to the renowned karateka who created and refined the art through the centuries. They are a lasting gift from the legends of the past to generations they would never know—a bequest through which we can glimpse the minds and culture of those pioneers who shaped this way of life. Kata are the canvasses on which these ancient karate practitioners composed the art of karate-dō. They are an enduring treasure that we can behold and enjoy as well as participate in and share with future generations. Kata are the core, the essence, the beauty, the tradition, the legacy—the heart—of karate-dō.

The traditional kata were created during a turbulent period of Okinawan history, while the Satsuma clan of Kyūshū, Japan, held the island under subjugation. These kata became the repository for the storehouse of knowledge passed down by the ancients. The idea for kata may have actually originated before a system of writing reached the Ryūkyū Islands. It certainly served as a means of preserving and imparting self-defense techniques in secrecy. Legends suggest that ancient Okinawan *odori* (festival dances) were actually kata performed to music, which permitted them to be practiced and taught even under the watchful eyes of the Satsuma overlords, but this may be apocryphal.

Given this history, the techniques in kata were obviously designed to disable or kill an attacker in mortal combat. They were tested and proved in real life-or-death battles against both armed and unarmed aggressors. If the techniques worked, they were preserved in a kata by the survivor and passed on to their disciples.

Until the late nineteenth century it was rare that a teacher would truly know more than a handful of kata. This is because kata contain the entire art of karate-dō, encompassing the full spectrum of both gōhō ("hard" methods, such as punching and kicking) and jūhō ("soft" methods, like joint locks, throws, and chokes). What the pioneers of old gained through a lifetime of study of just a few kata, we now learn through the practice of the great many kata that they cumulatively passed down to the world.

Kata are solo exercises, so their advantage over various forms of kumite is that they can be practiced alone and at almost any time or place. This also means that kata practice requires—and therefore instills—patience, persistence, and discipline. While the different varieties of kumite provide a real opponent, kata must be performed by visualizing the adversaries involved, which stimulates the imagination. Kata also possess a meditative quality, since the mind must be sharply focused to simultaneously remember the movements in their proper sequence and visualize the attackers, requiring that distractions be completely shut out. Additional concentration and mental stimulation come from the contemplation and analysis (bunkai) of the movements to determine their practical application (ōyō) while performing a kata.

There are many ways to classify kata. One of the earliest was to categorize them by their origins as Naha-te, Shuri-te, or Tomari-te. For decades this was thought to relate to the primary town in the area in which they were created, those being the capital city of Shuri, the port city of Naha, and the interisland port of Tomari, just north of Naha. In more recent times, this idea has been brought into question. These three terms appear to have been used first during a demonstration of karate held in 1927 for Kano Jigoro, the creator of jūdō. The performers were Mabuni Kenwa, Kyan Chōtoku, and Miyagi Chōjun, who at that time lived in Shuri, Tomari, and Naha, respectively. It is possible that instead of describing the origins of the kata they performed, these designations may have simply referred to where the three representatives lived. Regardless of how the use of these terms came about, they are still widely used today to categorize kata.

The classification preferred by the authors groups kata by their lineage (*kei*) rather than geographic origin. In this method, kata that were either created by or transmitted primarily by Itosu Ankō, for example, are known as Itosu-kei kata. For a style named in honor of two of its major source sensei, this seems a more logical choice.

Ōyō no Jūyōsei
THE IMPORTANCE OF ŌYŌ

The overriding factor in kata training and performance is ōyō (practical application). The movements in a kata must be performed in a manner that reflects the way those movements would be used in combat. It is not sufficient to merely perform with grace, balance, good posture, speed, and power. The kamae (structure), speed, timing, and performer's state of mind must coincide as closely as possible to how the technique would be applied in actual combat. You cannot just look like you're in combat; you must *be* in combat against an invisible opponent. Otherwise, you are just performing a dance without music and training yourself to lose a fight. This is why kata performance is pointless without diligent bunkai (analysis) and practice of ōyō with a training partner who is behaving in a realistic manner. This concept is so vital that there is a name given to this imaginary opponent: *kasō teki* ("hypothetical enemy").

Kankyū ni Tsuite
UNDERSTANDING TEMPO

It is therefore bunkai and ōyō that should determine the tempo of every kata. While kata designed for beginners follow a steady, plodding pace and each movement is performed with equal speed and force, this is not true of intermediate and advanced kata. The distinctive feature of advanced kata is that they include all the elements of a realistic battle, which is exemplified in changes in tempo (*kankyū*).

Tempo in a kata has the same characteristics as tempo in music and is more than simply rhythm. The richness of a musical piece comes from changes in its beat, the rise and fall of its pitch, the swell and wane of volume, the interplay of staccato and smoothness in transitions from note to note, and the variety of contrasts and harmonies between the different tones and instruments.

The same elements exist in kata, which at different points incorporate both power and subtlety, tension and relaxation, explosive speed and methodical restraint, overpowering aggression and supple yielding, sequences that are quick and choppy, others that are smooth and gliding, graceful transitions, large robust techniques and intricate motions, variations in angles of movement and turning direction, shifts from sturdily braced stances to nimble dance-like footwork, and light agile strikes contrasted with heavy devastating blows. These are the elements a karate practitioner uses to bring a kata to life. But those changes and transitions are not arbitrary, nor are they merely to display the karateka's virtuosity and artistry. They must be the product of realism—the ebb and flow of battle, not merely contrived to impress observers or tournament judges.

Renshū no Junjo
PROGRESSION OF TRAINING

It is impossible to develop all of these aspects of kankyū and realistic application right from the start. They develop over time as you advance in your training. One aspect of this progression, *dai, kyō, soku, kei* (big, powerful, fast, light), was previously described, as well as its more advanced counterpart, *shō, jū, chi, kan* (small, soft, slow, heavy). The order in which kata are introduced to students is designed to facilitate this progression. Coupled with frequent bunkai and experimentation with ōyō, your performance of kata will steadily show greater realism if you keep that goal in mind.

The first kata ordinarily taught to beginners are the "Kihon" kata. Some dōjō teach as many as twelve of these. The "Kihon" kata are not really kata at all. They are patterns of footwork and movement whose purpose is to train new students in the basic concepts of kata performance—kamae, tai sabaki, kihaku, kankyū, chakugan, and so forth—which is why the authors often refer to them as katachi, rather than kata, to help students clearly distinguish between the two concepts.

In Shitō-Ryū we next introduce the Heian kata (called Pinan in Okinawa), which are Itosu-kei (or Shuri-te) kata, plus one or two Mabuni-kei kata, like Shinsei and Kenshū. This is the phase at which kankyū based on ōyō should be emphasized in your training and begin to show in your performance. As an example, figure 16.1 is the sequence of movements for the kata Heian Nidan.

As students reach intermediate level, the curriculum includes more Higaonna-kei (or Naha-te) kata, which many students find more challenging due to their greater emphasis on breath control and alternation between tensing and relaxing the entire body. Some of these include Sanchin, Saifa, and Seienchin.

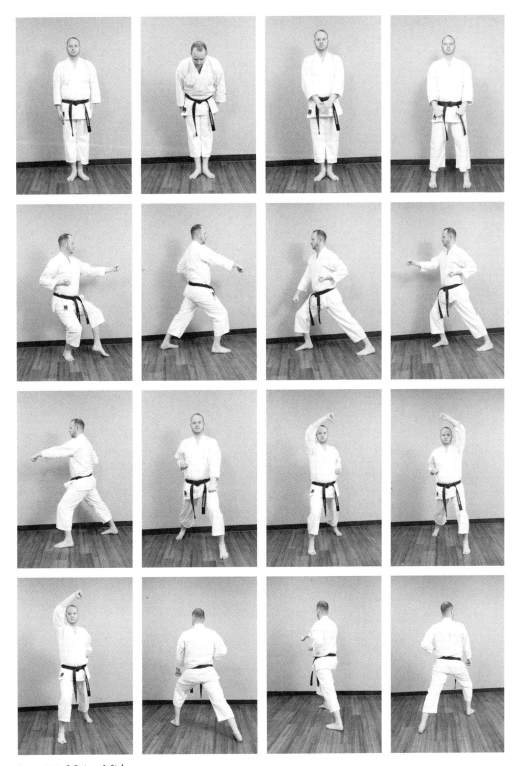

Figure 16.1 Heian Nidan.

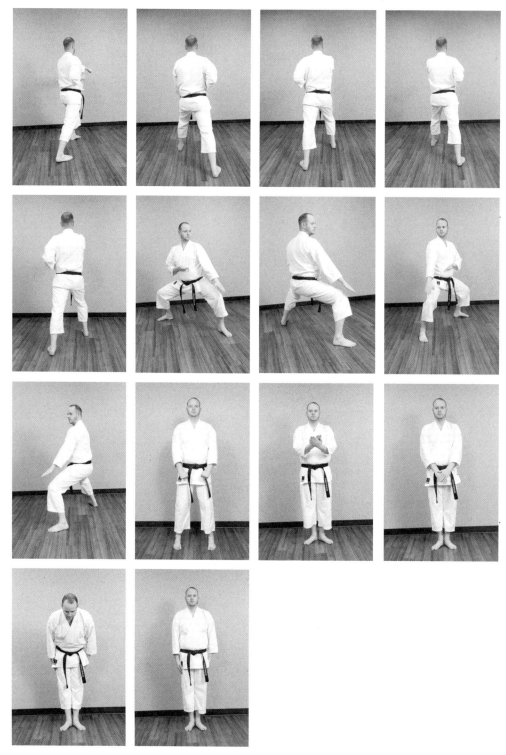

Figure 16.1 *(continued)*

As *yūdansha* (black belts), still more challenging Itosu-kei, Higaonna-kei, Mabuni-kei, Aragaki-kei, and Matsumura-kei kata are added to the karateka's repertoire. A few Matsumora-kei (or Tomari-te) kata such as Tomari Bassai as well as several *sankō* ("consultation") kata borrowed from other styles are also incorporated into the training.

With more than sixty kata in the Shitō-Ryū curriculum, it would be impossible to present and described them all in a single-volume work like this, so we have instead presented only one representative kata to serve as an example. In addition, it is impossible to learn a kata from reading a book. Although videos provide a more complete visualization of the speed, tempo, footwork, and techniques of kata, it is also impossible to learn kata from videos.

There is a Japanese saying that applies to learning complex and multifaceted skills like kata: *manabu no tame ni hyakkai, jukuren no tame ni senkai, satori no tame ni manga okonau* ("a hundred times to learn, a thousand times for proficiency, ten thousand repetitions for complete understanding"). Another popular concept prior to World War II was *ichi kata san nen* ("one kata, three years"). It was generally believed that to master a single kata took three years of diligent training. If a karateka performs a kata ten times per day, it would take ten days to perform it one hundred times, a hundred days to perform it one thousand times, and a thousand days—just under three years—to perform it ten thousand times.

To practice a kata ten times, we recommend performing it slowly three times, each time checking for proper stance, balance, breath control, and other technical issues. Then perform the kata three more times, slightly faster, still concentrating mainly on correct technique. Lastly, perform the kata four times at full speed, thinking less about the technical aspects and instead visualizing the kasō teki (virtual opponent) and focusing on realistic timing, speed, zanshin, combat effectiveness, and kiai.

SHITŌ-RYŪ KATA LIST
ITOSU-KEI

- Kihon (up to 12)
- Heian (Pinan) (1–5)
- Naifanchi (Tekki) (1–3)
- Jutte
- Jion
- Jiin
- Rohai (1–3)
- Bassai (Dai, Sho)
- Kōsōkun (Dai, Sho)
- Gojūshihō

MATSUMURA-KEI

- Matsumura no Bassai
- Matsumura no Rohai
- Wanshū
- Chintō
- Chinte

MABUNI-KEI

- Shinsei
- Kenshū
- Juroku
- Matsukaze
- Kenpaku
- Kensho
- Myojo
- Aoyagi
- Hopposho
- Shinpa
- Shiho Kōsōkun

HIGAONNA-KEI

- Saifa
- Sanchin
- Tenshō
- Sanseiru
- Seipai
- Shisōchin
- Seienchin
- Kururunfa
- Seisan
- Suparinpei

ARAGAKI-KEI

- Sōchin
- Unsū
- Niseishi

In addition to the sixty kata listed above, the curricula of some Shitō-Ryū dōjō include several sankō kata, such as:

- Tomari Bassai
- Pachū
- Heiku
- Paiku
- Anan
- Aragaki Niseishi
- Chatanyara Kūshankū
- Annanko
- Nipaipō
- Haffa
- Hakkaku (Hakutsuru)

Bunkai to Ōyō

Analysis and Application

Bunkai
ANALYSIS

Many of the techniques in kata were long considered secret. In some cases, the nature of the technique was even disguised in some way as it was performed in the kata. To this day, many kata contain techniques that remain secrets in the sense that they are not readily apparent to an untrained observer. This is why the key to understanding and performing kata is bunkai—the study of the application of movements and combinations within kata. The word *bunkai* has the same root as the Japanese term for frame-by-frame instant replay. It means to take apart and analyze, so it implies a minute study of each movement in the kata in order to understand its purpose and its proper relationship to the other movements in the kata.

In a traditional dōjō, bunkai is a combination of instruction and investigation. The sensei will fully explain the application of many movements so the student can begin to understand the principles that govern the construction of kata. However, the sensei will often give only hints and suggestions regarding other techniques. This forces the student to study, contemplate, and experiment in order to discover the deeper meaning, nuances, and variations of technique concealed within the kata.

The application of a traditional kata typically has three increasingly deep levels of insight and development: basic, intermediate, and intended variations.

The simplest level of bunkai is the obvious technique. In essence, this is the application that an untrained observer would visualize for the technique: what looks like a block is a block; what looks like a punch is a punch; and what looks like a kick is a kick. This is sometimes referred to as *omote* ("surface") or *shoden* ("first communication") bunkai.

A more abstract understanding appears at the intermediate level. At this level, kata have subtler shades of meaning that appear to be "hidden behind" or "beneath the surface" to the beginner. One example that appears to be hidden beneath the surface is the *chūdan geri* that is implied, but not always performed, whenever Neko-Ashi Dachi appears in a kata. This type of bunkai is sometimes called *ura waza* ("obscured technique") or *chūden* ("intermediate communication") bunkai.

The third type of bunkai is typically called *kakushide* ("hidden hands") or *okuden* ("deep communication") bunkai. Most kata contain techniques for which their true nature cannot be determined by direct observation—movements that have no obvious application, or the apparent (omote) application simply is not practical or effective against a real attack. In order to understand the bunkai for these techniques, the specific type of attack for which it was designed must be determined. Often, these techniques are kansetsu waza (joint-lock techniques), osaekomi waza (grappling), or nage waza (throws) that either look vaguely like some form of strike or block or are an inexplicable pose. Kata contain many such movements that either have no obvious use or simply would not work if performed in the manner practiced in the kata. These are challenging mysteries to unlock.

In some cases, the attack for which a waza is intended can be inferred from other techniques in the kata. The movements immediately preceding or following a technique often give clues suggesting that the opponent is attempting to strike, grab, or choke you from a particular angle. With this information, it is often possible to determine the nature of the attack for which a "secret" technique was designed. However, some waza require that a knowledgeable sensei disclose the type of attack so that the hidden meaning of a waza can be discovered.

Bunkai is a pointless exercise unless it is accompanied by training in ōyō—the practical application of kata techniques to realistic self-defense situations.

Ōyō
PRACTICAL APPLICATION

Ōyō is the aspect of training in which you apply the lessons and discoveries from bunkai against realistic attacks by a training partner. In some respects, ōyō is the purpose and goal of all karate training: to be able to use the lessons learned in the dōjō to defend your life or protect the lives of others. But in another sense, ōyō may be the least important aspect of training, because it should and will be so seldom, if ever, used.

For intermediate and advanced students who have gained proficiency in the maai (distance control and timing) of kihon, most yakusoku kumite training should focus on ōyō. Ippon kumite and sambon kumite are vital for beginners to develop essential distance, timing, kamae (structure), and correct tai sabaki (body movement) in the performance of kihon. The next phase of training is to use yakusoku kumite to learn to actually use the techniques contained in kata.

Initially, yakusoku kumite is entirely choreographed. Both participants know in advance how uchikata will attack and how shikata will defend. This type of yaku-soku kumite should be used to practice every sequence of a kata in order to fully understand it. Once a karateka has become proficient in most or all techniques from a given kata, uchikata should use any attack from that kata so that shikata must respond more spontaneously. This form of yakusoku kumite is still choreographed in the sense that uchikata and shikata are defined in advance and shikata knows that the attack will be from a given kata. Shikata simply doesn't know in advance which of those attacks will be used. At a more advanced level, uchikata employs an attack from any kata in which uchikata has trained so that shikata must react even more sponta-neously. At this level, yakusoku kumite approaches the realism of a true self-defense situation. The only element of choreography involved is that both know in advance that uchikata will attack and shikata will defend.

Tekiō
ADAPTATION (VARIATIONS)

Tekiō means "adaptation" or "variation." Another common term for variation is *henka*, but *henka* has a connotation of "strange" or "unusual" that does not suit the nature and purpose of tekiō. Tekiō fall into two categories: (1) variations from the specific move-ments in a kata, such as changing a chūdan oizuki to a jōdan hirabasami uchi, and (2) practicing possible follow-up or finishing techniques for the movements contained in a kata, such as adding a fumikomi (stomp) to the opponent's throat following a throw or takedown performed in the kata.

Since tekiō are normally practiced during yakusoku kumite, they provide oppor-tunities for students to express their individuality and experiment. For example, a certain kata might contain just a single block or single counterpunch, but during tekiō training, you might add a throwing technique followed by a simulated disabling or killing strike to the opponent on the ground. Tekiō are limited only by your imagina-tion and the effectiveness of the techniques you choose, and they should be incorpo-rated into yakusoku kumite training by intermediate and advanced karateka.

Jirei
EXAMPLES

To help explain the process involved in bunkai and ōyō, we will use a movement from the kata Heian Nidan as an example, describe how to examine the movement in detail, analyze it (bunkai), and then practice a practical application of that movement with a training partner (ōyō), as well as add a variation (tekiō) to the technique.

Figures 17.1–3 depict the first sequence of movements in the kata Heian Nidan presented in chapter 16: turning 90 degrees to the left with uchi-otoshi, followed by oizuki.

Figures 17.1-3 First sequence of Heian Nidan.

The omote explanation of the uchi-otoshi in figure 17.2 is to block an attack coming from the left side in the manner shown in figure 17.4, then counterattack with oizuki.

Figure 17.4 Blocking attack with uchi-otoshi.

One possible ura waza is to use the identical movement as the kaihō waza kote mawari-hineri to escape from an opponent's wrist grab, as shown in figure 17.5.

Figure 17.5 Using uchi-otoshi as kote mawari-hineri escape.

Another example from Heian Nidan is the series of blocks depicted in figure 17.6.

Figure 17.6 Blocking sequence in Heian Nidan.

The omote interpretation of this sequence is gedan barai followed by three successive age uke performed while stepping forward to keep forcing the opponent off-balance and stumbling backward. While this has merit as a basic strategy, it lacks the element of ichi geki hissatsu—placing the opponent in an indefensible position. A more practical interpretation found by applying the ura waza ("obscured technique") principle is depicted in figures 17.7–17.8.

Figures 17.7-8   Age uke and wantō uchi from Heian Nidan.

In this interpretation, the first two blocks are age uke (fig. 17.7) to drive the opponent back, followed by wantō uchi (fig. 17.8), which renders the opponent incapable of continuing. Even more aggressive would be a single age uke, followed by two wantō uchi, one to each side of the opponent's jaw.

Another example of ura waza from Heian Nidan can be found in the movements depicted in figure 17.9.

Figure 17.9   Final sequence from Heian Nidan.

The typical omote explanation of these movements is a series of four consecutive gedan shutō uke. However, this interpretation once again fails to incapacitate the opponent. One possible ura waza for these gedan shutō uke is depicted in figures 17.10–14.

Figures 17.10-14 Final gedan shutō uke used as kuchiki daoshi.

In this interpretation, as uchikata attacks with oizuki, shikata deflects the punch with the leading arm while stepping into Shiko Dachi (fig. 17.11). At that point, kuzushi (destabilizing) has already been initiated by shikata pressing their knee into the side of uchikata's knee and pushing uchikata rearward with their arm. Shikata completes kuzushi and tsukuri (setup) by grabbing uchikata's leg (fig. 17.12). The kuchiki daoshi throw is completed (kake) by lifting uchikata's leading leg (fig. 17.13) while driving uchikata's torso to the floor with a downward sweep of the arm, finishing in the position shown in figure 17.14. If the impact on the floor or the ground has not already incapacitated uchikata, any number of follow-up techniques (tekiō) can be used once uchikata is down.

An example of kakushide (hidden hands) might be the posture shown in figure 17.15. Heian Yondan, Heian Godan, Naifanchi Shodan, Bassai Dai, Kōsōkun Dai, and several other kata all contain a posture with both hands drawn to one side of the body in this manner, sometimes called *morote hikite* (both hands pulling).

Figure 17.15 Morote hikite position.

Depending on the movements that either precede or follow this posture, it can have many applications. It can be used to yank an opponent off balance and into a strike or throw, or to gain control of an opponent's hand or wrist as part of a kansetsu waza (joint lock technique) or osaekomi waza (grappling technique). In figure 17.16 it is being used for *ushiro hadaka jime* (rear naked choke) to render an opponent unconscious.

Figure 17.16   Ushiro hadaka jime.

Thus, a major reason some techniques are called "kakushide" is that their meaning and use cannot be determined from simple observation, like omote waza, or by considering more practical uses for them, like ura waza. Instead, they must be understood in the context of the movements before or after them in the kata, and their purpose is thus hidden from direct observation. One of the best ways to discover the ura waza and kakushide in kata is through the use of yakusoku kumite during the bunkai process, experimenting with ways a movement in a kata might be applied to a variety of attacks.

Bunkai and ōyō are the essence of karate training. It is only through diligent bunkai and ōyō training that the meaning and purpose of karate are revealed. However, finding the meaning of movements in a kata is the least important aspect of bunkai and ōyō. Their greatest value lies in providing a methodology and a habit of thoroughly analyzing behavior, which allows the karateka to more fully understand the actions of other people and thereby improve personal relationships. Ultimately, it provides us with a method by which to understand and improve our own attitudes, behavior, and character.

Chapter Eighteen

人殺し技

Hitogoroshi Waza

Killing Techniques

Karate is the art of killing. It developed over a period of centuries in the Ryūkyū archipelago, a chain of islands stretching from a little northeast of Taiwan to just south of Kyūshū. These islands were rich in natural beauty and resources and were within easy sailing distance from China, Southeast Asia, Japan, and a multitude of Polynesian islands. Karate developed at a time when many of these surrounding kingdoms were seeking expansion, conquest, and plunder, so for centuries they were under imminent threat of invasion or piracy from any direction. In addition, it developed during the period in which the individual island kingdoms of the Ryūkyūs were conquering one another to form larger kingdoms consisting of clusters of islands, eventually consolidating into just three multiple-island kingdoms by 1322 and ultimately to a single unified kingdom in 1429.

So karate did not develop as a sport. Nor was it created for protection against playground bullies or muggers. In modern times, street fights or barroom brawls come closest to the purpose for which karate was designed, but its real purpose was for life-and-death combat. Its objective was not to score a point, fend off a sucker punch from a drunk, or beat a street thug into submission, but to kill a mortal enemy by any means necessary. It was not designed to be graceful and artistic but rather brutal, bloody, and savage, ending with eyeballs dangling from their sockets or lying in the dirt, bones shattered, joints dislocated, ligaments torn, throats crushed, and men screaming and thrashing in their death throes. Prior to 1900, kumite was not a sporting event; it was savage combat, horrifying and sickening to witness. It was illegal because someone invariably died or was permanently disabled. Either way, a family lost its breadwinner and was financially and emotionally devastated by kumite. The folklore of karate is replete with tales of karate masters who killed one or more opponents in kumite.

In modern times, there are some who scoff at these stories and consider them exaggerations. But the fact is that even if some of their legendary deeds have been embellished over the years, the karate masters of old indeed killed and maimed their opponents. Another legend that is often dismissed as myth is *san-nen goroshi* or *go-nen goroshi*—the ability to execute a strike that causes the opponent to die three or even five years later. It has only been in recent times that medical advances have allowed us to understand how these strikes actually worked and prove such techniques to be possible, rather than mere fables. It has now been medically proved that by striking certain nerve points, bursting blood vessels, or damaging internal organs, a person can die days, weeks, even years later from sepsis, edema, or gradual deterioration of vital organs resulting from these injuries. The many recent cases of delayed brain damage from concussions among professional athletes are conclusive proof of this. A hundred or more years ago, physicians lacked both the knowledge and diagnostic technologies to detect the resulting ailments and treat them. Now the symptoms can be detected and correctly interpreted, making the aftereffects of these strikes readily curable in most cases.

The importance of these legends is in understanding their purpose. Today, when fame—and even infamy—is a quick path to riches, tales of incredible deeds and prowess could be used to increase one's celebrity for profit. But a hundred or more years ago, in isolated areas like the Ryūkyū Islands, there was no monetary gain to be made from such exaggerations. So tales of karateka employing lethal techniques were told for a nobler and more pragmatic purpose: they served as a warning about the dangers and consequences of careless or vindictive use of the deadly art of karate.

Why do you suppose that the legendary karate masters each only had a handful of students at one time? Was it because they really weren't as famous as legend has made them out to be? Or because people back then weren't as interested in learning karate as people are today? No. Prior to the twentieth century, karate sensei were afraid that a student might misuse their teachings to kill or disable someone unjustly. In those times, to be accepted for instruction by a reputable sensei, a potential student had to have a hoshōnin, a sponsor and guarantor. The hoshōnin had to be someone of high standing and impeccable reputation in the community, such as a government official or village head. And the hoshōnin wasn't merely giving a character reference or a letter of recommendation; they were personally guaranteeing the proper conduct of the student. If the student did someday misuse what they had been taught, the hoshōnin would be personally and professionally ruined—and perhaps held legally responsible—as a result. It was not taken lightly, and only a few were able to secure a hoshōnin in order to obtain instruction in karate.

Karate should still be such a terrifying art! If practiced correctly, just like the karateka of old, we should all be afraid to ever use it, except as an absolute last resort. And when we train in the dōjō, that fear should make us practice with unwavering focus, care, and respect for our training partners.

KILLING TECHNIQUES IN KATA

Every technique in every kata is a killing technique if applied in the necessary manner. Notice that we do not say "the appropriate manner" but "the necessary manner." This is a deliberate word choice. In our modern world, it is rarely appropriate to kill, but it is sometimes necessary. Following are just a few examples of techniques that are common to many traditional karate kata and that can kill or disable an opponent.

In figure 18.1, the attacker's punch is being diverted by *osae uke* (suppressing block) with the left hand, while a strike (here *hiraken tsuki*, middle-knuckle spear-hand) is made to the throat. This technique or a variation of it is found in many traditional kata, such as Pachū and Jitte.

Figure 18.1 Potentially lethal strike with hiraken tsuki.

The strike to the throat can itself be lethal if delivered with enough force to damage the esophagus or crush the hyoid bone and prevent breathing (see the close-up in fig. 18.2). But even if this strike is not immediately fatal, by temporarily impairing the opponent's breathing, it provides a few seconds of opportunity to follow up with a lethal technique while the opponent is unable to defend against it. This is a clear example of ichi geki hissatsu. The technique produces a certain kill, either initially or by momentarily preventing the opponent from being able to defend against the fatal follow-up strike.

Figure 18.2 Hiraken tsuki close-up.

Another fairly straightforward example of ichi geki hissatsu is depicted in figure 18.3. Here the opponent's attack has been deflected and their arm grabbed by kakete uke, followed by a strike to the vagus nerve by shutō uchi. This type of counterattack is found in many traditional karate kata, including Kenshū, Kōsōkun (Kūshankū/Kankū) Dai, Tomari-Bassai, and others.

Figure 18.3 Potentially lethal strike with shutō uchi.

With sufficient force and precision, this strike by itself could be fatal. However, more often it will only temporarily stun the opponent, allowing a fatal blow to be made immediately afterward. In addition, the vagus nerve is located in the jugular foramen in the area being struck, and it is the only nerve that is connected directly to the brain stem. The vagus nerve is composed of 80–90 percent afferent nerve fiber, which is sensory fiber conducting information about the state of the body's major organs to the brain. Since the defender's left hand is also applying pressure to the nerves of the attacker's forearm, a powerful strike to the vagus nerve can confuse the brain and disrupt the functioning of one or more internal organs—an action that is sometimes called a kyūsho waza (nervous-system attack) in Japanese. This has the potential to impair a vital organ such as the liver or spleen.

If not diagnosed and treated, the attacker would gradually weaken and could eventually die—long after the kyūsho waza was delivered—from any number of severe disorders that can result from impaired function of the liver, pancreas, spleen, or gallbladder. A hundred years or more ago, such disorders would have been almost impossible to diagnose or treat. With modern diagnostic and imaging technologies, such long-term effects can be diagnosed and cured if medical treatment is sought. Nevertheless, due to the gradual onset of symptoms, a person's health and quality of life might easily be diminished for months or even years by a careless or overzealous application of this technique during practice.

There are many techniques, such as *hirabasami* or *yubibasami* (pictured in fig. 18.4), that are performed in only a few kata. Both of these techniques are designed to crush the windpipe—hirabasami by the force of the strike to the throat and yubibasami by powerfully squeezing and twisting it. Yubibasami is performed in the kata Seisan.

Figure 18.4   Yubibasami.

However, both yubibasami and hirabasami are implied in practically every kata we perform. This is the principle of tekiō (adaptations or variations). Tekiō is the fundamental concept that every technique in a kata—and especially the most basic and common techniques, like chokuzuki and choku geri—can be adapted slightly to address different conditions. So, when we perform chokuzuki chūdan (middle-level straight punch) in Heian Nidan, we must be prepared to alter it to jōdan (high level) or nakadaka ippon-ken (middle-knuckle-protruding fist) if the circumstances warrant. Thus, tekiō provides the understanding that anytime an opponent is vulnerable to it, we can substitute hirabasami or yubibasami for a more basic tsuki (thrusting strike), like a punch in a given kata.

Either hirabasami or yubibasami can be fatal if delivered with sufficient power directly to the windpipe. And even if the technique is slightly deflected or its power dissipated by an opponent's attempt to block or evade it, it will leave the opponent choking or gasping for breath and temporarily unable to defend effectively against a follow-up strike, once again exemplifying ichi geki hissatsu.

A similar example is yonhon nukite tsuki (four-finger spear-hand thrust). Nukite tsuki is a familiar technique to most karateka, and it is found in numerous kata, including Heian Shodan, Heian Sandan, Kōsōkun Dai, Tomari-Bassai, Gojūshihō, and many others. Legends of the lethality of nukite tsuki include claims that it can be used to penetrate the body cavity and tear out the heart or other vital organs. Such claims not only appear spurious, as there is no credible evidence that they have been, or can be, performed, but are unnecessary exaggerations. Even without penetrating the body, yonhon nukite tsuki can be a devastating technique.

Although it is theoretically possible to strike with sufficient force with nukite tsuki to rupture the carotid artery or other major blood vessel, it is an unlikely outcome. More often, nukite tsuki serves as a precision strike rather than a power strike, inflicting sufficient pain to a nerve point (kyūsho) to temporarily disable or disorient the opponent so that a killing blow can be delivered unimpeded. The principle of tekiō allows it to be substituted for any more basic tsuki kata (thrusting attack), and vulnerable targets include the throat and anterior sides of the neck, armpits, and inner thighs—any soft-tissue area in which the nerves run close to the surface.

Common variations of nukite tsuki include ippon nukite (one-finger spear-hand) and nihon nukite (two-finger spear-hand).

Typically, these are used to attack the opponent's eyes because it takes very little power to inflict extreme pain or severe damage to the eyes. A strike that compresses the eyeball no more than a half inch is completely debilitating. Another half inch can cause irreparable damage and blindness. These variations of nukite tsuki do not occur in many kata. However, Chinte is one of the few kata in which nihon nukite tsuki is actually practiced, and ippon nukite tsuki is employed in some versions of Unsū (Unshū). But the principle of tekiō makes these strikes applicable to any kata where the circumstances would warrant its use. Although rarely fatal by itself, an ippon or nihon nukite strike to the eyes would clearly render an opponent incapable of defending against a killing blow, and would constitute ichi geki hissatsu.

In addition to hand strikes, many other parts of the body can be used for ichi geki hissatsu. As shown in figure 18.5, for instance, a powerful blow to the jaw or to the side of the head with the elbow can kill or incapacitate an opponent. In this case, the strike is made to the jaw while pulling the adversary's head sharply forward to increase its impact and torsion on the spinal cord, which is extremely susceptible to damage. If not immediately fatal, such a blow will either temporarily or permanently stun the opponent. This particular strike is found in many kata, including Heian Yondan, Naifanchi Shodan, Kōsōkun Dai, Bassai Dai, and others in which a lateral hiji ate is employed.

Figure 18.5 Hiji ate.

In those kata, the hiji ate strikes the palm of the other hand, which represents pulling the opponent into, or holding the opponent in place during, the strike. Thus, ōyō for this strike allows for pulling the opponent's head forward, as shown in figure 18.5, stretching the spinal cord and causing it to twist as the blow is struck—and thus maximizing the resulting damage to the spine and nervous system.

A similar principle is employed when the head is pulled fiercely downward into a rising hiza ate (knee strike). This technique, found in Heian Yondan and other traditional kata, is far more damaging than it might at first appear. The blow from the knee alone against the side of the head, particularly at the temple, can be enough to stun—or in some cases kill—the opponent. But the severe concussion caused by hiza ate is only part of the damage caused by this technique. As the head is yanked downward, it is also twisted violently to the side, placing severe torsion to the spine an instant before the impact of the knee drives the head upward, causing lateral torsion on the same section of the spine. This sudden, powerful bidirectional movement will either sprain or break the neck of the opponent.

One of the best examples of a technique that is rarely lethal in and of itself and yet should definitely be considered ichi geki hissatsu is kansetsu geri (joint kick). As shown in figure 18.6, kansetsu geri is completely debilitating to an opponent. Dislocating a major joint like the knee not only immobilizes the opponent but also inflicts unbearable pain, rendering them almost completely helpless. Even if the kansetsu geri is unsuccessful in dislocating the targeted joint, it will normally cause the opponent to lose balance or fall—either of which will leave them exposed to a lethal follow-up technique. Kansetsu geri are found in numerous traditional karate kata, including Bassai Dai, Sanseirū, Pachū, and many others.

Figure 18.6   Kansetsu geri.

The most common kick found in traditional kata is choku geri (straight kick). The majority of kata contain at least one choku geri. The main targets for choku geri include the pubic symphysis, groin, and inner thighs. None of these targets is likely to produce a fatality, yet a forceful kick to any of them is sufficient to be considered ichi geki hissatsu. For instance, a kick to the groin will cause such intense pain that the opponent will be unable to defend against a subsequent strike of any kind. A kick to the inner thigh, where main nerve branches serving the legs lie close to the surface, is nearly as painful and will normally cause the leg to buckle and no longer support the opponent. A powerful choku geri to the pubic symphysis is capable of breaking the cartilage connection and possibly the bone itself, which is not only immediately debilitating but will also incapacitate the opponent for weeks.

These examples serve to illustrate another key point: like the hands, the feet also have multiple striking surfaces. Any of these striking surfaces might be employed in a given situation, based on the location and angle of attack for the target area being struck. The side of the foot (sokutō) was used for the kansetsu geri, while the top of the foot (sokkō) was used for the kick to the groin. For a kick to the pubic symphysis, the ball of the foot (jōsokutei) would be used. Once again, when practicing kata it should be remembered that while choku geri might be the kick normally performed in a given kata, the actual target and angle of attack may dictate that a different kicking surface or other variation of the kick be used.

The foregoing contact areas are by no means an exhaustive listing but include the majority of those found in the most widely practiced kata. As you study advanced kata and their ōyō, you will discover a myriad of additional striking areas and ways to employ them.

Ken o Koroshi, Ki o Koroshi, Waza o Koroshi
KILL THE WEAPON, KILL THE SPIRIT, KILL THE TECHNIQUE

We do not have to directly kill the body to achieve ichi geki hissatsu. There are three other methods: *ken o koroshi* (kill the fist), *ki o koroshi* (kill the spirit), and *waza o koroshi* (kill the technique). Destroying the opponent's weapon—their striking hand or arm, or their kicking leg or foot—can render them helpless to defend themselves further.

Many kata contain techniques to perform ken o koroshi (kill the fist, meaning kill the weapon). A method found in many kata is to damage the opponent's striking arm. In some kata, like Nipaipō and Shisōchin, instead of merely blocking the opponent's punch, the defender traps the fist with one arm and strikes just above the elbow with uchi uke (striking block) using the other arm. The blow is delivered just as the opponent's arm has reached full extension, elongating the tendons around the elbow and making it especially vulnerable to dislocation. Dislocating the elbow not only renders that arm useless for further attack but inflicts extreme pain that impairs the opponent's ability to defend against counterattack. The shutō uke performed in numerous kata can be used as a variation of this, as depicted in figure 18.7.

Figure 18.7 Using shutō uke for ken o koroshi.

Another common method of ken o koroshi is the yoko gedan barai in Shiko Dachi found in many kata. Figure 18.8 shows how gedan barai can be used as an elbow dislocation, often following a strike to the face, as in the kata Shinsei and Seienchin.

Figure 18.8   Using gedan barai for ken o koroshi.

Several other kata provide additional methods of elbow or shoulder dislocation, including Seipai (fig. 18.9) and Kururunfa (fig. 18.10). Obviously, an opponent whose arms have been disabled is helpless, which is undoubtedly why techniques of this kind are found in so many kata.

Figure 18.9 Seipai
elbow dislocation.

Figure 18.10 Kururunfa
elbow dislocation.

Ki o koroshi (kill the spirit) is achieved by breaking the opponent's confidence. This is achieved with a combination of physical skill, relentless seme, and overwhelming kihaku that crushes the opponent's spirit and makes them feel incapable of defeating you.

Waza o koroshi (kill the technique) is accomplished through superior use of maai (distance control) and sen (initiative) that makes it impossible for the opponent to mount a successful attack. This is a major reason that various forms of kumite are so vital to karate training. Mastery of maai is mastery of the opponent through waza o koroshi.

A basic example of waza o koroshi using maai and sen is depicted in figures 18.11–12. Uchikata, on the left, is poised to attack. Sensing uchikata's intention, shikata drives forward, intercepting uchikata in mid-stride and striking with jōdan oizuki (fig. 18.12), thus destroying uchikata's technique.

Figures 18.11-12 Waza o koroshi.

The practice of kata is much more than the memorization and repetition of a specific sequence of techniques. The purpose of practicing of kata is to understand and be capable of using its ōyō—the pragmatic application of its techniques to produce ichi geki hissatsu. If you do not yet understand how a technique in a kata will render your opponent incapable of defending against your counterattack, you do not yet understand the kata.

The training required to learn the sequence of movements in a kata, practice them sufficiently to become proficient in them, perform the bunkai (analysis) of those techniques, and train until they become an instinctive response to simulated attacks in yakusoku kumite, jūhō, and jiyū kumite takes years. The ancient saying *ichi kata san nen* ("one kata, three years") is no exaggeration.

In order to unlock the okuden bunkai and many of the deadliest techniques of karate-dō, you must practice, analyze, and experiment with the kata for years. This may seem like reinventing the wheel, but karate has always been intended as a process of discovery, not explanation. Centuries ago, karate sensei understood that knowledge that comes without effort or sacrifice is not appreciated or retained as readily as knowledge that must be earned. So we encourage you to begin exploring the mysteries of kata today!

By now it should be clear that the essence of karate is ichi geki hissatsu, meaning both that a single counterattack should result in a certain kill, and perhaps more importantly, that our response to the opponent's first attack should be so devastating that it leaves them incapable of launching a second attack.

Too many students mistake ichi geki hissatsu as merely encompassing techniques that are so powerful that one blow will kill an opponent, or that the strike is so powerful that it can penetrate through the opponent's block. Such notions are only a superficial understanding of a certain kill in one attack. The true meaning of ichi geki hissatsu is employing a technique that is so effective that the opponent cannot successfully defend against it.

CONCLUSION
KARATE-DŌ IS THE ART OF KILLING

The concept of ichi geki hissatsu is fundamental to every aspect of the art: physical combat, strategy and tactics, ideology, personal character, and the spirit. It is important to remember that the main purpose of the art is to develop your skills to such a lethal level that you never have to use them. The fact that you can kill with a single blow does not mean you must kill. In fact, it should make you hope you never have to use it in earnest.

Every karateka faces two possible paths: katsujinken (the life-giving fist) or satsujinken (the death-inducing fist). A life literally depends on the choice we make in a fraction of a second after being attacked. Which will *you* choose? The dire implications of that question alone should terrify you!

Chapter Nineteen

組手

Kumite

Sparring

INTRODUCTION

No matter how solid your proficiency in fundamentals may become, the practice of kihon alone at the expense of applying the principles of footwork, timing, balance, and distance control against an opponent will not enable you to prevail in self-defense situations.

In most traditional dōjō, the first step in developing footwork, balance, and timing is idō kihon. Literally translated, idō kihon is "moving basics," but in practice, idō kihon should entail much more than simply performing basic blocks, punches, and kicks while moving from stance to stance. To be most instructive, your practice should involve the integration of stances, directional movement, and body-shifting (tenshin) together with realistic combinations of blocking and counterattacking techniques. For this reason, we prefer to think of and practice idō kihon as "combinations" rather than merely "moving basics."

A step further than idō kihon is training with a partner to practice proper defending and counterattacking distances, to hone reactions to attacks with realistic speed and timing, and to learn correct positioning to strike appropriate target areas on real opponents of varying sizes. Practicing predetermined attack-and-defense maneuvers with a partner is generally referred to as yakusoku kumite (prearranged sparring), which in turn falls into three major categories:

1. *ippon kumite* (one-step sparring)
2. *sambon kumite* (three-step sparring)
3. *yakusoku kumite* (prearranged sparring other than ippon or sambon kumite)

From the very onset of karate training, the above three forms of kumite should be practiced in conjunction with one another, each increasing in difficulty and realism as the student's competence improves.

For the beginning student these early stages of practice are far from realistic since the primary goal is to begin developing timing and distance-control under highly controlled conditions. As students advance, the complexity and difficulty of the techniques and footwork steadily increases, together with the degree of realism in the training exercises. As students approach black belt, ido kihon involve intricate footwork and evasion methods and utilize advanced blocking and counterattacking techniques. These sophisticated techniques are also employed in both ippon kumite and sambon kumite, along with a variety of yakusoku kumite exercises to resemble realistic "street defense" situations.

Yakusoku Kumite
PARTNER TRAINING

Yakusoku kumite can be a stimulating and rewarding training method when used imaginatively. Yakusoku kumite is not constrained by the formality of ippon or sambon kumite. Instead, it can involve attacks against a walking or seated defender, attacks that imitate a robbery, attacks involving simulated weapons, attacks by multiple opponents, and similar situations beyond the parameters and structure of other forms of partner training. Most importantly, it should be used to practice the ōyō of techniques found in kata.

IPPON KUMITE: *ONE-STEP SPARRING*

This is the most basic form of partner training. At the beginning levels it is highly structured so that students know exactly what to expect and how to react. This provides a vital measure of safety while beginning students are trying to learn the rudiments of timing and distance-control. As students progress, the degree of structure can be modified to resemble unexpected attacks to create a more realistic environment, while ippon kumite should also incorporate body-shifting (tenshin) techniques as soon as students have grown accustomed to linear movement, as depicted in figures 19.1–6.

Figures 19.1-6 Example of ippon kumite.

In the example, after the formal courtesies, uchikata (left) and shikata (right) both take Heikō Dachi at uchima (striking distance) as their preparatory kamae (fig. 19.1). Uchikata steps back into Zenkutsu Dachi with gedan barai and kiai (fig. 19.2). The kiai serves as a warning for the safety of shikata. Uchikata then steps forward with the prearranged attack—in this case chūdan oizuki in Han-Zenkutsu Dachi, which shikata defends with any technique they choose. In this instance, shikata uses gedan barai, immediately followed by chūdan gyakuzuki (fig. 19.3).

As students progress in skill and experience, the variety of attacking techniques employed by uchikata increases to include all basic hand strikes and kicks. Shikata may respond to uchikata's predetermined attack with any defensive technique they choose. Shikata should kiai on the final movement of their counterattack as a signal to uchikata that it is safe to disengage. The variety of defensive techniques and counterattacks also increases as students progress. Gōhō, jūhō, and combinations of the two should be employed.

After the final counterattack by shikata, both partners step back in Jiyū Kamae and return to their starting positions with zanshin, as shown in figure 19.5. It is vital to habitually behave as if your training partner will attack again if you provide the slightest opening or opportunity. The participants return to Heikō Dachi (fig. 19.6) in preparation for the next round, taking turns in the roles of shikata and uchikata.

SAMBON KUMITE: *THREE-STEP SPARRING*

Sambon kumite (fig. 19.7) is essentially a modification of ippon kumite, designed to add the factor of multiple attacks by the practice aggressor. One of the shortcomings of ippon kumite is that a real attacker would seldom try only a single attacking technique but would instead follow up with one or two additional strikes. Sambon kumite adds this element to the training program, while maintaining the safety of the structured environment of yakusoku kumite. In its earliest phases, sambon kumite will often employ repetitions of the same attacking technique, gradually advancing to widely varied combinations.

Figure 19.7 Example of sambon kumite.

GOSHINJUTSU: *SELF-DEFENSE TECHNIQUES*

A form of yakusoku kumite that some dōjō practice as a separate activity is goshinjutsu (self-defense techniques). The concept is to set up common contemporary self-defense scenarios, like purse-snatching, parking-lot assault, kidnap attempts, and the like so that students can practice defensive and counterattacking techniques.

JIYŪ KUMITE: *FREE SPARRING*

Soon after karate-dō was introduced into Japanese universities early in the twentieth century, karate instructors began to develop kumite into a form of safe karate practice. By 1935, jiyū kumite (free sparring) was being routinely practiced at many, if not most, university karate clubs in Japan. In November 1936 the All-Japan Collegiate Karate Union was formed, and soon after, the various clubs regularly met for what was termed *kōkan geiko* ("exchange training"), but which were actually loosely controlled tournaments. As the popularity of karate-dō rapidly spread in the 1950s, tournament kumite (jiyū kumite) quickly gained in popularity as well, so the establishment of widely accepted contest rules and governing bodies was inevitable. By the early 1960s, tournament kumite was so popular that the Zen Nippon Karate-dō Renmei (Federation of All-Japan Karate-dō Organizations, commonly called FAJKO) was organized in 1964 to establish consistent rules and judging criteria that would apply to all the major styles represented in karate competition. By 1970 the practice of karate-dō and tournament competition had grown so popular internationally that the World Union of Karate Organizations (WUKO) was formed to disseminate standardized tournament rules throughout the world. Kumite is now a significant feature of karate tournaments ranging from small dōjō matches to massive international championships involving thousands of competitors.

Whether for sport or for self-defense on the streets, the principles of victorious kumite are the same. The difference is whether or not there are rules. Winning in kumite starts from the ground up. It begins with stance (kamae), controlling the distance from your opponent (maai), footwork and timing, speed, and determination to win. It starts from the ground up, but it works from the top down. Your attitude, determination, discipline, strategy, and technical knowledge—the mental aspects of the art—are what propel your body to victory.

Kamae ni Tsuite
PROPER STRUCTURE

Structure, called kamae in Japanese, is literally the foundation for victorious kumite. With the proper foundation, you have mobility, speed, power, balance, timing, and protection against attack. The principle underlying a correct Jiyū Kamae (Sparring Stance) is always to be ready for attack or defense. Kamae is a joint effort of the mind and body.

Kokoro gamae ("heart structure") means having the mind focused on victory. So, while you are setting your feet, testing the feel of the floor, and raising your hands into position for kumite, set your mind and attitude resolutely on winning.

Jiyū Kamae (fig. 19.8) is a variation of Han-Zenkutsu Dachi that provides the best combination of stability and mobility, but with the heel of the rear foot slightly elevated and the leg bent to provide even greater spring for charging forward. Your weight should be distributed about 60 percent on the front leg and 40 percent on the rear leg, so you are already encroaching into your opponent's space, yet you should feel as if you could instantly spring in any direction. Do not lean forward! This invasive shift of your weight is accomplished by bending the front knee so your whole body is lowered, not by leaning forward. Your back must be kept straight.

Your hips should be turned outward a little more than in Han-Zenkutsu Dachi, so your upper body is slanted to reduce your frontal target areas. This angling of the upper body is called hanmi. Keep your behind slightly tucked in so that your hips are not drawn away from your opponent and your posterior does not protrude. Withdrawing the hips (called *heppiri-goshi*—"cowardly hips") not only tilts your body forward but impairs your stability, reduces your speed of movement, and robs your techniques of hip-rotation power.

Protect the ribs of your forward side by keeping your elbow tucked close in—about one fist's distance from the floating ribs—and your fist at about chin level. This leaves almost no exposed target area on the leading edge of your body and prevents a direct punch to the face without impairing your own view. The trailing fist should be held about midway between the solar plexus and the elbow of the front arm to close off any openings to the front of the body. Your shoulders should be square, not hunched in, so the chest is open for ease of breathing. The shoulders must also be relaxed. Tension in the shoulders raises them and impedes movement of the arms. Both hands should be aligned directly toward the opponent's centerline (seichūsen).

The seichūsen of the body is an imaginary vertical line that leaves half of the visible width of the body on each side of it. Thus, when you are directly facing someone, your centerline splits you in half, passing directly through your nose and belly button.

If you turn 45 degrees to the side, your seichūsen bisects the forward eye and a point halfway between your belly button and hip on the leading side.

Face directly toward the opponent with your head upright and neck straight. Your chin should be slightly tucked in, but without tilting the head downward. Keep your facial muscles relaxed and without noticeable expression. Furrowed eyebrows are a sign of excessive body tension and wasted energy. Instead of being intimidating to an opponent, they are a sure sign of anxiety and self-doubt. A calm, unreadable expression is far more disconcerting than a grimace.

Figure 19.8 Jiyū Kamae.

From this basic posture, you will continually adjust your angle of stance, distance from the opponent, arm and hand positions, and leading foot to react to the shifting and movement of your adversary. Until the moment that you initiate an attack or counterattack, you will constantly be adapting to the opponent so that you are always in a position to attack instantly while being fully shielded against an attack.

Maai ni Tsuite
CONTROLLING DISTANCE

Success in kumite is determined primarily by distance. The contestant who controls the distance controls the outcome of the match. Whoever can first enter into striking distance with an effective technique wins, so maai (confrontation distance) is the fundamental science of kumite. The basis of maai is found in three crucial components: (1) speed—to close distances faster; (2) range—to cover more distance in a single movement; and (3) angle—to shift to an angle that allows you to strike the opponent while preventing the opponent from striking you.

Basic sparring distance is issoku ichi geki no maai, "one stride away from attacking." Another frequently used term for this is *uchima*. An easy way to measure this distance is for both opponents to extend their leading arms until their fists touch while in Jiyū Kamae. From this distance, one combatant must take a full step in order for either of them to strike the other. For adults, this places their front feet about four feet apart.

The essence of maai, then, is to remain closer to your opponent than they are to you. This makes you safe from attack while keeping your opponent within your attacking range. Therefore, you must either be able to cover the distance separating you faster than your opponent, or to travel more distance at the same speed as your opponent.

Stance (kamae) is the first secret to maai. Keeping your stance forward, as we described earlier, so that you are already encroaching into the opponent's protective zone, places you effectively closer than an opponent whose weight is shifted back. With both knees bent, you can launch yourself forward with greater speed than could someone in a stiff stance.

The front knee is especially crucial to kamae, and therefore to maai. With the front knee bent well forward, you are extremely mobile. Without moving your feet, you can shift your body backward nearly two feet to avoid an attack, then instantly drive forward to deliver a counterattack. This alone effectively places you two feet closer to your opponent than they are to you. With your center of gravity ahead of the midpoint between your feet, you are in a position similar to that of a sprinter in the running blocks, ready to catapult yourself toward the target with more effective use of the driving power of both legs.

A forward-bearing stance is also one of the first manifestations of kihaku (strong spirit). Confidence, coupled with unwavering determination to win, will impel you toward your opponent. Strong ki also suppresses the opponent's spirit, either physically pressuring them back through encroachment, or by intimidating the opponent into losing confidence. If your opponent is held at bay by your kihaku, then you have gained the advantage in maai. It is said that Miyamoto Musashi exuded such overpowering ki that even his mightiest and bravest adversaries felt like mice cowering under the gaze of a starving lion when they faced him in battle. It is a serious mistake to overlook or underestimate the value of kihaku in kumite.

Giryō (superior proficiency) is another key factor in maai. The discipline to invest more hours and more effort in training pays dividends in greater expertise. The countless repetitions that lead to faster movement, longer strides, and faster reflexes are rewarded with victory over opponents who lack the determination and discipline to push themselves. In championship-level matches, the margin of victory is often only hundredths of a second, but those precious hundredths of a second were gained through an investment of hours of training.

A margin of tenths or hundredths of a second is often the difference in reaction time. *Shunpatsu ryoku*, or reflex speed, is therefore another crucial aspect of maai. If you move with equal speed and cover the same distance as your opponent, but you react first, you will obviously strike first. Quick reflexes are, quite simply, the product of experience. Each time you face an opponent in training, you improve your ability to judge an opponent's intentions, timing, speed, and range. Once you have developed fast reflexes, you must be prepared mentally—with determination and kihaku—and physically—with solid basics, good kamae, and superior skill (giryō)—to take the correct action that your reaction has initiated.

Sen ni Tsuite
USING INITIATIVE

In kumite, victory is exclusively the result of sen: initiative. This would seem axiomatic since you cannot win solely through defense. You must make some kind of attack or counterattack—thus using initiative—in order to defeat an opponent. Of course, proper technique, accuracy, speed, timing, and power are all part of the equation as well, but none of these factors have any effect without the initiative (sen) to carry them out.

This initiative in karate-dō is extremely subtle and has two distinct shadings: *sen no sen* (preemptive initiative) and *go no sen* (counterattack initiative). The common thread is that both counterattacking and preemptive attacking involve initiative—moving to the opponent. The major difference between the two is in the timing of the attack. A good karateka can employ either sen no sen or go no sen so that an opponent cannot readily anticipate which type of initiative they will face.

Go no sen, counterattacking initiative, is more commonly used by beginning and intermediate karate practitioners because it is easier to learn. However, go no sen is not waiting for the opponent to attack and then blocking and counterattacking. Instead, go no sen is counterattacking at the same instant the opponent attacks.

Figure 19.9 is an example of go no sen, in which the karateka at right waits for the opponent's attack, blocks it, then counterattacks with gyakuzuki. This defensive strategy is usually ineffective in kumite. Nimble opponents can dart away quickly enough after their attack has been blocked to evade the counterattack.

Figure 19.9 Go no sen, example 1.

Figure 19.10 depicts a more effective application of the go no sen concept. At the same moment the student at the left begins their attack, the defending student moves in to meet the attack with a simultaneous *sashite uke* and gyakuzuki counterattack, using the opponent's attacking momentum to close the distance and to add force to the counterattack. The goal of go no sen is to react so swiftly to the opponent's attack that your counterattack lands at the same moment the opponent's strike would have landed.

Figure 19.10 Go no sen, example 2.

Another go no sen method that results in the attacker being struck at the moment they would have delivered their intended blow is shown in figure 19.11. In this scenario, the karateka on the right uses tenshin (evasion) to step slightly off-line from the opponent's attack, so it misses by the barest of margins. Without blocking, the karateka on the right counterattacks with sokutō geri to the ribs.

Figure 19.11 Go no sen, example 3.

A more advanced, and even more exactingly timed, form of initiative is the pre-emptive counterattack, which is often called sen no sen. Sen no sen requires sensing the opponent's intention to attack and initiating the counterattack an instant before the opponent's attack is actually launched, as shown in figure 19.12.

Figure 19.12 Sen no sen.

In sen no sen, the karateka on the right sensed the opponent's intention to attack and lunged forward with a jōdan oizuki counterattack a split second before the opponent began their attack.

Sen no sen requires exquisite sensitivity to the opponent's body language and anticipation of their reactions. The Japanese sometimes call this sensitivity *teki no shinchi o minuku*, or "reading the opponent's mind." Of course, this skill does not involve any paranormal ability to read an adversary's thoughts, but rather the experience from years of training to anticipate an opponent's intentions to such an extent that the preemptive counterattack makes it appear like mind-reading.

In sen no sen especially, it is often best to precipitate the opponent's attack in order to more easily anticipate it and make a timely counterattack. This is done by combining timing and distance (maai), either in the form of a fake, a stutter-step, a timing change, or an encroachment into the attacking range of the opponent.

While this is a relatively simple concept to state in theory, it can only be achieved in practice through countless hours of repetitive training in the dōjō. It requires the discipline to endure hundreds of early failures before your senses and technique are honed to the point at which you can succeed more often than fail in this strategy, which is why sen no sen is primarily a tactic of more advanced karateka, who first perfected the use of go no sen.

In the final analysis, the terms *go no sen* and *sen no sen* are meaningless. There are really only two counterattacking methods: *go* and *sen*. You are either waiting to act until the opponent begins their attack (go) or you are preemptively counterattacking before the opponent begins to move (sen). Everything is merely a variation of one or the other.

Shin-Gi-Tai
MIND-TECHNIQUE-BODY

Flawless kumite is the product of the integration of the mind, technique, and the body. Mental preparation alone, without solid technique or physical conditioning, will not prevail against another trained karate practitioner. Similarly, technical proficiency without the knowledge and spirit to apply it, and the physical ability to carry it out, will fail. Neither will a strong body, without an equally strong mind and the technical expertise, be sufficient to triumph over a skilled karate practitioner.

The most important of these three elements is shin (mind). As we mentioned in chapter 7, *shin* is an alternative pronunciation of 心 (kokoro), and it is a concept vital to much of martial arts philosophy. We examined ken shin ichi nyo, for instance, in chapter 6, as well as the subject of kokoro itself. There are a number of other related concepts, like *shin-ki-ryoku* (mind-spirit-power), that are similar to, or interrelated with, each other. Kokoro is the heart—literally and figuratively—of ichinen (determination), and determination is the foundation of kumite.

Without the determination to win, you should not even face an opponent in kumite. In truth, if you have not decided that you will win, you have decided that you will lose. No amount of training and no extreme of technical knowledge will be of any value if you have not decided to use them to achieve victory.

We often tell students that in any given match, the person who will win is the one who is most determined. Students sometimes misunderstand this to mean that all they have to do is face their opponent with a resolute spirit and they are assured of victory. This is not what we mean at all.

Determination to win means having the discipline to prepare to win. Preparation is an investment in your future success. It is not the strength of will during kumite which brings success; it is the hours invested perfecting the basics, practicing techniques again and again until they become instinctive, which results in victory. Those hours of diligent training spent long before the kumite match begins are the product of true determination.

An aspect of mental training that receives little attention in most of the articles and books we have read is the philosophy of karate-dō. While many references touch on some of the subjects we have discussed in this book, few make the connection between philosophy and technique in a broad sense. An integral part of technique is the character of the karate practitioner employing it. If their character is seriously flawed, then the technique will be equally flawed.

This is why it is so important to pursue perfection of character in life, and it is the reason why karate-dō is a way of life rather than simply a collection of self-defense techniques.

The philosophical foundation of karate-dō is precisely that: a foundation. It must be the basis for all mental development, and that mental development flows into technique. Punches and kicks thrown in rage or hatred are far less effective that those employed in the calm and relaxed state of heijōshin. Not only does anger cause excessive muscle tension, which robs techniques of their power, but it constricts blood vessels, impeding the flow of oxygen and releasing toxins into the bloodstream. It also creates tunnel vision and slows thinking and reaction time. An attack motivated by hatred or jealousy is always inhibited, if only slightly, by the nagging doubts of a guilty conscience, and is physically damaging as well.

The philosophy of karate-dō leads to pure motives, which permits techniques to be employed with complete confidence and peace of mind. Knowing that you are justified in defending yourself, you can unleash the full combined power of your mind, spirit, and body without the shackles of guilt. With a relaxed mind, your reflexes and intellect will be operating at peak efficiency, and your body will be unhampered by toxins. Without this philosophy, there is both the subconscious restraint of guilt and the physiological hindrances reducing the speed, power, and accuracy of your techniques.

Kihon o Manabu
EMPHASIZE THE FUNDAMENTALS

Victory in kumite against a veteran challenger cannot be achieved by flamboyant or intricate techniques. There are no secret attacks that no one can block. Instead, the true secret of success in kumite is emphasis on the fundamentals. Only by perfecting your use of correct stances, refining the mechanics of movement and footwork, undertaking constant repetition to increase your speed and power, and achieving flawless control of timing and distance with your opponent can you consistently achieve victory in kumite. The secret of kumite, then, as with all other aspects of karate-dō, comes back to discipline and determination.

If you have sufficient resolve to practice the fundamentals when your opponents are practicing the spectacular crowd-pleasing techniques, and the discipline to train harder and practice longer than your adversaries, then you can be assured of victory over them.

TOURNAMENT KUMITE

There is a major difference between what we refer to as "traditional kumite" versus "sports kumite." Traditional kumite can be witnessed through watching the karateka performing good, focused, and powerful effective technique as one would observe in a true combat situation. This is true budō. For this type of kumite, it is imperative that the karateka be trained under the watchful eye of a traditional kumite instructor. Winning in traditional kumite is based on what is called *ippon shobu* (one-point match), meaning "one encounter, one chance," the same principle as ichi geki hissatsu. The mental focus during these types of matches necessitates the determination to win a life-or-death encounter. Through this type of training, one will develop compassion and respect for one's opponent.

Sports kumite is based on fundamentals that emphasize explosiveness, speed, flexibility, plyometrics, and overall physical conditioning. The matches are determined by the continual scoring of points throughout the match. This allows an athlete the ability to improve the outcome after an initial point loss. For this type of training, a well-developed coaching system as well as a Western-style coach is the preferred method of instruction. The mental focus of the sports kumite athlete is the unwavering determination to win. This develops a mental attitude that one can overcome great obstacles through hard work and committed practice.

TO COMPETE OR NOT TO COMPETE

That is the question. Knowing that a major emphasis of this book is that karate is not a sport, you may be wondering why we devoted so much of this chapter to the topic of tournament kumite. Our misgivings are chiefly a matter of the degree of emphasis placed on sports karate. Based on decades of personal observation, we are convinced that excessive emphasis on sports competition is contrary to the purpose of karate, but that does not mean that competitive sparring cannot be a part of a well-rounded, effective training regimen.

Occasionally entering a competition in order to experience the pressure of an opponent attacking with full speed and power, as if trying to kill you, and testing your reactions and state of mind under those conditions, can be a valuable learning and training tool, provided you remain cognizant of the limitations that are imposed on technique for safety reasons. So we do not discourage students from participating periodically in tournaments.

What we believe is detrimental about competitive karate is when winning tournaments becomes the major focus of training. When that occurs, far too much emphasis is placed on techniques and strategies that are ineffective in real combat but can score points under the tightly controlled conditions and rigid rules of tournament play. An allegory would be to devote most of your time and training to preparing for and winning squirt gun fights. The skills and strategies applicable to squirting an opponent with a water pistol with an effective range of ten feet or less are wholly inadequate for a real gunfight at twenty yards.

Karate-dō to Kobujutsu
Karate and Ancient Weapons

KARATE WEAPONS

Beginning with the deluge of martial arts movies in the late 1960s, scenes such as the flamboyant nunchaku wielding of Bruce Lee have made the ancient weaponry of Okinawa nearly as well known in the western hemisphere as karate-dō itself. Most people with an interest in any type of martial arts have at least a passing familiarity with such Okinawan weapons as the bō, sai, nunchaku, tonfa, and kama. Even those who would not recognize their names have seen these weapons employed in action movies. Many of these weapons actually predate the emergence of karate-dō—including its earlier forms as te or Okinawa-te—by several centuries.

Since the stances, turns, principles of movement, and kata of these Okinawan weapons are visually similar to those of karate-dō, most people (other than budōka) have come to think of them as "karate weapons." Many instructors even incorporate training in one or more of these weapons into their karate curriculum, as if the two disciplines were a single combined art. The fact that most karate tournaments offer opportunities to compete in weapons or "kobudō" divisions may also foster this impression. Such confusion is one reason that every karateka should understand something of the weapons arts of Okinawa and their relationship with karate.

Weapons, in a general sense, are called *buki* in Japanese. The martial arts performed with buki are called kobudō, which translates literally as "ancient peacemaking ways," or kobujutsu ("ancient peacemaking arts"). Kobudō itself has two major types: Nippon kobudō (Japanese kobudō), and Okinawa (or sometimes Ryūkyū) kobudō

(kobudō of Okinawa or the Ryūkyū Islands). These two major categories are dramatically different.

Nippon kobudō are the ancient weapons arts that developed on mainland Japan. They are chiefly the weapons of the samurai, which include the sword (iaijutsu and kenjutsu), the spear (yarijutsu or sōjutsu), the halberd (naginata-jutsu), the six-foot staff (bōjutsu), the four-foot staff (jōjutsu), the bow and arrow (kyūjutsu), the police truncheon (juttejutsu), as well as many specialized weapons, like the *sode-garama* ("sleeve-tangler"), too numerous to cover here. In addition to the weapons themselves, Nippon kobudō encompasses such military disciplines as horsemanship (bajutsu) and swimming in armor (suieijutsu), among many others. Most of these arts evolved into highly systematized schools of instruction with strict protocol and formality in their training, as befitted the dignity, demeanor, and high social status of the samurai caste and their wide-ranging roles as professional soldiers, government administrators, and diplomats.

Okinawa kobudō, on the other hand, are defensive arts that utilize a variety of tools and implements as makeshift weapons. Some of these articles could be found on any farm or fishing boat, such as poles (*bō*), sickles (*kama*), wooden handles (*tonfa*), hoes (*kuwa*), flails (*nunchaku*), pitchforks (*nunte*), and oars (*eku* or *kai*). The two major exceptions were the *sai*, a police truncheon, and the *sansetsu-kon*, a three-section staff brought to Okinawa by Chinese emissaries and military officials.

It is a mistake to think that because most of these implements were used by farmers and fishermen, they were weapons of Okinawan peasants. They were simply items that people could quickly and easily get their hands on in an emergency. The arts of Okinawa kobudō that gradually developed using these tools as weapons were the arts of the Okinawan military and police. What began as the use of improvised weapons was carefully studied and systematically developed into refined combat arts that employed readily available tools.

Okinawa was but one of some 35 to 40 inhabited islands among the roughly 140 that form the Ryūkyū archipelago. If there is any real distinction today between Okinawa kobudō and Ryūkyū kobudō, it is chiefly in name only. While there may be minor differences in posture, movement, or the weapons utilized, the major elements of both Ryūkyū kobudō and Okinawa kobudō are virtually identical, including their kata.

As in every other part of the world, the earliest settlers of the Ryūkyū Islands probably employed their hunting and cultivating implements for self-defense, so it is almost certain that kobudō was Okinawa's original native combat system, and its origins date back at least five thousand years. Many of the Okinawan folk dances, some of which may be as much as a thousand years old, pantomime the use of these implements. As we noted previously, there is such a remarkable similarity between the traditional festival dances of Okinawa and the kata of Okinawan martial arts that it is unlikely the two developed independently of each other.

Little historical information on early Okinawan culture has survived the ravages of conquest and war, so it is difficult to accurately reconstruct the social and political climate of the island before its alliance with the Ming Dynasty of China in 1372. The available evidence suggests, however, that Okinawan society and government were considerably less rigidly structured than Japan at that time. Okinawa was also militarily inferior, both in terms of weaponry and sophistication, so it is unlikely that the *anji* (nobles) or bushi of Okinawa were as culturally refined or as highly trained as their Japanese counterparts of the late fourteenth century.

With the arrival of the Thirty-Six Families from China in 1393, the Okinawans were formally introduced to Chinese culture, philosophy, and martial arts. Along with the empty-handed art of chuan fa (kempō) undoubtedly came several Chinese weapons arts, including the bō (six-foot staff), which had been a favorite of itinerant Buddhist monks for hundreds of years, and the Chinese equivalent of the sai. Under the intensified tutelage of the Thirty-Six Families, upper class Okinawans undoubtedly refined te to a much greater degree than had previously ever been accomplished, and Okinawa kobudō along with it.

The formalization of te received additional stimulus when the Japanese King Shō Hashi unified the three Ryūkyūan kingdoms into a single domain in 1429 and banned the possession of all bladed weapons. This edict had little effect on Okinawan peasants, who had not generally owned such weapons prior to the prohibition, but it may well have provoked the nobility to study unarmed self-defense with greater zeal and to become proficient in the use of the improvised weapons of kobudō.

By the time Okinawa was conquered by the Satsuma clan (*han*) of Kyūshū 180 years later, tremendous advances had been made in Okinawan culture. When Shimazu Iehisa, leader of the Satsuma han, reinstated and rigorously enforced a total ban on weapons, his action precipitated a further increase in budō training in two key respects. First, it gave rise to a certain amount of underground resistance among Okinawan nobles and warriors, who were now forbidden to own the weapons befitting their offices, and which had formerly symbolized their status. Secondly, the presence of Satsuma samurai as occupation forces exposed the upper classes of Okinawa to the rigorous, highly systematic training systems and family schools (ryū) that typified classical Japanese budō.

Proof of this influence is that Jigen-Ryū kenjutsu, the primary style of swordsmanship and bōjutsu practiced by the Satsuma han of Kyūshū, is still widely practiced on Okinawa today. Furthermore, Funakoshi Gichin, in his well-known book *Karate-dō Hitosuji*, points out that many Okinawan shizoku (nobility and disarmed warriors), like his own sensei, Azato Yasutsune, received classical training in such Nippon kobudō as bajutsu (horsemanship), kyūdō (archery), and kendō (swordsmanship) during the nineteenth century.

Another source of mainland Japanese weapons were the *yakunin* (constables), who were charged with keeping the peace under Satsuma rule. The yakunin were generally so adept with the *jutte* that they were a match for all but the most formidable sword-wielding samurai. The jutte, a weapon similar to the sai, was not only the primary weapon of the yakunin but also served as their official badge of office. It is probable that many Okinawan nobles and bushi were trained in the use of the jutte or sai so that they could assist in maintaining law and order among their people under Satsuma dominion.

Thus, there were ample reasons that the officers and nobles who developed karate-dō into the art we know it today were also involved in the parallel development of Okinawa kobudō. This theory is supported by the nature and evolution of the traditional kata of these arts. Karate masters such as Sakugawa Kanga, Chatan Yara, and Hamahiga, for instance, are known to have created kata for both karate-dō and Okinawa kobudō—particularly the bō, sai, and tonfa.

In the early twentieth century, the members of the Karate Kenkyū-Kai, who met in Mabuni Kenwa's garden, routinely trained with the weapons of Okinawa kobudō. The stances, turning methods, and *embu-sen* (performance lines) of the kata for karate and Okinawa kobudō are nearly identical. From all of this evidence, it seems clear that the two arts developed together, and chiefly by the same men.

However, that does not mean that Okinawa kobudō is the art of "karate weapons." The two are separate, but complementary, arts. Since most Okinawan dōjō have long incorporated Okinawa kobudō into their curricula, along with karate-dō, it is natural for neophytes to assume that these were karate weapons and therefore perceive Okinawa kobudō as an aspect of the art of karate-dō. Unfortunately, many observers have taken this assumption to an extreme and expect that to be a true karateka one must also be adept in Okinawa kobudō. This is not the case and should not be an expectation. Karate-dō and Okinawa kobudō are each complete and comprehensive arts unto themselves.

On the other hand, since many of the techniques in karate kata are intended for use against opponents wielding various weapons from both Nippon kobudō and Okinawa kobudō, it certainly makes sense for a karateka to have a solid working knowledge of Okinawa kobudō in order to better understand and apply those techniques. In addition, there are many ways in which training in Okinawa kobudō supplements training in karate, so we do recommend—but not require—students to learn at least the fundamentals of Okinawa kobudō.

Mabuni Kenwa is so well known and highly revered as the founder of Shitō-Ryū and famous for his unsurpassed encyclopedic knowledge of karate kata that many people are unaware that he was equally renowned and respected in his time for his extensive knowledge and expertise in Okinawa kobujutsu. So, it is entirely fitting that karateka training in Shitō-Ryū also develop at least a cursory knowledge of Okinawa kobujutsu.

The study of these weapons arts also offers a fascinating insight into human ingenuity and provides a foundation for adapting modern tools and household objects for use as weapons of self-defense in an emergency.

Okinawa Kobudō no Buki
WEAPONS OF OKINAWA KOBUDŌ
BŌ: *STAFF*

The bō is one of the most ancient and universal of all Okinawa kobudō weapons. A staff of six feet or greater length has been employed as both a weapon and tool from the very dawn of recorded history. Staves have been documented as both weapons and tools common throughout Europe, Africa, the Middle East, and Asia for as long as those regions have been populated. As a result, at about the time that kobudō was developing into a full-fledged martial art in the Ryūkyū Islands, the staff was enjoying widespread popularity as a self-defense weapon in the British Isles, as evidenced by the tales of Little John's besting of Robin Hood in a duel of staves around the time of the Crusades.

Shown in figure 20.1 is a standard-length bō, sometimes referred to as a *rokushaku* (six-foot-long) bō. Slightly taller than the average person who wielded it, the bō has many noncombative uses, such as a drying pole for laundry, meats, hides, and pelts;

a walking stick for travelers desiring an extra margin of protection from beasts or attackers; and a carrying pole for shouldering buckets of dyes, excrement, and other material the bearer does not want staining garments or contacting the body.

Figure 20.1 Bō.

The rokushaku bō also approximates the length of a yari (spear) and may have been used to practice sōjutsu in a manner comparable to the way a *bokken* (wooden sword) has been used for centuries in the dōjō for safety in kenjutsu and iaijutsu training. Thus many of the blocking, thrusting, and disarming techniques of the bō may have been derived from sōjutsu. Similarly, the *hasshaku* (eight-foot-long) bō may be an adaptation of the naginata (halberd) of the samurai. Generally, the bō of mainland Japan are about 1 to 1¼ inches in diameter along their full length, while the Okinawan bō are frequently tapered at both ends, so that each tip is ½ to ¾ inches in diameter, while the center third is 1 inch or slightly more in girth. Ideally the bō should be 6 to 12 inches taller than the person bearing it.

There are over twenty-five classical kata for the bō, most or all of which (like Sakugawa no Kon) originated from the shizoku tradition. These traditional kata, arranged alphabetically, include:

Aragaki no Kon

Chatan Yara no Kon

Chinen Shikiyanaka no Kon

Choun no Kon

Hassu no Kon

Kachin no Kon

Kobō no Kon

Kongo no Kon

Rufa no Kon

Sakugawa no Kon

Sesoko no Kon

Shimajiri no Kon

Shiromatsu no Kon

Shirotaru no Kon

Shishi no Kon

Shukumine no Kon

Shūshi no Kon

Soeishi no Kon

Sueyoshi no Kon

Tokumine no Kon

Tsuken no Kon

Tsuken Sunakake no Kon

Ufugushuku (Ōshiro) no Kon

Urasoe no Kon

Yonegawa no Kon

For several of the bō kata listed, there are also shō (lesser) and dai (greater) variations, as in Sakugawa no Kon Shō and Sakugawa no Kon Dai. In most cases, these variations were not created by the originator of the kata but by those who subsequently conceived one or more equally effective alternatives to the techniques originally contained in the kata and incorporated them into their instruction.

SAI: *THREE-PRONGED TRUNCHEON*

The sai is another weapon whose origins clearly include some degree of crossover between the nobility and peasants of ancient Okinawa. While the sai undoubtedly employs principles and methods derived from the mainland Japanese jutte, the ancient Chinese utilized a weapon shaped nearly the same as the sai, and the *manji-sai* (swastika-shaped sai) is close in appearance to a type of gaff sometimes used by Okinawan fishermen.

Figure 20.2 Sai.

The most common shape of sai is illustrated in figure 20.2. It is a three-pronged instrument about 17 inches in overall length. The center tine is usually sharpened to a point for stabbing an opponent while the two shorter outer tines are normally blunt. In addition to stabbing, the long tine can be used for striking with great effect as well as blocking against a steel or hardwood weapon. The U on either side of the center prong is useful for trapping an opponent's weapon, particularly a bō or other wooden-handled implement, and the blunt end of the handle (the *kashira* or *tsuka-gashira*) causes devastating injuries when employed in a punching technique.

Among the more than ten classical sai kata are:

Chatan Yara no Sai	Jigen no Sai
Sanchō Sai	Tsuken Shitahaku no Sai
Hamahiga no Sai	Kogusuku (Kojo) no Sai
Shinbaru no Sai	Ufuchiku no Sai
Hantagawa no Sai	Matsuhiga no Sai
Tawada no Sai	Yaka no Sai
Ishikawa Guwa no Sai	Nichi Sai
Tokuyama no Sai	

TONFA: *HANDLE*

The tonfa is most likely a weapon of peasant origins, adapted for use by Okinawan bushi. Sometimes called *tunfa*, *tuifa*, or *tonkua* in the Okinawan dialect, it probably originated as the handle for turning a small grinding wheel, and its first uses were likely spontaneous reactions to attacks. Once the tonfa came to the notice of the Okinawan bushi, its use was not only systematized to conform to principles of budō, but it was most likely modified in subtle ways to improve its effectiveness. This is

Figure 20.3 Tonfa.

suggested by the fact that tonfa are normally used in pairs as weapons but singly on a grindstone. Thus the weaponized version of the tonfa probably would not actually fit or turn a grinding wheel, but it looked enough like a standard millstone handle to pass casual inspection by government officials enforcing the various weapons bans.

As used in Okinawa kobudō, the tonfa, pictured in figure 20.3, ranges from 18 to 21 inches in overall length, so that when gripped by its protruding handle, it extends just beyond the elbow. The shorter end of the tonfa should extend 2 to 3 inches beyond the fist so that it can be used for devastating strikes. The handle, which projects at a right angle from the body of the tonfa, is used to swing the tonfa in a circular pattern that can produce high speeds and tremendous striking power.

There are only a few traditional kata for the tonfa, such as Hamahiga no Tonfa, Kanagushuku (Kinjō) no Tonfa, and Yara Guwa no Tonfa.

KAMA: *SICKLE*

The kama is another common tool of the farmer. A handheld sickle consisting of a curved blade about 9 inches long attached to a wooden handle some 16 to 17 inches in length, the kama required no modification to be an effective weapon. The kama is razor-sharp along its inside edge and was used in harvesting a variety of grains, including rice, millet, and wheat.

As used in kobudō, the kama's handle is roughly the length of the forearm, as depicted in figure 20.4. The kama is an extremely potent weapon. Its blade is used for slashing attacks directed at the opponent's neck, arms, midsection, groin, and legs. Those deep gashes that did not quickly kill an opponent left them hamstrung, an amputee, or immediately disabled in some fashion. The wooden handle can be used to block a variety of attacks, either extended from the fist or running along the

Figure 20.4 Kama.

forearm, and the crux at which the blade joins the handle can be used to catch and swing aside an opponent's weapon. Both the butt of the handle and the top (*mune*) of the blade can also be used to deliver punching counterstrikes.

The *furigama* (swinging kama) is a twentieth-century invention, probably modeled after the mainland samurai's *kusarigama* (kama on a chain). The handles of two kama are connected by a 10- to 12-foot length of rope so that one or both can be swung rapidly in circular and figure-eight movements similar to those performed with the nunchaku. While the furigama has been popularized by its appearance in martial arts movies, it is not a common Okinawa kobudō weapon.

The rare traditional kata for the kama include Kanegawa no Kama and Tozan (Toyama) no Kama.

EKU: *OAR*

The eku, shown in figure 20.5, is the standard type of boat oar used by Okinawan fishermen. Sometimes also called *kai* or *yeku*, the eku is usually about 6 feet long, roughly the same length as a bō. About half that length is the handle, and half is the broad "blade" of the oar. The handle section is about the same diameter as a bō, while the blade is about 6 inches wide. Both the edges and tip of the blade are usually less than ½ inch thick, so they will readily break bones or even split the skin upon striking.

Figure 20.5 Eku (kai).

Little or no modification was required to make the eku an effective weapon, and its first uses in self-defense were probably spontaneous reactions to attack. Many of the offensive and defensive techniques of the bō have been adapted to the eku, with the strikes having an even more devastating impact due to the greater weight of the eku.

In addition, the blade of the eku can be used to fling sand or debris at the attacker in a technique called *sunakake*.

The traditional kata for the eku include Tsuken Akacho no Eku and Tsuken Sunakake no Kon.

Sunakake means "sand-scooping," so it is probable that Tsuken Sunakake no Kon was originally an oar kata that was practiced with a bō, since the bō and eku are about the same length. Many students of Okinawa kobudō first practice eku kata using a bō.

NUNCHAKU: *FLAIL*

The Okinawan farm weapon best known outside Japan is probably the nunchaku. Sometimes crudely referred to as "num-chucks" or just "chucks," this weapon has been featured in numerous martial arts and action movies since first being introduced to Western audiences by the late Bruce Lee. A more formal term for nunchaku is *sōsetsu kon* ("equal-length sticks"). The prevalence of nunchaku in action films of the 1970s made them such a popular street weapon in the United States that many states made their possession a crime.

Figure 20.6 Nunchaku (sōsetsu kon).

It is likely that early nunchaku were much shorter than those shown in figure 20.6, making them easier to conceal in the sleeves or sash of traditional Okinawan clothing. Modern nunchaku are customarily elbow-length.

The specific origins of the nunchaku are uncertain. It is likely that none of the current theories are entirely correct. While this weapon appears to have been adapted from the Chinese *san setsu kon* (three-sectioned staff), with which Okinawans were probably familiar for the previous thousand years, it is also unique to Okinawa in several respects. There are several farm implements that could have been modified into nunchaku. Ancient Okinawan horse bridles used a pair of sticks similar in appearance to nunchaku joined by a section of horsehair rope as the bit and reign attachment. A flail-like instrument called a *mochi* has been used for centuries to beat the husks off several types of grains, but most mochi consist of a short handle joined by rope to a longer flail. Okinawan farmers also used two pieces of wood, often bamboo, joined by a short string at one end, to strip certain grains from their stalks or to peel bark from slender branches. Any or all of these implements could have been adapted into a weapon based on the san setsu kon.

The principal benefits of the nunchaku are its ease of concealment and the incredible force generated by the whipping motion with which it is used to strike. It provides great versatility in blocking, since either wooden handle can be used to block or swipe away a strike, or both handles can be crossed like an X to trap an opponent's weapon. The nunchaku was probably the ancient Okinawan equivalent of the switchblade—a weapon that could easily be concealed on the body, grasped with little noticeable movement, and suddenly used with devastating effectiveness.

There are no traditional kata for the nunchaku. All nunchaku kata currently practiced were created after World War II.

Shitō-Ryū no Kyūchi

The Dilemma for Shitō-Ryū

As we come to the concluding chapters of this book, having presented our case for changing how karateka perceive and train in Shitō-Ryū, we think it important to reflect on the future of both the art as a whole and our style in particular.

Our research into the history and origins of karate-dō has convinced us that prior to the twentieth century, there were no styles of karate in the sense we use that term today. There was only karate (tōde). There were many sensei, and they didn't all teach the same kata or teach kata to be performed the same way as other sensei, but what they taught was simply karate. Even well into the early twentieth century, karate pioneers like Funakoshi Gichin, Miyagi Chōjun, Mabuni Kenwa, Motobu Chōki, and others who wrote the first books on karate voiced objection to the notion that there were different styles or schools of karate like there were of kenjutsu on mainland Japan. The Karate Kenkyū-Kai in which most of these pioneers were members was a melting pot of karate masters who met regularly and openly shared their knowledge and ideas, but none of them claimed to lead a style or school of the art.

Then something changed. As some of the Okinawan karateka moved to the mainland of Japan, they began to be pressured to establish names for their schools, or "styles," as was the mainland custom. They soon adopted other mainland customs, like the karate-gi, wrapped with a black or white obi. They began issuing rankings and *menjō*, which had never been done in Okinawa before that. By the early 1930s they had agreed to change the way *karate* was written from 唐手 (Chinese hands) to 空手 (empty hands), and they had all given their styles names that remain in use to this day: Shōtō-kan, Gōjū-Ryū, Wadō-Ryū, Uechi-Ryū, Shōrin-Ryū, and so forth. Mabuni Kenwa first named his style Hankō-Ryū ("half-hard style"), but soon changed it to Shitō-Ryū ("Itosu-Higaonna style"), as it is known today.

However, Shitō-Ryū is not just the combined teachings and kata of Itosu Ankō and Higaonna Kanryō. It contains kata that Mabuni sensei learned from many others, including Aragaki Seishō, Kyan Chōtoku, Gō Kenki, and Aragaki Ankichi at a minimum. It also contains at least ten kata that Mabuni himself created between 1915 and 1940.

Then came the war: World War II changed everything for karate-dō. Several of the legendary masters died during the war years. The Dai Nippon Butoku-Kai was permanently closed. Japan came under occupation by the armed forces of the Allied nations. Karate training wasn't permitted to resume until 1953, and by law it could not conduct any form of "militaristic" training. Foreign service members soon discovered karate and joined local dōjō. Green-colored belts were added. Mabuni Kenwa created what may have been the first comprehensive written syllabus for karate instruction. When those foreign students returned to their home countries, they took karate with them, and it began to spread throughout the world.

As prosperity returned to the Allied nations, karate styles became increasingly important. Business growth in those countries made brands more important. Americans, especially, wanted to think they were buying the best brand, whether it was automobiles, televisions, appliances, clothing, or breakfast cereal. Karate "styles" are the brands of karate. It would never occur to anyone to look for the best brand of swimming or the best brand of tennis because there are no brands or styles of swimming or tennis. But since there were different styles of karate, one of them had to be the best—or so logic would seem to dictate.

Complicating matters for Shitō-Ryū, Mabuni Kenwa died on May 23, 1952, just as much of this was occurring. The elder son, Mabuni Kenei, should have been the rightful heir to the Shitō-Ryū style, but he had not trained with his father as consistently as the younger son, Mabuni Kenzō, so their mother arranged for Kenzō to take over the hombu dōjō in Ōsaka and supported his claim to leadership of the style. Mabuni Kenei, of course, disputed this claim, so Shitō-Ryū split into two factions. The one led by Mabuni Kenzō took the name Seitō ("authentic") Shitō-Ryū and the other group, jointly led by Iwata Manzō and Mabuni Kenei, called itself the Japan Karate-dō Kai.

Another notable Shitō-Ryū group that rose to prominence in the 1950s was the Seishin-Kan, founded in 1940 by Kokuba Kōsei. Among his senior students was Hayashi Teruō. When Kokuba sensei died in 1959, Hayashi sensei was appointed technical adviser of the Seishin-Kan, a position he held until leaving the organization in 1970 to found Hayashi-Ha Shitō-Ryū. Shimabukuro Masayuki became a student of Hayashi Teruō in 1963 and remained with Hayashi sōke until 1995 when he aligned with Mabuni Kenzō and Seitō Shitō-Ryū.

Hayashi sōke drew criticism from some circles for founding his own branch of Shitō-Ryū, for making minor alterations in some of the Shitō-Ryū kata, for incorporating several kata from the Ryūei-Ryū style into Hayashi-Ha Shitō-Ryū, and for becoming heavily involved in tournament competition. In the 1980s and 1990s, Hayashi sōke's students dominated many of the major karate tournaments worldwide, and their success was largely responsible for Shitō-Ryū becoming the second most popular style of karate.

Mabuni Kenzō and Seitō Shitō-Ryū were a stark contrast to Hayashi-Ha. Mabuni sōke refused to engage in tournament competition and proudly followed his father's original written syllabus completely unchanged. Hayashi sōke died in 2004 and Mabuni sōke passed away in 2005, leaving Shimabukuro Hanshi without a karate sensei for the last seven years of his life. Despite having aligned with Mabuni Kenzō and preferring Mabuni's overall approach to karate-dō in general and Shitō-Ryū in particular, Shimabukuro Hanshi continued to include the Ryūei-Ryū kata added by Hayashi sōke in his teaching curriculum.

And that is what has created a dilemma for Shitō-Ryū. With at least five organizations teaching and promoting the style we call Shitō-Ryū, which of them—if any—is now actually seitō (authentic) Shitō-Ryū? A strong argument can be made for any of them. On the one hand, following Mabuni Kenwa's written syllabus to the letter passes on the founder's teachings and legacy exactly as he created it, which certainly makes it authentic in that sense. On the other hand, the founder himself altered the style considerably from the curriculum and teachings that had been passed on to him by his sensei. He too added kata from other styles as well as adding kata of his own creation, just as Itosu Anko had done before him. So continuing to expand the style in a manner similar to the founder's actions seems equally authentic. After all, a ryū is a living organism that adapts, changes, and alters course as it flows from one generation to the next. If it ceases to grow and change, if each successive generation is prohibited from adding its own "DNA" to the gene pool of the ryū, is it still alive? Is it still a ryū? Or has it stagnated and either gone into hibernation or died?

While you ponder those questions, we will raise another. Shimabukuro Hanshi essentially did what Mabuni Kenwa did: he blended the styles of his two major teachers and added his own knowledge gained from personal research to form the teachings we have presented in this book. Isn't that also the function and purpose of a ryū? Isn't that also authentic, inasmuch as it follows the founder's model and tradition? Should Shimabukuro Hanshi's legacy rightfully be called Shimabukuro-Ha Shitō-Ryū?

We will leave that question for others to debate and decide. The answers are not as important as the thought you give to the questions as you consider for yourself what it really means to be a ryū in the twenty-first century. The journey is often more important than the destination, and contemplating the question can be more beneficial than finding the answer.

Shitō-Ryū no Yōten

Summary of the Shitō-Ryū System

One of our goals was to provide readers with a comprehensive training curriculum in the art of Shitō-Ryū karate-dō. We believe that goal was achieved in the content of chapters 10 through 19. The following is an outline of that curriculum for quick reference:

IPPAN GENSOKU: *GENERAL PRINCIPLES (CHAPTER 10)*

- *chikara* (power)
- *tai sabaki* (body movement)
- *shisei* (posture)
- *chakugan* (eye contact)
- *maai* (distance control)
- *seme* (pressure or intimidation)
- *zanshin* (situational awareness)
- *machigai* (mistakes)

SAHŌ TO REIHŌ: *PREPARATION AND ETIQUETTE (CHAPTER 11)*

- *sōji* (clean-up)
- *sahō* (preparation)
- *reihō* (etiquette, formal and informal)
- *mokusō* (meditation)
- *dōjō kun* (code of the dōjō)

KIHON: *FUNDAMENTALS (CHAPTER 12)*

- *karada no buki* (body weapons)
- *kamae* (structure and stances)
- *ashi sabaki* (footwork)
- *hojo undō* (strength training)
- *danryoku* (stretching)
- *kitae* (hardening of contact surfaces)

BŌGYŌ WAZA: *DEFENSIVE TECHNIQUES (CHAPTER 13)*

- *uke kata* (blocking methods)
- *tenshin* (evasion)

KŌGEKI WAZA: *OFFENSIVE TECHNIQUES (CHAPTER 14)*

- *tsuki kata* (punching and thrusting)
- *uchi kata* (striking techniques)
- *keri kata* (kicking techniques)
- *hiji ate gōhō* (five ways of elbow striking)

JŪHŌ: *SOFT TECHNIQUES (CHAPTER 15)*

- *ukemi* (breakfalls)
- *kaihō waza* (escaping techniques)
- *nage waza* (throws)
- *osaekomi waza* (grappling)
- *tenshin* (evasion)

KATA: *TEMPLATES (CHAPTER 16)*

- Itosu-kei
  - Kihon (up to 12)
  - Heian (Pinan) (1–5)
  - Naifanchi (Tekki) (1–3)
  - Jutte
  - Jion
  - Jiin
  - Rohai (1–3)
  - Bassai (Dai, Sho)
  - Kōsōkun (Dai, Sho)
  - Gojūshihō
- Matsumura-kei
  - Matsumura no Bassai
  - Matsumura no Rohai
  - Wanshū
  - Chintō
  - Chinte
- Mabuni-kei
  - Shinsei
  - Kenshū
  - Juroku
  - Matsukaze
  - Kenpaku
  - Kensho
  - Myojo
  - Aoyagi

- Hopposho
- Shinpa
- Higaonna-kei
  - Saifa
  - Sanchin
  - Tenshō
  - Sanseiru
  - Seipai
- Aragaki-kei
  - Sōchin
  - Unsū

- Shiho Kōsōkun

- Shisōchin
- Seienchin
- Kururunfa
- Seisan
- Suparinpei

- Niseishi

In addition to the kata listed above, the curricula of many Shitō-Ryū dōjō include several additional kata, borrowed from other styles. These kata are often called sankō ("consultation") kata, because they provide access to techniques not found in the core curriculum. Some examples include:

- Tomari Bassai
- Pachū
- Heiku
- Paiku
- Anan
- Aragaki Niseishi

- Chatanyara Kūshankū
- Annanko
- Nipaipō
- Haffa
- Hakkaku (Hakutsuru)

BUNKAI TO ŌYŌ: *ANALYSIS AND APPLICATION* (*CHAPTER 17*)

- *bunkai* (move-by-move analysis)
- *ōyō* (practical application)
- *tekiō* (variations and adaptations)

HITOGOROSHI WAZA: *KILLING TECHNIQUES* (*CHAPTER 18*)

- finding hitogoroshi waza in kata
- practicing hitogoroshi waza during kumite training

KUMITE: *SPARRING (CHAPTER 19)*

- *yakusoku kumite* (choreographed sparring)

  - *ippon kumite* (one-step sparring)

  - *sambon kumite* (three-step sparring)

  - *goshinjutsu* (self-defense techniques)

  - *jiyū kumite* (free sparring)

- *go* versus *sen* (reactive versus proactive)

KARATE-DŌ TO KOBUJUTSU: *KARATE AND ANCIENT WEAPONS (CHAPTER 20)*

- *bō* (six-foot staff)

- *sai* (three-pronged truncheon)

- *tonfa* (wooden handle)

- *kama* (sickle)

- *eku* (oar)

- *nunchaku* (flail)

In addition to the foregoing curriculum for the physical aspects of karate training, in chapters 2 through 9 we have provided an equally comprehensive explanation of the major philosophical, mental, and spiritual elements that are essential to karate training.

Chapter Twenty-Three

武士の心得

Bushi no Kokoro-e

Precepts of the Bushi

This book contains enough information on karate as the art of killing to last several lifetimes. It will take a dozen years of training to become adept at the physical techniques alone, and decades more to master them and imprint them with your own personality and spirit. The philosophy contained in this book is condensed from the lives of many of Japan's greatest bushi, and it would be the height of arrogance for any of us to presume that we could assimilate all of it in a single lifetime. Even the authors reread their own works routinely to remind themselves of the ideals and principles they have chosen to follow in life.

Bear in mind that we have only presented the major tenets of karate philosophy in this volume. An authoritative and exhaustive study on the philosophy of karate-dō would require a work of encyclopedic proportions, so this should not be your only reference, but one of many. This manual can serve you for a lifetime of training, enjoyment, and personal enrichment. It is not merely a handbook on karate. As the bushi of old so well understood, all of its principles can be applied to the challenges and aspirations of our everyday lives.

The authors began work on this book when they were both roughly sixty years of age and both recognized that they were entering the final stages of life. They wrote it in order to leave a legacy—not only for their karate students and fellow karateka around the world but for their own descendants as well. We tried to create a book worthy of being passed on from generation to generation—a book you can pass on to your children when the time comes, and they can pass on to their children in much the same way the art of karate-dō itself has been passed from generation to generation, flowing endlessly with the ryū.

We began the book by outlining major concepts and general principles about karate-dō and about life. Karate-dō is, after all, ultimately about life—a life that is more abundant and fulfilling. We close by providing some practical ways to apply those ideas to your everyday activities both inside and outside the dōjō—ways we know can help you achieve true victory over the circumstances and adversities we all face in our family lives, social relationships, jobs, and ambitions, and to bring you and those around you greater joy and fulfillment.

Bushi no Kokoro-e
TWENTY-ONE PRECEPTS OF THE BUSHI

1. Know yourself. (*Jikō o shiru koto*)

   The foundation of all personal growth is to truly know yourself—that which seems both good and bad in yourself. To understand your faults as well as your virtues allows you to begin working to remedy your faults, strengthen your virtues, and find ways to work around those aspects of your personality and character that you may be unable to change.

2. Always follow through on commitments. (*Jibun no kimeta koto wa saigo made jikkō suru koto*)

   A commitment is essentially a promise you make to yourself. Commitments can be as shallow and short-lived as going on a diet or as deep and lasting as marriage: the marriage vow is the promise you make to your spouse; the marriage commitment is the promise you make to yourself. Each unfulfilled commitment is a personal failure that can be deeply disappointing and damaging to your self-esteem. Think carefully before you make any commitment. Make only those commitments that are truly valuable to you. And don't overburden yourself with so many commitments that you are doomed to failure from the start.

3. Respect everyone. (*Ikanaru hito demo sonke suru koto*)

   If you have gained nothing else from this book, the concept of respect should be indelibly etched into your mind. The true bushi, as we have often stated, respected even their enemies. Respect for others—for their ideas, beliefs, culture, and human rights—is the bridge to mutual understanding and ultimately to peaceful coexistence with others.

   Respecting someone is not the same as admiring them. You can respect someone else's basic humanity—their right to hold different ideas and perspectives from yours—without agreeing with them. Remember, a bushi even respects their sworn enemies.

4. Hold strong convictions that cannot be altered by your circumstances. (*Kankyō ni sayu sarenai tsuyoi shinnen o motsu koto*)

It's one thing to develop strong convictions; it's quite another to hold to those convictions even when it appears foolish in the eyes of the world to do so. We now live in an era in which welfare and insurance fraud are commonplace roads to financial success, where television and movies have glamorized promiscuity to an extent that sexually transmitted diseases are epidemic, where the majority of premature deaths are the direct result of lifestyle choices, where ease and comfort are more highly revered than hard work and sacrifice, and where commitment to family and traditional values are publicly ridiculed.

The easy way to deal with social, cultural, and political pressure is to capitulate to it and abandon those convictions that others criticize or denigrate. Incredible strength of conviction is necessary to withstand such social and economic pressures—pressures that have led our present generation into a malaise of alcohol and drug abuse, immorality, greed, laziness, and self-indulgence that is out of control and bringing the entire world to ruin.

5. Don't make an enemy of yourself. (*Mizu kara teki o tsukuranai koto*)

Don't be your own worst enemy! Jealousy, greed, and self-pity will ensure that you have plenty of enemies if you try to accomplish something worthwhile with your life. If you treat people with respect and compassion, you won't add to the number of your opponents by your own attitude.

6. Live without regrets. (*Koto ni oite kōkaisezu*)

This is a double-edged admonition. First, don't wallow in regret over your past mistakes. Take responsibility for them and learn from them—and then put them behind you. Accept the fact that the past cannot be undone, find something of value (such as a lesson learned) in your mistakes, and go forward with the knowledge that you have taken another step toward perfection of character.

Second, if you know—or even suspect—that you will regret an action you are considering, don't do it! Heed the warning of your conscience in advance. As you strive toward improving yourself and grow in compassion and self-awareness, you will find that your conscience allows you to make fewer and fewer regrettable decisions.

7. Be certain to make a good first impression. *(Hito to no deai o taisetsu ni suru koto)*

As the old saying goes, "First impressions are lasting impressions." A good first impression is a barometer of the kind of life you are leading. If you consistently leave good impressions on those you meet, it is likely that you are living a more fulfilling and positive life than someone who consistently leaves a poor first impression.

8. Don't cling to the past. *(Miren o motanai koto)*

This is more than simply not regretting the past; it means to let go of both the good and the bad. All too often we meet people who sacrifice their own present or future because they are still mired in the past. Their stories of "the good old days" are a telltale sign that nothing of import is occurring in their lives now.

Our past is a good history lesson, and it is as valuable as a road map to our future. But in order to move ahead, we must let go of past glories as well as past failures.

9. Never break a promise. *(Yakusoku o yaburanai koto)*

To be a person of character, you must say what you mean and mean what you say. It is really that simple. Don't make promises you can't or won't keep, and if you do make a promise, do whatever is necessary to keep it. Remember: the disappointment and distrust caused by only one broken promise can undo ten years of kept promises.

10. Don't depend on other people. *(Hito ni tayoranai koto)*

This precept is a bit paradoxical. We cannot succeed in life without the help of others. We cannot have fulfilling relationships with other people without allowing them to become deeply involved in our lives. Yet we must not depend on them!

What this really means is that we must take personal responsibility for our lives. Children depend on their parents, but adults must be responsible for themselves. We cannot rely on family, friends, or the government to take care of us, direct us, or make us happy. With realistic expectations of others, we will feel genuine gratitude for their contributions, and we will avoid anger and disappointment if others let us down.

11. Don't speak ill of others. *(Hito o onshitsu shinai koto)*

If you have a grievance with someone, the respectful and proper way to deal with it is to speak directly with that person, not about that person to others.

Compassionate confrontation is the core of good relationships. It is easy to compliment people, but it takes real courage and true friendship to openly discuss with others the things that bother you. Yet we can only have deep friendships if we are willing to take the emotional risks of raising difficult issues and settling them. If we do, then both people benefit. If we don't, both will suffer.

12. Don't be afraid of anything. *(Ikanaku koto ni oite mo osorenai koto)*

Fear robs you of heijōshin and prevents you from thinking clearly and reacting naturally. It ignites the fight-or-flight reaction, yet often neither fighting nor fleeing is the most beneficial response. This is especially true of the flight response since our avoidance of all but physical danger usually takes the form of emotional barriers or escapism into drug and alcohol use or submission to cult behavior.

It is always preferable to face your problems, whether they are physical dangers or the everyday obstacles and challenges of life. After all, as a bushi, you have already conquered the fear of death and are instead pursuing a noble death (see chapter 2). So, since you do not fear death, why should you fear anything that life might throw your way?

13. Respect the opinions of others. *(Hito no iken o soncho suru koto)*

The opinions of others have been shaped by a lifetime of experience and thought, just as yours have. It is important not to preconceive different opinions or ideas as "wrong." The other person's opinion may be just as well substantiated as your own—perhaps even more so. If you can set aside your desire to be "right" and focus only on the opinion that has the most value, you will find your attitude encourages others to share their ideas freely, which will in turn provide you with greater insight and more options from which to choose.

Remember the lesson of Takeda Shingen, who encouraged and rewarded dissent among his subordinates. It was that very trait that made him one of the greatest leaders in history.

14. Have compassion and understanding for everyone. *(Hito ni taishite omoiyari o motsu koto)*

True compassion cannot be achieved without deep understanding of human nature and motivations, so this precept implies the need to really know people. This is especially crucial for leaders, and it can be seen in such examples as Takeda Shingen, Abraham Lincoln, and countless others. Those who take a genuine interest in people inspire great loyalty, dedication, and desire to succeed. There is great truth in the axiom "People don't care how much you know until they know how much you care."

Compassion is the key to discovering what motivates people. If you sincerely care, you will be interested enough to learn their deepest desires, hopes, and fears and eventually grow to understand them. Compassion is also the key to developing healthy and harmonious relationships with family, friends, and your spouse, and the key to appreciating and validating the points of view and feelings of others, even if they differ from yours.

15. Don't be impetuous. *(Karuhazumi ni koto o okosanai koto)*

The bushi of old were bound by a strict code of honor and lived in a society in which the slightest insult could result in a duel to the death. In such times, the implications of every action had to be carefully considered beforehand. The slightest mistake could cost you your life and bring about the ruination of your family. Even though the consequences are not as severe, it is not so different today. Rash decisions or words can cost a new job or a promotion; impulsive financial decisions can throw your family into bankruptcy. Things posted on social media can result in lost opportunities. If you maintain heijōshin and do not allow your emotions and impulses to dictate your decisions, you will enjoy greater abundance in all aspects of life.

16. Even little things must be attended to. *(Chiisa na koto demo taisetsu ni suru koto)*

There is a common saying, "Take care of the little things, and the big things will take care of themselves." There is a great deal of truth in this dictum. If unattended, the little things in life soon compound into big things. Just as small physical tasks, such as personal and financial details, can add up into serious problems if not taken care of, a series of seemingly insignificant emotional hurts will quickly escalate into major conflicts.

It is not always necessary to personally perform the little tasks; it is only important to see that they get done. If your lifestyle requires you to concentrate on major issues, then you must delegate the small tasks and ensure that they are done.

17. Never forget to be appreciative. *(Kansha no kimochi o wasurenai koto)*

A sincere word of thanks is often better than payment for a favor done. Most of us enjoy helping others and gain a sense of satisfaction in knowing that we have done something unselfish, but we also quickly grow tired of doing things for people who do not show any appreciation for our efforts. If we show genuine appreciation for the assistance of others, there will always be friends willing to help us through difficult times. But if we fail to show our appreciation, we will quickly become known as a "taker," and our acquaintances will lose all respect for us.

This is also a prime example of taking care of the little things. Just the simple courtesy of a "thank you" to a friend or loved one, if left unsaid, can build up into great anger and discontent with time and repetition. But that same simple courtesy, if never forgotten, will keep our friends and family steadfast by our side even through the darkest of times.

18. Be first to seize the opportunity. *(Hito yori sossenshi kōdō suru koto)*

We must not act impetuously. But once we have reached a well-considered decision, we must act quickly and precipitously. As the old saying goes, "Opportunity knocks but once." We usually get only one chance, and that chance only lasts for a limited time.

This is a lesson we practice often in karate-dō. Our opponent will give us few opportunities to win the encounter, and those opportunities will last only moments at best. So we must seize an opportunity the instant it arises. The same holds true in business and other areas of life. True opportunities will be rare and short-lived, so we must be prepared for them and act swiftly when they are presented.

19. Make a desperate effort. *(Isshō kenmei monogoto o suru koto)*

Here is another lesson directly from karate training. In important matters, a "strong" effort usually results in only mediocre results. Whenever we are attempting anything truly worthwhile, our effort must be as if our life is at stake, just as if we were under physical attack. It is this extraordinary effort—an effort that drives us beyond what we thought we were capable of—that ensures victory in battle and success in life's endeavors.

20. Have a plan for your life. *(Jinsei no mokuhyō o sadameru koto)*

If you don't know where you are going, how will you know when you get there? To have a plan for your life is such an obvious admonition that it almost seems ludicrous to mention it here. Yet sadly, fewer than 10 percent of us have a clear written plan for our lives. And of those who do have some kind of plan, fewer than 10 percent have planned for anything other than just the financial aspects. The average person spends more time planning a holiday weekend than in planning their whole life.

While financial matters are an important part of an overall life plan, it is equally—if not more—important to set goals for all the other areas of your life. The necessities of life keep financial matters at the forefront of our thoughts, so having specific goals for the other areas of our life helps prevent financial matters from crowding everything else out. Your life plan should also be written, so that you can use it as a road map to your achievements and to help keep you accountable for staying on track.

However, a good life plan does not have to be highly detailed. An outline is usually sufficient. At a minimum, it should include specific goals and timetables for achieving them, in the following areas:

1. Family goals: This broad category concerns such issues as family relationships, marriage, children, where you will live, and most other lifestyle decisions.

2. Social involvement: Your social life can include clubs, social status, and political involvement, and will often affect such areas as recreation, charitable activities, and the like.

3. Personal accomplishments: These are your "trophies," how you want to leave your mark on the world, what you will be remembered by.

4. Financial objectives: This area should focus primarily on the income and expenses you generate. The things you purchase and own (cars, home) are planned under other categories. Your financial plan outlines how you will obtain the money needed to acquire those things that you have planned for elsewhere.

5. Intellectual development: This should include goals for both formal education (high school, college, advanced degrees) and informal areas (topics you might study—even become expert in—outside academic institutions).

6. Emotional maturity: Just as it helps to have definite, measurable objectives in financial areas, you should plan for your emotional maturation. How will you ensure that you continue to mature and improve your character? Will you attend courses, read self-help books, or join organizations that promote this? How will you establish an underlying philosophy or ethical basis by which to guide your behavior?

7. Spiritual growth: You will not be a whole person until you have resolved your quest for meaning in life. You must deal with the issues that most of us consider "religious": Is there a god? How does the existence or nonexistence of god affect my life and behavior? Is there a hereafter? What will become of my soul when my body dies? Do I need to make spiritual preparations for the afterlife? What is my role in the universe? Why am I here? Is there a purpose to life beyond mere carnal pleasures? Are there moral absolutes? By what spiritual path can I find these answers?

These questions require deep soul-searching and careful investigation. You must be careful to seek truth rather than what is popular, self-serving, or convenient to believe. And your quest for the answers to such crucial spiritual questions should be at least as well planned as your family vacation.

To help you focus on what is truly important to you, as opposed to those things that would merely be nice to accomplish if you had a chance, just ask yourself this question: "If I died at the end of this (day, week, month, year), what accomplishments would leave me with absolutely no regrets?"

Ask this question for your long-term (five-, ten-, and twenty-year) goals, medium-term (one- to three-year) goals, and short-term (weekly, monthly, quarterly) plans. Then, use the answers to set your truly important objectives for each of these planning periods.

This is truly a bushi's perspective—the perspective of a warrior who routinely faced the real possibility of untimely death. If you knew with certainty that you would die exactly one week from today, just think what you would really do during those final seven days. You would make sure that all your personal and financial affairs were as orderly as possible, so as not to inconvenience your heirs. Petty squabbles and hurt feelings would suddenly seem inconsequential, and you would spend hours cherishing the company of your closest friends and loved ones. And you would probably take the time to do one or two really important things that you always wished you had done. Those are precisely the types of things your short-term objectives should concentrate on.

On the other hand, if you knew you would die in exactly three years, you would plan more types of activities and goals. You would set aside money for events planned months ahead. You might schedule a dream vacation to some distant land or devote several months to working for a cause you believe in deeply. These are appropriate medium-range goals.

Lastly, if you know you would die in exactly ten or perhaps twenty years, you would make other, more far-reaching plans and prioritize them differently. You might plan a dream home to share with your family for the last ten of those twenty years, or establish a fund for your children's college education, or set aside time to research and write a book, or plan a change of careers.

This is truly the secret of living without regrets. If you lived each day as if you were scheduled to die at midnight that night, you would make sure you spent every waking hour accomplishing only the most important things in life, and you would devote the most time possible to the people who mean the most to you. At the end of such a day, you would have no regrets.

Regardless of whether the goals you set are lofty or simple, once you have established a plan for your life, your next step is to begin applying the other principles in this book to accomplishing that plan. Chief among these is always follow-through on commitments. Having made a commitment to achieve your written goals, don't stop working toward them, especially when you encounter setbacks.

Not everything you try in life will succeed. The more you try to accomplish, the more failures you will experience. The most successful people in the world are the ones who have failed the most often, because they have tried more things. You cannot allow failures, obstacles, and setbacks to affect your confidence and desire to succeed. Remember: the only people who never fail are the ones who never try.

In karate there is no such thing as a draw. In every battle, you either win or lose, and to lose is to die. The same is essentially true for your ambitions in life. There is no middle ground: you either succeed or fail.

You can think of your life plan like a marathon race: you must complete all twenty-six miles. If you don't cross the finish line, it doesn't matter if you ran only ten miles or all but the last ten feet, you still didn't finish—you didn't run a marathon. A 10K run is still a major accomplishment, but it isn't a marathon. And when you are running a marathon, the judges don't hand out 10K medals to the ones who don't finish.

So treat your life plan like karate-dō—don't accept anything less than winning. In this way you will be sure you achieve your goals. This also means you must plan thoughtfully. Set realistic goals and know what you really want to accomplish. Also, set only those goals that you are willing to sacrifice everything that isn't one of your goals to achieve. If you are really willing to settle for completing a 10K run instead of a marathon, then make a 10K run your life goal. Don't have "marathon" in your plan and think it will be all right to fall back to a 10K. It won't be. At your very core, you will think of yourself as a failure if you do not accomplish what you set out to do. It is much better, in every way, to have a 10K goal and push on to run a marathon than to have a marathon goal and fall short with a 10K. Conversely, if a marathon is really what you have your heart set on achieving, then make it your goal, and then make a desperate effort to finish the race.

21. Never lose your "beginner's spirit." (*Shoshin o wasurubekarazaru koto*)

This admonition is much deeper than it seems at first. On the surface it means to maintain the freshness and excitement that you bring to any new endeavor as a beginner. Don't lose your eagerness to improve and learn and experience. And don't lose a beginner's humility and openness to instruction. But it also means never to lose touch with the basics in any area of life.

It is so easy to find ourselves caught up in the complexities of modern living that we lose track of the basics—those elements that bring true meaning and joy to life: love and friendship, an appreciation of nature, gratitude for all the blessings we enjoy, and enjoyment of the simple things of life itself.

In times of stress, difficulty, and setbacks, keeping your beginner's spirit means to go back to the fundamentals to find the solutions to your problems. The answers are seldom found in the complexities. Our hardships and failures are usually the result of losing touch with the basic principles of life, not the intricacies and minor details.

When adversities arise, you can actually use these twenty-one precepts as a diagnostic tool to find the area of life in which you may have gotten off track. Just start at the top and start asking yourself the questions: Do I truly know myself? Have I followed through on all my commitments? Have I been disrespectful to someone? As you work your way down the list, if you are honest with yourself, you will probably find the cause of your difficulties.

LIFE'S LABORATORY

The precepts of Bushi no Kokoro-e apply as aptly to life in general as to karate-dō specifically, from knowing yourself to keeping your beginner's spirit. One of the major benefits of karate training, then, is the opportunity to use the dōjō as a laboratory in which to experiment with, test, and perfect these principles under controlled circumstances. Once refined, you can then apply them in your own life.

Every day we can improve our character and experience the value of these concepts in the microcosm of the dōjō. We can learn by trial and error under the caring, corrective eye of our sensei and in the company of understanding and compassionate fellow students who share our struggle with the same lessons—before attempting to apply them in the broader world of daily life.

RISE ABOVE THE ORDINARY

Animals live only day by day or even hour by hour, driven by instinct and reaction to their environment, and satisfied with whatever outcome befalls them. Only humans have freedom of choice, the ability to set goals, to establish principles and ideals by which to live, and to strive for an improved life despite the obstacles and circumstances of their environment. It is this very ability that creates stress, worry, fear, and uncertainty, but it is also this ability that allows us to persevere and overcome the trials of life and experience true victory and joy.

Those who have neither hope nor ideals to live by are living only on the level of brute animals. Your first step in rising above a primitive existence is to establish strong convictions that will form the basis for an enriched and rewarding life and give you the emotional stamina to endure its hardships and trials.

A person of high ideals and character appreciates the laws of nature and the fundamental laws and mores of their society. Even if you disagree with how some of these laws are enforced or applied, such principles give you a foundation for exercising sound judgment, even in complex and difficult circumstances. If you really know yourself and have compassion for yourself (as well as others), then every action or decision you make will polish your character—even those that turn out adversely—because you will accept responsibility and continue to strive for improvement.

It is this strength of character and commitment to continual improvement that will set you apart from the ordinary and mundane, and allow you to remain unaffected by your environment and circumstances. With a spirit of purpose and a dedication to continual self-improvement, you will learn to benefit almost equally from adversity as from success. When you can do this, you will no longer find your emotions rising and falling with your changing fortunes. You will know and experience heijōshin.

To perfect our character, to fulfill our purpose in life, to live up to our fullest potential, we must not allow ourselves to be held back by imaginary restraints. We must always be willing to try, and be willing to try again. We cannot allow a previous setback, failure, or humiliation condition us not to try again. How many wallflowers have missed out on a "yes" from the person of their dreams only because they first got a "no" from another, and were never willing to risk another minor humiliation? To become all that you are capable of being takes tremendous courage. You must be willing to risk all that you already are.

Saigo no Hito Koto

Concluding Thoughts

Kantan na michi o susumeba, jinsei wa muzukashii;
muzukashii michi o susumeba, jinsei wa kantan desu.
If you take the easy path, life is difficult;
If you take the difficult path, life is easy.

The meaning of this proverb is fairly obvious. But, like all of bushidō philosophy, it has deeper and more subtle shadings of meaning the more it is contemplated. If we take the easy path—the path of leisure and inaction, avoiding confrontation and unpleasant situations, ignoring problems, and doing less than our best—we create difficulties for ourselves and allow problems to worsen. If we instead take the difficult path—the path of hard work and action, confronting the unpleasant people and situations in our lives, nipping problems in the bud, and doing our best at all times—then we remove or minimize many of the difficulties and obstacles of life. The latter is the path of the budōka.

A closely related adage is:

Yū wa yasuku; okonai wa muzukashii.
Okonai wa yasuku; satoru koto muzukashii.
Talk is easy; action is difficult.
Action is easy; enlightenment is difficult.

At the obvious level, this maxim tells you to get busy right now with your karate training. Thinking or talking about it are worthless unless you do something about it. So begin and persist in your training. Take action!

As you do so, the truth of the second half of the saying will become apparent. Compared to motivating yourself to action, the Herculean task of acquiring true understanding of karate-dō will prove to be a lifelong endeavor. If you are diligent in your training and attempt to practice bushidō in daily life, you will soon discover a subtler truth: that knowing bushidō and being able to explain it ("talk") is simple compared to applying it consistently in everyday life. Likewise, as you begin to apply bushidō on a daily basis, you will find that a true understanding of its limitless depth and applicability is a monumental but worthy undertaking.

Your journey will be fraught with difficulty, frustrations, adversities, and setbacks—bruises, blisters, aches, and painful nicks on the body as well as the soul—but liberally seasoned with incomparable joys and triumphs. It is a journey of self-discovery, self-enrichment, and the discovery and enrichment of others. Join us on this journey of victorious living!

後書

Atogaki

Afterword

This book was literally ten years in the making. Hanshi and I began work on it in late 2009. Its original concept was significantly different from what it became in the process of writing and revising the first five or six chapters in 2010 and 2011. Hanshi and I both faced severe challenges throughout that period, and our work was sporadic. Those challenges came to a head in 2012 with Hanshi's untimely death and my untimely layoff from my primary job.

In the aftermath of Hanshi's death, I lost the will to continue for several years. We had completed a little more than half the manuscript, had outlined the remaining chapters, and I had gathered a mountain of notes from our many telephone conversations, but without Hanshi to share the process with, I didn't have the heart to continue. He had not only been my sensei for twenty-three years, he had been my mentor and closest friend. *Karate As the Art of Killing* had been *our* work, *our* vision, but *we* no longer existed. And I didn't want to continue it alone.

The event that motivated me to resume work on *Karate As the Art of Killing* was the 25th Anniversary Edition of *Flashing Steel.* My own health was failing. Between 2012 and 2016 I had suffered two heart attacks, congestive heart failure, and nearly died three times on the operating table during open-heart surgery, so I was acutely aware of my own mortality and that I had only limited time left in which to accomplish anything I believed to be meaningful. When the opportunity arose to update *Flashing Steel,* I seized upon it as a way to complete Hanshi's legacy in the art of iaijutsu and present it to the world in lasting form. As the editing of *Flashing Steel* was coming to a close, I realized that by completing *Karate As the Art of Killing,* I could do the same for Hanshi's legacy in the art of karate-dō that we both loved so much. With renewed purpose, I enthusiastically seized the opportunity.

It took me more than six months just to assemble the preliminary drafts and my copious notes and chapter fragments into a cohesive manuscript for submission to the publisher. Many times during the process I simply set it aside for days—sometimes weeks—at a time, feeling drained and unable to continue. For most of that time, I attributed my lack of enthusiasm to writer's block or old age and fatigue, but as I was working frantically in the final days to complete the manuscript, I realized that the cause of my reticence was something much deeper than mere writer's block or the distractions of the COVID-19 pandemic and its effects on my work, social life, and finances. It was something far more personal than that. I didn't *want* to complete this book!

I most certainly wanted to see it in print, but I didn't want to finish it. Not because I'm lazy or a procrastinator, but because finishing it would mark the end of my relationship with Shimabukuro Hanshi. Writing *Flashing Steel, Katsujinken,* and *Karate As the Art of Killing* provided the most intimate contact I had with Hanshi. We spent hours each week, month after month, sharing our deepest thoughts about budō and life. Discussing, debating, laughing, and often sharing personal experiences that left one or both of us in tears. *Karate As the Art of Killing* was the last book we started together, and deep in my psyche I felt that as long as it remained a work in process, Hanshi was still alive for me in mind and spirit. He was still speaking into my thoughts, instructing me, guiding me on the keyboard, correcting me, counseling me, and even encouraging me. Deep down, I never wanted that to end.

My reluctance to let go of Hanshi, to bring my work with him to a close, made *Karate As the Art of Killing* the most arduous project I've ever written. I began writing short stories at the age of eight or nine, after being scolded by my mother for wasting my intellect and imagination after I complained to her that I was bored. Writing has always come easily for me. The words usually pour out onto the page. Not so with *Karate As the Art of Killing.* Even though I had extensive notes and had completed nearly half the book prior to Hanshi's death, I still had to drag every word from my mind against what I now realize was almost insurmountable subconscious resistance.

Once I understood what was holding me back, I was able to reconcile myself to the completion and publication of *Karate As the Art of Killing* being the end of a major chapter in my life, and move on. The words again flowed, as they are doing right now.

In the closing chapter of this book we ask the reader the question, "If you were given only one week to live, what would you do?" After outlining some possible answers, we conclude with, "or would you do nothing different than you had done the previous week, or the week before that? That would indicate that your lifestyle had produced heijōshin." Right up until just days before being admitted to hospice care, Hanshi was doing exactly what he had done the week before, and the week prior to that—traveling and teaching the arts he loved to the people he loved. He didn't just write and lecture about the life and principles of a bushi, he *lived* the life and principles of a bushi.

In 2013, the Dai Nippon Butoku-Kai posthumously inducted Shimabukuro Masayuki Hidenobu Hanshi into their Hall of Fame for his lifetime of contributions to the arts and people he loved. Deservedly so. His life and his achievements stand as an inspiration to all who would strive to live by the highest principles and values of bushidō—a life that was imbued with its spirit and actions, a life that produced a legacy that lives on in his body of work and in the hearts of the thousands of students worldwide whom he trained.

When describing Hanshi's accomplishments, the tendency is to focus on the many awards, accolades, honors, rankings, and titles that were bestowed on him and the number and importance of his achievements. But the real measure of his life is the impact he had on the lives of others. Everyone who came in contact with him walked away better for having met or known him. His life—his words of wisdom and encouragement, his acts of kindness and compassion toward others—improved the lives of thousands of people around the world. And that is the hallmark of a life of genuine importance. A life truly well lived.

He was the sage; I am merely the scribe. My goal in completing *Karate As the Art of Killing* and finally getting it into print as closely to our original intent as possible was to create a lasting tribute to the life, work, teachings, and memory of Shimabukuro Hanshi—a work that would be truly worthy of him. As I write these final passages, it is with a sense that I could and should have done more—that he deserves better than what I am capable of producing. But I have done my best, and now that it is going to press, I think he would be pleased with the result. He would certainly be polite enough to say so, while I will continue to wonder.

Japan's feudal system was officially abolished in 1871, and in 1876 the former samurai were abolished. Although the spirit of the samurai was resurrected in the postwar era, legally and factually the samurai no longer exist. The principles of bushidō do live on, but the bushi themselves faded into history long ago. Or so they say. I know that bushi can and do live on today. I know because I walked alongside a true bushi for more than twenty years, training with him, dining with him, traveling with him, facing some of life's greatest challenges and difficulties with him, laughing with him, rejoicing with him, and occasionally crying with him. Such men still do walk the earth, and if you are ever privileged to encounter one, it will change your life forever, as it has mine.

The book you now hold in your hands explains all the character traits, principles, ideals, and wisdom to live such a remarkable and meaningful life yourself, if you wish to do so. It includes a detailed program of training and personal growth by which you too can develop those traits—all presented in the teachings and thoughts of a man who actually did it—who lived a life that exemplified heijōshin and bushidō. Every time you return to its pages, you will have another encounter with such a man through the words he wanted to share with the world.

My time with Hanshi has come to an end. With the completion of *Karate As the Art of Killing*, I now pass him on to you and to future generations through these pages.

APPENDIX
細足情報

Hosoku Jōhō
Supplemental Information

The authors' first collaboration was for *Flashing Steel: Mastering Eishin-Ryu Swordsmanship*, the number-one selling book in the English language on the subject of iaijutsu (drawing the samurai sword). The first edition, published in 1995, was 268 pages in length, about 66,000 words, with 438 photographs and illustrations. Over the course of two subsequent editions, *Flashing Steel* has expanded to 568 pages, 129,000 words, and 2,407 photographs and illustrations in its *25th Anniversary Memorial Edition*, published in 2020.

In 2006 the authors published their first book on traditional karate-dō, titled *Katsujinken: Living Karate & The Way to Self-Mastery*. *Katsujinken* has been well received and is now in its fourth printing.

連絡先
Renrakusen
CONTACT INFORMATION
JIKISHIN-KAI INTERNATIONAL

5505 Clairemont Mesa Boulevard
San Diego, CA 92117
USA
Shimabukuro Kanako, *dōjō-chō* (director)
Richard Madriaga, chief instructor
(858) 560-4517
(858) 354-1342
http://facebook.com/sandiegokarate858

NIPPON BUDŌ SEISHIN-KAN

PO Box 8684
San Antonio, TX 78202
USA
Leonard J. Pellman, *kanchō* (managing director)
(210) 591-7551
kancho@seishin-kan.org
www.seishin-kan.org
https://facebook.com/NipponBudoSeishin-Kan

用語集
Yōgoshū

GLOSSARY OF COMMON TERMS USED IN KARATE-DŌ

PART I—GENERAL TERMS AND CONCEPTS

Japanese　　　　　　　　　　　　　　　　　**English**

RŌMAJI	日本語	PRONUNCIATION	TRANSLATION
aiki	合気	eye-key	blending/uniting with opponent's energy
aisatsu	挨拶	eye-sahts	courteous (formal) greetings
aite	相手	eye-teh	other person, training partner ("companion hand")
aiuchi	合い打ち	eye-oo-ch'	simultaneous strike(s), mutual kill
aka(i)	赤(い)	ah-kah(ee)	red
aka(i)	紅(い)	ah-kah(ee)	dark red
bōgu	防具	bow-goo	protective equipment
bushi	武士	boo-sh'	peacemaker, protector
bushidō	武士道	boo-sh'-doe	Way of the peacemaker
dan	段	dawn	level, step
danketsu	団結	dawn-ketts	unity, togetherness
dantai	団体	dawn-tye	group, team, together
dō	道	doe	way, path, The Way
dōjō	道場	doe-joe	training place ("place of the Way")

(continues)

Japanese			English
TERM (RŌMAJI)	日本語	PRONUNCIATION	EQUIVALENT
dōjō-chō	道場長	doe-joe-choe	head of the *dōjō* (*chief instructor*)
dōjō kun	道場	doe-joe koon	Code of the Dōjō
embu	演武	em-boo	performance of bujutsu
embu sen	演舞線	em-boo-sen	line, direction, or sequence of performance
enzan no metsuke	遠山の目付	en-zahn no meh-ts'keh	distant gaze ("eyes fixed on distant mountains")
fudoshin	不動心	foo-doe-sheen	immovable or indomitable spirit
fundoshi	褌	foon-doe-sh'	loin cloth (underwear)
futari	二人	f'-tah-ree	two people
futari geiko	二人稽古	f'-tah-ree gay-koe	training with a partner
gasshuku	合宿	goss-shoo-k'	training camp
geta	下駄	geh-tah	Japanese wooden clogs (for rainy, muddy conditions)
gi	着	gee	clothing, uniform (generic term)
go	後	go	after, later (implies reacting to opponent)
go	五	go	five
goshin	護身	go-sheen	self defence
goshin jutsu	護身術	go-sheen jewts'	self-defence technique(s)
hachi	八	haw-ch'	eight
hai	はい	high	yes
han	半	hahn	half, halfway
han	藩	hahn	the territory controlled by a *daimyō* (similar to a county)
hambun	半分	hawm-boon	one-half (a piece)
heihō	兵法	hey-hoe	military methods (martial arts)
henka	変化	hen-kah	variation, alteration
hikiwake	引き分け	hee-kee-wah-kay	drawn match, tie game
hiku	引く	hee-koo	to pull

Japanese **English**

TERM (RŌMAJI)	日本語	PRONUNCIATION	EQUIVALENT
hira	平	hee-raw	flat, level, even
hō	法	hoe	method, technique
ichi	一	each'	one
ii	いい	ee	good
iie	いいえ	ee-eh	no (said rarely, generall impolite)
ippon	一本	eep-pone	one point
itadaku	頂く	ee-tah-daw-koo	to receive (a gift, etc.)
itai	痛い	ee-tye	painful
jaken	邪拳	jaw-ken	evil fist (a strike made unjustly)
jibun	自分	jee-boon	self, by oneself, alone
jikiden	直伝	jee-key-den	direct heritage (personal legacy)
jikishin	直心	jee-key-sheen	pure heart, mind, and spirit
jiko	自己	jee-koh	self, oneself
jitsu	実	jee-ts'	truth, fact(s)
jitsu	術	jee-ts'	art (alternate pronunciation of *jutsu*)
jōzu	上手	joe-zoo	skillful
jūji	十	jew	ten
jūban	襦袢	jew-bahn	*samurai* undershirt
jūdō	柔道	jew-doe	Way of yielding
jūhō	柔道	jew-hoe	method(s) of yielding
jūji	十字	jew-jee	the kanji (symbol) jū (十)
jūjutsu	柔術	jew-jew-ts'	art of yielding
jutsu	術	jew-ts'	art
jutte	十手	jute-teh	steel police weapon ("ten hands")
kachi	勝	kaw-ch'	victory
kagami	鏡	kah-gah-mee	mirror
kami	神	kah-mee	God, deity, gods

(continues)

Japanese			English
TERM (RŌMAJI)	日本語	PRONUNCIATION	EQUIVALENT
kamiza	上座	kah-mee-zah	"upper seat" (a place of honour for symbols of a *dōjō*)
kamon	家紋	kah-moan	family symbol, family crest
kankyū	緩急	kahn-kyoo	rhythm, tempo ("slow and fast")
karate	唐手	kaw-raw-teh	karate (pre-1930 kanji)
karate	空手	kaw-raw-teh	karate (post-1930 kanji)
karate-dō	空手道	kaw-raw-teh-doe	Way of karate
karate-jutsu	空手術	kaw-raw-teh-doe	Art of karate
kata	型	kah-tah	template of techniques
katachi	形	kah-tah-ch'	pattern of movements
katana	刀	kah-tah-nah	sword
katate	片手	kah-tah-teh	one-handed
katsu	勝つ	kaw-ts'	to win (verb)
katsu	活	kaw-ts'	live, life, alive, living
katsujin ken	活人拳	kaw-ts'-jean ken	life-giving (live saving) fist
keiko	稽古	kay-koe	training
keiko-gi	稽古着	kay-koe-gee	training clothes, uniform
ken	剣	ken	sword
ken	拳	ken	fist
kendō	剣道	ken-doe	sport based on *kenjutsu*
kenjutsu	剣術	ken-jew-ts'	art of *samurai* sword combat
kesa	袈裟	keh-saw	a monk's tunic covering only one shoulder
ki	気	kee	spirit, energy
kigurai	気位	key-goo-rye	poise, dignity, bearing
kihaku	気迫	kee-hawk'	intense spirit
kihon	基本	key-hone	fundamentals, basics, foundation
kime	決め	kee-meh	focus, precision
kimaru	決まる	kee-maw-roo	Inevitable, inevitability

Japanese			English
TERM (RŌMAJI)	日本語	PRONUNCIATION	EQUIVALENT
kimono	着物	kee-mow-noh	clothing (general term)
kiru	斬る	kee-roo	to kill (verb)
kobushi	拳	koe-boo-sh'	fist
kōdansha	後輩	koe-dawn-shah	high-ranking student
kōhai	後輩	koe-high	junior student
kōhaku	赤白	koe-haw-k'	red-and-white (red versus white match)
kokoro	心	koe-koe-roe	heart (also mind or spirit)
kokoro-e	心得	koe-koe-roe-eh	principles, precepts, ideals
kokyū	呼吸	koe-kyoo	breath control ("exhale and inhale")
koryū	古流	koe-r'yoo	old style, old school, ancient ways
kōsa	交叉	koe-saw	crossed (wrists, legs, arms, fingers, etc.)
ku	九	koo	nine
kyū	九	kyoo	nine
kyū	級	kyoo	rank, grade
ma	間	mah	distance, interval
maai	間合い	mah-eye	distance control
mazakai	間境	mah-zah-kye	safe distance (boundary)
meijin	名人	may-jean	famous/renowned person (master)
me tsuke	目付	meh ts'-keh	eye contact ("affix the eyes")
mitori geiko	看取り稽古	mee-toe-ree gay-koe	learn by observation ("train by capturing with the eyes")
mokusō	黙想	moe-k'-so	focusing the mind ("silent thought")
mon	紋	moan	emblem, symbol, crest, logo
montsuki	紋付	moan-ts'-kee	jacket with family crest imprinted or embroidered
musha	武者	moo-shaw	a peacemaker, a *budōka*
musha shugyō	武者修行	moo-shaw shoo-gyo	training journey
mushin	無心	moo-sheen	empty mind (limitless mental capacity)

(continues)

Japanese   **English**

TERM (RŌMAJI)	日本語	PRONUNCIATION	EQUIVALENT
ni	二	knee	two
o-	お	oh	honorific (extra polite)
ō-	大	owe	big, large, great
obi	帯	oh-bee	belt, sash
onore	己	oh-no-reh	self, oneself
onore ni katsu	己に活	oh-no-reh knee kawts'	conquer oneself
rakkan shugi	楽観主義	rock-kahn shoo-gee	optimistic attitude
rei	礼	ray	respect
reigi	礼儀	ray-gee	respectfulness, politeness
reihō	礼法	ray-hoe	acts of respect
reishiki	礼式	ray-shee-kee	formal etiquette
renshū	練習	ren-shoo	training for mastery ("polishing")
riron	理論	ree-roan	principles, concepts
ritsurei	立礼	ree-ts'-ray	standing bow
roku	六	roe-k'	six
ryaku	略	r'yah-koo	fusion of technique
ryoku	力	r'yoe-koo	power
ryū	流	r'yoo	style, school, system, teachings, ("flow")
ryū-ha	流派	r'yoo-hah	schools, styles, branches, and divisions (as a whole)
sahō	作法	saw-hoe	preparation (mental, physical, and spiritual)
san	三	sawn	three
satsujinken	殺人拳	saw-ts'-jeen-ken	murdering fist (fist used to harm others)
seimei	生命	say-may	life, living, being alive
seishin	正心	say-sheen	pure, true, righteous heart
seito	生徒	say-toh	student, pupil
seitō	正統	say-toe	traditional, authentic, classic

Japanese			English
TERM (RŌMAJI)	日本語	PRONUNCIATION	EQUIVALENT
seme	攻め	seh-meh	maintain pressure on opponent ("attack")
sempai	先輩	sem-pie	senior student
sensei	先生	sen-say	teacher, instructor ("previously born")
setsudo	節度	seh-ts'-doh	discipline
shi	四	shee	four
shiai	試合	shee-eye	match, contest, tournament
shichi	七	shee-ch'	seven
shihan	師範	shee-hahn'	senior teacher (master)
shikata	仕方	sh'-kah-tah	user (person using technique being practiced)
shin	心	sheen	heart, mind, spirit
shinobi	忍	shee-no-bee	stealth (also a term for *ninja*)
shinobu	忍ぶ	shee-no-boo	move stealthily (verb)
shinsa	審査	sheen-saw	test, examination (for rank promotion)
shintō	神道	sheen-toe	native Japanese religion
shiro(i)	白(い)	shee-roh(ee)	white
shisei	姿勢	shee-say	posture, bearing
shisei	至誠	shee-say	sincerity, integrity
shizentai	自然体	shee-zen-tie	natural stance, posture ("natural body")
shōbu	勝負	show-boo	a match, bout, or round in a contest ("victory-defeat")
shoshinsha	初心者	show-sheen-shaw	beginner, person with beginner's spirit
sōke	宗家	sow-keh	hereditary leader (grandmaster)
sōshi	創師	sow-sh'	founder
sōshihan	総師範	sow-shee-hahn	headmaster ("general instructor")
suigetsu	水月	swee-geh-ts'	the moon's reflection in water ("water moon")
suishin	水心	swee-sheen	mental agility ("water mind")
sun dome	寸止	soon doe-meh	stop within an inch

(continues)

Japanese | **English**

TERM (RŌMAJI)	日本語	PRONUNCIATION	EQUIVALENT
tachirei	立ち礼	tah-ch'-ray	standing bow
taikai	大会	tie-kye	convention, tournament ("large meeting")
tanren	鍛錬	tahn-ren	hard training ("tempering" or "forging")
teki	的	teh-kee	enemy, opponent
tsukekomi	付け込み	ts'-keh-koh-mee	seize the opportunity/initiative
tsukeru	付ける	ts'-keh-roo	to affix, stick to, connect (verb)
uchikata	受ち方	oo-ch'-kah-tah	receiver (person receiving technique being practiced)
uchikata	打ち方	oo-ch'-kah-tah	striker (person receiving technique being practiced)
uke	受け	oo-keh	receive, block, intercept, deflect
ukemi	受身	oo-keh-mee	controlled falling ("receiving body")
uki	受き	oo-key	receiver, assistant (slang term)
ushiro	後ろ	oo-shee-roe	rear, rearward, backward
uwagi	上着	oo-wah-gee	*gi* jacket ("upper clothing")
wa	和	wah	peace, harmony (also nickname for Japan)
wa	輪	wah	ring, ring-shaped
waza	技	wah-zah	technique
yama	山	yah-mah	mountain
yama bushi	山伏	yah-mah boo-sh'	hermit priest(s)
yamato	大和	yah-mah-toh	a nickname for Japan
yon	四	yone	four
yūdansha	有段者	you-dawn-shaw	a person holding *dan* rank
yūkata	浴衣	you-kah-tah	an evening-wear *kimono*
yūkyūsha	有級者	you-cue-shaw	a person holding *kyū* grade
zanshin	残心	zahn-sheen	"leave mind" (awareness of surroundings)
zōri	草履	zoe-ree	Japanese thong-sandals

PART II—COMMON INSTRUCTIONAL COMMANDS

Japanese			**English**
TERM (RŌMAJI)	日本語	PRONUNCIATION	EQUIVALENT
abunai	危ない	ah-boo-nye	dangerous (be careful)
agura	胡坐	ah-goo-rah	sit cross-legged
ashi hantai	足反対	ah-sh' hahn-tye	switch (leading) feet (positions)
dame	駄目	dah-meh	forbidden (stop immediately)
hairei	拝礼	high-ray	venerating bow (to founder, dojo emblem, dignitaries, etc.)
hajime	始め	ha-jee-meh	begin, start, first time
~hantai	反対	hahn-tye	switch (hands, feet, places, etc.)
kamaete	起立	kaw-mah-eh-teh	ready stance (lit. "structure")
ki o tsuke	気を付け	Key oh ts'-keh	attention (stand at attention)
ki o tsukete	気を付けて	Key oh ts'-keh-teh	be careful, watch out
kiritsu	起立	kee-ree-ts'	stand up, standing
mawatte	回って	maw-watt-teh	turn, turn around
mokusō	黙想	moe-k'-so	focusing the mind ("silent thought")
mokusō yame	黙想止め	moe-k'-so yah-meh	cease *mokusō*
moto no ichi	元の位置	mow-toe no ee'ch'	(return to) original position
naotte	直って	nah-oat-teh	finish
otagai ni	お互いに	oh-tah-guy-nee	face toward, facing toward
rei	礼	ray	respect
seiretsu	整列	say-reh-ts'	line up ("adjust alignment")
seiza	正座	say-zah	sit on heels with feet flat ("true sit")
shirei	師礼	shee-ray	bow to instructor
sōji	掃除	Sow-jee	clean up
suwatte	座って	soo-watt-teh	sit down, be seated (command)

(continues)

Japanese			English
TERM (RŌMAJI)	日本語	PRONUNCIATION	EQUIVALENT
tsuzukete	続けて	ts'-zoo-keh-teh	continue
yame	止め	yah-meh	stop (command)
yasunde	休んで	yah-soon-deh	rest, relax (command)
yōi	用意	yoe-ee	prepare ("use thought")
zarei	座礼	zah-ray	seated (kneeling) bow

PART III—STANCES, MOVEMENT, AND DIRECTION

Japanese			English
TERM (RŌMAJI)	日本語	PRONUNCIATION	EQUIVALENT
agura	胡坐	ah-goo-rah	sit cross-legged
age	上げ	ah-geh	upward, rising, lifting
ashi barai	足払い	ah-sh' bah-rye	foot/leg sweep
~ashi mae	足前	ah-sh' mah-eh	(left, right~) foot forward
ashi sabaki	足捌き	ah-sh' saw-bah-kee	footwork
ato de	後で	ah-toe deh	after, afterward
awase ni	合わせに	aw-wah-seh knee	together with~ (simultaneously)
choku	直	choke	straight, direct
chūdan	中段	chew-dawn	middle level, mid-height
dantai embu	団体演舞	dawn-tye em-boo	group/team performance (in formation)
embu sen	演舞線	em-boo-sen	line, direction, or sequence of performance
gedan	下段	geh-dawn	low-level
go	後	go	after, later (implies reacting to opponent)
gyaku	逆	gyah-koo	reverse, reversed, opposite

Japanese			English
TERM (RŌMAJI)	日本語	PRONUNCIATION	EQUIVALENT
gyaku-te	逆手	gyah-koo teh	reversed-hand(s)
hachi-ji dachi	八字立ち	haw-ch'-jee daw-ch'	hachi-shaped (八) stance
han	半	hahn	half, halfway
hanmi	半身	hahn-mee	angled (half-turned) body
hanmi kōkutsu dachi	半身後屈立ち	hahn-mee	angled body rear-bent stance
han-kōkutsu dachi	半後屈立ち	hahn-koe-kuts' daw-ch'	half rear-bent stance
han-zenkutsu dachi	半前屈立ち	hahn-zen-kuts' daw-ch'	half front-bent stance
heikō	平行	hey-koe	parallel
heikō dachi	平行立ち	hey-koe daw-ch'	parallel stance (shoulder width)
heisoku	平足	hey-soak'	feet parallel (side-by-side)
heisoku dachi	平足立ち	hey-soak' daw-ch'	feet parallel stance
hidari	左	hee-daw-ree	left, leftward
hidari heikō dachi	左平行立ち	hee-daw-ree hey-koe daw-ch'	left-facing parallel stance
hiki	引き	hee-kee	pulling
hikite	引き手	hee-kee-teh	pulling hand
hiku	引く	hee-koo	to pull
hiraki ashi	開き足	hee-raw-key ah-sh'	side-step, side-stepping
jōdan	上段	joe-dawn	upper level
kamae	構え	kah-mah-eh	structure (of the body)
katate	片手	kah-tah-teh	one-handed
kiba dachi	騎馬立ち	key-bah daw-ch'	horse-riding stance
kiza	跪座	kee-zah	sit like *seiza*, but on the balls of the feet
kōkutsu dachi	後屈立ち	koe-kuts' daw-ch'	rear-bent stance
kōsa	交叉	koe-saw	crossed (wrists, legs, arms, fingers, etc.)
kōsa dachi	交叉立ち	koe-saw daw-ch'	crossed-leg stance

(continues)

Japanese   **English**

TERM (RŌMAJI)	日本語	PRONUNCIATION	EQUIVALENT
koshi mawari	腰回り	koe-sh' mah-wah-ree	hip rotation
mae	前	mah-eh	front, frontward
mae ni	前に	mah-eh nee	in front of
maai	間合い	mah-eye	distance control
mawari~	廻り	mah-wah-ree	turning~ or spinning~
migi	右	mee-gee	right, rightward
migi heikō dachi	右平行立ち	mee-gee hey-koe daw-ch'	right-facing parallel stance
morote	両手	mow-row-teh	both hands (simultaneously), two-handed
musubi dachi	結び立ち	moo-soo-bee daw-ch'	joined (heels) stance
naifanchi dachi	ナイファンチ立ち	nye-fawn-ch' daw-ch'	Naifanchi (kata name) stance
naka	中	nah-kah	center, middle, inside, within
nami heikō dachi	並平行立ち	nah-mee hay-koe daw-ch'	normal parallel stance
neko-ashi dachi	猫足立ち	neh-koe awsh' daw-ch'	cat-foot stance
okuri ashi	送り足	oh-koo-ree ah-sh'	front foot leads moving forward; rear foot leads moving backward
omote	表	oh-mow-teh	front (visible/obvious) side
otagai ni	お互いに	oh-tah-guy-nee	face toward, facing toward
re-no-ji dachi	レの字立ち	reh-no-jee daw-ch'	re (レ) shaped stance
ryōte	両手	r'yoe-teh	(using) both hands
sagi-ashi dachi	鷺足	saw-gee awsh' daw-ch'	crane (heron) foot stance
saki	先	saw-kee	edge
sanchin dachi	三戦	Sawn-cheen daw-ch'	Sanchin (kata name) stance
seichūsen	正中線	say-chew-sen	center line
seitai	正体	say-tie	face straight on, not angled ("true body")

Japanese			English
TERM (RŌMAJI)	日本語	PRONUNCIATION	EQUIVALENT
seiza	正座	say-zah	sit on heels with feet flat ("true sit")
sen	先	sen	before, prior (implies initiative or preemption)
shiko dachi	四股立ち	sh'-koe daw-ch'	four-ply stance
shisei	姿勢	shee-say	posture, bearing
shita	下	sh'-tah	below, beneath
shizentai	自然体	shee-zen-tie	natural stance, posture ("natural body")
shōmen	正面	show-men	center of the face ("true face")
suri-ashi	摺り足	soo-ree ah-sh'	move by sliding feet on the floor
suwari	座り	soo-wah-ree	sitting, seated
soete	添えて	so-eh-teh	reinforced, reinforcing, supported, stabilized
tachi (dachi)	立ち	tah-ch' (daw-ch')	stance, standing, upright
taishite	対して	tye-sh'-teh	face toward, facing toward
tatehiza	立膝	tah-teh-hee-zah	sitting with one knee raised ("upright knee")
tsugi-ashi	次足	tsoo-gee ah-sh'	another term for *yori ashi*
tsukeru	付ける	ts'-keh-roo	to affix, stick to, connect (verb)
ue	上	oo-eh	up, upward
uki-ashi dachi	浮足立ち	oo-key-awsh' daw-ch'	floating-foot stance
ura	裏	oo-raw	back (unseen) side
ushiro	後ろ	oo-sh'-row	rear, rearward, back, behind
waki	脇	wah-kee	side, beside
yoko	横	yoh-koh	sideways, sideward
zenkutsu dachi	前屈立ち	zen-kuts' daw-ch'	front-bent stance

PART IV—MAJOR PARTS OF THE BODY AND STRIKING TARGETS

Japanese			English
TERM (RŌMAJI)	日本語	PRONUNCIATION	EQUIVALENT
ago	顎	ah-go	chin, jaw
ashi	足	ah-sh'	foot, feet
ashi	脚	ah-sh'	leg(s)
ashikubi	足首	ah-sh'-koo-bee	ankle(s)
atama	頭	ah-tah-mah	head
dō	胴	doe	torso
ekika	腋窩	eh-key-kah	armpit
hana	鼻	haw-naw	nose
hara	腹	haw-raw	abdomen
hiji	肘	hee-jee	elbow
hiza	膝	hee-zaw	knee
jōwan	上腕	joe-wahn	upper arm
kansetsu	関節	kahn-sets'	joint(s)
kata	肩	kah-tah	shoulder(s)
kawan	下腕	kah-wahn	lower arm
ken	拳	ken	fist(s)
kobushi	拳	koe-boo-sh'	fist(s)
kokan	股間	koe-kahn	groin
kokoro	心	koe-koe-roe	heart
koshi	腰	koe-sh'	hip(s)
kote	小手	koe-teh	forearm
kuchi	口	koo-ch'	mouth
kubi	首	koo-bee	neck
me	目	meh	eye(s)
men	面	men	face
mimi	耳	mee-mee	ear(s)

Japanese   **English**

TERM (RŌMAJI)	日本語	PRONUNCIATION	EQUIVALENT
mine	峰	mee-neh	spine, center of the back
mune	胸	moo-neh	chest, bosom, breast
nodo	喉	no-doe	throat
shōmen	正面	show-men	center of the face ("true face")
soto momo	外腿	sow-toe mow-mow	outer thigh
soto ude	外腕	sow-toe oo-deh	outer arm
suigetsu	水月	swee-geh-ts'	solar plexus, abdominal nerve centre
sune	脛	soo-neh	shin
tanden	丹田	tahn-den	lower abdomen
te	手	teh	hand(s)
uchi mata	内股	oo-ch' mah-tah	inner thigh
uchi ude	内腕		
ude	腕		
yokomen	横面	yoh-koh-men	side of the face/head (usually temple)

PART V—STRIKING SURFACES OF THE BODY

Japanese   **English**

TERM (RŌMAJI)	日本語	PRONUNCIATION	EQUIVALENT
Ashi no meishō	脚の名称	ah-sh' no may-show	Striking surfaces of the legs and feet
hiza	膝	hee-zaw	knee
jōsokutei	上足底	joe-soak-tay	ball of the foot
kakato	踵	kah-kah-toe	heel (back edge)
kasokutei	下足底	kah-soak-tay	bottom of the heel
koshi	腰	koe-sh'	hip

(continues)

Japanese			English
TERM (RŌMAJI)	日本語	PRONUNCIATION	EQUIVALENT
sokkō	足甲	soak-koe	top (instep) of the foot
sokutō	足刀	soak-toe	edge (blade) of the foot
sune	脛	soo-neh	shin
tsumasaki	爪先	ts'-mah-sah-key	tip of the (big) toe
ura sokuto	裏足刀	oo-raw soak-toe	Inner edge of the foot
Atama no meishō	頭の名称	ah-tah-mah no may-show	Striking surfaces of the head
ago	顎	ah-go	chin or jaw
gaku	額	gah-koo	forehead
kōtōbu	後頭部	koe-toe-boo	back of the head
zentōbu	後頭部	zen-toe-boo	forehead (alt. term)
Te-ude no meishō	手腕の名称	teh no may-show	Striking surfaces of the hand(s) and arm(s)
boshi	母指	bow-sh'	thumb ("father finger") [alt. term]
haishu	背手	high-shoo	back of the hand (flat/open)
hiji	肘	hee-jee	Elbow [common term]
hiraken	平拳	hee-raw-ken	middle knuckles ("flat fist")
hitosashi ippon-ken	人指一本拳	h'-toe-saw-sh' eep-pone-ken	mid-knuckle of forefinger
ippon ken	一本拳	eep-pone ken	protruding knuckle fist
ippon nukite	一本抜き手	eep-pone new-key-teh	one-finger (forefinger) spearing-hand
kata	肩	kah-tah	shoulder(s)
ken	拳	ken	fist(s)
kentsui	拳槌	ken-tsoo-ee	hammer fist
kobushi	拳	koe-boo-sh'	fist(s)
koken	弧拳	koe-ken	top of the wrist
kumade	熊手	koo-mah-deh	bear's paw (nukite with fingers spread)

Japanese			English
TERM (RŌMAJI)	日本語	PRONUNCIATION	EQUIVALENT
nakadaka ippon-ken	中高一本拳	nah-kah-dah-kah eep-pone-ken	mid-knuckle of middle finger
nihon nukite	二本抜き手	knee-hone new-key-teh	two-finger spearing-hand
nukite	抜き手	new-key-teh	spearing-hand (general term)
oya-yubi	親指	oh-yah yoo-bee	thumb ("boss finger") [common term]
seiken	正拳	say-ken	forefist ("true fist")
shōtei	掌底	show-teh	palm-heel (base of the palm)
shutō	手刀	sh'-toe	edge (blade) of hand, knife-hand
tateken	縦拳	tah-teh-ken	vertical fist (thumb on top)
uraken	裏	oo-raw-ken	back-fist
ura shutō	裏	oo-raw sh'-toe	reverse knife-hand (ridge-hand)
wantō	手刀	wahn-toe	edge (blade) of the forearm
yonhon nukite	四本抜き手	yone-hone new-key-teh	four-finger spearing-hand
yubi	指	yew-bee	finger(s)
yubisaki	指先	yew-bee-saw-k'	fingertip(s)

PART VI—ATTACK AND DEFENSE TECHNIQUES

Japanese			English
TERM (RŌMAJI)	日本語	PRONUNCIATION	EQUIVALENT
bōgyo waza	防禦技	bow-gyoe wah-zah	defensive technique(s)
dome	止め	doe-meh	block, stop, prevent
harai (~barai)	払い	haw-rye (~bah-rye)	sweep, sweeping
harai uke	払い受け	haw-rye oo-keh	sweeping block
kaihō waza	解放技	kye-hoe wah-zah	escaping techniques
tenshin	転身	ten-sheen	evasion, dodging ("body turning")

(continues)

Japanese   **English**

TERM (RŌMAJI)	日本語	PRONUNCIATION	EQUIVALENT
uke	受け	oo-keh	receive (an attack)
uke kata	受け方	oo-keh kah-tah	receiving method(s)
ukekomi	受け込み	oo-keh-koh-mee	deflect and suppress
ukemi	受け身	oo-keh-mee	breakfalls
ukenagashi	受け流し	oo-keh-nah-gah-sh'	flowing deflection ("flowing reception") of an attack
kōgeki waza	攻撃技	koe-geki wah-zah	offensive technique(s)
ate	当て	ah-teh	strike(s) {noun]
atemi waza	当身技	ah-teh-mi wah-zah	body striking technique(s)
kansetsu waza	関節技	kahn-sets wah-zah	joint (manipulation/dislocation) technique(s)
~keage	蹴上	keh-ah-geh	up-swinging kick
~kekomi	蹴込	keh-koe-mee	thrusting kick
~keri (~geri)	蹴り	~keh-ree (~geh-ree)	kick(s) [noun]
keri kata	蹴り方	keh-ree kah-tah	kicking method(s)
kyūsho waza	急所技	kyoo-show wah-zah	vital point techniques
me tsubushi	目潰し	meh ts'-boo-sh'	"destroy the eyes" (blind or obstruct opponent's vision)
~nage	投	~nah-geh	throw(s) [noun]
nage waza	投げ技	nah-geh wah-zah	throwing methods
~osaekomi	抑え込み	oh-saw-eh-koe-mee	Grapple, hold, pin down, trap [noun]
osaekomi waza	抑え込み技	oh-saw-eh-koe-mee wah-zah	grappling/wrestling methods
~shime (~jime)	絞め	~shee-meh (~jee-meh)	strangle, choke, chokehold
shime waza	絞め技	shee-meh wah-zah	strangling/choking method(s)
tsuki	突き	tsoo-kee	thrust or punch
tsuki kata	突き方	tsoo-kee	thrusting/punching method(s)
uchi	打ち	oo-ch'	to strike, to hit
uchi kata	打ち方	oo-ch' kah-tah	striking method(s)

Japanese			English
TERM (RŌMAJI)	日本語	PRONUNCIATION	EQUIVALENT
shūshoku go	修飾語	shoo-show-k' go	modifying words
age	上げ	ah-geh	rising, lifting, upward
ai	合い	eye	together, mutual
awase	合わせ	ah-wah-seh	simultaneous, together, matching
choku	直	choke	straight, direct
furi	振り	foo-ree	swinging, whipping, shaking
fumi	踏み	foo-mee	stomping, smashing underfoot
gobu	五分	go-boo	half-inch
gyaku	逆	gyah-koo	reverse, reversed
gyaku-te	逆手	gyah-koo teh	reversed hand(s)
heikō	平行 or 並行	hay-koe	parallel
issun	一寸	ees-soon	one inch
jūji	十字	jew-jee	cross-shaped (十)
jun	順	june	standard
~kaeshi (~gaeshi)	返し	~kah-eh-sh' (~gah-eh-sh')	return, reverse direction, twist backward
kagi	鈎	kah-gee	right angle, hooking, hooked
kakete	掛けて	kah-keh-teh	grasping, seizing, holding
kakiwake	掻き分け	kah-key-wah-keh	spreading apart, separating, prying
kizami	刻み	key-zah-mee	jabbing, chopping
kōsa	交差	koe-saw	crossed, crossing
mawari	廻り	mah-wah-ree	spinning, rotating
mawashi	回し	mah-wah-shee	turning
mikazuki	三日月	mee-kah-zoo-key	crescent moon shaped
morote	両手	mow-roe-teh	two-handed, using both hands
nagashi	流し	nah-gah-sh'	flowing, blending, redirecting
naname	斜め	nah-nah-meh	diagonal, diagonally

(continues)

Japanese   **English**

TERM (RŌMAJI)	日本語	PRONUNCIATION	EQUIVALENT
nidan	二段	knee-dawn	two level (high-low)
oi	追い	oy	pursuing, lunging toward
osae	押さえ	oh-saw-eh	holding down, pressing down, smothering
otoshi	落とし	oh-toe-sh'	downward, falling, dropping
ryōte	両手	r'yoh-teh	two-handed, using both hands
sasae	支え	saw-saw-eh	supported, braced
soete	添えて	so-eh-teh	reinforced
sukashi	透かし	s'-kah-sh'	skidding, sliding ('thinning out")
sukui	掬い	s'-koo-ee	scooping
tobi	飛び	toe-bee	jump, jumping ("flying")
tobi-koeru	飛び越える	toe-bee-koe-eh-roo	jump over
ura	裏	oo-raw	opposite side, back, reverse direction
wa	輪	wah	ring (O) shaped
yama	山	yah-mah	mountain (山) shaped

Using the words listed in this glossary, the term for most karate techniques can be readily determined or translated by using the appropriate word or words from Part III (stances, movent, and direction), Part IV (parts of the body and target areas), Part V (striking surfaces) and Part VI (techniques and modifiers), as in the examples below:

PART III	PART V	PART VI	TECHNIQUE
yoko	sokutō	kekomi	side foot-edge thrust kick
mae	nakadaka ippon-ken	oi-zuki	frontal mid-knuckle fist lunging punch
mae	sokutō	tobi-geri	frontal foot-edge jumping (flying) kick
hidari	kentsui	otoshi-uchi	left hammer-fist downward strike

D

dachi. *See* stances
Dai Nippon Butoku-Kai, 16, 24, 328
daikentō (fore-fist), 149
Dalberg-Acton, John, 22
danketsu shin (spirit of unity), 74–76
danryoku (flexibility), 197
defense, principles of, 202
defensive techniques. *See* bōgyō waza
dependability, 135
deshi, 6
difficulties, as medicine, 58–59
distance control. *See* maai
dōjō
    definition of, 6, 23
    function of, 23–24
    as life's laboratory, 76, 345
dōjō kun, 23–24, 145–46

E

effort. *See* kihaku
egen (knowing eyes), 51, 53
ego, controlling, 99–100
eku (oar), 324–25
empathy, 134–35
empi (elbow), 160–62
enzan no metsuke, 119
escape techniques. *See* kaihō waza
etiquette. *See* sahō to reihō
eye contact. *See* chakugan

F

faithfulness. *See* chūgi
fear, 339
Federation of All-Japan Karate-dō Organizations (FAJKO), 303
feet, striking surfaces of, 166–68
fight-or-flight response, 65–66
first impressions, importance of, 338
fist
    making, 150–51
    striking surfaces of, 149–60

fixation. *See* kime
flexibility. *See* danryoku
fukushiki kokyū (abdominal breathing), 109–10
fulfillment. *See* kofuku
Funakoshi Gichin, 14, 16, 41, 201, 318, 327
fundamentals. *See* kihon
furi uchi, 236
furigama (swinging kama), 324
Fu-Rin-Ka-Zan banner, 74–75
furisute uke (shaking-off block), 221

G

gaku (forehead), 169
gedan barai (low-level sweep), 203, 296
gendai-ryū, 3
gi (righteousness), 45–46
giryo (doubt), 126
giryō (superior proficiency), 306–7
Go Dō Shin (Five Paths of the Spirit), 128
Gō Kenki, 31, 32, 328
go no sen, 307–8, 309
gobuzuki, 230
gōhō, 4
Gōjū-Ryū, 16, 24, 29, 148, 195, 198, 326, 327
goshinjutsu, 92, 303
grappling techniques. *See* osaekomi waza
gyaku mikazuki geri (reverse crescent kick), 246
gyakuzuki (reverse punch), 229

H

ha, 3
Hachi-ji Dachi (Hachi-Shaped Stance), 174–75
haishu uchi, 236
haitō, 157
Hamahiga, 318
Hanashiro Chōmo, 14, 24, 30, 41
hand, striking surfaces of, 149–60
Handen Shūju Sei, 35–36

hangeki (counterattack), 202
Han-Kōkutsu Dachi (Half Rear-Bent Stance), 180–81
Han-Zenkutsu Dachi (Half Front-Bent Stance), 178–79
happō, 187
harai uke (sweeping block), 203
hardening. *See* kitae
Hashiba Hideyoshi, 39
Hayashi Teruō, 32, 33, 328, 329
Hayashi-Ha Shitō-Ryū, 328–29
head, striking surfaces of, 169–70
heart. *See* kokoro
Heian Nidan, 274, 275–76, 282–86
heijōshin (peace of mind), 64–71, 81–82
heijutsu no sambyō, 126
Heikō Dachi (Parallel Stance), 172–73
heikōzuki (parallel punch), 230
Heisoku Dachi (Closed-Feet Stance), 172
hen doku i yaku, 58–59, 72
Hidari Heikō Dachi (Left Angled Parallel Stance), 173–74
Higaonna Kanryō, 14, 29, 30, 31, 32, 41, 42, 328
hiji ate, 249–51, 293
hiji-sasae uke (reinforced-elbow block), 220
hikite (pulling hand), 113–14, 192–95
hip rotation. *See* koshi mawari
hira-basami (hand scissors), 159, 232, 291, 292
hira-ken (middle-knuckle spear-hand), 157
hiraken tsuki, 289–90
hitogoroshi waza (killing techniques). *See also* ichi geki hissatsu
    history of, 287–88
    in kata, 289–95
    methods of, 295–98
hitosashi ippon-ken (fore-knuckle), 153–54, 230
hiza (knee), 165
hiza ate (knee strike), 165, 243–44, 293

筆者紹介
Hissha Shōkai
ABOUT THE AUTHORS

Shimabukuro Masayuki
Hidenobu Hanshi.

The life and achievements of **Masayuki Shimabukuro** were so significant and plentiful that they are difficult to summarize in just a few paragraphs. He was born on March 27, 1948, in Ōsaka, and followed his lifelong passion for traditional Japanese budō right up to his untimely death on September 7, 2012. He devoted himself to the mastery and promotion of budō, and eventually became one of the most highly respected authorities on budō in the world—of his or any other time.

He began his budō training with jūdō in school but soon gravitated to karate-dō. He became a direct student of Hayashi Teruō, founder of Hayashi-Ha Shitō-Ryū, in 1965, and continued training with Hayashi until 1996, the year he became a direct student of Mabuni Kenzō, son and successor to Mabuni Kenwa, the creator of Shitō-Ryū. By the time of his death, he had achieved rankings of 8th dan in Musō Jikiden Eishin-Ryū iaidō, 8th dan in Shitō-Ryū karate-dō, 7th dan in Shindō Musō-Ryū jōjutsu, and the title of Hanshi in both iaidō and karate-dō, the highest title awarded in traditional Japanese budō. He had students and affiliated dōjō throughout North America as well as in Europe, Asia, Central America, South America, and Australia. He was featured on the cover of *Black Belt* magazine several times and was named its Weapons Instructor of the Year in 2006.

More than his many awards and accomplishments, his life was a testimony to his resolute effort to the life of a samurai—a life lived by the precepts of bushidō for the purpose of serving and benefiting others. His warm smile, his gracious and caring attitude, his love of budō, and his zeal to see budō reach the largest possible audience and improve the world are the things for which he should be remembered. The high rankings, titles, and accolades he received in life, and his posthumous induction into the Dai Nippon Butoku-Kai, are merely the tangible evidence of the tremendous impact he had on the people who knew him and trained with him.

People of his stature and influence are precious and all too rare, and it was truly a privilege to have walked by his side for a time.

Leonard J. Masanobu Pellman shihan.

Leonard J. Pellman was introduced to budō at the age of fourteen when, in 1966, after years of suffering persistent bullying in school, his parents enrolled him in a jūdō program in San Diego. He continued his jūdō training and was introduced to kendō at Toyokawa High School while an exchange student to Japan in 1968. While there, his host family arranged for him to train on Saturdays at a Shōtō-kan dōjō in the nearby city of Toyohashi, which further whetted his appetite for karate-dō.

His lifelong training in karate-dō began in January 1971 when he enrolled in the karate class at San Diego State University. His roommate was a member of the karate club at the University of California, San Diego, and Pellman occasionally participated in seminars taught by guest instructors like Nishiyama Hidetaka and Richard Kim at UCSD. In 1973, Pellman returned to Japan for nine months of intensive training as an uchideshi (live-in student) in karate-dō, kendō, Okinawa kobujutsu, and aikidō. While there, his exchange student "sister" married his aikidō sensei. At their wedding, her uncle performed a demonstration of iaidō—a common custom at traditional Japanese weddings—sparking Pellman's interest in that art as well.

Upon his return to San Diego in 1974 he resumed his karate training. His first sensei died of stomach cancer in 1984, so Pellman trained with his most senior student for an additional four years. In late 1988, Shimabukuro Hanshi began teaching iaidō on Saturdays at the dōjō where Pellman was training in karate and Okinawa kobujutsu. Not long after beginning to train in iaidō under Shimabukuro Hanshi, Pellman also began training in Shitō-Ryū karate-dō, Okinawa kobujutsu, and jōjutsu with him.

Pellman opened his first dōjō, the Skyline Karate Club, in February 1989. When Shimabukuro Hanshi established the Jikishin-Kai International (JKI) in 1992,

Pellman changed the name of his dōjō to Nippon Budō Seishin-Kan and was among the first dōjō to affiliate with the JKI. Thereafter he trained almost exclusively with Shimabukuro Hanshi. In 1996, Pellman became one of the first budōka to create a website, the Web-Dōjō.

Pellman shihan continues to serve as dōjō-chō (chief instructor) of the Nippon Budō Seishin-Kan and its San Antonio affiliate, Victory Dōjō, teaching iaidō, jōjutsu, kenjutsu, and aiki-jūjutsu in addition to karate-dō and Okinawa kobujutsu. He also maintains an active presence on social media and an extensive internet presence promoting traditional Japanese budō. In July 2021, Pellman shihan was inducted into the United States Martial Arts Hall of Fame.

About North Atlantic Books

North Atlantic Books (NAB) is a 501(c)(3) nonprofit publisher committed to a bold exploration of the relationships between mind, body, spirit, culture, and nature. Founded in 1974, NAB aims to nurture a holistic view of the arts, sciences, humanities, and healing. To make a donation or to learn more about our books, authors, events, and newsletter, please visit www.northatlanticbooks.com.